IN THE MIDST OF MIDST OF PERPETUAL FETES

This book was

the winner of the

JAMESTOWN PRIZE

for 1995.

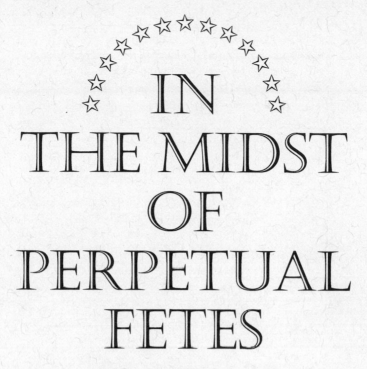

IN THE MIDST OF PERPETUAL FETES

THE MAKING OF AMERICAN NATIONALISM, 1776–1820

DAVID WALDSTREICHER

Published for the

Omohundro Institute of Early American History and Culture,

Williamsburg, Virginia,

by the University of North Carolina Press,

Chapel Hill and London

The Omohundro Institute of
Early American History and Culture is sponsored
jointly by the College of William and Mary and the
Colonial Williamsburg Foundation.
On November 15, 1996, The Institute adopted the
present name in honor of a bequest
from Malvern H. Omohundro, Jr.

Set in New Baskerville type by Tseng Information Systems
Manufactured in the United States of America

Library of Congress Cataloging in Publication Data
Waldstreicher, David.
In the midst of perpetual fetes : the making of American nationalism,
1776–1820 / by David Waldstreicher.
p.   cm.
Includes bibliographical references (p.   ) and index.
ISBN 978-0-8078-2384-2 (cloth : alk. paper).
— ISBN 978-0-8078-4691-9
(pbk. : alk. paper)
1. United States—Politics and government—1775–1783.   2. United
States—Politics and government—1783–1865.   3. Nationalism—
United States—History—18th century.   4. Festivals—Political
aspects—United States—History—18th century.   5. Political
culture—United States—History—18th century.   6. Nationalism—
United States—History—19th century.   7. Festivals—Political
aspects—United States—History—19th century.   8. Political
culture—United States—History—19th century.   I. Omohundro
Institute of Early American History and Culture.   II. Title.
E210.W35   1997   97-18908
973—dc21   CIP

The paper in this book meets the guidelines
for permanence and durability of the Committee on Production
Guidelines for Book Longevity of the Council on Library Resources.

This volume received indirect support from
an unrestricted book publication grant awarded to the Institute
by the L. J. Skaggs Foundation of Oakland, California.

12 11 10 09 08   8 7 6 5 4

For

Blanche *and* Joel Waldstreicher

and in loving memory of

Minnie *and* Morris Waldstreicher

☆ ☆ ☆

ACKNOWLEDGMENTS

Like the rituals and the accounts of them that are the focus of this study, scholarship cannot be produced alone: so it is a pleasure to thank those who have knowingly proceeded with me in this work. Those who have done so unknowingly are thanked in the footnotes.

Fellowships from the Mellon Fellowships in the Humanities, the American Antiquarian Society, the American Philosophical Society, the Virginia Historical Society, and the National Endowment for the Humanities supported me materially during the research and writing of my dissertation and its revision into its present form. I would particularly like to thank the staff of the American Antiquarian Society, especially Georgia B. Barnhill, Joanne Chaison, John Hench, Thomas Knoles, and Dennis Laurie. Roy E. Goodman and Martin Levitt of the American Philosophical Society helped make my stay in Philadelphia enjoyable and productive, as did Philip Lapsansky of the Library Company of Philadelphia at a later date. Bennington College provided me with a home and an institutional base as I researched and wrote further: the collegiality and good faith of Marc Lendler, David M. Luebke, Mansour Farhang, Elizabeth Tingley, Ronald Cohen, and Sally Sugarman helped keep me going and made my two years in Vermont an invaluable learning experience.

This study would not have been possible without the great librarians and archivists of America, who saved and microfilmed aging documents and, especially, newspapers. But if you can't find it, or if the supporting cast isn't there to help, it might as well not be there. I would like to thank the librarians and workers at the institutions mentioned above and at the New-York Historical Society; the Connecticut Historical Society; the New Haven Colony Historical Society; the Historical Society of Pennsylvania; the Library Company of Philadelphia; the Virginia Historical Society; the Virginia State Library; the Historical Society of York County, Pennsylvania; the Special Collections Library, Duke University; the New York State Library, Albany; the Albany Institute of History and Art; the South Caroliniana and Thomas Cooper libraries, University of South Carolina; the Charleston Public Library; the South Carolina Historical Society; the Ohio Historical Society; the Cincinnati Historical Society; the University of Cincinnati Library; the Kentucky Historical Society; the University of Kentucky

Library; the New York Public Library; the Georgia Historical Society; the Massachusetts Historical Society; the Boston Public Library; Temple University Library; Sawyer Library, Williams College; Crossett Library, Bennington College; and Beinecke, Cross Campus, and Sterling Memorial Libraries, Yale University. I spent the most time in the microforms division in the bowels of Sterling Library: thanks are due to Kevin Pacelli and his staff for cataloging, finding, and refiling many microfilms, microfiche, and microcards for me over the years.

I am deeply grateful for the imprimatur of the Omohundro Institute of Early American History and Culture and for the support of its director, Ronald Hoffman. Fredrika J. Teute, Editor of Publications, has been a careful, farsighted critic and a true friend: may our conversations long continue. Gil Kelly is a far better copyeditor than I could have deserved, and not at all nearsighted in any way that matters. An earlier version of the first chapter appeared in the *Journal of American History,* LXXXII (1995–1996), 37–61, and I would like to thank its editors, David Thelen and David Paul Nord, for permission to reprint and, with readers John L. Brooke and Robert A. Gross, for help along the way.

My greatest intellectual and professional debts are to the teachers, scholars, and colleagues who supported this project and its author. Before I could do more than imagine graduate school, Hugh M. Grey showed me what rigorous historical thinking—and creative teaching— can do. At the University of Virginia, Dante Germino personified the value, and fun, of talking and thinking about politics; Jessica Feldman saw to it that I kept studying literature, and made me a better reader; Stephen Innes nurtured my interest in the American Revolution and introduced me to social history. It's been a long road since their classrooms, but their lessons stay with me.

In 1989, Edward Countryman came to Yale for just one term but made all the difference. The original idea for the project came out of his seminar and the good talks we had about why the Revolution mattered. He followed its gestation long-distance from Warwickshire and Dallas; I hope he still recognizes and likes it now, for there are only two people I have ever permitted to nickname me, and he is one. David Brion Davis, who labored as the director of the dissertation that became this book, also saw the potential of the subject matter and gave generously of his wise counsel and sensitive readings. Those who know David Davis or his works know what a gift his sense of irony, and demand for subtlety, can be, and I can only hope that some of it has rubbed off. Jean-Christophe Agnew's artful investigations of some early drafts continued to work their magic years later. Bryan Wolf provided an example of broad-mindedness and creativity at a time when this project was still being formulated. Ann Fabian lent her sharp eye and some very timely encouragement. John Demos and Harry S. Stout saw the thing whole; their comments, and those of Philip J. Deloria, Christopher Grasso, and Stephen R. Grossbart at later stages, helped me present it more effectively in the end. Benjamin Filene, Peter P. Hinks, Sylvie Murray, Corey Robin, Nikhil Pal Singh, Michelle Stephens, Glenn Wallach, Shane White, Lane Witt, and Rosemarie Zagarri read drafts of individual chapters and pushed me to consider different possible audiences. John Brooke, Dickson D. Bruce, and especially Simon P. Newman and Shane White generously shared their work in progress, which enabled me to shape Chapters 3 and 6 so as to complement their own ventures, all of which I greatly admire.

Conversations with Steven Bullock, Reeve Huston, and Nikhil Singh helped me to articulate what this work means to me, and what I hope it might mean to others. Gunther Peck discussed the meaning of all our work at many of New Haven's wondrous diners; he also offered incisive, thorough critiques of every chapter as it was written. He has been a remarkable friend and comrade, and I thank him for marching and munching with me at the intersections of history, politics, personality, and pancakes.

Diane Simon read drafts of early chapters and provided years of invaluable personal support, for which I will always be grateful.

For a quarter of a century Minnie and Moe Waldstreicher, of blessed memory, were my living guides to the past. They showed me how to listen to the silences as well as the sounds, to understand the gestures as well as hear the words. I owe them my ear, and some of the better voices in my head.

Joel and Blanche Waldstreicher taught me to read, took me to my first parades, purchased my first history books, and schlepped me to many a patriotic and political landmark. They listened sympathetically during the throes and, for longer than I had any right to expect, made everything I did seem okay. Whatever comes of this is thanks to them.

☆ ☆ ☆

CONTENTS

☆ ☆ ☆

ILLUSTRATIONS

IN THE
MIDST OF
PERPETUAL
FETES

☆　☆　☆

INTRODUCTION

THE PRACTICES OF NATIONALISM

When a modern-day organizer of a national victory celebration looked for a model of successful patriotic and political pageantry, he found it in the Grand Federal Procession that marked the ratification of the Constitution in 1788. As Barnett Lipton, chief coordinator of New York City's Operation Welcome Home festivities at the end of the Persian Gulf War in 1991, told the story:

> In the olden days essentially what happened is they just reached out to every group around town and said, what can you do for this parade? Everybody came up with their own thing. And that parade was wonderful because there was a story built in. Nobody wrote it, but it emerged.
>
> *　*　*
>
> Here's a case in point: the butchers participated in the parade by having two oxen which they brought down the street and they had a banner between their horns. And one said ANARCHY and the other said CONFUSION. And it was "The Death of Anarchy and Confusion Shall Feed the Poor." After the parade, they slaughtered the oxen and fed them to the poor.[1]

Like the citizens who marched in and watched the 1788 parade, Lipton was aware that parading is politics. The butchers were participating in the ratification of the Constitution, and they knew it. Marching with their cleavers in the Grand Federal Procession, the butchers demonstrated their everyday contribution to the health of the polity: they as-

---

1. Mark Sussman, "Celebrating the New World Order: Festival and War in New York," *Drama Review,* XXXIX, no. 2 (Summer 1995), Lipton quoted at 157–158. Lipton also produced the Constitutional Bicentennial parade in Philadelphia in 1988, which included a reenactment of the Grand Federal Procession. For the mass-mediated (and conservative) nature of those reenactments, see Susan G. Davis, "'Set Your Mood to Patriotic': History as Televised Special Event," *Radical History Review,* no. 42 (1988), 122–143.

serted the importance of their productive labor as well as the political clout of artisans like themselves.[2]

But in choosing the names Anarchy and Confusion for their cattle, the butchers were being more than clever, and more than even casually political. They were taking part in an allegorical battle over the meaning of the Constitution and the identities of those who opposed and those who supported its ratification. This battle had filled the newspapers in Philadelphia and beyond for months before Federalists linked the celebration of the Constitution with the Fourth of July in what became known as the greatest civic event Philadelphia had ever seen. Francis Hopkinson, the architect of that celebration, led the way in depicting the Antifederalists as disorderly, animalistic anarchists in essays, songs, and parables. When the butchers slaughtered Anarchy and Confusion, they symbolically and politically slaughtered their opponents. They were also proclaiming a new American unity. And they had a wonderful time doing it.[3]

Like the Constitution itself, this new unity could not appear to be written by an individual like Hopkinson, or a social group like the parading artisans: it had to "emerge," as Lipton remarked about the Gulf War festival. That political desire—the desire for spontaneous emergence—helps explain why Americans seem drawn to national celebration as a political strategy. This study is about the festive innovations through which Americans of the early Republic practiced a divisive politics and a unifying nationalism at the same time. I examine that am-

2. Eric Foner, *Tom Paine and Revolutionary America* (New York, 1976), 206–209; Sean Wilentz, *Chants Democratic: New York City and the Rise of the American Working Class, 1788–1850* (New York, 1984), 87–97; Edward Countryman, *The American Revolution* (New York, 1985), 214–219, 226–227.

3. [Francis Hopkinson], *Account of the Grand Federal Procession . . .* [Philadelphia, 1788]; Hopkinson, "The New Roof: A Song for Federal Mechanics," "Objections to the Proposed Plan of a Federal Government," in *The Miscellaneous Essays and Occasional Writings of Francis Hopkinson, Esq.* (Philadephia, 1792), II, 320–321, 329; Hopkinson, *The Comical Spirit of Seventy-Six: The Humor of Francis Hopkinson,* ed. Paul M. Zall (San Marino, Calif., 1976); Vera Brodsky Lawrence, *Music for Patriots, Politicians, and Presidents: Harmonies and Discords of the First Hundred Years* (New York, 1975), 106–109; Francis Hopkinson, "Grand Antifederal Procession," Hopkinson Family Papers, XIII, Historical Society of Pennsylvania, Philadelphia; *New Hampshire Spy* (Portsmouth), Aug. 26, 1788. As Lester H. Cohen observes, the Philadelphia procession "serves, then, as one example of how the Federalists self-consciously created the myth of consensus" ("The Myth of Consensus and the Antifederalists," *Proteus*, IV, no. 2 [Fall 1987], 15).

biguous middle ground of parades, spectatorship, and politics, which remains a site of national identity, effective political action, and mass-mediated delight. I specifically trace the development of nationalism in the United States to celebratory activities like the parades of 1788. Insofar as I explore nationalist rituals in depth, I do so in order to relate them to an evolving political culture: indeed, to understand their crucial role in that political culture. I am less interested in the emergence of "American identity," or even in the rites of that identity, than in the relationship of nationalist ideology to political practice in the United States. In reconsidering nationalism in terms of its practices as well as its ideas, this work attempts to comprehend the everyday interplay of rhetoric, ritual, and political action that permitted the abstractions of nationalist ideology to make real, effective, practical sense.

It is my hope that a closer look at the early Republic's politics of celebration will change our view of what nationalism has been in the United States. The battles over patriotism and the national culture in our own time (however each of us might have participated in them) make it all the more important to understand how much of American politics has turned on these politically potent and multiply mediated gestures of celebration and mourning. Nationalism in America hasn't been a great idea that has waxed and waned, something that people truly had or did not have. It has been a set of practices that empowered Americans to fight over the legacy of their national Revolution and to protest their exclusion from that Revolution's fruits. It is not inherently reactionary or progressive; like other nationalisms, its political meanings are multiple, even contradictory, and can be shown to have changed radically over time.[4] Thus, it will be instructive, first, to see how, by stressing the ideological nature instead of examining the everyday practice, we have misunderstood American nationalism.

Despite a surge of interest and the appearance of a number of path-breaking historical and theoretical works, our understanding of nationalism still derives from nineteenth-century idealism. "The nation is a soul, a spiritual principle," wrote Ernest Renan, one of the first scholar-critics of nationalism, in 1882. For Max Savelle, writing in the late 1940s, nationalism was "a component element in the 'mind' of a

---

4. R. Radhakrishnan, "Nationalism, Gender, and the Narrative of Identity," in Andrew Parker et al., eds., *Nationalisms and Sexualities* (New York, 1992), 82.

people," "a psychological phenomenon. . . . a sort of synthesis of idea, emotion, and ideal."[5] To be sure, a rising interest in secular ideologies during the Cold War added some sophistication. But this sophistication, by which nationalism (like communism and other bad -isms) was seen as a pathology, did not truly redefine the subject of inquiry. Indeed, what was "ideology" for others was for America a naturally occurring, healthy, reasonable idealism. According to Henry Steele Commager, the dominant form of American nationalism arose from America's peculiar conditions and was not imposed upon it; and thus it escaped the pathologies of other, bad nationalisms (read fascism and communism) that were based on romantic associations "with the past, with reaction, with religion, with the military, or with class consciousness." Whether applauded or dissected, nationalism remained a great idea, to be studied as a Great Idea.[6]

Because of this definition of nation, the study of nationalism be-

5. Ernest Renan, "What Is a Nation?" in Homi K. Bhabha, ed., *Nation and Narration* (London, 1990), 19; Max Savelle, *Seeds of Liberty: The Genesis of the American Mind* (1948; rpt. Seattle, Wash., 1965), 554.

Especially useful works on nationalism include Benedict Anderson, *Imagined Communities: Reflections on the Origin and Spread of Nationalism,* rev. ed. (London, 1991); E. J. Hobsbawm, *Nations and Nationalism since 1780: Programme, Myth, Reality* (New York, 1990); Etienne Balibar, "Racism and Nationalism" and "The Nation Form: History and Ideology," in Balibar and Immanuel Wallerstein, *Race, Nation, Class: Ambiguous Identities* (London, 1991), 37–67, 86–106; Marc Shell, *Children of the Earth: Literature, Politics, Nationhood* (New York, 1993); Craig Calhoun, "Nationalism and Difference: The Politics of Identity Writ Large," in Calhoun, *Critical Social Theory: Culture, History, and the Challenge of Difference* (Oxford, 1995), 231–282.

6. Henry Steele Commager, "The Origins and Nature of American Nationalism" (1953), in Commager, *Jefferson, Nationalism, and the Enlightenment* (New York, 1975), 157–196, quoted at 195. Eighteen years later, surveying the American "quest for nationhood," Clinton Rossiter concluded that the idea of "the American mission stimulated a healthy nationalism that fell short of unthinking chauvinism and an exuberant expansionism that fell short of imperial conquest" (*The American Quest, 1790–1860: An Emerging Nation in Search of Identity, Unity, and Modernity* [New York, 1971], 134). This tendency persists in modern writings on contemporary nationalisms, in which liberal, civic nationalism is identified with the the West, and backward, ethnic nationalism with the the third world. The tendency of scholars to distance themselves from the phenomenon of nationalism contributes to the Western demonization of postcolonial nationalist movements. See Alok Yadav, "Nationalism and Contemporaneity: Political Economy of a Discourse," *Cultural Critique,* no. 26 (Winter 1993/1994), 191–229; Will Kymlicka, "Misunderstanding Nationalism," *Dissent,* XLII (1995), 130–137.

came inextricably entangled with the search for the "national mind" or character—an intellectualization of the nineteenth-century search for the national soul in folk cultures. Professional historians and scholars in new fields like American Studies probed the national psyche and became cutting-edge practitioners, as well as occasional critics, of nationalism. By 1963, the rather unscientific basis of the enterprise left David M. Potter in a quandary. How, he wondered, could one name the nation and not be used by it? How could one study nationalism without creating it?[7]

An idealistic definition of nationalism created particular difficulties for those concerned with American nationalism. During the 1950s, a formidable body of literature insisted that America itself was primarily an idea. A comparative perspective, encouraged by American dominance of the West and the growth of totalitarian others in the East, led historians like Richard Hofstadter to conclude that American politics and culture had been marked by a lack of the solid social forces of class inequality that characterized European history: "It has been our fate as a nation, not to have ideologies but to be one."[8] Hofstadter lamented many aspects of the American ideology, but the very structure of his famous quip reveals its indebtedness to a particular Cold War story about America's absolute difference from Europe and the East. Because America was its own ideology, it did not need—or have—"ideologies."

The generation of historians who followed Hofstadter have shown

7. Rupert Wilkinson, *The Pursuit of the American Character* (New York, 1988); David M. Potter, "The Historian's Use of Nationalism and Vice Versa" (1963), in Don E. Fehrenbacher, ed., *History and American Society: Essays of David M. Potter* (New York, 1973), 60–108.

8. Hofstadter quoted in Hans Kohn, *American Nationalism: An Interpretative Essay* (1957; New York, 1961), 25. It should be stressed that when Hofstadter described American ideological consensus he was usually criticizing it, both on its own terms and for what it masked. See Hofstadter, *The American Political Tradition and the Men Who Made It* (New York, 1948). Thus it is all the more disappointing to see Michael Kazin repeating this quote uncritically to conclude an appreciative essay on social historians' efforts to write histories of patriotism that go beyond the assumptions of the consensus school ("The New Historians Recapture the Flag," *New York Times Book Review*, July 2, 1989, 1). Even worse, a later prominent comparative study of nationalism makes America the ideal type in an avowedly idealist interpretation, citing the same Hofstadter line approvingly while asserting that nationalism, though "an explanandum in every other case, . . . in the American society, is an independent variable." See Liah Greenfeld, *Nationalism: Five Roads to Modernity* (Cambridge, Mass., 1992), 402.

that Americans did indeed have ideologies, ranging from far left to far right. Moreover, as some of Hofstadter's own later work suggested, the *interaction* of radical and reactionary ideologies with nationalism has been a recurring trend in American history. "America" was an ideology, but Americans also had ideologies; and, if there is any exceptional character to American cultural and political development, it ought to be sought in the relationship between nationalist ideology and those other ideologies (and realities) that buffeted the myths of national homogeneity and consensus. Too often, American nationalism has been taken at its word and examined alone, as an idea that waxes and wanes, and not in relation to other identities, beliefs, and practices.[9] For example, local, regional, and national identities existed simultaneously, complementing or contesting one another; nationalism is always one of several ideologies in a larger cultural field. If nationalist rhetorics and practices are just one among the many "struggles for recognition" in public life, it follows that nationalism is a political strategy, developed differently at different times by specific groups, responding to the strategies of other groups.[10] Nationalist discourses and practices seek to

9. Richard Hofstadter, *The Paranoid Style in American Politics* (New York, 1967); David Brion Davis, ed., *The Fear of Conspiracy: Images of Un-American Subversion from the Revolution to the Present* (Ithaca, N.Y., 1971); Michael Paul Rogin, *Ronald Reagan, the Movie, and Other Episodes in American Political Demonology* (Berkeley, Calif., 1987), 272–300.

For works that began to overcome the tendency to isolate nationalism but that remained bogged down by the idealist conception of nationalism, see Yehoshua Arieli, *Individualism and Nationalism in American Ideology* (Baltimore, 1964); Paul C. Nagel, *This Sacred Trust: American Nationality, 1798–1898* (New York, 1971); Nagel, "Historiography and American Nationalism: Some Difficulties," *Canadian Review of Studies in Nationalism*, II (1974–1975), 225–240. Richard W. Van Alstyne defined nationalism in terms of imperialism in *Genesis of American Nationalism* (Waltham, Mass., 1970). Nationalism was tied to the emergence of racial and gendered identities by Lawrence J. Friedman, *Inventors of the Promised Land* (New York, 1975); and Elise Marienstras, *Nous, le peuple: les origines du nationalisme américain* (Paris, 1988). For an overview of the literature and a cultural geographer's perspective, see Wilbur Zelinsky, *Nation into State: The Shifting Symbolic Foundations of American Nationalism* (Chapel Hill, N.C., 1988).

10. Pierre Bourdieu, *In Other Words: Essays towards a Reflexive Sociology* (Stanford, Calif., 1990), 22.

Potter made the point about complementary and contrasting ideologies with respect to northern and southern regional identities in "Historian's Use of Nationalism," in his *History and American Society*, ed. Fehrenbacher, 60–108; see also

create what they promote—the nation—but in this they hardly differ from any other group political strategy.

The particular strategies of early American nationalists derived from a particular moment in world history. Older approaches to that nationalism tended to ignore the international trends of "the age of the democratic revolutions" (perhaps better termed the age of the nationalist democratic revolutions). Newer scholarship stresses that the invention of modern democracy in the late eighteenth century was inextricably tied to the creation of newly coherent national peoplehoods whose will, it was believed, ought to be expressed in national political institutions. A "dramatically new political culture" emerged in both France and England during this era, despite these nations' very different political histories. Petitions, huge outdoor meetings, committees of correspondence, and innovative uses of the press energized older customs like ritualized crowd actions.[11] The new reality of the age was much more

---

Robert H. Wiebe, *The Segmented Society: An Introduction to the Meaning of America* (New York, 1975), 46, 98–102; Thomas Bender, *Community and Social Change in America* (1978; rpt. Baltimore, 1982), 87–89.

11. On older approaches, see R. R. Palmer, *The Age of the Democratic Revolutions: A Political History of Europe and America, 1760–1800,* 2 vols. (Princeton, N.J., 1959, 1964). Dominant approaches to the American Revolution do place it explicitly in a European intellectual context, that of "republicanism." Yet the latter interpretive tradition, which arose at about the same time that "nationalism"-as-ideology began to exhaust itself as a subject of historical inquiry, has been remarkably disinclined to come to grips with nationalism, even to the point of denying its existence in late-eighteenth-century America. For signs of change, however, see Edmund S. Morgan, *Inventing the People: The Rise of Popular Sovereignty in England and America* (New York, 1988), 263–287; Michael Warner, *The Letters of the Republic: Publication and the Public Sphere in Eighteenth-Century America* (Cambridge, Mass., 1990); and Peter S. Onuf and Nicholas G. Onuf, *Federal Union, Modern World: The Law of Nations in an Age of Revolutions, 1776–1814* (Madison, Wis., 1993).

On a new political culture, see Lynn Hunt, *Politics, Culture, and Class in the French Revolution* (Berkeley, Calif., 1984), 15; Linda Colley, *Britons: Forging the Nation, 1707–1837* (New Haven, Conn., 1992). Colley argues that it was in large part England's conflicts with France that catalyzed these developments.

On older customs and innovative political practices, see E. P. Thompson, *The Making of the English Working Class* (New York, 1963); Mona Ozouf, *Festivals and the French Revolution,* trans. Alan Sheridan (Cambridge, Mass., 1988); Colin Lucas, ed., *The French Revolution and the Creation of Modern Political Culture,* II, *The Political Culture of the French Revolution* (Oxford, 1988); Robert Darnton and Daniel Roche, eds., *Revolution in Print: The Press in France, 1775–1800* (Berkeley, Calif., 1989);

than the idea of the nation: it was the new political practices justified in the name of the nation and its people.

The rites of nationhood are best understood in the context of this broad range of popular activities, often festive or celebratory, that constituted political action between elections. Too often, an anthropological understanding of such ritual has led scholars to view American holidays in isolation both from the customary and innovative behavior of early modern crowds and from the ritualized rhetoric and behaviors that made up an expanding sphere of politics. From its beginning, the Fourth of July—itself the model for an expanding calendar of post-Revolutionary festivals—drew upon these traditions and innovations. Much as the Fourth improvised upon the old holiday of the King's Birthday, the new American nationals demonstrated their joy or sorrow in a wide range of political events and anniversaries. These nationalist celebrations consisted of far more than parades: there were orations, celebratory dinners at which politically rousing toasts were given, and printed commentary on all of these in their wake. Such rituals might have aspired to a unity beyond political division, but, because of their origins and the political needs of various groups, they did not and could not merely reflect ideological consensus. Instead, they engendered both nationalism and political action.

This irony has been lost on even the most prescient students of American culture. Perhaps because our expectations of nationalist ritual have been formed by the relentlessly (but really only seemingly) depoliticized celebrations of a later day, scholars still recoil at the inescapably partisan parades of the early Republic. In a work otherwise sensitive to the value of conflicts over the meanings of patriotism and national memory, Michael Kammen writes: "Perhaps the most notable aspect of Independence day in our early history was *not* that it became an occasion for consensus, but rather that for a while memory frequently fell victim to fierce factional disputes. Partisanship and mutual recriminations became the order of the nation's natal day, rather than

---

Jeremy Popkin, *Revolutionary News: The Press in France, 1789–1799* (Durham, N.C., 1990); Ruth Bogin, "Petitioning and the New Moral Economy of Post-Revolutionary America," *William and Mary Quarterly*, 3d Ser., XLV (1988), 391–425; Kathleen Wilson, *The Sense of the People: Politics, Culture, and Imperialism in England, 1715–1785* (New York, 1995); Charles Tilly, *Popular Contention in Great Britain, 1758–1834* (Cambridge, Mass., 1995).

reciprocal congratulations based upon shared legends."[12] Politicization
here victimizes "memory," which must be completely shared and consensual in order to be truly national; as a result, a familiar dichotomy
recurs: parades are really something other than politics.

This study argues nearly the opposite: that relentless politicization
gave nationalist rituals their most important meanings. Conflict produced "the nation" as contestants tried to claim true American nationality and the legacy of the Revolution. Sacvan Bercovitch may be right
to maintain that "the rites of assent" ultimately contained all dissent
within an all-embracing American ideology.[13] But, if we leave it at that,
we miss the very real difference that nationalist contest and its parades
have made in American history.

Social historians have led the way in drawing attention to such parades,
and this study would never have been written had it not been for their
example. In the early 1980s Sean Wilentz showed how the festivals
of New York City's artisans broadcast the collective identities of their
trades as well as a sense of citizenship grounded in the craftsman's
useful labor, the independence of the manly producer, and pride in the
American Revolution. These workers took to the streets to equate their
class vision with American republicanism. But when the artisan class
began to split into entrepreneurial masters and deskilled journeymen,
these "artisan republican festivals" became expressions of class conflict,
"a transformation of the rituals of mutuality into declarations of class."[14]

Other scholars have found "a complex process of inclusion, exclusion, influence, and planning" in nineteenth-century urban street the-

12. Michael Kammen, *Mystic Chords of Memory: The Transformation of Tradition in
American Culture* (New York, 1991), 49. For similar critical remarks on early Fourth
of July celebrations, see Robert Pettus Hay, "Freedom's Jubilee: One Hundred Years
of the Fourth of July, 1776 to 1876" (Ph.D. diss., University of Kentucky, 1967);
Diana Karter Appelbaum, *The Glorious Fourth: An American Holiday, an American History* (New York, 1989).

13. Sacvan Bercovitch, *The Rites of Assent: Transformations in the Symbolic Construction of America* (New York, 1993), 49.

14. Sean Wilentz, "Artisan Republican Festivals and the Rise of Class Conflict
in New York City, 1788–1837," in Michael H. Frisch and Daniel J. Walkowitz, eds.,
Working-Class America (Urbana, Ill., 1983), 37–77, quoted at 56; Wilentz, *Chants
Democratic.*

ater, as different groups reacted to each other. At their best, modern studies go beyond showing how one group used parades and reveal festive culture instead as an arena where classes, sexes, and ethnic groups fought their relations out.[15] Close attention to given locales over time has made these insights possible. Yet the methods of the community study draw our attention away from cultural and political phenomena that transcended and transformed the local. Where historians of nationalist ideas erred by assuming national uniformities, social historians' insistence upon local experience makes nationalism comprehensible only as an abstraction. Insofar as they see nationalism as a lived reality, they see it mainly as a screen or vehicle for the working out of more grounded social realities. Larger cultural processes are ignored, just as historians of ideology ignored local constituencies and political practices.

Nationalism, the ideology of the "imagined community," is certainly an abstraction, but it is imagined and practiced locally in distinct, changing ways by different groups for a variety of purposes. How can we do justice to the history of something so imaginary and yet so grounded? To overcome this dilemma, it is helpful to return, for a moment, to the Grand Federal Processions of 1788. The processions transcended local significance because they were repeated, recorded, and reinterpreted: as each state ratified the Constitution, Federalists in all the other states reprinted accounts of the faraway festivals in their local newspapers and celebrated again. The local uses of the streets reverberated nationally.

During the late eighteenth and early nineteenth centuries, newspapers transformed the very rituals that they might seem to merely describe. In an important sense, American parades were always media

15. Susan G. Davis, *Parades and Power: Street Theatre in Nineteenth-Century Philadelphia* (Philadelphia, 1986), 5; Roy Rosenzweig, *Eight Hours for What We Will: Workers and Leisure in an Industrial City, 1870–1920* (New York, 1983), 65–90, 153–168; Mary Ryan, "The American Parade: Representations of the Nineteenth-Century Social Order," in Lynn Hunt, ed., *The New Cultural History* (Berkeley, Calif., 1989), 131–153; Ryan, "Ceremonial Spaces: Public and Private Women," in *Women in Public: Between Banners and Ballots, 1825–1880* (Baltimore, 1990), 19–57; David G. Hackett, "The Social Origins of Nationalism: Albany, New York, 1754–1835," *Journal of Social History*, XXI (1987–1988), 659–681; Scott C. Martin, *Killing Time: Leisure and Culture in Southwestern Pennsylvania, 1800–1850* (Pittsburgh, Pa., 1995), 71–101. For an overview of this literature, see John Bodnar, *Remaking America: Public Memory, Commemoration, and Patriotism in the Twentieth Century* (Princeton, N.J., 1992), 21–38.

events.[16] By thinking of newspapers as mere documentary windows onto the scenes and symbols of parades, social historians have largely ignored the printed discourse that surrounded these events and gave them extralocal meaning. From the beginning, celebrants of the nation took their cues from printed sources. They improvised upon events they read about and then publicized their own interventions in public life. If we restrict our inquiries to the parade itself, we rely on a narrowly anthropological definition of ritual that does not do justice to the cultural complexity, much less the political significance, of modern American celebrations.[17]

This study views ballads, broadsides, orations, and newspaper report-

16. Michael McGerr shrewdly notes: "The denigration of popular demonstrations as 'media events' is one more way in which contemporary discourse robs Americans of their political heritage. The presence of reporters and cameras seemingly deprives an activity of its legitimacy; apparently people are supposed to watch 'events,' not to create them" ("Political Styles and Women's Power, 1830–1930," *Journal of American History*, LXXVII [1990–1991], 879). David Chaney and James Carey have argued that the notion of ritual can itself be applied to the very processes of mass communication: see Chaney, "The Symbolic Form of Ritual in Mass Communication," in Peter Golding et al., eds., *Communicating Politics: Mass Communications and the Political Process* (New York, 1986), 115–132; Carey, *Communication as Culture* (London, 1989), chap. 2. In any case, the ritualization of reportage (not to mention the skepticism about it) is nothing new, and there can be no easy separation of authentic ritual or political actions from inauthentic media events. Instead, we should explore the changing nature of this mediation for insights into the specific character of ritualized performances and their extralocal political effects.

17. For examples of this anthropology, which has yet to overcome its own restrictive definitions of rituals as "relatively closed phenomenal worlds," see Victor W. Turner, *The Ritual Process: Structure and Anti-Structure* (Chicago, 1969); Turner, ed., *Celebration: Studies in Festivity and Ritual* (Washington, D.C., 1982); John J. MacAloon, ed., *Rite, Drama, Festival, Spectacle: Rehearsals toward a Theory of Cultural Performance* (Philadelphia, 1984); Alessandro Falassi, ed., *Time out of Time: Essays on the Festival* (Albuquerque, N.M., 1987); Don Handelman, *Models and Mirrors: Towards an Anthropology of Public Events* (Cambridge, 1990), quoted at 16. A partial exception is David I. Kertzer, *Ritual, Politics, and Power* (New Haven, Conn., 1988). Other anthropologists who labor in the interdisciplinary field of cultural studies have produced excellent case studies that explicitly deal with the representation of festivals and that place both festivals and representations of them in larger cultural and political contexts. See especially Virginia R. Dominguez, *People as Subject, People as Object: Selfhood and Peoplehood in Contemporary Israel* (Madison, Wis., 1988); Richard Handler, *Nationalism and the Politics of Culture in Quebec* (Madison, Wis., 1989); Robert Cantwell, *Ethnomimesis: Folklife and the Representation of Culture* (Chapel Hill, N.C., 1993).

age as nationalist practices, every bit as much as the processions they announced, punctuated, and described. They did more than spread nationalism: they constituted a national popular political culture. In the first chapter I argue that the colonists of mid-eighteenth-century British America drew upon a rich spectrum of celebratory and anti-celebratory, or mourning, rituals through which they expressed their approval or disapproval of political institutions and events. These rites, as performed and printed, were the building blocks both of the whig rebels' resistance to the British Empire and, after 1776, of American nationhood. With the Declaration of Independence, the revolutionaries turned the King's Birthday festival into a funeral for monarchy. British tradition made it possible for the warring whigs to celebrate an American future.

Chapter 2 takes up the post-Revolutionary crisis of the 1780s: how nationalist rites were employed to stymie disorderly expressions of political differences. Members of the upper classes staged impressive displays of patriotic sensibility in an attempt to domesticate the Revolution. These patriotic spectacles were responding to a threefold crisis of representation during the postwar years, as political language, personal identity, and paper currency all seemed to have lost their secure foundations in reality. As part of the debate over the ratification of the Constitution, Federalists seized upon these celebratory forms in an effort to create unanimity, or at least the appearance of it, in favor of the new federal government. They did marginalize their Antifederalist opponents, but their intervention in the politics of the streets would have been unthinkable without the very development that elite federalism was designed to control: the truly revolutionary participation of large numbers of people in politics.

During the 1790s, nationalist celebrations became a key locus of the continuing battle over the nature of political participation. Both nascent parties invented new rites that expressed their different views: the Federalists' tributes to Washington, the Democratic-Republicans' fetes in honor of the French Revolution, both parties' competing July Fourth celebrations, and the national fasts and thanksgiving days Federalists developed to wed nationalism and religion to the state. After 1800, the Republicans pioneered election-oriented festivals that helped legitimate key innovations in local political organizing. Chapters 3 and 4 trace the subtle yet deeply charged relationship between nationalist partisan subcultures and local political practice. Owing to the elite orientation of their preferred sources, most political historians have concluded that only political leaders had a national perspective; I try to show that celebrations and the printed discourse that suffused them made it possible for large numbers of people—men and women—to practice nationalism and local politics simultaneously. To see the contemporary public sphere in the intersection of local rites and an expanding print culture illuminates much about early national political culture, including the seemingly paradoxical existence of partisanship alongside nationalist denials of party legitimacy, and how partisan competition helped keep women and blacks beyond the pale of citizenship.

The last two chapters stress other effects of America's competitive, nationalist political culture, effects that surpassed the intentions of its most able practitioners. By the time that the white nationalists of the American Colonization Society seized the mantle of the nation in their efforts to cleanse the United States of its free African American population, abolitionists had already begun to use Fourth of July rhetoric and rituals to protest the existence of slavery in a free country. Free blacks themselves exposed the hypocritical rhetoric of Independence but simultaneously appropriated the forms of white nationalism—parades, oratory, and print culture—to create their own diasporist African nationalism. Black celebrations of the end of the slave trade, along with the reactions of whites to them, speak volumes for the remarkable openness as well as the tragic limitations of nationalist politics.

For even American politics is always about limits as well as new beginnings; yesterday's successful strategy engenders today's crisis and tomorrow's political tragedy. The unavoidable reality of regional differences in early national America created problems and opportunities for people in both parties and in each section of the country. With varying success, New England, western, and southern regionalisms developed in dialogue with nationalist practices; each sought to express that nationalism. The triumphs of southern Jeffersonians over New England Federalists during the first two decades of the nineteenth century might only have set the pattern for the sectional partisan battles that led to the Civil War. The resolutions of such conflicts seemed to lie in the frontier, where insecure patriots celebrated themselves as the advance guard of the American nation and were joined, through print, by easterners (north and south) intent on their own role in the westward-moving American future. But rather frank attempts to dissolve regional conflict through celebrations of economic development, as in the spectacles of progress and improvement that marked events like the opening of the Erie Canal, only reveal, in retrospect, how the practices of nationalism provided for both divisive activity and real consensus. American minorities, be they partisan, racial, regional, might have found themselves limited by the rites of national assent, but the creators of whatever consensus did emerge repeatedly found that they could not truly celebrate their way into a future without differences—which is to say, without politics.

The practices of nationalism are political practices; to ignore the politics of the parade is to miss its very reason for being. Moreover, those who see nationalism as a realm of unthinking consensus, and therefore as neither interesting nor politically useful, have conceded too much to those who have used parades to recreate that myth of consensus. Americans left and right appear to share an ambivalence regarding the nationalist practices that seem somehow removed from politics but that are actually among our oldest political tools. Ironically, this ambivalence—the denial of the political that legitimates creative political practice—is one of the contributions of the founding fathers, some of whom would have preferred that politics remain their more or less exclusive domain.

This study traces the enabling and paralyzing contradictions of American political culture to the conjoined emergence of popular politics and the rituals of national identity. It is this conjunction—the local and the national, the politicized and the consensual—that inspires the remarkable creativity and the profound ambivalence I see as equally crucial aspects of whatever American political tradition can be said to exist. We have only begun to comprehend this ambivalence, even as Americans continue the creative, festive practice. But, by comprehending it, we might become more self-conscious, and more honest, practitioners.

REVOLUTION, NATION, STATE

THE
REVOLUTIONARY
POLITICS OF
CELEBRATION

In a famous letter home just after the Continental Congress declared American national Independence, John Adams predicted: The anniversary of the Declaration "will be the most memorable Epocha, in the History of America.—I am apt to believe that it will be celebrated, by succeeding Generations, as the great anniversary Festival. It ought to be commemorated, as the Day of Deliverance by solemn Acts of Devotion to God Almighty. It ought to be solemnized with Pomp and Parade, with Shews, Games, Sports, Guns, Bells, Bonfires and Illuminations, from one End of this Continent to the other from this Time forward forever more."[1] Adams, of course, proved to be almost as prophetic as he had wished. But why did he expect—insist, even—that national Independence be celebrated by "Pomp and Parade," everywhere, forever?

By the late 1760s Adams had learned the uses of festivity in the struggle against British imperial authority. He understood how politicized anniversaries wedded tradition to innovation, broadcasting potentially controversial statements in well-known, even beloved cultural forms, like toasts and newspaper accounts. During the Revolutionary struggle, Adams and his fellow patriots relied upon a dynamic relationship between local street theater, print culture, and the imagined community of the Revolutionary American nation.[2] As the very practices of

1. John Adams to Abigail Adams, July 3, 1776, in L. H. Butterfield et al., eds., *The Adams Family Correspondence* (Cambridge, Mass., 1963–), II, 30.

2. David W. Conroy, *In Public Houses: Drink and the Revolution of Authority in Colonial Massachusetts* (Chapel Hill, N.C., 1995), 265–268. On nationalism and print

nationalism, these celebrations and publications drew upon the politicized rituals that Britons had been employing for more than a century.
The mobilization of citizens to celebrate patriotic occasions, with the
reprinting of accounts of these events, helped make an intercolonial
resistance movement possible.

As developed and modified by patriots after 1776, these rites of celebration, publication, and republication became capable of resolving
certain problems of the American Revolutionary struggle. Celebrations
and printed accounts of them embodied and emboldened a nationalist ideology that made consensus the basis of patriotism. Indeed, by
fostering an idea of the nation as extralocal community and by giving
ordinary people the opportunity for local expression of national feeling, this reciprocal influence of celebrations and print literally and
figuratively papered over the disturbing class resentments (expressed
in the antiaristocratic language of the Revolution) that had energized
much of the populace in the first place.[3] By the 1790s these resentments
would reemerge in festive culture, as nationalist celebrations provided
a venue for recasting them as national, partisan political divisions. Yet
during the war years, past and present divisions between plebeians and
elites, and among elites themselves, were absorbed by the direct link
between the people and the nation whose Independence they repeatedly celebrated. Through crucial displacements of space and time, the
local came to represent the national while the present gave proof, not
of the past, but of the future. Spread by print, the unruly rites of rebellion could serve as ruling rites of assent.

ANCIENT RITES

Controversies over what the English should celebrate and how they
should celebrate it date back to the sixteenth century, the era when

culture, see especially Benedict Anderson, *Imagined Communities: Reflections on the
Origins and Spread of Nationalism*, rev. ed. (New York, 1991), 9–65; Michael Warner,
The Letters of the Republic: Publication and the Public Sphere in Eighteenth-Century America
(Cambridge, Mass., 1990).

    3. On class and the Revolution, see Gary B. Nash, *The Urban Crucible: The North-
ern Seaports and the Origins of the American Revolution* (Cambridge, Mass., 1986); Allan
Kulikoff, *The Agrarian Origins of American Capitalism* (Charlottesville, Va., 1992),
99–151; Alfred F. Young, ed., *The American Revolution: Explorations in the History of
American Radicalism* (DeKalb, Ill., 1976); Young, ed., *Beyond the American Revolution:
Explorations in the History of American Radicalism* (DeKalb, Ill., 1993).

the cultural project of inventing nationhood began to take its many forms. Protestant reformers "inveighed against the licentiousness that was associated with popular festivity" and attacked the saints' days that dotted the Roman Catholic calendar. Not surprisingly, new secular anniversaries, commemorating such events as the accession of Elizabeth I, royal birthdays, and military victories, followed fast on the suppression of church-sponsored revelry. During the 1620s, William Laud (later archbishop of Canterbury) and his followers made a concerted effort to combine approved old-church holidays with the new rites of the state, such as the observance of the King's Birthday. In doing so, Laud and his followers hoped to resolve the diverging preferences of royalty, churchmen, lords, gentry, and common folk by remarrying the sacred and the secular. For example, Gunpowder Day (or Guy Fawkes Day, November 5, commemorating the rescue of the church and state from a Popish plot) replaced Halloween. High Church ritual returned to official favor, and the relatively new state-sponsored red-letter days took on the appearance of the old saints' days, including orchestrated synchronized bell ringings.[4]

The deep social and cultural conflicts of the mid-seventeenth century only raised the stakes of this "politics of mirth." Puritans campaigned against festivals; non-Puritan elites and plebeians championed them. During the English Civil War itself, both Cavaliers and Roundheads perceived an affinity between traditional festivity and the Royalist cause. The first modern revolution profoundly politicized cultural forms. In this case it was the counterrevolutionaries who favored the cultivation of traditional revelry, such as morris dancing. Yet celebrations were never merely tools used by political factions to gain followers: they were actual enactments of ideological alternatives.[5] Elites, middling sorts, and common people alike invented traditions of ritual and counterritual that symbolized the worlds they had lost and the worlds they hoped to create.

Long after the English Civil War, celebration continued to be an

4. Richard Helgerson, *Forms of Nationhood: The Elizabethan Writing of England* (Chicago, 1992); David Cressy, *Bonfires and Bells: National Memory and the Protestant Calendar in Elizabethan and Stuart England* (Berkeley, Calif., 1989), 4, 52 (quote), 34–92; David Underdown, *Revel, Riot, and Rebellion: Popular Politics and Culture in England, 1603–1660* (New York, 1985), 70.

5. Leah S. Marcus, *The Politics of Mirth: Jonson, Herrick, Milton, Marvell, and the Defense of Old Holiday Pastimes* (Chicago, 1986); Underdown, *Revel, Riot, and Rebellion,* 44–72, 103, 240, 275.

important site of the struggles among patricians and between patricians and plebeians. As the gentry gradually withdrew from face-to-face relationships with their social inferiors through the eighteenth century, they also encouraged a flood of festive creativity and used such occasions to stage conspicuous displays of their generosity. Common folk matched the gentry's creativity. Anniversary observances of Queen Anne's coronation and the King's Birthday sparked opposition celebrations that turned riotous in 1715; thereafter, on Restoration Day (December 5, marking the return of a Stuart king, Charles II, to the throne), pro-Tory crowds smashed unilluminated Whig windows; the military dispersed demonstrations held on the birthday of the Stuart Pretender, James II. Ballads, always a staple of festive culture, once again became key expressions of political opinion. Printed and then hawked in the streets, these songs mingle oral and print culture: "Through the new media of journalism, urban festival reached an expanding audience." Augustan England's calendar of politicized holidays was in fact a precondition of the new political culture coalescing in taverns, coffeehouses, and newspapers. Even the new, bourgeois public sphere, organized around clubs and polite letters, can be seen as a locus for relating and debating the deeds of a politically active populace as well as the doings of an increasingly powerful central government.[6] And, thanks to the press, the meanings of celebration began to travel the sea and back, on the same ships that brought news of changes in imperial policy to the inhabitants of colonial British America.

Whether they adopted or refused the rites of church and crown, the American colonists participated in the same festive battles over the character of sacred and secular community. Some historians have seen the calendar of seventeenth-century America as "the dullest in Western

6. E. P. Thompson, *Customs in Common: Studies in Traditional Popular Culture* (New York, 1991), 45–94; Robert W. Malcomson, *Popular Recreations in English Society, 1700–1850* (Cambridge, 1973); Nicholas Rogers, *Whigs and Cities: Popular Politics in the Age of Walpole and Pitt* (Oxford, 1989), 9, 25–29, 53–61, 350–386, quoted at 353; John Brewer, *Party Ideology and Popular Politics at the Accession of George III* (New York, 1976), 150; Linda Colley, *Britons: Forging the Nation, 1707–1837* (New Haven, Conn., 1992); Kathleen Wilson, *The Sense of the People: Politics, Culture, and Imperialism in England, 1715–1785* (New York, 1995). For the concept of the bourgeois public sphere, see Jürgen Habermas, *The Structural Transformation of the Public Sphere,* trans. Thomas Burger (Cambridge, Mass., 1989).

civilization." Underpopulation and the hardships of settler life certainly limited public life in the early seventeenth century. But the dearth of holidays was also a conscious choice on the part of the New England Puritan leadership, a choice among alternatives in a shared Anglo-American culture. Political and religious differences led some colonists to revel while others expressed themselves by ignoring the occasion. In 1663, the Virginia House of Burgesses declared that the date planned for a foiled servants' rebellion should "be annually kept holy . . . in a perpetual commemoration": we can be fairly certain that Virginia's many indentured bondpersons found little in this to celebrate, but the declaration itself tells us much about the uses of commemoration in the expression of political differences. After news arrived at Jamestown of the Restoration of Charles II, for example, the inhabitants heard music, danced, and fired guns; but there was little in the way of revelry among the sympathizers of Cromwell in Massachusetts. Later, during the imperial reorganization known as the Dominion of New England (1686–1689), Governor Edmund Andros's regime promoted royal birthday parades and church services for the anniversary of the execution of Charles I, much to the irritation of many colonists. Some New Englanders resisted by calling fast days to counter the Dominion's festivals and thanksgivings.[7]

By the eighteenth century, even New Englanders participated fully in the Anglo-American politics of celebration. Guy Fawkes Day, for example, evolved into a popular way of expressing anti-Catholicism. Through the flexible form of the effigy of the Pretender (false nobleman as well as Popish usurper), some colonists criticized secular as well as religious aristocracy. Moreover, as Richard L. Bushman has shown, eighteenth-century Massachusetts possessed a monarchical political

7. David Freeman Hawke, *Everyday Life in Early America* (New York, 1988), quoted at 91; Robert Middlekauff, "The Ritualization of the American Revolution," in Stanley Coben and Lorman Ratner, eds., *The Development of an American Culture* (Englewood Cliffs, N.J., 1970), 32–33; Michael Zuckerman, "Pilgrims in the Wilderness: Community, Modernity, and the Maypole at Merry Mount," *New England Quarterly*, L (1977), 255–277; Edmund S. Morgan, *American Slavery, American Freedom: The Ordeal of Colonial Virginia* (New York, 1975), 246; Lyon G. Tyler, "Virginia under the Commonwealth," *William and Mary Quarterly*, 1st Ser., I (1892–1893), 196; Cressy, *Bonfires and Bells,* 196–202; Richard P. Gildrie, *The Profane, the Civil, and the Godly: The Reformation of Manners in Orthodox New England, 1679–1747* (University Park, Pa., 1994), 89; Stephen Foster, *The Long Argument: English Puritanism and the Shaping of New England Culture, 1570–1700* (Chapel Hill, N.C., 1991), 238–239.

culture, complete with celebrations that expressed the mutual dependence of king and people. In colonial America as in the mother
country, the deference of plebeians to patricians, and the rivalries
among patricians themselves, gained expression when common people
watched, or cheered, their betters performing the ceremonies of public life. Court days and elections more closely resembled early modern
carnival than today's orderly behind-the-curtain voting rites, insofar as
these public events brought high and low into deeply charged, face-
to-face, ritualized encounters. If these events were local in focus, they
nonetheless existed on the same imperial calendar, on a continuum
with officially sanctioned celebrations of empire and monarchy.[8]

Even the New Englanders' dull calendar seems less so when we consider the legacy of fast days and thanksgivings that encouraged political
expression in the form of toasts and sermons. Popular tradition persisted, and Puritans did not so much eradicate these festive forms as
channel them into godly practices, like the Sabbath. Religiously sanctioned feasting and fasting rites remained quite popular among the
godly and the profane alike, not least because of their adaptability to
civil controversies. In 1750, on the anniversary of the execution of
Charles I, Jonathan Mayhew explicitly attacked the "slavish" doctrine
of submission to secular authority that many other preachers promul-
gated annually on that date. According to John Adams, Mayhew's published sermon was "read by everybody"; it became one of the most
famous texts of the nascent resistance movement.[9]

8. Peter Shaw, *American Patriots and the Rituals of Revolution* (Cambridge, Mass.,
1981); Alfred F. Young, "English Plebeian Culture and Eighteenth-Century American Radicalism," in Margaret Jacob and James Jacob, eds., *The Origins of Anglo-
American Radicalism* (London, 1984), 185–212; Paul A. Gilje, *The Road to Mobocracy: Popular Disorder in New York City, 1763–1834* (Chapel Hill, N.C., 1987), 28–
36; Richard L. Bushman, *King and People in Provincial Massachusetts* (Chapel Hill,
N.C., 1985); Gordon S. Wood, *The Radicalism of the American Revolution* (New York,
1992), 11–92; Conroy, *In Public Houses*, 57–58, 160; Steven C. Bullock, *Revolutionary
Brotherhood: Freemasonry and the Transformation of the American Social Order, 1730–1840*
(Chapel Hill, N.C., 1996), 73–79; Edmund S. Morgan, *Inventing the People: The Rise
of Popular Sovereignty in England and America* (New York, 1988), 174–208; Rhys Isaac,
The Transformation of Virginia, 1740–1790 (Chapel Hill, N.C., 1982), 110–114, 252–
254.

9. Harry S. Stout, *The New England Soul: Preaching and Religious Culture in Colonial
New England* (New York, 1986), 6; David D. Hall, *Worlds of Wonder, Days of Judgment:
Popular Religious Belief in Early New England* (New York, 1989), 166–172; Gildrie, *The

But Mayhew's sermon was hardly the first time that festivity and publication had crystallized controversies over the nature of government and the extent of British liberties. The famous 1734 libel trial of John Peter Zenger, printer of the *New-York Weekly Journal,* followed his publication of broadside ballads that celebrated the victory of insurgent candidates for the Common Council. The songs ridiculed a feast held by the losers in honor of the governor and the obsequious address that they had presented to him and published in the rival *New-York Gazette.* Zenger's anonymous balladeer praised those who voted for the opposition:

> Your votes you gave for those brave men
>   who feasting did despise;
> And never prostituted pen
>   to certify the lies
> That were drawn up to put in chains
> As well our nymphs as happy swains;
>   —with a fa la la.

The song itself linked political writing and feasting; it continued, through a logic of inversion, the very celebration and printed commentary that it lambasted. Chief Justice James De Lancey ordered the offending broadside to be burned, setting off a debate in the courts and the papers over the freedom of the press. In the *Weekly Journal,* the defenders of published satire explicitly compared themselves to the "patriot whigs" of seventeenth-century England.[10]

Many colonists, then, were already proving adept at using British tradition to their own ends. As the examples of Zenger and Mayhew indicate, this tradition included both festive practice and printed commentary in several genres. Printed texts such as Zenger's broadsides and Mayhew's sermon enabled the politics of celebration to be not only

---

Profane, the Civil, and the Godly, 111–130; Jonathan Mayhew, *A Discourse, concerning Unlimited Submission and Non-Resistance to the Higher Powers . . .* (1750) (Boston, 1818), iv, 37–39, 43–46; Patricia U. Bonomi, *Under the Cope of Heaven: Religion, Society, and Politics in Colonial America* (New York, 1986), 195–197 (Adams quoted at 197); "A Republican," *Boston Gazette, and the Country Journal,* Jan. 31, 1785.

10. James Alexander, *A Brief Narrative of the Case and Trial of John Peter Zenger, Printer of the New York Weekly Journal* (1735), ed. Stanley Nider Katz (Cambridge, Mass., 1963), 109, 116, 221 n.2; Patricia U. Bonomi, *A Factious People: Politics and Society in Colonial New York* (New York, 1971), 114–117.

a local but also an extralocal, even imperial, politics, since both protests questioned the authority of British appointees in the colonies. This
repeated move from performance to print and back epitomized a profound, complex set of cultural forms in which traditional festivals were
inverted into dirges and then reinverted to become celebrations, only
to be improved upon in song, in dance, in the streets, in church, and,
once again, in print. The coming decades would reveal celebration and
print to be not just available political resources but necessary ones for
those who would resist imperial authority.

FESTIVITY AND THE ORIGINS OF AMERICAN POLITICS

During the 1760s, American colonists adopted a very British politics
of opposition. The colonists' rich spectrum of celebratory and mourning rituals articulated the overlapping series of polarities that, taken
together, constituted the political culture of Anglo-America: whig versus tory, Protestant versus Catholic, Dissenter versus High Church,
better versus lower sorts, English versus French or Irish, male citizens
versus effeminized others. The sheer number of possible oppositions,
representing the real diversity of Anglo-American society, made the
politics of celebration a fertile occasion for the making and unmaking
of political alliances such as the church-and-king crowds led by tories.
One of the root meanings of the verb *to celebrate,* after all, is to publicize, to make known; through toasts and other celebratory declarations,
whigs and tories alike made known their allegiances.[11]

Much like the anti-Puritan mirthmakers of the seventeenth century
and the Country party pamphleteers of the early eighteenth, these colonial whigs justified their noncompliance with state regulations through
references to ancient British customs and liberties. The American "rituals of revolution" drew on a popular political culture that was satu-
rated by controversies with economic roots: for example, in wars and
their attendant taxes. In the era of the decidedly international Seven
Years' War, it did not take the mind of a James Otis to understand that
these economic consequences had an imperial dimension, for Britons

11. Bernard Bailyn, *The Ideological Origins of the American Revolution* (Cambridge,
Mass., 1967); Shaw, *American Patriots and the Rituals of Revolution;* Ann Fairfax
Withington, *Toward a More Perfect Union: Virtue and the Formation of American Republics* (New York, 1991), 92–143; Ruth H. Bloch, *Visionary Republic: Millennial Themes
in American Thought, 1756–1800* (New York, 1985), 53–74.

in the colonies and at home. British Americans occupied a marginal position with respect to centers of power, not unlike that of England's Country-thinking gentry, the artisan political parvenus associated with John Wilkes, or the disenfranchised participants in London crowds. All these groups claimed, with some plausibility, to be the true representatives of "the people" and the nation while arguing for measures that addressed their particular political and economic needs. We should not be surprised, then, to see colonists drawing on the forms of street theater as well as the patterns of thought of their predecessors in contests with British central authority. Thus a *North American's Almanack* of 1775 described the "antient Whigs" not just as those who stood against the "Court" interest but as Scotsmen who "held meetings." American whigs adopted the Wilkesites' celebrations of Wilkes and execrations of Lord Bute, festive practices that borrowed from traditional holiday celebrations and the rituals of royalty. Like the Wilkesites, the colonial rebels pursued in their celebration an alliance, however uneasy, between the middling interests and the popular interest against a real and an imaginary aristocracy. They could do so and still be loyal to Mother England precisely because such ritual protests were performed in the name of English tradition and its guardian, the king. With the king on their side, the lower classes could take the rhetorical high ground, even against the king's men.[12]

The first and most important example of celebration and mourning as loyal protest would be the street theater surrounding the Stamp Act crisis. In addition to symbolically killing and burying stamp distributors, angry colonists announced and performed "the funeral of Liberty." They took this metaphor into the streets in actual funeral processions. Patriots inverted traditional rituals to depict a political world turned upside down. These rites expressed a stance and a program: Liberty could be revived before her internment, just as aristocratic stamp

12. John Brewer, "Commercialization and Politics," in Neil McKendrick, Brewer, and J. H. Plumb, *The Birth of a Consumer Society* (Bloomington, Ind., 1982), 197–262; T. H. Breen, "'Baubles of Britain': The American and British Consumer Revolutions of the Eighteenth Century," *Past and Present*, no. 119 (May 1988), 73–104; John Brewer, *The Sinews of Power: War, Money, and the English State, 1688–1783* (New York, 1989); Samuel Stearns, *The North American's Almanack, and Gentleman's and Lady's Diary, for . . . 1776* (Worcester, Mass., 1775); Pauline Maier, *From Resistance to Revolution: Colonial Radicals and the Development of American Opposition to Britain, 1765–1776* (New York, 1972), 161–197; Shaw, *American Patriots and the Rituals of Revolution*, 48–73.

men could repent. If the Stamp Act spurred rites of mourning, the act's repeal spelled celebration. The first crowd actions resisting the act and its repeal (August 14, 1765, and March 18, 1766) were later memorialized as patriot holidays, solemnized by pilgrimages to the Liberty Tree and ratified by public toasts to ancient British liberties and the king who upheld them.[13]

Toasts possessed the dialogic character often found in early modern literature: every word is an object that can be made to look ridiculous. Offered daily in taverns, toasts were often the centerpiece of festive dinners. A toast could be a celebration or an abnegation, an invocation of praise or blame: tories themselves came to be known according to whom they toasted, when, and how. The Revolutionary committees that were organized to enforce nonimportation and boycott of British goods punished two sorts of acts: noncompliance, and slander of the patriot cause. Often such slander consisted of a toast in the form of a curse, such as this one from the war years: "The Continental Congress, with all their subordinates, may their commissions prove death warrants, and their sword belts be exchanged for halters." Such strong sentiments gained at least some of their bluster from strong drink. Yet taverns were far more than places to imbibe. Men repaired there to read the newspapers and discuss politics: they were ideal sites for these public acts of affiliation.[14]

Another kind of celebratory inversion put to effective use by the rebels was tarring and feathering. This most humiliating of rituals actu-

13. Withington, *Toward a More Perfect Union,* 144–184; Arthur M. Schlesinger, *Prelude to Independence: The Newspaper War on Britain, 1764–1776* (1957; rpt. Boston, 1980), 76–78; Philip Davidson, *Propaganda and the American Revolution, 1763–1783* (Chapel Hill, N.C., 1941), 174–179; Frank Moore, comp., *Diary of the American Revolution, from Newspapers and Original Documents* (New York, 1860), I, 127; Shaw, *American Patriots and the Rituals of Revolution,* 182; Beverly Orlove Held, "'To Instruct and Improve . . . to Entertain and Please': American Civic Protests and Pageants, 1765–1784" (Ph.D. diss., University of Michigan, 1987), chaps. 2–3.

14. M[ikhail] Bakhtin, *The Dialogic Imagination: Four Essays,* ed. Michael Holquist, trans. Caryl Emerson and Holquist (Austin, Tex., 1981), 49–50; "Loyal Constitutional Toasts and Sentiments," in *Loyal and Humorous Songs, on Requested Occasions* (New York, 1779), 53; Withington, *Toward a More Perfect Union,* 219–220; Robert McCluer Calhoon, *The Loyalists in Revolutionary America, 1760–1781* (New York, 1973), 399; Richard J. Hooker, "The American Revolution Seen through a Wine Glass," *WMQ,* 3d Ser., XI (1954), 64–65; Peter John Thompson, "A Social History of Philadelphia's Taverns, 1683–1800" (Ph.D. diss., University of Pennsylvania, 1989), 58–118; Conroy, *In Public Houses.*

ally reversed the coronation ceremony: transgressors were crowned with goose quills. Rather than proceeding through town to a symbolic center, tories were marched out of town, sometimes permanently. Again and again, the feathered tories were described as getting "a new set of clothes," "in the new style." The desire for unwarranted social distinction—the basic explanation tories themselves gave for discontent among the people—was thus secured onto the tory body politic. *They* were the would-be aristocrats, enemies of communal good and the republican ideal. Whether or not a true American invention, tarring and feathering drew on the conventions of satirical prints, in which political offenders appeared as geese, and "turned the prints into real life." Moreover, the connection between political tracts and street politics was not lost on rebel crowds. When a stamp man or an author was not available, they often tarred and feathered a pamphlet instead.[15]

These rituals certainly "dramatized" Revolutionary politics, and their description in the press certainly gave them extralocal consequences as they were mimicked or improved upon elsewhere. Yet the coherence of the process arose, not from the simple addition of celebration and printed discourse, but from their mutual reinforcement, so that it becomes hard to tell where the ritual or the reportage begins or ends. The reciprocal constitution of celebration and print may be seen in a fascinating piece of newspaper satire that appeared shortly after Independence. This report is said to come from a London paper of six months earlier; it announces a special joint celebration, in the empire's capital, of the anniversaries of "Saint YANKEY's day" and the skirmish at Lexington. According to the author of the pseudocommentary, all "loyal friends of government" from America (that is, the tories) would celebrate the auspicious day. The collected exiles and their friends would join in procession from the Crown and Anchor, in the Strand, to Saint Dunstan's, where they would hear a sermon by "Rev. Mr. CORIOLANUS, from New York." The procession would be joined later by a "Reverend band of Martyrs" from Saint Paul's, and by none other than former Massachusetts governor Thomas Hutchinson, in the role of "St. Yankie."[16]

15. Shaw, *American Patriots and the Rituals of Revolution*, 185–188; Withington, *Toward a More Perfect Union*, 226, 229, 231–237; Schlesinger, *Prelude to Independence*, 223.

16. Isaac, *Transformation of Virginia*, 248–260; *Freeman's Journal, or New-Hampshire Gazette* (Portsmouth), Sept. 28, 1776.

Dressed "in his speckled velvet," the most prominent American loyalist in the imaginary procession carries "Machiavelli's works richly gilt and lettered, in his right hand, and [is] supported" on each side, lest he falter, by his predecessor and his successor in tyranny, Governor Francis Bernard and General Thomas Gage, "both of them in armor." Bringing up the rear would be "mandamus counselors," judges of the imperial admiralty courts, "Fugitive Clergy," "American commissioners of revenue," and all their administrative servants, "dressed as harlequins." Finally, following the colonial officials who justified and enforced Parliament's taxes, and marching a quickstep "Yankee Doodle," would be the "hypocritic merchants" who claimed to be patriots but doubled as informers. They proceed with black veils on their faces. The author did not forget to ask the presumed audience—the nobility—to caution their coachmen "not to stop up the passage in the narrow part of the strand."[17]

This fiction of celebration ridicules a would-be king and the political placemen who have alienated the colonists. Real Massachusetts patriots solemnly marked the anniversary of Lexington; but, after years of funereal rites that commemorated the passage of the Stamp Act and the Boston Massacre, they imagined their opponents turning it into a festival—a saint's day. This allusion to the Anglicization of Popish ritual and its royalist overtones would not have been missed by Protestant colonists. Nor would they have mistaken the path of the procession, which marked the participants as pro-Restoration, church-and-king martyrs. Even in supposedly celebrating their Yankeeism, the experts in official ritual get it all wrong. The procession is at once too stately and too clownish. Officers of the crown appear as fools while two-faced Americans are shamed in echoes of both carnival (the harlequin dress) and the ritual punishment of transgressors, such as tarring and feathering.[18]

17. *Freeman's Journal, or New-Hampshire Gazette,* Sept. 28, 1776.

18. "Coriolanus" of New York, the minister who gives the sermon, is probably the Reverend Charles Inglis, the Anglican tory who had written against Paine's antimonarchical *Common Sense* (Philadelphia, 1776). He would later use the anniversary of the "martyrdom" of Charles I (January 30) in British-occupied New York to compare the Revolution to the "unnatural rebellion" of the Puritans. See Inglis, *The Duty of Honouring the King, Explained and Recommended* . . . (New York, 1780). British opponents of the American war incorporated the colonists' grievances into celebrations and boycotted certain national anniversaries (Wilson, *The Sense of the People,* 241, 245).

On these traditions of carnival and ritual punishment, see Peter Stallybrass and

FIGURE 1. *The Repeal; or, The Funeral Procession of Miss Americ-Stamp.*
1766. Courtesy American Antiquarian Society

The misrule here is the pretension of elites, their self-aggrandizement in the shadows of church and king.

Said to be written by an authentic Briton, this anticelebratory satire ridicules tories for adhering to bad British forms of culture. They are shamed before American patriots, but the printed nature of this exercise makes it possible to throw them onto London streets. With reference to more than a century of political events and celebratory practices, the story invents an aristocratic, High Church tory alternative to patriot ritual, thus making the punishment tories faced before and after 1776—ritualized ridicule and real exile—fit their crimes. Such a spoof of excessive Britishness, of course, could be executed (or understood) only by those steeped in the dense symbolic order of Anglo-American popular political culture. Its appearance in a newspaper suggests that print and the rituals of revolution fed one another, increasing both the geographical reach of ideology and the opportunities for local practice.

Allon White, *The Politics and Poetics of Transgression* (Ithaca, N.Y., 1986); Natalie Zemon Davis, *Society and Culture in Early Modern France* (Stanford, Calif., 1975).

For the revolutionaries, the Anglo-American politics of celebration tethered popular sovereignty, resentment against aristocratic privilege, and the idea of American unity to everyday issues and local public life. The ideology of Revolutionary resistance made sense because its practice was openly participatory and local. Yet the rites as well as the rights continued to be derived nationally, from the British past. The common past made it possible for the British colonists to contest the present. This linkage of past and present, venerated and rehabilitated in every patriotic performance, had to be broken if that seeming oxymoron, a new nation, was to come into being. How did the revolutionaries of 1776 finally use the past to invent the future? The answer, of course, lies with the king. From being the great protector who legitimized the execration of other (British) enemies, George III became the soul of Britain itself, reconstituted as *the* enemy. His funeral became the national birthday.

CELEBRATING THE AMERICAN FUTURE

Celebrations were no afterthoughts to Independence. They were anticipated, deliberate, necessary responses to the Declaration of Independence. By the summer of 1776, Independence had been in the air for at least a year, and the Continental Congress had already declared two national fast days, July 20, 1775, and May 17, 1776.[19] Yet on sending out the printed Declaration, the Congress did not recommend fasting, mourning, bell ringing, or any other observance. Congress would not— could not—order the nation to celebrate its own birth. The new nation could not exist until the people spontaneously celebrated its existence, until evidence of this nationwide celebration appeared in print.

The Declaration of Independence signaled the ultimate rejection of England: it thrust all grievances onto the person of the king. Consequently, its public proclamation set off public vilifications of the king's body. New Yorkers tore down the equestrian statue of George III and hacked it to pieces; in other places the monarch's picture and royal arms were ceremoniously burned.[20] Many scholars have observed in

19. Moses Coit Tyler, *The Literary History of the American Revolution, 1763–1783,* 2 vols. (New York, 1897), II, 284; *In Congress, Saturday, March 16, 1776 . . .* (Philadelphia, 1776).

20. *Dunlap's Pennsylvania Packet, or the General Advertiser* (Philadelphia), July 8, 15, 1776; *Boston-Gazette,* July 22, 1776; *New-England Chronicle* (Boston), Aug. 1, 1776;

these king-killing rituals "the symbolic transfer of sovereign power from the king to the people of the American republic." Yet these founding rituals drew less on some "prehistoric human past" of ritual murder than on a quite historic recent past of British monarchical political culture.

For this king killing was not only a murder: it was also a *funeral*. At Huntington, Long Island, they took down the old liberty pole (topped with a flag dedicated to liberty and George III) and used the materials to fashion an effigy. This mock king sported a wooden broadsword, a blackened face "like *Dunmore's* [slave] Virginia regiment," and feathers, "like *Carleton* and *Johnson's* savages." Fully identified with the black and Indian allies his generals had enlisted to fight the Americans, wrapped in the Union Jack, he was hanged, exploded, and burned. Like the corpse of Liberty after the Stamp Act, George III was "laid prostrate in the dirt," his remains set afire. In Savannah he "was interred before the Court House." With their town lit up at night in honor of the occasion, Baltimoreans saw "the effigy of our Late King . . . carted through the Town, and committed to the flames, amidst the acclamations of many hundreds—the just reward of a tyrant." Only the people presided at such rites.[21] And whether the deceased arrived dead or was killed on the spot, this was no ordinary funeral: it inverted and transformed the King's Birthday celebration. The two most often mentioned aspects of this Independence Day, the bonfires and the bells, had been center-pieces of those festivals.

Compressing the cyclical political calendar, the Americans' funeral

Dixon and Hunter's *Virginia Gazette* (Williamsburg), July 29, 1776; *Norwich Packet* (Conn.), July 15, 1776; Larry R. Gerlach, ed., *New Jersey in the American Revolution, 1763–1783: A Documentary History* (Trenton, N.J., 1975), 225–226; Robert Pettus Hay, "Freedom's Jubilee: A Hundred Years of the Fourth of July, 1776–1876" (Ph.D. diss., University of Kentucky, 1967), 1–14; Fletcher Melvin Green, "Listen to the Eagle Scream: One Hundred Years of the Fourth of July in North Carolina, 1776–1876," in Green, *Democracy in the Old South and Other Essays,* ed. J. Isaac Copeland (Nashville, Tenn., 1969), 112–113; Bushman, *King and People,* 225. On king-killing rituals, see Winthrop D. Jordan, "Familial Politics: Thomas Paine and the Killing of the King, 1776," *Journal of American History,* LX (1973–1974), 294–308.

21. Peter Force, ed., *American Archives,* 5th Ser., 3 vols. (Washington, D.C., 1848–1853), I, 144, 543, 643; *Boston-Gazette,* July 22, 1776; Moore, ed., *Diary of the American Revolution,* I, 284. Many of these accounts of the reception of the Declaration are most readily available in John H. Hazelton, *The Declaration of Independence: Its History* (New York, 1906), 240–281.

for monarchy necessitated a birthday for the Republic. Unlike the Stamp Act funerals, which had also turned funeral into festival, jubilation at the Declaration rites was immediate and continuous, not deferred until the resurrection of the ancient liberty's corpse. Thus the preservation of birthday cheer at a funeral without solemnity: this death meant eternal life, the life of a new nation and its people. A few days after New Yorkers heard the Declaration of Independence and toppled the equestrian statue of George III—built in gratitude for the repeal of the Stamp Act—a correspondent expressed no doubt of the place of the event in history:

> The fourth instant was rendered remarkable by the most important event that ever happened to the *American* Colonies; an event which will doubtless be celebrated through a long succession of future ages, by anniversary commemorations, and be considered as a grand era in the history of the *American* States.

Nationhood could not fail to occur if left to the *people* who had demonstrated their assent. Even if in the present there were still thirteen colonies, in the future there would be independent states. Instead of toasting the king, patriots in Boston drank "prosperity and perpetuity to the U.S.A."[22]

The Declaration spoke for the people, or at least for their representatives: it assumed a performative aspect.[23] But the newspaper texts spoke as well, in response to the people's ritualized demonstration of their assent. If the rituals of national birth in effect ratified the act of declaring Independence, the printed descriptions of these rituals also were crucial, and not merely supplemental. They too confirmed the people as the authors of Independence, if not of the Declaration of Independence. To understand these links it is necessary to see newspaper accounts of celebrations less as objective reportage than as rhetoric. In

22. Force, ed., *American Archives*, 5th Ser., I, 144, 174, 425–426; Dixon and Hunter's *Virginia Gazette*, July 29, 1776; *A Proclamation for a Day of Public Humiliation, Fasting, and Prayer* [Watertown, Mass., 1776]; State of Massachusetts-Bay, *A Proclamation for a Day of Public Thanksgiving and Prayer* [Boston, 1776]; *Boston-Gazette*, July 18, 1776.

23. Stephen E. Lucas, "Justifying America: The Declaration of Independence as a Rhetorical Document," in Thomas W. Benson, ed., *American Rhetoric: Context and Criticism* (Carbondale, Ill., 1989), 67–130; Jay Fliegelman, *Declaring Independence: Jefferson, Natural Language, and the Culture of Performance* (Stanford, Calif., 1993).

this case, they are a genre unto themselves, a genre that defines what it ostensibly describes. These printed accounts were fundamental to a celebratory political culture: they enacted American belonging, and they fulfilled the prophecies of Independence. Reporting celebrations, they inspired new ones and thus new reports of celebrations.

The generic newspaper accounts of the response to the Declaration always stress the voluble and visible assent of the people. At Easton, Pennsylvania, on July 8, the "great number of spectators" who heard the Declaration "gave their hearty assent with three loud huzzahs, and cried out, 'May *God* long preserve and unite the Free and Independent States of *America.*'" The people of Trenton responded to the declaration "with a loud acclamation." The sounds and sights, as reported, confirmed the cross-class unity of the day. In Providence: "The Declaration was received with joy and applause by all ranks." The Committee of Safety in Halifax County, North Carolina, asked both "freeholders and Inhabitants" to attend their public reading. This was not to be taken for granted. The shadow of the unruly crowd hung over these ritual and rhetorical demonstrations of the new order. An account of the celebration in Richmond, Virginia, expressed relief: "Although there were near 1000 people present, the whole was conducted with the utmost decorum; and the satisfaction visible in every countenance sufficiently evinces their determination to support [Independence] with their lives and fortunes." In Boston, "undissembled festivity cheered and brightened every face." By contrast, pictures of the king and tories were everywhere taken down: their faces were not to be seen.[24]

These rhetorical appeals to sight, to the sensory experience of seeing, are one of the ways in which the newspapers successfully bridged street theater and the act of reading (itself a visual experience). In this respect, printed accounts acted nationally as the personal display of sentiment—the huzza, the toast, the beaming countenance—acted locally: both taught patriotic feeling and action even while demonstrating that such virtue already predominated across class boundaries in those places where "joy and festivity pervaded all ranks of people." Readers as far away as Philadelphia learned that in Savannah "a greater

24. Moore, ed., *Diary of the American Revolution*, I, 284; Force, ed., *American Archives*, 5th Ser., I, 119–120, 136, 418–419, 425–426, 582; *Boston-Gazette*, July 22, 1776; Hazelton, *Declaration of Independence*, 259, 273; Tyler, *Literary History of the American Revolution*, II, 160–161.

number of people than ever appeared on any occasion before, in this province" came out to witness the symbolic funeral of George III. The corollary, invoked explicitly in this case, was that America would be great among the nations.[25]

Reports of celebrations elsewhere demonstrated the simultaneity of national action and the pervasiveness of national sentiments. The *Virginia Gazette* in Williamsburg went to the trouble of reproducing accounts of the Declaration celebrations from New York City and from Trenton and Princeton, New Jersey, while the *Norwich Packet* in Connecticut relayed an account that came all the way from Williamsburg. This pattern continued during the war years. A Charleston paper in 1779 carried an account of the Philadelphia Fourth of July celebration—five weeks later. The *Pennsylvania Journal* of Philadephia reprinted descriptions of the Fourth of July from distant Richmond as well as nearby Trenton.[26] The printed description of local display was thus the perfect way to spread nationalism. The same vehicle that reported the local and present-oriented recent past could make the extralocal future self-evident.

Unfortunately for the patriots, nationalist celebrations and publications could not alone win the War of Independence, much less guarantee present unity and future glory. Charles Royster rightly observes: "Many revolutionaries tried to win independence by declaring it over and over. In the search for signs of grace, they often convinced themselves, for a while, that words were works." The decade's worth of politicized celebration and printed commentary of the resistance movement probably made it seem as if street theater combined with printed words *was* the most effective of political works. This is why the ardent celebrating continued, and even multiplied, after July 4, 1776. Having affirmed the righteousness of their Revolution by their manner of receiving the good news, patriots linked an increasingly interregional war effort to their local experiences by holding "continental" fasts and thanksgiv-

25. *Pennsylvania Evening Post* (Philadelphia), July 9, 1779; Moore, ed., *Diary of the American Revolution,* I, 284.

26. Dixon and Hunter's *Virginia Gazette,* July 29, 1776; *Norwich Packet,* Aug. 12, 1776; *Gazette, of the State of South-Carolina* (Charleston), Aug. 11, 1779; *Pennsylvania Journal and the Weekly Advertiser* (Philadelphia), July 17, 1782. On imagining national community in simultaneous time and space, see Anderson, *Imagined Communities,* chap. 2; Mona Ozouf, *Festivals and the French Revolution,* trans. Richard Howard (Cambridge, Mass., 1988), chaps. 6–7.

ings, by celebrating anniversaries of war victories and Independence, and by mourning defeats and heroic deaths.[27] The Declaration of Independence celebrations and the Fourth of July anniversaries that came to follow them annually were only models for the national celebrations that filled the war years with sets of thirteen gunshots and lists of thirteen toasts.

More important, then, than the speed with which the Fourth of July celebration spread or even the local variations in the celebrations is the very generic quality of the commentary around these celebrations: the vagueness—the intentional obscurity—of the printed reports. The summation of the report on the July 4, 1777, celebration in Philadelphia was typical in its guarantees: "Every thing was conducted with the greatest order and decorum, and the face of joy and gladness was universal." The overwhelming intent of these rites was unity. As a result, the achievement of sameness in these rites—such as the ubiquitous use of the number thirteen, one for each state—proved that national unity existed.[28] And the generic descriptions, which so frustrate the scholar looking for regional variation or local detail, were chosen deliberately, for the same reason.

27. Charles Royster, *A Revolutionary People at War: The Continental Army and American Character, 1775–1783* (Chapel Hill, N.C., 1979), 107; John Beebe, Jr., Diary, July 4, Nov. 2, 1780, New York State Library, Albany; Harold B. Hancock, ed., "The Revolutionary War Diary of William Adair," *Delaware History,* XIII (1968), 163, 165; *The Diary of Matthew Patten of Bedford, N.H.* (Concord, N.H., 1903), 381, 393, 399, 409, 413, 423, 439; Jonathan Clark Diary (transcript), July 4, 1778, Oct. 17, 1779, July 4, 1780, Mar. 31, Apr. 29, 1783, Filson Club Library, Louisville, Ky.

28. *Pennsylvania Journal,* July 9, 1777, rpt. in *Pennsylvania Packet,* July 15, 1777, *Norwich Packet,* July 21, 1777, and elsewhere. An observer of a celebration of the French alliance in 1778 noted: "Some of the ancients were not more attached to their mystical figures than many of the moderns. We of America have our number THIRTEEN. The officers approached the place of entertainment in different columns, thirteen abreast, and closely linked together in each other's arms. The appearance was pretty enough. The number of officers composing each line, signified the thirteen American States; and the interweaving of arms a complete union and most perfect confederation." See *New-York Journal, and the General Advertiser* (Poughkeepsie), June 15, 1778, reprinted in Frank Moore, comp., *The Diary of the American Revolution, 1775–1781,* abr. and ed. John Anthony Scott (New York, 1967), 303. Of course, the use of numbers owed more to recent British political culture, in which numbers like fifteen and forty-five had deep political resonances. See John Brewer, "The Number 45: A Wilkite Political Symbol," in Stephen B. Baxter, ed., *England's Rise to Greatness, 1660–1763* (Berkeley, Calif., 1983), 349–380.

In a hundred birthdays and funeral rites the patriots built an experiential and a discursive basis for the belief that "the nation" existed and could be spoken of, that there was a national mind that thinks, a national character with a virtuous heart. Massachusetts patriots took the lead in turning local episodes into occasions for Revolutionary—and by extension national—memory. Since 1770 they had marked the Boston Massacre with dirges and orations on the dangers to liberty posed by a standing (that is, British) army. The Sons of Liberty in Boston and elsewhere kept up the August 14 and March 18 Stamp Act holidays. Evidence shows also that Lexington was only the first battle to be commemorated annually. In June 1777 Charleston's Palmetto Society established itself to commemorate the June 28, 1776, victory at Sullivan's Island. After bell ringing in the morning, a church service and oration in honor of the militia, and intermittent gun blasts by the boats in the harbor, three hundred Charlestonians headed to the fort for a dinner party. Two other groups dined together (one at the local liberty tree), and fireworks closed the festivities. Likewise, as early as 1778 and 1779 the inhabitants of Bennington and Saratoga sponsored civic feasts and orations that underscored the national significance of local victories. Local attachments were no prerequisite, though: American patriots as far away as Saint Croix celebrated the anniversary of Lexington.[29]

More common, especially as the Continental army fared better, were the assertions of spontaneous rejoicing when news arrived of a patriot victory. According to the *Boston Gazette*, all of Cambridge was illuminated the evening word came of General John Burgoyne's defeat at Saratoga in October 1777. Correspondents stressed the immediacy of popular demonstration. Even more than the judicious preservation of anniversaries, spontaneous joy revealed cross-class unity in the Conti-

---

29. *Gazette, of the State of South-Carolina,* June 9, 30, 1777, June 29, 1778; *Boston-Gazette,* Aug. 19, 1776, Mar. 10, 1777; Phillips Payson, *A Memorial of Lexington Battle . . .* (Boston, 1782); Jeff Hyson, "The Spirit of the Times: Anniversary Sermons at Lexington, 1776–1783," paper, Yale University, 1989; Oliver Hart Diary, June 28, 1779, South Caroliniana Library, University of South Carolina, Columbia; "Celebration in 1778 of the Bennington Victory of 1777," Vermont Historical Society, *Collections,* I (1870), 251–270; Nathan Fiske, *An Oration Delivered at Brookfield, Nov. 14, 1781, in Celebration of the Capture of Lord Cornwallis . . .* (Boston, 1781); Israel Evans, *A Discourse Delivered near York in Virginia, on the Memorable Occasion of the Surrender . . .* (Philadelphia, 1782); *Independent Gazetteer; or, the Chronicle of Freedom* (Philadelphia), Apr. 19, May 31, 1783; *New-Jersey Gazette* (Trenton), Apr. 23, 1783; *Independent Ledger, and American Advertiser* (Boston), July 14, 1783.

nental cause. On June 25, 1779, a citizen of Portsmouth, New Hampshire, received a personal letter from General Horatio Gates: "I do most heartily congratulate you upon the *Success* of our *Arms* in South Carolina, which I think finishes the British Empire in AMERICA." "Immediately," the account reads, bells began to ring and continued to ring all day, interspersed with the firings of cannon.[30]

Residents of Portsmouth heard the news by word of mouth and responded with joyous noise. An extralocal audience received the news (or at least a reminder) of the victory and the news of celebration, at once, through print. The two became one. Yet this particular description, from the perspective of a gentleman, reveals the dependence of planned festivals on the more spontaneous (and inclusive) demonstrations of assent. Only *after* describing the immediate revelation of patriotic joy does the author describe the gathering at the State House of the "most respectable gentlemen . . . whose smiling countenances evidenced the sincerity of their Hearts." The toasts these worthies offered were not solely for their own consumption; described as public, they were "accompanied with three Huzzas in and out of Doors." The subjects are unquestionably members of the upper classes, but their sincere displays of patriotic emotion are ratified by the populace at large.

Who were the possessors and performers of political virtue? The people "out of Doors"? Or did they merely recognize it when they saw it? Despite a consensus that the people were the source of political legitimacy, the character and limits of popular action remained unresolved. Two years earlier in Portsmouth, on the first anniversary of the Fourth of July, Captain Thompson had somehow succeeded in getting "all the friends of American independency" on board his Continental ship in dock. But then who were the "large concourse of people" on the wharf who vociferously approved the thirteen guns fired? Likewise, if ritual dinners occurred during daylight hours, the citizens appeared to ratify the sentiments of the toast givers by participating in illuminations and fireworks at night.[31] In Revolutionary rhetoric and practice there remained a vagueness, an indeterminacy about who were "the people"

30. *Boston-Gazette,* Oct. 27, 1777, Oct. 19, 1778; *New-Hampshire Gazette; or, State Journal, and General Advertiser* (Portsmouth), June 29, 1779.

31. *Freeman's Journal, or New-Hampshire Gazette* (Portsmouth), July 12, 1777; *New-Jersey Gazette* (Newark), July 8, 1778.

and who were "the citizens," or true political actors. This dilemma would plague American republicanism for many years to come.

Different definitions of "the people" and citizenship coexisted uneasily within the Revolutionary alliance. Rituals and published descriptions of rituals often betrayed uncertainties whether all the "people" were "citizens" even while they seemed to resolve the question. Early Fourth of July celebrations were attempts to establish (or reestablish) an organic link between elite and populace and among the elites themselves, ratifying both popular sovereignty and the most tasteful displays of patriotic affiliation. They did so by deferring controversial questions of political participation and local control in favor of self-evident displays of national unity. The thirteen toasts generally offered (one for every state in the new union) not only spread Revolutionary ideology: they also promoted *national* pride. Rather than moving organically from local to national identifications, the toasts moved from the national back to the local, making the local part of, or evidence for, the greater national entity. Invariably, the first toasts laud the United States, the Congress, the Continental army, George Washington, the holiday itself—all *national* institutions. Only afterward did they (sometimes) move on to praise "the State of New Jersey," the "brave militia," or "our officers and privates" who fought at the battle of Monmouth Courthouse.[32] In the story told by these toasts, the original source of joy is always national. Local luminaries and events prove virtuous by attachment to the glory of America.

The muster of the militia on the Fourth of July, the new national holiday, was a particularly appropriate way to consolidate local leadership while nationalizing popular sovereignty. On the morning of Independence Day 1779, in Boston, the militia paraded and performed a mock engagement before "a vast concourse of spectators." Afterward, one hundred patriots ate under a tent in the Commons. Again attendance and display prove the constancy of Revolutionary sentiments:

> The spirit of the people never appeared at once more elated and firm than upon this happy occasion: An unaffected joy was diffused thro' the countenances of the generality of the citizens—intermix'd with such composure and decency as afforded a most agreeable indication of their entire satisfaction in this glorious revolution, and

32. *New-Jersey Gazette,* July 8, 1778.

that the true republican principles were not only well understood but highly relish'd.[33]

The "generality" of citizens not only comprehend republicanism but show joy on their faces and "decency" in demeanor, a remarkable statement of optimism in so large and troubled a city as Revolutionary Boston. Coming at a time of military setbacks, when the sustaining virtues of the populace seemed doubtful, rhetoric here functioned as self-fulfilling prophecy, in that its local details, such as the smiling faces, were meant to inspire what they described. Virtue is apparent in the response to nationalist ritual; thus virtuous patriots would be citizens devoted to the needs of the nation.

Another way to ensure that celebration served virtue was to follow the dicta of republican simplicity. Sometimes this was a necessity. A citizen of Newport, Rhode Island, reported in 1780 the thirteen gun blasts fired by the French ships in the harbor as well as "other such demonstrations of joy as the embarrassed circumstances of the town would admit." As secretary of the Philadelphia Council shortly after the British evacuation in 1778, Timothy Matlack made it publicly known that "because of the heat and 'scarcity' of candles, and other considerations," the council suggested that residents forbear from Fourth of July illuminations. But moderation in celebration could also be a matter of careful political balance, a way to maintain a semblance of the unity that the celebrations were supposed to demonstrate. The "other considerations" Matlack alluded to almost certainly included the need to consolidate an upper class that had divided during the recently ended occupation of the city by British troops and the need to calm the plebeian anger that, on previous holidays, had been directed against Quakers and quondam tories. This anger, after all, could take on disruptive and divisive overtones, as when Philadelphia crowds had broken unilluminated Quaker windows on the previous July 4 or when, on that same Fourth in 1778, crowds had marched a prostitute through the streets sporting a mockery of the fashionable headgear tory-sympathizing women had worn during the British occupation.[34]

33. *Independent Ledger, and American Advertiser* (Boston), July 12, 1779; *Boston Gazette,* July 12, 1779.

34. *Pennsylvania Journal,* July 26, 1780; *Pennsylvania Packet or the General Advertiser* (Philadelphia), July 4, 1778; *Pennsylvania Ledger,* Dec. 6, 1777; David S. Shields and Fredrika J. Teute, "The Meschianza's Meaning: 'How Will It Sparkle—Page

Some controversy attended the question of whether the Continental Congress should sponsor fireworks and festivities. William Henry Drayton urged the measure; his fellow South Carolinian Henry Laurens argued that such "fooleries" had brought down the republics of ancient Greece. For the most part, leaders resolved this problem by imagining their holidays to be sacred—and thus solemn. A Newburyport gentleman wrote that the Fourth of July spurred his town to comply with state requests to send more men off to battle. After an oration, fifty-nine were chosen to march off in the morning; local men of property showed their zeal by pledging to make good on the soldiers' pay. The writer found this to be evidence of true virtue, perhaps because the ritual included all classes while maintaining differences of rank: "Plato thanked heavens he was born in the age of Socrates: I give thanks that I was born an American; that I lived in the hour of the separation of America from Britain, and that I have seen the exertions of my country in the cause of freedom, that rival the boasted patriotism of antiquity." [35]

Yet the mythic "patriotism of antiquity" was not the only kind that helped achieve American Independence, and some early skeptics underscored this by reminding others of the time-tested relationship of celebration to crowd action and drink. After the first Fourth of July, Continental Congress member William Williams of Connecticut wrote home to Jonathan Trumbull: "Yesterday was in my opinion poorly spent in celebrating the Anniversary of the Declaration of Independence . . . a great expenditure of liquor, powder etc., took up the Day and of candles thro the City good part of the night." He added, "I suppose and I conclude much Tory unilluminated glass will want replacing." [36] A broadside circulated in Philadelphia after the victory at Yorktown pleaded:

> Those Citizens, who choose to ILLUMINATE on the GLORIOUS OCCA-SION, will do it this evening at Six, and extinguish the lights at Nine o'clock.
>
> Decorum and harmony are earnestly recommended to every Citizen and a general discountenance to the least appearance of riot.

the Future?'" paper presented at the Organization of American Historians annual meeting, Chicago, April 1996.

35. Edmund S. Morgan, *The Challenge of the American Revolution* (New York, 1976), 124; *Boston Gazette,* July 10, 1780. On pageantry as a possible locus of Old World decadence, see Held, "'To Instruct and Improve,'" 167–168.

36. Charles Warren, "Fourth of July Myths," *WMQ,* 3d Ser., II (1945), 255.

Patriot leaders wanted order, but they needed popular celebration and its impolite reversals. Such expressions of praise and insult, bringing down the high and mighty, remained the main mode of distancing whig from tory, a distinction that itself rested on the whig assertion of the people's authority. Again and again, patriot rhetoric and ritual taught the lesson of leadership gone wrong, a homily that resonated with the precarious situation of the whig leadership itself. At Princeton in 1778, the inhabitants found particular pleasure in firing the thirteen cannon, "being some of the brass field-pieces taken from General Burgoyne, *one* of the three *conquerors* of *America*." At the celebration of the peace proclamation in April 1783, inhabitants of Newport, Rhode Island, saw an effigy of Benedict Arnold hanged and then blown apart. Three years after the Treaty of Paris ended the War of Independence, in Northumberland County, Pennsylvania, one could still find "Colonel JOHN BULL . . . unanimously placed on the wheatsack."[37]

This celebratory mode is captured in a 1776 "new favorite song at the American Camp." Sung to the tune of the "British Grenadiers," it inverts all things British, truly turning the world upside down.

> Your dark unfathom'd Councils, our weakest Heads defeat,
> Our Children rout your Armies, our Boats destroy your Fleet;
> And to complete the dire Disgrace, cooped up within a Town,
> You live the scorn of all our Host, the Slaves of WASHINGTON.

Even the "weakest" have a hand in the prostration of the British elite. The story that is told here gives primary agency to the people. Yet the end result is the upraising of a new George, whose elite status is inseparable from that of the new nation.

> Great Heaven! is this the Nation, whose thundering Arms were
>   hurl'd,
> Thro' Europe, Afric, India; whose Navy rul'd the World;
> The Lustre of your former Deeds, whole Ages of Renown,
> Lost in a moment, or transferr'd to US and WASHINGTON.

The British past has passed from relevance. Pausing for a moment to assure the listener that freedom, not mere glory, inspires the American, the song concludes:

37. *Illumination . . . Surrender of Lord Cornwallis . . .* ([Philadelphia], 1781); *New-Jersey Gazette*, July 8, 1778; "Newport, April 26," *Independent Gazetteer* (Philadelphia), May 17, 1783, July 29, 1786.

Proud France should view with Terror, and haughty Spain should
  fear,
While every warlike Nation would court Alliance here,
And ———, his Minions trembling, dismounted from his T———,
Pay homage to *AMERICA,* and glorious WASHINGTON.[38]

This is the heady, king-killing optimism of 1776; yet with the French
alliance, international recognition reinforced these boastful wishes. As
William Stinchcombe and Beverly Orlove Held have shown, elaborate
celebrations of the Treaty of Amity and Commerce, King Louis's birthday, and the birth of the dauphin helped to prove Americans' sincere
loyalty to their new ally and to define American national identity against
a common enemy. Furthermore, the French provided a helpfully different flavor of gentility, enabling the elite in Philadelphia and elsewhere
to retain their stylishness while distancing themselves from tories. Celebrating the alliance at Washington's camp, "through the whole, there
was a remarkable style of looks and behavior, undebauched by British
manners or British entertainments." The French ministry in America
did its part by sponsoring orations and festivities on the Fourth of July
as well as on French red-letter days. Though it required considerable
ideological agility to explain how the Popish French monarchy could
truly rejoice at the spectacle of the republican United States (and vice
versa), the symbolic and actual presence of the French at these celebrations helped to keep the focus national and to fix the burden of
opprobrium on the common enemy, England.[39]

French support turned a traditional, Catholic enemy into a friend
and, in doing so, reinforced a key idea in the development of American
nationalism: that America was at the center of a world stage, acting out
God's plan. Here national celebration became the site of that peculiar

38. The blanks are for the omitted "George" and his "throne." Jonathan Mitchell
Sewall, *Gen. Washington, A New Favourite Song at the American Camp* ([New York],
1776). For a variant, see Vera Brodsky Lawrence, *Music For Patriots, Politicians, and
Presidents: Harmonies and Discords of the First Hundred Years* (New York, 1975), 63.

39. William C. Stinchcombe, "Americans Celebrate the Birth of the Dauphin,"
in Ronald Hoffman and Peter J. Albert, eds., *Diplomacy and Revolution: The Franco-
American Alliance of 1778* (Charlottesville, Va., 1983), 39–71; Held, " 'To Instruct and
Improve,' " 254–310; *Pennsylvania Packet*, Feb. 18, 1779, in Moore, ed., *Diary of the
American Revolution*, II, 134; Seraphin Bandot, *Discours prononcé le 4 juillet . . .* (Phila-
delphia, [1779]); *Boston Gazette,* June 17, 1782; *Thomas' Massachusetts, New-Hampshire,
and Connecticut Almanack for . . . 1780 . . .* (Worcester, Mass., 1779); Isaac Weston,
The Massachusetts Almanack for . . . 1783 (Salem, Mass., [1782]).

confluence of whig politics and millennial thought. Millennial thought in this context did not require (though it often included) belief in the coming of God's rule on earth; rather, the political millennium was characterized by an overriding confidence in the future. "I congratulate you on our glorious prospects," said David Ramsay in one of the first Fourth of July orations to be published.

> When I anticipate in imagination the future glory of my country, and the illustrious figure it will soon make on the theatre of the world, my heart distends with generous pride for being an American. What a substratum for empire! . . .
> . . . Our Independence will redeem one quarter of the globe from tyranny and oppression, and consecrate it the chosen seat of Truth, Justice, Freedom, Learning and Religion.

In newspapers, such sentimental paeans to the American future are often juxtaposed with mock funerary announcements like "Old England's Last Will" (see Figure 2).[40]

Nationalist movements often require traditions, inventing them out of whole cloth, if necessary. But the American revolutionaries already had a tradition: an English tradition of revelry and rights that Independence had rendered suddenly problematic. For the American patriots after 1776, then, the more unprecedented everything appeared, the better. Appropriating the oldest English commemorative rituals and rhetoric, celebrants of the nation during the war struggled to keep the character of a first celebration by always celebrating the *future*—a strategy that helped deflect the difficulties of a less-than-perfect present. "A second celebration already has the character of a reification," Paul Ricoeur tells us; communities usually celebrate the past in order to legitimate the present.[41] Through their celebrations of each

40. Jeffrey H. Richards, *Theater Enough: American Culture and the Metaphor of the World Stage, 1607–1789* (Durham, N.C., 1991), chaps. 9–11; Bloch, *Visionary Republic*, 75–93; Michael Lienesch, *A New Order of the Ages: Time, the Constitution, and the Making of American Political Thought* (Princeton, N.J., 1988); David Ramsay, *An Oration on the Advantages of American Independence* . . . (Charleston, S.C., 1778), 20–21; *Boston Gazette*, July 26, 1779; *Freeman's Journal: or, The North-American Intelligencer* (Philadelphia), Oct. 3, 1779; *Epitaph: Indignant Reader, Whoever Thou Art, More Especially an American* . . . (Philadelphia, 1782).

41. Anderson, *Imagined Communities*, 67–111; Eric Hobsbawm and Terence Ranger, eds., *The Invention of Tradition* (Cambridge, 1983); Paul Ricoeur, *Lectures on Ideology and Utopia*, ed. George H. Taylor (New York, 1987), 261.

EPITAPH.

INDIGNANT Reader,
Whoever thou art, more especially an
AMERICAN,
Lift up thine eyes, be thankful, rejoice, and behold!
on a level with former
Tyrants,
Knock'd down and tumbled in the dust,
like his equestrian statue at
New-York.
Relinquished, utterly rejected, and deposited,
as a security for
AMERICA,
In sackcloth and ashes, *stratum super stratum,*
corruption with corruption,
Food for profligate *Ministers,* corrupt *Parliaments,*
bloody rapacious *Nabobs,* venal *Placemen,*
time-serving *Pensioners,* and deceit-
ful, bribing, pretending
peace-making
Commissioners.
The residuum and political remnant of

George the III.

Button-Maker;

An enemy to liberty, an ungrateful, inexorable
TYRANT,
Of inglorious memory, and an eternal disgrace to those
(who are falsely) called the
Lord's Anointed!

In him was completely verified that saying of
St. Paul's,
" Evil communication corrupts good
manners."

A king, who, while on his earthly throne, pursued various villainous schemes to obtain,
Arbitrary Power,
And that divinity of all Tyrants
GOLD!
By fleecing, in the most
shameful manner his subjects,
to support luxury, ambition, balls, af-
semblies, theatres, concerts, routs, races,
bal-pares, cornelli-masquerades, Stratford-jubi-
lees, Ranelagh-regattas, effeminate Ita-
lian fidlers, emasculated singers, and
the whole complicated round of
Nocturnal Pleasures.

Making baubles of the laws of the land,
A joke of liberty and property,
Foot balls of petitions and remonstrances,
Kicking heels overhead, religion, justice and humanity,
Turning topsy-turvy, charters and bills of right.

Like NERO, burning cities through wantonness,
starving, poisoning, smothering, putting thousands to
the sword, and, wading knee deep with secret
pleasure, in the blood of his subjects
to gratify a brutal devilish
Revenge;
Like SYLLA and CESAR, bribing parliaments,
and feasting soldiers, (the execrable instruments
of his tyranny) with visionary confiscated
lands of the friends of
Liberty.
Like JAMES II. dispensed with the laws, and
made continual innovations upon the
Constitution.
Like CHARLES I. raised a rebellion in the land.
Like CARACALLA, loaded the people in all the
provinces, with grievous, arbitrary taxes, to
reduce them to a state of poverty and
Vassalage.
Like PHARAOH, hardening his heart, and con-
tumaciously persisting, though often admo-
nished of the fatal
Consequences.
Like CALIGULA, overflowing with vanity and
pride, commanded his image to be set up in the
Temple;
So he, (as though making it a point to
affront his maker) by suffering him-
self to be addressed by the
blasphemous title of
" Most Sacred Majesty,"
Like HIMSELF only, by swearing, while he
wore the crown, and carried the sword, his
subjects should bow down in
" Unconditional Submission,"

'Till they were humbled, and brought under his
FEET.
Like a LION, greedy of his prey;
And,
Like a CORMORANT, never satisfied, although
crammed with millions, gorging and disgorging
extegally, and eternally craving more.
So that
His sceptre became broken,
His crown transformed into a fool's cap,
And his THRONE,
(the throne of his ancestors)
which in ancient days was the seat of regal power,
the meridian and pinnacle of human glory,
visibly declining, and in all human probability,
(unless a miracle interpose, which cannot be expected
in his favour)
will shortly become a Foot-stool to the most christian,
most illustrious, and most invincible,
LOUIS XVI.

Now Reader attend!

On the ever memorable and auspici-
ous 4th day of July, in the year of our Lord, 1776,
after near a sixteen years tyrannical reign, it
was declared unto this second Nebuchadnezzar, even while his fleet and army were riding, (as he thought)
TRIUMPHANTLY at
New-York,
casting forth their threats,
and bellowing out death and
destruction, by the voices and
hand-writing of THREE MILLION of
AMERICAN FREEMEN (Tories excepted)
" Thy kingdom is departed from thee."

Thus, a most glorious
INDEPENDENCY
Commenced,
And the period of his tyrannical race being ended,
after galloping through and trampling under
foot the precepts of the
Constitution,
His popularity spent, hated, despised, contemned and
justly cast off by his American subjects, he
funk to his deserved insignificancy and
obscurity; over a free people
to reign no
more.

Yet, by a fatality peculiar to himself, did this frantic,
infatuated, inflexible, pertinacious Briton pursue, with diabolical rage and unrelenting fury, the Ignis Fatuus of
AMERICA,

By sending his impotent fleets and armies to burn,
plunder, desolate, and lower round her coasts,
to gain (if possible) advantage, like the
elder Satan, who scaled the walls of
Paradise.

But, behold ! in due time, (even while his hopes
and expectations were raised to the highest pitch,
from false intelligence of detestable Refugees,
those shooters of fine beards, arrows and
death, emphatically called Vipers,
and the lying spirit of an infernal
RIVINGTON !
which had gone forth)
By the permission of kind
PROVIDENCE,
The directing hand of a Godlike Hero !
A mighty
WASHINGTON!
And the generous assistance of our magnanimous
ALLY,
The Ignis Fatuus led him on to his destruction,
be sidder'd him,
His fleet was beaten, taken, and scatter'd,
A bloody CORNWALLIS Burgoyn'd,
As was some time before,
A BURGOYNE Cornwallis'd,
And their whole armies
CAPTIVATED.
In consequence
of which (shewing
not the least disposition
towards amendment or re-
pentance) he became spiritless,
exhausted, perturbated, mortified, dis-
tracted, humbled, and seized with fits of
trepidation, " demoniac piteously, moping-
melancholy, and moon-struck madness,"
HE FELL UNPITIED,
mourning over, and shedding
thirteen bitter tears, for his
lost colonies, and took
precipitant to rise
no more ;

And the gate of America, immediately closed,
for ever against him; of which the fall
of a jewel from his crown, (on his
coronation day) was a type,
a forerunner, a sad
Omen !
which, (although me-
lancholy in its nature) crea-
ated an universal joy, among
the powers of EUROPE, and him-
self the laughing stock of the nations of the
EARTH.
A Memento-mori, and an instructive lesson to future
Tyrants.

Neither was his
Omnipotent Parliament
Less agitated by the shock, in the PANDEMONIUM,
Rueful countenances succeeded whispers,
Groans, fighs, and an hideous gabble ensued,
Horrible distractions, discord, and despair started up,
Followed by a hum, like the sound of mighty waters;
Pride, fury, and disappointment together rose, in the
character of the
Minden-Hero,
with crest erect, loud storming
War! War! War!
But on the sudden appearance of
Independence,
Who gave him a frown,
Pride fell back, fury hood transfix'd, and disappoint-
ment disappointed, staggered, hung down his
head, and became instantaneously
DUMB.
BOREAS rose next, with a subtile, keen edge,
and with the voice of thunder, blew his last blast;
but on an oblique view of
General Washington's Picture,
the Thunderer (expiring in an echo) grew insensibly
moderate, reluctantly soften'd, and faintly
and inarticulately breathed
Peace! Peace! Peace!
Now a jangling noise, now various sentiments started
up, and as various interpretations (for " a house
divided against itself cannot stand") 'till
confusion on confusion rolled, like the
waters of the ocean disturbed by
a mighty leviathan, & closed
the scene in a downright
hubbub of various langu-
ages, resembling those
at the confusion of
BABEL.

Thus was begun,
And by a progressive series of remarkable events,
continued and brought about,
The most wonderful Revolution
since
Noah's Flood ;
And out of the ruins of a cast off, sunken reprobate
Monarchy,
ascended upwards
(like the smoke of an
accepted sacrifice, and with
radiant light, like the beams of the
sun in his meridian splendor, spreading
every way instantaneous, like a shooting star,
to the wonder and joy of the whole universe)
thirteen glorious Republics.

May the Light above,
far more resplendent than the flashes of his favourite
gunpowder,
GRANT,
That his deeds be recorded in the memory of all true
patriots, until the general conflagration, reunification,
and renovation of all things, never to be thought
of, but to be execrated, by true Americans,
whom he hath, and those whom he would have
plundered; and that like
NEBUCHADNEZZAR I.
his hairs may grow as eagles feathers,
his nails like birds claws, and instead of grass his food be thistles,
to graze on, not seven only,
but seventy times seven
years, thrice told, on
the summit of the
highest mountain
in North Britain,
but never like
him to reign
again.

PHILADELPHIA:
Printed by F. Bailey, in *Market-Street,* 1782.

FIGURE 2. *Epitaph:* "Indignant Reader. . . ." *Philadelphia, 1782.*
Courtesy Library Company of Philadelphia

remarkable Revolutionary event, American nationalists repeatedly enacted the founding. In the present there was an army to support, and class-based cultural rifts dividing decorous diners from riotous revelers. In the future there were unanimity, prosperity, nationhood—and none of these problems. Thus the problems of the present were incidental, local, passing, past.

A closer look at an almost unexplored genre of popular literature—the almanac—helps illustrate this diversion of attention from the local present to the national future. Like newspapers, almanacs can be read by historians for evidence of beliefs and deeds; and, like newspapers, they functioned prescriptively in their own time, enacting and encouraging new ways of thinking in time and space. If newspapers used the recent past to construct the present as news, almanacs relied on representations of the past and the present to plan the future.[42] Through the dual logic of celebration and execration, almanacs turned British memory into American millennialism, sacralizing a national future in festive culture.

What literature could be more locally oriented than the almanac? Virtually all almanacs of the 1770s were aimed at a particular city, colony, state, or region. Often they include lists of court days and local, county, and state civil officers. Yet British almanacs before and American almanacs after the Revolutionary era also fostered a national outlook. Almanacs included reminders of national festive occasions; as such they linked the rhythms of local life to official acts of national commemoration. Listing different holidays, changing the chronicle of history's remarkable events, featuring pro-British and anti-French essays, these pre-Revolutionary "colonial weekday bibles" promoted not just the imagination but the practice of national time.[43]

42. My understanding of time and genre in eighteenth-century print culture, particularly in relation to the emergence of "news," has been influenced by J. Paul Hunter, *Before Novels: The Cultural Contexts of Eighteenth-Century British Fiction* (New York, 1990), 89–109, 167–194; David Paul Nord, "Teleology and News: The Religious Roots of American Journalism, 1630–1730," *JAH*, LXXVII (1990–1991), 9–38.

43. Bernard Capp, *English Almanacs, 1500–1800: Astrology and the Popular Press* (Ithaca, N.Y., 1979), 80, 286; Jon Stanley Wenrick, "For Education and Entertainment: Almanacs in the Early American Republic, 1783–1815" (Ph.D. diss., Claremont Graduate School, 1974), 256; Marion Barber Stowell, *Early American Almanacs: The Colonial Weekday Bible* (New York, 1977). My conclusions are based on a complete survey of the almanacs for the period 1775–1783 reproduced in

Up to 1776, most almanacs noted a range of traditional English festive days on the monthly calendar, along with religious days, astronomical observations, and meteorological predictions. Not all such holidays
were celebrated in the colonies or observed widely, but the almanac
nonetheless reveals that royal and ecclesiastical anniversaries were still
considered remarkable. The frontispiece of John Anderson's *Almanack*
(published in Newport, Rhode Island) for 1776 declared the coming
year to be the "16th in the reign of George III." Inside, Anderson
notes the following political anniversaries: January 18 ("Queen's birthday kept"), January 30 (Charles I beheaded), April 27 (final defeat of
the Jacobite rebels at Culloden in 1746), May 29 (birthday and Restoration of Charles II), June 4 (birthday of George III), August 12 (prince
of Wales born), September 22 (coronation of George III), October 25
(accession of George III), November 5 (Gunpowder Plot Day), and
November 23 (defeat of Jacobite rebels at Preston in 1715).[44]

Yet this list of British red-letter days also includes March 18, the anniversary of the repeal of the Stamp Act. The next year, many almanacs
would carry the anniversary of the battle at Lexington. Other patriot
almanac makers were already playing down the king's days, including
only January 30 (the "execution" or "martyrdom" of Charles I, which
could be and was interpreted either way), Coronation Day of George III
(the most official of the royal anniversaries), and the old New England
favorite, Gunpowder Plot Day.[45] Few offered the traditional genealogical register of British royalty that year, and one, Nathan Daboll, delegitimized the whole genre:

A Genealogical Account of the KINGS of ENGLAND

George the Third, grandson of George the 2d, the son of George the
First, who was cousin to Queen Anne, the daughter to King James the

the microfiche edition of *Early American Imprints, 1639–1800, Based on the Thirteen-
Volume Charles Evans Bibliography, Including Supplements and Corrections to Evans* (New
Canaan, Conn., 1985–).

44. John Anderson, *An Almanack and Ephemeris, for . . . 1776* (Newport, R.I.,
1775); *Anderson Improved: Being an Almanack, and Ephemeris, for . . . 1775* (Newport,
R.I., [1774]). Almanacs for the year were published during the autumn of the previous year.

45. [Nathan Daboll], *Freebetter's New-England Almanack, for . . . 1776* (New London, Conn., [1775]); Samuel Stearns, *North American's Almanack . . . for . . . 1775*
(Boston, [1774]); [Nehemiah Strong], *An Astronomical Ephemeris, Kalendar, or Almanack, for . . . 1776 . . .* (New Haven, Conn., 1775).

2d, who was son to Charles the First, the son of James the First, who was third cousin to Elizabeth, the daughter of Henry the Eighth, who was son to Henry the Seventh, the cousin to Richard the Third, who was uncle to Edward the Fifth, who was son to Edward the Fourth, the cousin to Henry the Sixth, who was son to Henry the Fifth, the son to Henry the Fourth, who was the grandson of Edward the Third, the son of Edward the Second, son to Edward the First who was son to Henry the Third, the son of King John, who was son to Henry the 2d, the cousin of Stephen, who was nephew to Henry the First, the son of William the Conqueror, who was a SON OF A WHORE.

Similarly, *George's Cambridge Almanack* announced itself for "the Sixteenth of the Reign of George III. . . . And the First Year of the bloody and unnatural Civil War in America, commenced by the *British* King's, or Ministerial Troops." George also advertised full treatment of the events of April 19 (Lexington) — "a day that ought and will be handed down to ages yet unborn."[46]

After Independence, most almanacs superimposed the national birth upon the king's death, now declaring the year on the frontispiece as "Being the FIRST YEAR OF AMERICAN INDEPENDENCE."[47] Here independence is described as a state existing, not a work to be accomplished or an event (even though July 4 would soon be the most uniformly noted date on the calendars). The meaning of these changes did not escape the notice of the British and their sympathizers, as this note from a British paper shows:

A gentleman, who was a prisoner in America, has brought to Whitehaven, a Boston almanac for the year, in which the days of his Majesty's birth, accession, etc., are not marked as usual, but the particular days relative to Oliver Cromwell instead of them. The year

46. [Daboll], *Freebetter's New-England Almanack, for 1776;* Daniel George, *George's Cambridge Almanack; or, The Essex Calendar, for . . . 1776* . . . (Salem, Mass., [1775]). For a notation about June 4: "George III tyrant born 1738," see [Ezra Gleason], *Bickerstaff's Boston Almanack, for . . . 1777* . . . (Boston, [1776]). The post–Fourth of July issue of the *North-Carolina Gazette* (New Bern) announced that on July 4, 1778, "the RISING STATES of America entered the THIRD year of their INDEPENDENCE" (July 11, 1778).

47. [Ezra Gleason], *Bickerstaff's Boston Almanack, for . . . 1777* . . . (Salem, Mass., [1776]). Beginning on Jan. 5, 1779, the *New-Hampshire Gazette* (Portsmouth) carried on its masthead the notice, "Third Year of American Independence."

is denoted by the "first of American Independence, which began July 4, 1776."[48]

During the war, which holidays to mark became a tough issue of personal allegiance, and of sales, for almanac makers. Some avoided the issue by excising the British calendar and keeping only the most ideologically labile of Anglo-American anniversaries, January 30 and November 5.[49] More, though, gradually replaced even these dates with those of the Boston Massacre, the battles at Lexington and Concord, the Stamp Act and its repeal, the British evacuation of Boston in 1776 and of Philadelphia in 1778, the anniversary of the treaty with France, the burnings of towns, and literally dozens of battles as they occurred.[50]

48. Moore, ed., *Diary of the American Revolution*, I, 423. Some of the New England almanacs explicitly embrace the Cromwellian legacy; see n. 47, above, and Benjamin West, *Russell's American Almanack, for . . . 1782 . . .* (Boston, [1781]). See also Young, "English Plebeian Culture and American Radicalism," in Jacob and Jacob, eds., *Origins of Anglo-American Radicalism*, 198–200. Tories made the connection explicit in songs denouncing the "Roundhead Pest." Sheldon S. Cohen, ed., "The Connecticut Captivity of Major Christopher French," *Connecticut Historical Society Bulletin*, LV (1990), 176–177.

49. [David Rittenhouse], *The Lancaster Almanack for . . . 1779 . . .* (Lancaster, Pa., [1778]); Samuel Stearns, *North American's Almanack, for . . . 1777* (Worcester, Mass., 1776). Often the notation evolved from "Charles I martyred" to "Charles I exec[uted]" or "Charles I beh[eaded]." Richard Saunders (pseud.), *A Pocket Almanack for the Year 1776* (Philadelphia, 1775); Saunders, *Poor Richard Improved: Being an Almanack and Ephemeris . . . for . . . 1777 . . .* (Philadelphia, [1776]). Joseph Crukshank of Philadelphia printed almanacs with no holiday notations for a largely Quaker audience: see [William Andrews], *Poor Will's Almanack, for . . . 1781 . . .* (Philadelphia, [1780]).

50. Timothy Trueman, *The New-Jersey Almanack for . . . 1779 . . .* (Trenton, N.J., [1778]); [Benjamin West], *Bickerstaff's New-England Almanack, for . . . 1776* (Norwich, Conn., [1775]); [William Andrews], *Poor Will's Pocket Almanack, for . . . 1782* (Philadelphia, [1781]); Thomas Fox, *The Wilmington Almanack, or Ephemeris for . . . 1781* (Wilmington, Del., [1780]); Daniel Sewall, *An Astronomical Diary; or, Almanack for . . . 1783 . . .* (Portsmouth, N.H., [1782]); [David Rittenhouse], *Weatherwise's Town and Country Almanack, for . . . 1782 . . .* (Boston, [1781]).

One almanac author, "John Tobler" of South Carolina, included only Protestant holidays, July 4 and August 23, for 1779. But in the next year's issue, during his state's occupation by British forces, he included January 30 and the Queen's Birthday. The next year he added June 20 ("Reb rep. at Stono 1739") and December 29 ("Savannah taken 1779"). The 1783 issue declares "the 7th year of American Independence" and notes only American holidays and recent battles. See Tobler, *The South-Carolina and Georgia Almanack, for . . . 1779 . . .* (Charleston, S.C., [1778]);

By 1780 American almanac makers had revived the old practice of listing history's "Memorable events." Some of these consisted solely of Revolutionary events. More often they start with the Creation and merge sacred and secular progress. Depending on the proclivities of the printer, they may emphasize biblical dates, the years of scientific discoveries like those of Nicolaus Copernicus or Johann Gutenberg, key dates in Anglo-American history, or a combination of these. But whatever the earlier dates included, these chronicles always end with the important dates of American history since 1775. Sometimes these lists of recent history dwarf the ancient past with dozens of citations, as if to highlight the newness of the new dispensation. Moreover, virtually no regional focus appears in the different almanacs' chronicles of the times. All Americans share in the accomplishments of the militia at Lexington or the Continental army at Saratoga.[51] God's and Albion's histories culminate in American Independence and national integration. History not only ratifies the present: history is the history of the present. The very printed texts by which provincials planned their local year told them they had a sacred history and a national future.

The thirteen pillars that grace the cover of the *Continental Almanac, for 1780* uniformly support a national arch; an angel trumpets the joyous news. An assumption of unity justifies the celebratory image, "mark[ing] the Empire which extends / With equal sweep through heavn's broad way, / From Lake Champlain to wide Savannah Bay" (see Figure 3).[52] Far from keeping provincial farmers focused on the agricultural season or the holy days of a shared religion, almanacs, like Anglo-American culture generally, gave colonists the resources to ex-

---

Tobler, *The South-Carolina and Georgia Almanack, for . . . 1780* (Charleston, S.C., [1779]); Tobler, *The South Carolina and Georgia Almanack, for . . . 1781 . . .* (Charleston, S.C., [1780]); [Tobler], *The Carolina and Georgia Almanack, or Ephemeris, for . . . 1783 . . .* (Charleston, S.C., [1782]).

51. [Richard Saunders], *Poor Richard Improved . . . for . . . 1782 . . .* (Philadelphia, [1781]); Andrew Ellicott, *The Maryland, Delaware, Pennsylvania, Virginia, and North-Carolina Almanack and Ephemeris, for . . . 1781 . . .* (Baltimore, [1780]); Jacobus Bumbo (pseud.), *The American Almanac, for . . . 1781 . . .* (Philadelphia, [1780]); [Samuel Stearns], *The Universal Kalendar, and the North American Almanack, for . . . 1784* (New York, [1784]); Hosea Stafford, *Stafford's Almanack; for . . . 1784* (New Haven, Conn., 1783).

52. [David Rittenhouse], *The Continental Almanac, for . . . 1780 . . .* (Philadelphia, [1779]); Lawrence, *Music for Patriots, Politicans, and Presidents*, 102–103. This image first appeared in the *United States Magazine*, January 1779.

THE
CONTINENTAL
ALMANAC,

FOR THE

Year of our LORD, 1782:
Being the *Second* after LEAP YEAR.
The Seventh Year of American Independence.

By *ANTHONY SHARP*, Philom.

PHILADELPHIA:
Printed and Sold by FRANCIS BAILEY, in
Market-street, between *Third* and *Fourth-streets*.

FIGURE 3. *The Continental Almanac, for the Year of Our Lord, 1782.*
Philadelphia, 1781. Courtesy American Antiquarian Society

pand politics and to develop a nationalist ideology and practice. The
patriots did not have to invent a politics of the calendar. Had they
not been so British, they could not have celebrated themselves into an
American future.

☆ ☆ ☆

The revolutionaries' nationalist ideology demanded the assent of a unified populace. For the moment this was all that was needed. The practices of nationalism provided a way to create that unity, even though
the acts of celebration themselves often exposed class and regional
differences that would haunt archnationalists during the coming decades. Nationalism and popular sovereignty were not the same thing:
the Revolution had been fought for both the principle of government
for the people and for national Independence. But a common enemy—
Old England—that could be made to represent an antipopular faction
enabled the patriot alliance to invent a nationalism that, ironically, depended upon ideologies and practices truly inherited from England.

That this nationalism rejected the past to embrace an uncertain
future does not lessen its importance in history. Indeed, the relationships between nationalist ideology, celebratory practice, and print help
explain why nationalism could earn the assent of revolutionaries without guaranteeing a national state or even anything more than a vague
commitment to popular sovereignty. The resolution of the continuing
debate regarding conflict and consensus in the history of the Revolution may lie in a recognition that, even while the patriots remained
divided among themselves, they practiced a new national unity. This
national unity could be seen on the streets, toasted in a tavern, and
read about in a newspaper; increasingly, each of these acts referred to,
and supported, the others. In themselves these activities required little
sacrifice, and were actually a great deal of fun; but they rarely existed
"in themselves," that is, without the politicized statements that made
them so pregnant with meaning. The politics of celebration succeeded
in being revolutionary precisely because it allowed for both the creation
of cross-class alliances and for the partial expression of class conflict,
as in the shaming of aristocratic tories.

Whatever social grounding and local reality American nationalism
actually possessed during the American Revolution lay, not in any truly
lasting political or ideological consensus, but in its practices: in the
gathering of people at celebratory events, in the toasts and declarations
given meaning by assent, in the reproduction of rhetoric and ritual in

print. The invention of the American nation involved the mixing of rites of assent with apparently rebellious rituals of opposition, thereby preparing Americans to practice an active and popular politics while celebrating their national Revolution. Thus American nationalism would thrive on the denial of the very things that had made it possible, of precisely what would continue to infuse it with effectiveness and ever-new meanings: that is, contest. The rites of assent were also rites of contest.

2

THE
CONSTITUTION
OF FEDERAL
FEELING

In their rituals and their rhetoric, the American revolutionists created a new public called the "nation." This public arose from a truly revolutionary expansion of politics. During the 1760s and 1770s, an increasing number of people participated in the resistance against Great Britain and in the battle over who should rule at home. Nationalist celebrations helped solidify the unstable Revolutionary alliance, drawing attention toward a glorious national future and away from the conflicts of the present.

Celebrations played a more complex role in the more complex political situation of the 1780s. The opposition logic and political practices employed against the crown came home as remarkably democratic state constitutions and popular legislative initiatives like debtor relief. To many of the elite, such measures looked like anarchy and put the future of the new nation at risk. Since John Fiske elected the phrase more than one hundred years ago, historians have generally and perhaps rightly echoed him and those elite citizens of the new nation in calling the era "the critical period of American history." For later students, the key dilemma has remained strikingly similar to the one facing the participants: whether the Federal Constitution was "the ideological fulfillment of the American Revolution," or a repudiation of the Revolution's democratic and local impulses.[1] The answer may depend on

1. John Fiske, *The Critical Period of American History, 1783–1789* (Boston, 1888); Gordon S. Wood, *The Creation of the American Republic, 1776–1787* (Chapel Hill, N.C.,

whether we merely take the Federalists at their word, or see the Federalists' words as deeds in a cultural context, as efforts to assert control over the expanded political world that they had (perhaps unwittingly) helped bring into being. When we concentrate on the real political and theoretical breakthroughs of the era, the framing behind closed doors in Philadelphia, we too easily obscure the participation of those out-of-doors, on both sides of the constitutional debate.[2]

The Great National Discussion over the Constitution should be seen as a struggle over the nature of the political, the spaces in which politics would happen, and the character of "the people" who would participate. The invention of a national political culture opened up a contest over what was being represented and who should represent it. This contest, as I will show, was part of a larger cultural crisis of representation,

---

1969), 393; Bernard Bailyn, "The Ideological Fulfillment of the American Revolution: A Commentary on the Constitution," in Bailyn, *Faces of Revolution: Personalities and Themes in the Struggle for American Independence* (New York, 1990), 226–278. This essay was reprinted as an afterword to a new edition of Bailyn's *Ideological Origins of the American Revolution* (1967), rev ed. (Cambridge, Mass., 1992). For other treatments of the founding as fulfillment and progress in treatment of the Revolutionary era, see Edmund S. Morgan, *The Birth of the Republic, 1763–1789,* rev. ed. (Chicago, 1977); Robert Middlekauff, *The Glorious Cause: The American Revolution, 1763–1789* (New York, 1982). For the classic statement of the opposing view, see Wood, *Creation of the American Republic,* 472–564. Other works offer a more nuanced view, akin to Wood's, with a greater stress on the "pyrrhic" nature of the victory of nationalist conservatives and with greater attention to the agency of the people out-of-doors. See Edward Countryman, *A People in Revolution: The American Revolution and Political Society in New York, 1760–1790* (1981; rpt. New York, 1989), 253; Countryman, *The American Revolution* (New York, 1985); Alfred F. Young, "The Framers of the Constitution and the 'Genius' of the People," with responses, *Radical History Review,* no. 42 (1988), 7–47; Colin Bonwick, *The American Revolution* (Charlottesville, Va., 1991).

2. A growing literature attributes the founders' "strategies of control" to their particular uses of republican ideology in general and print culture in particular. See Robert Ferguson, "We Hold These Truths: Strategies of Control in the Literature of the Founders," in Sacvan Bercovitch, ed., *Reconstructing American Literary History* (Cambridge, Mass., 1986), 1–29; Ferguson, "Ideology and the Framing of the Constitution," *Early American Literature,* XXII (1987), 157–165; Cynthia Jordan, " 'Old Worlds' in 'New Circumstances': Language and Leadership in Post-Revolutionary America," *American Quarterly,* XL (1988), 491–511; Michael Warner, *The Letters of the Republic: Publication and the Public Sphere in Eighteenth-Century America* (Cambridge, Mass., 1990), 97–117; Larzer Ziff, *Writing in the New Nation: Prose, Print, and Politics in the Early United States* (New Haven, Conn., 1991); Thomas Gustafson, *Representative Words: Politics, Literature, and the American Language, 1776–1865* (New York, 1992).

as wealth, personal identity, and even language itself appeared to have broken away from their moorings in reality. The critical period of the 1780s saw attempts to rein in these runaway representations. Celebrations and their circulation in print were key to this contest: they symbolically included and excluded particular groups while sanctioning the very acts of argument and affiliation that constituted citizenship.

Most importantly, the cult of true federal feeling suffused the politics of constitutional ratification. While this patriotic sentimentalism had little to do with the specific models of republican government offered up by Federalists and Antifederalists, it had everything to do with the temporary resolution of representational confusion and class conflict that the Constitution offered. Federalists looked to the display of festive joy as both evidence of national virtue and as a way to create that virtue, which they increasingly associated with their own movement to strengthen the national government. It is not that the debate over the form of the federal government was unimportant; rather, the mobilization of sentimental nationalism, with the concomitant identification of the Antifederalists as unfeeling "disorganizers," was crucial to what happened in 1788 and in the critical period as a whole. At the same time that Federalists interpreted republican political theory in terms of elite leadership and popular spectatorship, they enacted those arguments in sentimental spectacles.

Even as they tried to reform popular politics, then, those who fought for the Constitution fashioned their own styles of public celebration. These celebrations, culminating in the Grand Federal Processions of 1787–1788, relied upon the press in creative and consequential ways. Reports of celebrations helped create the sense that constitutional ratification, necessarily state by state, was actually a national movement, an inevitable expression of the national popular will. As it turned out, the new nationalist rhetoric and practices could not easily be extricated from substantive popular participation, though some tried. I will argue here that, after a concerted post-Revolutionary attempt to restrict the uses of public space, the representation of virtue, and the meaning of the Revolution, Federalists won their fight for a stronger national government only after they symbolically rebroadened the field of respectable, or virtuous, citizenry to include, first, women of the upper classes and, then, artisans and others of the "middling sorts." Whatever fulfillment and relief some watchers of the Grand Federal Processions might have felt, the vexing question of how to represent the people and the nation would remain quite open.

THE CRISIS OF VIRTUE AND THE VIRTUES OF "CRISIS"

British dumping of manufactured goods after 1783 caused "the new nation's first depression." But depression describes a national mood as much as an economic fact, and the mood of disappointment as a national phenomenon had a more complicated history than it might at first seem to have had. From the victory at Yorktown (September 6, 1781) to the final national Day of Thanksgiving for the peace (December 11, 1783), the mood under conscious construction had been millennial in reach, providential in origin, and human in execution. The awe with which commentators described America's new national past shaded into a remarkable optimism about the future. Americans would settle the continent. The trade of all Europe would flow to its ports.[3] Some orators attributed this future to the national character; others warned against such vanity.[4] The revival of the jeremiad, simultaneously celebrating the people and bewailing their fall, provided a fertile venue for grand speculation and prophylactic prophecy. But the jeremiad is only the best example of a cultural obsession with visions of progress and ruin. The war itself provided many examples of virtue exemplified and lost. As David Osgood put it, "Since the settlement of his own favored nation in Canaan, Providence has given to no people a fairer opportunity to secure national felicity." If only for this reason, Israel Evans maintained, the Americans needed to be more vigilant than ever.[5] Perhaps because expectations were so high, the rhetoric of crisis

3. Levi Frisbie, *An Oration Delivered at Ipswich . . . on the Twenty-ninth of April, 1783 . . .* (Boston, 1783); George Richards Minot, *An Oration Delivered March 5, 1782* (Boston, 1782); John Marsh, *A Discourse at Wethersfield, December 11, 1783* (Hartford, Conn., 1783); Merrill Jensen, *The New Nation: A History of the United States during the Confederation, 1781–1789* (New York, 1950), 245–246.

4. David Tappan, *A Discourse Delivered at the Third Parish in Newbury . . .* (Salem, Mass., 1783); Benjamin Hichborn, *An Oration, Delivered July 5th, 1784 . . .* (Boston, 1784).

5. Nathan O. Hatch, *The Sacred Cause of Liberty: Republican Thought and the Millennium in Revolutionary New England* (New Haven, Conn., 1977), chaps. 3–4; Michael Lienesch, *A New Order of the Ages: Time, the Constitution, and the Making of American Political Thought* (Princeton, N.J., 1988), 38–81; Ruth H. Bloch, *Visionary Republic: Millennial Themes in American Thought, 1756–1800* (New York, 1985), chap. 5; Israel Evans, *A Discourse Delivered in New-York . . . on the 11th December, 1783 . . .* (New York, [1784]), 13; Robert Smith, *The Obligations of the Confederate States of North America to Praise God* (Philadelphia, 1782); David Osgood, *Reflections on the Goodness of God . . .* (Boston, 1784), 31.

came to exceed anything heard or read during the most difficult war years.

Postwar realities tested the limits of Revolutionary millennialism. Could republican virtue be prevented from declining?[6] Wartime celebration had deferred the problem; the jeremiad froze it in a dialectic of millennial fantasy and apocalyptic fear. Postwar celebrations, however, went beyond both alternatives to situate virtue and the lack thereof. Though they continued to elaborate national identity, postwar celebrants no longer had the luxury of an outside enemy (or domestic tories) to provide an ideal contrast to native virtue. It became necessary to find the sources of virtue and corruption in order to see which would last—and to learn how to identify either by sight.

Two pieces of celebratory literature, from 1782 and 1786, reveal the terms of this shifting search for virtue. Both were first published in newspapers and presume the ability of the new republic of letters to promote national and futuristic thinking. Both projected their audience into the future by depicting the present as a ruin, a remain or memorial of a past age. Yet in other ways their predictions could not be more different.

In 1782, a fabricated excerpt from a future (1800) issue of the *Pennsylvania Gazette* appeared in a number of newspapers.[7] The news articles highlight joyous events from an imaginary millennium: an American alliance with Germany and reports of "the anniversary of the revolution in Ireland," spurred by the American example. The "Sons of St. Patrick" hold an entertainment for the president and Congress in the Federal City; all the nations of Europe (signifying America's allies) are toasted, except Britain. America redeems the world here, but the world pays tribute to America with thirteen toasts, much as the French had done in celebrations during the war. Most impressive is the monument dedicated to "J.D. G.W. and R.M. Esquires" (John Dickinson, George Washington, and Robert Morris):

In Honour of

THE AMERICAN *TRIUMVIRATE*

The First *began* with his letters,

6. On the question of time in republican thought, see especially J. G. A. Pocock, *The Machiavellian Moment: Florentine Political Thought and the Atlantic Republican Tradition* (Princeton, N.J., 1975); and Lienesch, *New Order of the Ages.*

7. *Massachusetts Gazette, or the Springfield and Northampton Weekly Advertiser,* July 9, 1782; *Salem Gazette* (Mass.), June 27, 1782.

The Second *Conducted* with his Sword,
The Third *finished* with his credit,
The American Revolution.
Reader!—Ask not their names. He is a
Slave who does not know them.
Ask not when and where they lived.—
Their days were measured by their Services to their
Country, and therefore they cannot
be numbered.
The *whole* World shared in their Benevolence, and
therefore America resigns to Humanity the
honor of claiming their Birth.
Ask not *when* they died—
ELOQUENCE, COURAGE AND INTEGRITY,
when they have for their Objects
the liberties of Mankind,
are
IMMORTAL

This imaginary monument substitutes for the memorials that the Congress in 1782 was actually too divided and impoverished to build.[8] It defers to the immediate future the unity and security necessary to such projects but makes that future certain and self-evident to everyone who will live in it. We, the readers, cannot mistake the meaning of the monument or the identity of those it commemorates: to fail to recognize public virtue would be akin to self-imposed enslavement. The conflicts within the patriot cause that haunted the war effort—between military men, merchants, financiers, men of letters, and politicians—appear not to have existed at all, as the pen is beaten into a sword that breaks into bank shares. The reader is told three times that the details don't matter: identity, place, and time are secured through universalization. The American Revolution will transcend its own geographic boundaries to redeem the world.

Four years later, several early supporters of a stronger national government published a verse series, *The Anarchiad*, in the *New-Haven*

8. On the Congress's resolutions to build monuments and failure to do so, see Beverly Orlove Held, "'To Instruct and Improve . . . to Entertain and Please': American Civic Protests and Pageants, 1765–1783" (Ph.D. diss., University of Michigan, 1987), 322–324.

Gazette, and Connecticut Magazine. Here John Trumbull, Joel Barlow, David Humphreys, and Lemuel Hopkins, all of whom had contributed to the literature of celebration during the Revolution, presented a wholly inverted, undone epic: an anticelebration of America. This narrative poem and explanatory notes allegorize the failures of Congress, of philosophical discourse, and of public finance. Much as celebratory orations had placed the Revolution in sacred and secular history, Trumbull and his fellow poets chronicle American history as the fall of empire and the fall of mankind.

Like the apocryphal reportage of 1782, *The Anarchiad* is presented as a document from another time, but in this case the past. From a darkly anti-American perspective, the poem monumentalizes the decline of the Republic, "the restoration of Chaos and substantial Night." [9] The great Anarch (the devil's monarch) supports "th' unfederal cause" and finds allies among pettifogging politicians, backcountry rebels, and scribblers for the popular press. These false patriots—not the Dickinsons, Washingtons, and Morrisses—are the actors in this world turned upside down. As "Democracy" rises, "public credit" sinks; in these dark scenes of fate, "mobs in myriads blacken all the way." *The Anarchiad's* villains are clearly identified, and its point could not be missed. As the American hero Hesper ends his soliloquy, "the voice of UNION calls. . . . 'YE LIVE UNITED, OR DIVIDED DIE.'" The highest virtues are national unity and respect for printed law and its makers.[10]

The opening lines of *The Anarchiad* cannot point to a Constitution that does not yet exist; instead, it names an anti-Constitution of Chaos: "Thy constitution, Chaos, is restor'd; / law sinks before thy uncreating

---

9. It is interesting that the document of future progress (1782) is print, from a newspaper; the document of real decline (1786) is represented as a manuscript, from the "American Antiquities."

Most famous of celebratory Revolutionary pieces are John Trumbull's *MFingal*, which depicts a celebration/rally that turns into a tarring and feathering, and Barlow's epic *Vision of Columbus*. On the Connecticut Wits and their politics, see Kenneth Silverman, *A Cultural History of the American Revolution* . . . (1976; rpt. New York, 1987), esp. 513–515; William C. Dowling, *Poetry and Ideology in Revolutionary Connecticut* (Athens, Ga., 1990); Vernon Louis Parrington, ed., *The Connecticut Wits* (1954; rpt. New York, 1969), 428.

10. Luther G. Riggs, ed., *The Anarchiad* (New Haven, Conn., 1862), 6, 63, 69. *The Anarchiad* appeared in the *New-Haven Gazette* in twelve installments from Oct. 26, 1786, to Sept. 13, 1787.

word." As one critic observes, the "furies" and anarchy "are most abused precisely for their manipulations of language."[11] Unlike the transparent initials and the epideictic rhetoric of the 1800 monument, in which the anonymous author wills his own, his readers', and his subjects' unification in death and ascent, anarchy's precisely named speakers and scribblers divide and conquer as "their arrows [drink] the flame / Of each unfederal politician's name." While there is a hint that Anarch's enemies, the forces of union, will win in the end, the framing of this mock epic actually inverts such other political paeans to the New World future as Philip Freneau and Hugh Henry Brackenridge's "Rising Glory of America" (1770) and Barlow's own *Vision of Columbus* (1787). The found manuscript appears in the *Gazette* under the heading "American Antiquities" but is discovered in the Ohio Country—the site of the nation's expansive future. Rather than belonging wholly to the future and instead of taking God's chosen people and the Roman republic as models, the would-be editor of *The Anarchiad* suggests that this epic poem and America were the model for the ancients. America has not merely fallen into the old cycle of rising and declining republics. It was the mother of them all.

Does discovering the past seal off the future? Not really, because there is no stable text to interpret. The editor repeatedly notes how dirty and illegible the manuscript is: we get only fragments in no particular sequence. The verse reports the past yet somehow predicts the *present* "blessings of paper money and confusion."[12] The imagined ancient text of 1786 is as incomprehensible as the imagined future newspaper of 1782 was transparent. Trumbull and his collaborators finally leave the future open by suggesting that the past as well as the present are negative examples. *The Anarchiad* is thus a late patriot version of what the tories had done a decade earlier when they satirized Revolutionary whigs for celebrating the wrong things. The poem takes such a complicated form because these post-Revolutionary wits had to restore, not a past, but a future. Like the tories, the Connecticut Wits saw virtue as a question of identity subjected to a crisis of representation. They portrayed a polity that had moved from order, benevolence, and transparency to disorder, venality, and illegibility.

Illegibility and false appearances are central themes of *The Anarchiad*,

11. J. K. Van Dover, "The Design of Anarchy: *The Anarchiad*, 1786–1787," *Early Am. Lit.*, XXIV (1989), 245.

12. Riggs, ed., *Anarchiad*, 7.

and for good reason. As Thomas Gustafson has observed, "In America, the pursuit of republican ideals has always been accompanied by attacks against false representation and fears of the people becoming the dupes of artful words and demagogues." The Revolution itself had begun as a protest against certain corruptions of political representation. Yet the poem joins contemporary efforts to relocate the precise sources of misrepresentation. The most obvious problem of representation is the unruly discourse of unvirtuous men. The second is these men themselves. The wrong people are taken for patriots and represent the people in places of public trust. Finally, emissions of paper money epitomize all personal and rhetorical inflations as the clamor for it becomes the most un-American of activities.[13] The themes of this conspiracy—paper money, inflated rhetoric, patriotic poseurs—add up to a post-Revolutionary crisis of representation. Real disorder and elite fears converged in a cultural obsession with the representation of wealth and property, representation in spoken and written words, and the self-presentation of persons.

The representation crisis was real, and the debate it spawned was thus part of the very phenomenon that critics of misrepresentations sought to address. These problems attending representation may be seen as subtexts of the more familiar struggles over political representation. But, since these comments on money, rhetoric, and identity appear right next to if not within constitutional debates in the press, it is more illuminating to consider each of them as individually important, albeit inseparable, aspects of a larger cultural moment in which the rapid expansion of political culture and the capitalist marketplace stretched many familiar ways of representing things, persons, and ideas to their limits and beyond.[14] They were certainly considered individually

13. Gustafson, *Representative Words*, 23, 138, 168; Edmund S. Morgan, *Inventing the People: The Rise of Popular Sovereignty in England and America* (New York, 1988); Silverman, *Cultural History*, 513.

14. An outstanding inquiry into some of these issues, and one that has influenced my approach to the topic, is Mark R. Patterson, *Authority, Autonomy, and Representation in American Literature, 1776–1865* (Princeton, N.J., 1988). Other scholars have usefully connected the changing phenomenologies of paper money and the self in capitalist culture, relating both to problems of literary representation. See Jean-Christophe Agnew, *Worlds Apart: The Market and the Theater in Anglo-American Thought, 1550–1750* (New York, 1986); Walter Benn Michaels, *The Gold Standard and the Logic of Naturalism* (Berkeley, Calif., 1987); and the criticism of Michaels

important, yet inseparable, in their time. During the 1780s, Federalists seized upon the same sorts of celebratory rhetoric and practice discussed earlier in a series of attempts to resolve these representational crises under the signs and symbols of the nation. Before analyzing these innovations in celebration, let us briefly consider the three representational dilemmas and some contemporary attempts to solve them.

☆   ☆   ☆

A March 1786 brief in favor of a stronger central government described the present time as "a critical period in the politics of America. . . . These states cannot remain free, and support a national character, without union" and obedience to the resolves of Congress. "If this were not the case," the writer adds, "Congress would be an empty name, and the federal government, a mere bubble."[15]

In one paragraph this writer hit on two key themes in the rhetoric of crisis: worthless language and unstable currency. During the 1760s and 1770s, tories had often complained about the "stupid jargon" of the patriots. Shocked by the street politics of the Revolutionary era, they contrasted their own printed, reasoned debate to the so-called demagoguery of the radical whigs. The very erudition of articulate loyalists reinforced their main point: that the revolutionaries were "a thoroughly plebeian movement." The illegitimacy of the patriotic movement lay in its reliance upon common people and loose language. In one tory song entitled "The Procession with the Standard of Faction," the New York radical Alexander McDougall is ridiculed for his lower-class origins, and Isaac Sears, another patriot leader, is denounced as a "marvellous Whorator."[16]

The real source of this rhetorical inflation was the desire and necessity of patriot leaders to persuade and exhort the populace. In the

---

in Fredric Jameson, *Postmodernism; or, The Cultural Logic of Late Capitalism* (Durham, N.C., 1991), 181–216. I am also indebted to conversations with Michelle A. Stephens.

15. *Maryland Gazette, and Baltimore General Advertiser*, Mar. 9, 1786.

16. "A Song, Wrote in the Spring of '76," *Pennsylvania Evening Post* (Philadelphia), Dec. 20, 1777; Philip Davidson, *Propaganda and the American Revolution, 1763–1783* (Chapel Hill, N.C., 1941), 298–313; Janice Potter, *The Liberty We Seek: Loyalist Ideology in New York and Massachusetts, 1765–1783* (Cambridge, Mass., 1983); Moses Coit Tyler, *The Literary History of the American Revolution, 1763–1783*, 2 vols. (New York, 1897), II, 52, 56–58; *Poems Serious and Sarcastical, Songs Loyal and Humorous, Constitutional Toasts and Sentiments, by a Briton in New-York* (New York, 1779), 73.

Revolution, the republic of letters "ballooned out to unmanageable proportions." If we take the number of newspapers as a measure, the arena for public discourse expanded even more rapidly in the 1780s than it had during the two decades before. The high Federalist reaction to this, usually dated to the 1790s, can be seen in full force in the newspapers of the mid-1780s. Among the "few events of 1786" thought worthy of remembrance, one writer found "men of neither *honour, honesty,* nor *decency,* talking of *virtue* and *merit.*" Already by 1787 some Federalists were challenging a key tenet of the republican public sphere: anonymity in print. According to the republican ideology of print culture in the eighteenth century, contributions to public debate, made for the good of the public, should be judged according to their own merit, not by the "private" identity of the author. Federalists, in the debate over the Constitution, began insisting that the real names of their opponents ought to be affixed to their newspaper essays so that their social standing could be taken into account.[17]

The measures for debtor relief and paper currency passed by state legislatures during the 1780s, another development inseparable from the political mobilization of the middling and lower sorts, also spurred nervous complaints by elites. The elaboration and diversification of business interests during the Revolutionary era gave life to conflicting theories regarding credit, debt, and paper money. The politics of debt had led some planters and merchants into revolution. But the new consumerism made possible by the war's end was a distinctly popular trend. Though renewed calls for frugality and virtue had some effect and the imbalance of trade lessened, specie still fled the country to pay foreign debts, and the squeeze forced the states into compensatory trade restrictions and paper emissions.[18]

17. Gordon S. Wood, "The Democratization of Mind in the American Revolution," in *Leadership in the American Revolution: Papers Presented at the Third Symposium, May 9 and 10, 1974* (Washington, D.C., 1974), 68–73, quote at 73; Richard D. Brown, *Knowledge Is Power: The Diffusion of Information in Early America, 1700–1865* (New York, 1989), 79; *Virginia Gazette, or, the American Advertiser* (Richmond), Oct. 25, 1786; Warner, *Letters of the Republic,* 34–72; John K. Alexander, *The Selling of the Constitutional Convention: A History of News Coverage* (Madison, Wis., 1990).

18. Gordon S. Wood, *Creation of the American Republic,* chap. 10; Wood, *The Radicalism of the American Revolution* (New York, 1992), 248–252; T. H. Breen, *Tobacco Culture: The Mentality of the Great Tidewater Planters on the Eve of the Revolution* (Princeton, N.J., 1985); Jensen, *The New Nation,* 177–344; Janet A. Riesman, "Money, Credit, and Federalist Political Economy," in Richard Beeman et al., eds., *Beyond Confed-*

These were local fights attuned to local interests, and the gentry might have been right to bewail the splintering of common goals. Paper money, which by its very nature conflated different kinds of proprietary and speculative wealth, directly threatened a landed gentry that based its claims to republican virtue on notions of land as the source of the commonwealth. In fact, their own speculations in real estate would have been enough to shake any sense of secure wealth and orderly progress.[19] The lines between owners of property, producers of wealth, and manipulating paper men blurred as never before when some of the very small farmers who were supposed to be the bulwark of Jefferson's Republic revolted against taxes that had to be paid in hard currency—which they neither possessed nor could easily acquire. How much things had changed by 1787 is evident in a bit of mock-celebratory verse against Shays's Rebellion that ridicules the Shaysites for claiming the Revolutionary mantle:

> Huzza my poe bankers! No taxes we'll pay!
> Here's a pardon for *Wheeler, Shays, Parsons* and Day.
> Fix green boughs in your hats and renew the old cause.
> Stop the courts in each County and bully the laws.[20]

The mere fact that a domestic opposition could claim a stake in the Revolution on this basis warranted concern over the nature of a unifying patriotism.

The unfinished business of the Revolution led all sides to continue to search for tories in disguise. Could patrotism be the first refuge of scoundrels? If so, what attributions of virtue could be trusted? Newspapers and almanacs warned readers to look out for fake patriots, counterfeiters, and seducers; these rogues made virtue all the more difficult to discern. The members of Congress, dining with the mayor of New York and the State Society of the Cincinnati on July 4, 1785, "en-

---

eration: Origins of the Constitution and American National Identity (Chapel Hill, N.C., 1987), 128–161.

19. Gordon S. Wood, "Interests and Disinterestedness in the Making of the Constitution" in Beeman et al., eds., *Beyond Confederation,* 72–73; Cathy Matson, "Public Vices, Private Benefit: William Duer and His Circle, 1776–1792," in William Pencak and Conrad Edick Wright, eds., *New York and the Rise of American Capitalism: Economic Development and the Social and Political History of an American State, 1780–1870* (New York, 1989).

20. *New Hampshire Spy* (Portsmouth), July 4, 1787 (from *Albany Gazette*).

joyed a degree of pleasure unknown to many pseudo citizens." But, unless reports greatly exaggerate, many men of paper wealth, false words, and dubious patriotism were enjoying themselves indeed.[21]

Separating the virtuous from the profligate had been a large part of Revolutionary nationalism. But what was often missing in the 1780s was the former confidence, amid the warnings, that the sunshine patriots would fade: that virtue would not only see the light but be seen in the light. New Hampshire July 4 revelers of 1783 toasted hopefully: "May the degenerate sons of America, who shrunk at the clouds of her distress, never bask in the rays of her glory." In Saint Croix, some formerly pro-British merchants joined in celebrating the anniversary of the Lexington battle, moving a patriot to assure a friend: "It will not be difficult to distinguish [the Tories]. . . . Like Cain, they will always have some mark easy to be discovered."[22]

By contrast, the author of a short essay, "On Sincerity," in the 1786 *New-England Almanack* actually expected duplicity. There was no easy way to separate the crisis of political virtue from all the inflated claims of an expanding market society.

> "*Sincerity is a jewel*," says the great man, when making a promise that he never intends to perform.—"*Sincerity is a jewel*," says the lover, when suing for happiness from the woman he is determined to ruin and abandon.—"*Sincerity is a jewel*," says the *hypocritically devout* female, while with a sanctimonious phiz she unworthily joins in the most sacred religious ordinances.—"*Sincerity is a jewel*," says this same paragon of female excellence, when assisting in a *disinterested* scheme to destroy her bosom friend.—"*Sincerity is a jewel*," says the mock patriot, when applying for the interest he means to abuse.— "*Sincerity is a jewel*," says the creditor to his debtor, while he knows a bailiff waits at the door to arrest him.[23]

---

21. "The Patriot, No. 1," *Freeman's Journal: or, the North American Intelligencer* (Philadelphia), Nov. 29, 1786; "Patriotism; or Liberty of the Press," *New-York Journal, and the General Advertiser,* Mar. 24, 1785; "Beware of Counterfeits," *New-Haven Gazette, and the Connecticut Magazine,* II (Oct. 11, 1787), 265–266; *Independent Gazetteer: or, the Chronicle of Freedom* (Philadelphia), July 9, 1785 (from New York).

22. *New-Hampshire Gazette, and General Advertiser* (Portsmouth), July 5, 1783; *Independent Ledger, and American Advertiser* (Boston), July 14, 1783.

23. "On Sincerity—A Shandean Rhapsody," in *The New-England Almanack . . . for . . . 1786 . . .* (Providence, R.I., 1786). On the market and crises of self-representation in the early Republic, see Michael Zuckerman, "A Different Thermi-

The insincere "lose that *confidence,* without which no dealing can be carried on by mankind." But the dealing only encourages the insincerity, the trade in misrepresentations. This is the old republican version of crisis rhetoric. It finds both virtue and venality in contemporary society, tying relations among men and women, and between the classes, to questions of private credit and public reputation. Perhaps most revealingly of all, it begins with an indictment of a lying "great man" and ends with an attack on creditors. And it hopes, against all hope, that further exposure will suffice.

The author of "On Sincerity" makes no distinction between the purveyors of bad credit and those who present false identities: they all say the same thing. The "mock patriot" is merely one among many poseurs who make capital out of insincere expressions of sincerity. For others, however, the failures of popular politics, exemplified by mushroom patriots gaining "interest" and speaking at great length in the streets and in the press, underscored the vices of the system. They worried less about irresponsible great men and cruel creditors and more about demagogues and debtors. Rather than giving up on the possibility of a virtuous republic, they refined older methods of embodying patriotism. Distancing themselves from the "jealousy" that had made a virtue of opposition and distrust, they sought a solution to the problems of loose language, fickle finances, and patriotic posing, and they sought it on a national scale.[24] One of the places they found it was in the politics of celebration.

dor: The Revolution beyond the American Revolution," in James Henretta et al., eds., *The Transformation of Early American History: Society, Authority, and Ideology* (New York, 1991), 170–193.

24. See the essays by "Nestor," *Carlisle Gazette, and the Western Repository of Knowledge* (Pa.), July 5, 19, 1786. On jealousy as a positive quality in earlier republicanism, see Bailyn, *Ideological Origins,* 144–159; James H. Hutson, "The Origins of 'The Paranoid Style in American Politics': Public Jealousy from the Age of Walpole to the Age of Jackson," in David D. Hall et al., eds., *Saints and Revolutionaries: Essays on Early American History* (New York, 1984), 342–360; Gordon S. Wood, "Conspiracy and the Paranoid Style: Causality and Deceit in the Eighteenth Century," *William and Mary Quarterly,* 3d Ser., XXXIX (1982), 401–441.

CELEBRATING NATURAL ARISTOCRACY:
FROM VIRTUE TO SENSIBILITY

Modern commentators on the *The Federalist* have devoted close attention to its rationale for enlarging "the practicable sphere of a republic." Large republics, believed Madison and Hamilton, generate a large pool of possible leaders, from which the truly virtuous may rise. The authors of *The Federalist* hoped to create the conditions for the emergence of a natural aristocracy, or meritocracy, to lead America into its republican future. In this they followed the hopeful orators of the early 1780s who foresaw rapid commercial development, unconcerned as they were for its effects on the division of wealth "in a country like this, which knows no distinction but that which arises from merit."[25]

We now know that inequities of wealth increased in mid-to-late-eighteenth-century America even as the sources of wealth diversified and mixed, competition increased, and a middling interest began to make itself felt. Many contemporaries knew this too. Yet the ideology of meritocracy played too important a role in the late-Revolutionary period to be easily dismissed as a timeless myth. Rather, we should see in that ideology an unstable alliance between an inchoate middling interest and various sectionally distinct, insecure landed gentries. Natural aristocracy was a solution to the weakness of the real American aristocracy and its delegitimization in Revolutionary ideology and experience.[26] For some celebrants of the Constitution in 1788, the Con-

---

25. Terence Ball, "A Republic—If You Can Keep It," in Ball and J. G. A. Pocock, eds., *Conceptual Change and the Constitution* (Lawrence, Kans., 1988), 148–151; Wood, *Creation of the American Republic*, 467–492; Hichborn, *An Oration,* 19.

26. Gary B. Nash, *The Urban Crucible: The Northern Seaports and the Origins of the American Revolution* (Cambridge, Mass., 1986); Rowland Berthoff and John M. Murrin, "Freedom, Communalism, and the Yeoman Freeholder: The American Revolution Considered as a Social Accident," in James H. Hutson and Stephen G. Kurtz, eds., *Essays on the American Revolution* (Chapel Hill, N.C., 1973), 279; Stuart M. Blumin, *The Emergence of the Middle Class: Social Experience in the American City, 1760–1900* (Cambridge, Mass., 1989), chap. 2; Allan Kulikoff, *The Agrarian Origins of American Capitalism* (Charlottesville, Va., 1992), 99–146.

On natural aristocracy: Gordon S. Wood, "Ideology and the Origins of Liberal America," *WMQ,* 3d Ser., XLIV (1987), 628–640; Albert Tillson, Jr., *Gentry and Common Folk: Political Culture on a Virginia Frontier, 1740–1789* (Lexington, Ky., 1991), 66, 85–86, 99; John M. Murrin and Gary Kornblith, "The Making and Unmaking of an American Ruling Class," in Alfred F. Young, ed., *Beyond the American Revolution: Explorations in the History of American Radicalism* (DeKalb, Ill., 1993), 27–

stitutional Convention itself symbolized this natural aristocracy. A virtuous elite constituted no threat to liberty, insisted Simeon Baldwin,
since "in these States the balance of property is wholly in favour of the
people.—Merit is the criterion of eminence, and the aristocratic influence is founded in superior wisdom and virtue." [27]

This kind of aristocracy had to be fashioned, but in a wholly natural way: it was not to be born, but rather made, like a merchant's good
credit. But credit could not be as secure as landed property: it had to
be *displayed*.[28] During the 1780s, public events like the Fourth of July
became an alternate venue for the establishment of that natural aristocracy—a meritocracy that would simultaneously reveal and recreate
itself through touching, unifying displays of virtue. We can see this in
the reportage of these explicitly nationalist rituals, which highlights
the participation of elites and formulaically stresses the unity they displayed and shared with the populace, the productive competition of
different groups' patriotic performance, participants' sincerity of feeling, and the equation of elite virtue with public order.

The most striking thing about post-Revolutionary celebrations and
the printed accounts of them is their sedateness. The seemingly restricted nature of the tavern-and-toasts gatherings of the 1780s has led
more than one historian to describe them as rather pallid affairs. Yet
it is not the absence of the populace from the streets that is revealed
in these accounts; it is the absence of the populace's importance to the
writers of accounts. Especially in sizable towns, nationalist celebrations
were actually overlapping sets of rituals: the muster of the militia, the
procession, an oration; the semipublic tavern gatherings and banquets;
and popular revelry, especially at night. By the mid-1780s a proliferation of short reports from smaller towns appeared in newspapers; they
often proclaimed precisely what editors cited them to prove: that the
Fourth was celebrated "everywhere." The companies whose toasts and

79. For a contrasting argument regarding the strengths of the elite, see Robert H.
Wiebe, *The Opening of American Society: From the Adoption of the Constitution to the Eve
of Disunion* (New York, 1984), chaps. 1–2.

27. Simeon Baldwin, *An Oration Pronounced before the Citizens of New-Haven, July
4th, 1788 . . .* (New Haven, Conn., 1788), 12.

28. For men who had risen in the Revolutionary era seeking to secure their
reputations "by cultivating the marks of gentility," see Alan Taylor, "From Fathers
to Friends of the People: Political Personas in the Early Republic," *Journal of the
Early Republic*, XI (1991), 465–491.

dinners made the papers, however, were generally "the most respectable characters."[29]

Apparently these "respectable characters" were not the entire body of citizens, much less "the people." Whoever they were, they appear to have taken as their models certain new groups on the public stage. One of these was the Society of the Cincinnati. A fraternity of officers from the Continental army who met annually on the Fourth of July, the Cincinnati did much to reestablish the solemnity and respectability of festivity in the eyes of the genteel. The Cincinnati quickly earned criticism for their militaristic trappings and hereditary succession of membership but succeeded nonetheless in establishing themselves on local landscapes with their annual meetings.[30] On Independence Day they waited on local officials and received official plaudits in turn. Wearing their army uniforms, they embodied the nation and personified its virtues. A witness of the proceedings of New York's Cincinnati in 1785 insisted, "Nothing could do more to honor human nature, than the brotherly love and unfeigned testimonies of veneration which each member of the Society demonstrated on the celebration of Independency on the 4th Instant." They, in turn, took full responsibility for encouraging honorable veneration. As William Jackson put it to his brethren Cincinnati in 1786, "How far our national character shall be established on the basis of virtue—and our public credit be supported with honor, will depend upon ourselves, and can only be chargeable upon our own neglect if unattained." The Cincinnati were early proponents of a stronger national government and did not fail to use the Fourth of July toasts to link national virtue to "an increase of energy" in federal government.[31]

29. Robert Pettus Hay, "Freedom's Jubilee: A Hundred Years of the Fourth of July, 1776–1876" (Ph.D. diss., University of Kentucky, 1967), 23, 26; *Pennsylvania Journal, and the Weekly Advertiser* (Philadelphia), July 19, 27, 1786; *Boston Gazette, and the Country Journal,* July 9, 1786; *Norwich Packet* (Conn.), July 22, 1784.

30. Pennsylvania Society of the Cincinnati, *Proceedings* (Philadelphia, 1785), 59; *Boston Gazette,* July 11, 1786; Charles Royster, *A Revolutionary People at War: The Continental Army and American Character, 1775–1783* (Chapel Hill, N.C., 1979), 353–358; Minor Meyers, Jr., *Liberty without Anarchy: A History of the Society of the Cincinnati* (Charlottesville, Va., 1984). Freemasons performed a similar function; they too relied on "sensible signs" to prove their own virtues and to educate their members and a wider audience who watched their spectacles. See Steven C. Bullock, *Revolutionary Brotherhood: Freemasonry and the Transformation of the American Social Order, 1730–1840* (Chapel Hill, N.C., 1996), 140.

31. *Extract from the Proceedings of the New-York State Society of the Cincinnati, Convened on the 4th of July, 1786* . . . (New York, 1786); W[illiam] Jackson, *An Oration,*

The 1780s also witnessed the revival and emergence of several fraternal organizations, including the Sons of Saint George, Saint Patrick, and Saint Andrew and the Masons. These voluntary groups and ethnic associations held their annual meetings on the old saints' days but positioned themselves as *American* sons of foreign fathers—and proved it by making thirteen toasts in the style of the Fourth of July. The Society of the Sons of Saint George took up the task of helping indigent British immigrants. Not "organized for the purpose of keeping alive any invidious national distinction," membership was yet restricted to the British-born and their sons. Revealingly, though, half of the one hundred names on one roll were "honorary" members. Local chapters used honorary memberships to raise the eminence of the fraternity. The most popular of these fraternal celebrants might have been the Sons of Saint Tammany, who did the immigrants one better by inventing a native American heritage. In Philadelphia they even invited six Seneca headmen to join their 1786 festivals. By the mid-1780s many almanacs listed its patron day—May 1—as a national festival.[32]

---

to Commemorate the Independence of the United States . . . (Philadelphia, 1786), 28; Joel Barlow, *An Oration, Delivered at the North Church in Hartford, at the Meeting of the Connecticut Society of the Cincinnati, July 4, 1787* (Hartford, Conn., [1787]), 11; *New-York Journal*, July 14, 1785.

32. *Virginia Gazette, or, the American Advertiser* (Richmond), July 16, 1785, Mar. 22, 1786; *New Jersey Journal, and Political Intelligencer* (Elizabethtown), July 8, 1784. The same was true for the Cincinnati. Limited to Continental army officers, it opened its doors for well-known—and wealthy—patriots like the financier Robert Morris.

On Sons of Saint Tammany: *Independent Journal: or, the General Advertiser* (New York), May 5, 1787; *New-York Journal*, May 22, 1788; *Father Tammany's Almanac, for . . . 1786 . . .* (Philadelphia, 1785); William Goddard, *The Pennsylvania, Delaware, Maryland, and Virginia Almanack for . . . 1787* (Baltimore, [1786]); Robert Andrews, *Virginia Almanack for . . . 1785* (Richmond, Va., [1785]); Mark Time, *The Pennsylvania Almanack for . . . 1787* (Philadelphia, [1786]); Samuel Stearns, *The Universal Calendar, and the North American Almanack, For . . . 1787 . . .* (Boston, 1787). Meeting on the banks of the Schuykill in 1785, Philadelphia Tammanyites cheered thirteen times but neither drank toasts nor paid court to the great: "Having no ambition to be greater, they determined not to be less than their fellow citizens" (*Freeman's Journal*, May 4, 1785). On the Tammany society and its cultural politics, see Edwin P. Kilroe, *Saint Tammany and the Origin of the Society of Tammany, or Columbian Order, in the City of New York* (New York, 1913), 84, 90–160; Philip Joseph Deloria, "Playing Indian: Otherness and Authenticity in the Assumption of American Indian Identity" (Ph.D. diss., Yale University, 1994), chap. 1; Roger D. Abrahams, "History and Folklore: Luck-Visits, House-Attacks, and Playing Indian in Early America," in

After 1783 these groups took up the most prominent celebratory spaces: through the streets, in places of worship, in taverns, and in the press. They identified explicitly with the nation, and they banished all semblance of partisan political disagreement. This, of course, had been a Fourth of July ideal since the beginning. But these celebrations also highlighted something that Revolutionary festivity could intentionally lack: order. Despite all the toasting, respectable citizens never got drunk, at least not in the published reports. Associating drunkenness and riot with the increasingly delegitimated crowd, accounts of the Fourth of July portrayed the order and decorum worthy of virtuous republicans. Only when the crowd was excluded was their disorder even mentioned. At the "pompously celebrated" New York Independence Day of 1787, "no one was admitted to the hall, without a card, by which means the auditory was brilliant and respectable." Outside the hall, "no unhappy accident took place, more than is customary at festivals of this nature, in populous cities, where all ranks partake of the copious libations of mirth and wine."[33]

Were we to take these accounts at face value, we might conclude that there were two distinct classes in post-Revolutionary America, the respectable and the not respectable, and that never the twain did meet. That the reality was much fuzzier may explain why the boundaries of respectability were continually being explored and shored up in both these celebrations and their published descriptions. Traditional rituals of exchange and deference, the older relationships of class, seem to have broken down. There are few examples of the gentility's providing punch for the people, a gesture that had characterized festive occasions in England and the colonies.[34]

Ralph Cohen and Michael S. Roth, eds., *History and . . . : Histories within the Human Sciences* (Charlottesville, Va., 1995), 268–295.

33. *New-York Journal,* July 5, 1787; *Independent Journal* (New York), July 7, 1787. On the delegitimization of the crowd after the Revolution see, especially, Paul A. Gilje, *The Road to Mobocracy: Popular Disorder in New York City, 1763–1834* (Chapel Hill, N.C., 1987); Thomas P. Slaughter, "Crowds in Eighteenth-Century America: Reflections and New Directions," *Pennsylvania Magazine of History and Biography,* CXV (1991), 3–34.

34. On changes in tavern-drinking habits, see David W. Conroy, *In Public Houses: Drink and the Revolution of Authority in Colonial Massachusetts* (Chapel Hill, N.C., 1995). One of the last treatings I have seen described occurred at a Marblehead celebration of the peace, an occasion that also included a traditional bonfire and a "burying of the hatchet" (*Salem Gazette,* May 1, 1783). Occasionally in the 1780s

The end of an older class system, with ties of deference and obligation between gentlemen (the "best") and the rest, has been persuasively described as the crucial transformation of the Revolutionary era. The Revolution's democratic impulses aspired to erase class, but at the same time its prevailing republicanism could not acknowledge the reality (much less the legitimacy) of any other kinds of interests.[35] This, it should be stressed, was an *ideological* transformation; in reality, class differences were being recognized—indeed, refigured—every day. Despite the egalitarianism surging from below, republicanism enabled already-recognized patriots to limit who counted in the public sphere. They could do so, not by *actually* representing the people, but by *virtually* representing the people's once and future virtue.[36] The high-toned celebrants of the 1780s stood for the people even as they excluded most people from active participation in their parades and evening balls. As "rites of assent," these festivals had decidedly different roles for elites and plebeians. The former performed the sacred rites; the latter, at most, demonstrated their assent. If the latter were really virtuous, they would assent by recognizing true virtue and showing their joy. If they were not now actually virtuous, they could be virtually represented by an actual aristocracy of virtue. If all ranks must share in the festivity, they need not share equally.

In practice, the organizers of nationalist celebrations tried to mediate between the classless meritocracy of their dreams and the divided

---

newspapers we see collections made to buy festive dinners for citizens in jail and their thankful toasts. This continues the jubilee aspect of Independence Day, but, given the increasing number of jailings for debt in the 1780s, the meanings of this largesse could have changed with the class identities of the recipients.

35. Wood, *Creation of the American Republic*, 606–615; Wood, *The Radicalism of the American Revolution*. For a similar assessment of French revolutionary republicanism and its failure to achieve a "liberal" representation of interests, see Lynn Hunt, *Politics, Culture, and Class in the French Revolution* (Berkeley, Calif., 1984), 229.

36. In playing with the terms "actual" and "virtual" in this way, I am alluding to the original controversy over representation in Parliament. During the 1760s, the colonists complained that the notion of virtual representation, by which any member of Parliament considered the interests, not of his own district, but of the whole realm, was precisely the fallacy that had led to unfair measures like the Stamp Act; see Morgan, *Inventing the People*, 240–245. It is worth considering whether the terms "virtual" and "virtue" had a very real connection, since in both cases it was only the presumption of elites of their own transcendent virtues that led them to believe in the particular fiction of "virtual" representation.

society they lived in. The most important development here was the didactic aspects of celebrations. By watching spectacular parades, the younger generation would be schooled in patriotism. In 1780, 1781, 1783, 1785, and 1786, the University of Pennsylvania held its public commencement exercises on Independence Day. In this and similar processions, students of all ages marched with their teachers. Like morning militia musters and speeches, such events spurred virtue and made it easier to include "almost all orders of citizens," if not as participants, then as spectators. The orations should be published, insisted one commentator, "so that the festival may always be recitative of the means by which it was produced, and the advantages which it bestowed: our youth will, by this means, be trained into the habits of thinking and speaking, becoming Republicans."[37]

What were these habits of thinking and speaking? Undoubtedly the would-be educators of the young Republic, like Noah Webster, hoped that the rising generation would "lisp the praise of liberty and of those illustrious heroes and statesmen who have wrought revolution in her favor." The stress on behavior and appearance at these festivals and their public nature point to efforts that went far beyond ensuring politically correct speech. If the rhetoric of these reports is to be taken at all seriously, it was national virtue itself that was being searched for in the faces and the general deportment of participants. For the nationalists of the 1780s, real virtue was not an abstract quality of moral character; it was experienced and seen as patriotic *feeling*. This quality of feeling was intimately bound up with every affective, natural tie among people.

37. *Pennsylvania Journal,* July 12, 1780, July 6, 1785, July 5, 1786, July 14, 1787; *Pennsylvania Packet or the General Advertiser* (Philadelphia), July 14, 1781, July 7, 1785; *Freeman's Journal* (Philadelphia), July 9, 1783; *United States Chronicle: Political, Commercial, and Historical* (Providence), July 20, 1786; *Connecticut Courant* (Hartford), July 14, 1788. On education for citizenship in the early Republic, see Gordon S. Wood, "Introduction," in Wood, ed., *The Rising Glory of America, 1760–1820,* rev. ed. (Boston, 1990), 7–8; Melvin C. Yazawa, "Creating a Republican Citizenry," in Jack P. Greene, ed., *The American Revolution: Its Character and Limits* (New York, 1987), 292–308. Peter S. Onuf observes: "Efforts to foster popular virtue, whether through state-supported religious or educational establishments, were premised on pessimistic assessments of the character of the American people. Popular ignorance was less a lack of information than a lack of respect for the well-informed and a natural disposition toward selfishness and licentiousness." Onuf, "State Politics and Republican Virtue: Religion, Education, and Morality in Early American Federalism," in Paul Finkelman and Stephen E. Gottlieb, eds., *Toward a Usable Past: Liberty under the State Constitutions* (Athens, Ga., 1991), 103.

"The spirit of friendship and military zeal and fortitude was manifest throughout" Philadelphia's 1786 Fourth of July celebration, "and where a soldier dropt a tear to the memory of his fallen friend, the audience shared in his sensibility." [38]

The 1780s appear to have been the high-water mark of the cult of sensibility in America. Far from a mere literary trend, this was a cultural imperative of international dimensions.[39] On the day before July 4, 1787, the editor of the *Salem Mercury* quoted the French philosophe Turgot on the need for "public spectacles." Such "sensible and striking objects" spur people to feel love, which leads to true patriotism. "Insensibly we learn to reunite under the same comprehensive idea, inhabitants of the country, and the country itself." The stakes here were too important to rely upon the unevenly distributed capabilities of the mind. Thomas Jefferson, for one, believed in the "moral sense," in sentiment as a faculty that operated through but was ultimately superior to intellect. More important, these affections were not private, as the nineteenth century came to think of them, but public. Social theories of the age homed in on the problem of education precisely because morality was thought to arise from the experience of "sociability." Selfishness, on the other hand, was privacy incarnate, the opposite of visible virtue. Whether figured as passion or (increasingly) as the height of calculation, self-interest was a problem to be exposed or to be reconciled with the public good.[40]

38. Noah Webster, *On the Education of Youth in America* (1787–1788; 1790), rpt. in Frederick Rudolph, ed., *Essays on Education in the Early Republic* (Cambridge, Mass., 1965), 65; *United States Chronicle* (Providence), July 20, 1786.

39. Historically oriented treatments include Colin Campbell, *The Romantic Ethic and the Spirit of Modern Consumerism* (London, 1987), 120–160; John Mullan, *Sentiment and Sociability: The Language of Feeling in the Eighteenth Century* (Oxford, 1988); Terry Eagleton, *The Ideology of the Aesthetic* (London, 1990), chap. 2; Dorinda Outram, *The Body and the French Revolution: Sex, Class, and Political Culture* (New Haven, Conn., 1989); Anne Vincent-Buffault, *The History of Tears: Sensibility and Sentimentality in France* (London, 1991); G. J. Barker-Benfield, *The Culture of Sensibility: Sex and Society in Eighteenth-Century Britain* (Chicago, 1992).

40. *Salem Mercury: Political, Commercial, Moral,* July 3, 1787. On the American scene I have profited from Garry Wills, *Inventing America: Jefferson's Declaration of Independence* (New York, 1978), 273–319; Daniel W. Howe, "The Political Psychology of *The Federalist,*" *WMQ,* 3d Ser., XLIV (1987), 485–509; Philip Greven, *The Protestant Temperament: Patterns of Child-Rearing, Religious Experience, and the Self in Early America* (New York, 1977); Jay Fliegelman, *Prodigals and Pilgrims: The American*

However natural, virtue, like a garden, could be cultivated. The right sensations awakened the moral sense and revealed its presence. Thus Americans of the respectable classes searched each other's countenance as they examined their own hearts for the signs of benevolence. Described in bodily sequence, sensations that awakened and strengthened the moral sense were perceived by the eye or the mind and channeled to the soul—the glowing heart, which then registered its true state in the radiant or beclouded face, the sparkling or tearful eye.

This "law of the heart" and the attendant "aestheticization of social life" helped the inchoate middle class (or, rather, parts of the older gentry allied with the newer commercial classes) to promote its own self-evident virtues as natural. In America, the sentimentalization of virtue permitted descendants of the Puritans to hope that the godly community (now the nation) would unite to praise God "with one heart and one voice." Republicanism's success signaled a more perfect union of virtuous hearts than had been possible under a king's domain. "A monarch's subjects may rejoice, in celebrating the anniversary of their sovereign's birth; but such joy cannot be compared to the veritable felicity which pervades the *souls* of real American Whigs, when they solemnize the *Birthday* of their country's freedom," averred a correspondent from Albany.[41]

Such affective ties were all the more important in a republican polity. When commentators waxed eloquent about Americans' patriotic feelings, they described both what they felt and what they believed it was necessary for citizens to feel, and to perceive. For David Ramsay, Independence Day marked nothing less than the freeing of the American heart. True virtue could now emerge, to see and be seen.

> In monarchies, an extreme degree of politeness disguises the simplicity of nature, and "sets the looks at variance with the thoughts"; in republicks, mankind appear as they really are, without any false colouring: In these governments, therefore, attentive observers have

Revolution against Patriarchal Authority (New York, 1982); Ruth H. Bloch, "The Gendered Meanings of Virtue in Revolutionary America," *Signs,* XIII (1987), 46–53; Jan Lewis, *The Pursuit of Happiness: Family and Values in Jefferson's Virginia* (New York, 1983), 141, 211–227.

41. Eagleton, *Ideology of the Aesthetic,* 44; Eliphalet Porter, *A Sermon, Delivered to the First Religious Society in Roxbury, December 11, 1783* . . . (Boston, 1784), 4; *Thomas's Massachusetts Spy; Or, the Worcester Gazette,* May 29, 1788.

an opportunity of knowing all the avenues to the heart, and of thoroughly understanding human nature.[42]

With artificial restrictions sloughed off, the rule of benevolence beckoned. Even commerce could be domesticated if true virtue flowed from the social and if virtuous education proceeded in public. Post-Revolutionary Americans could see in an expanded public sphere the opportunity for all to educate and exercise their reasonable and natural virtues. If the emergence of the nation made all this possible, truly there was something to celebrate. And celebrating itself would help make the nation great.[43]

Patriotic celebration became a cultural imperative in the 1780s, every bit as much as it had been a political imperative in the 1760s and 1770s. Just as in sentimental novels, the joyful tears spurred by sublime scenes of celebration were described in terms of exchange. Such exchange, good for all parties and resting on the expectation of unlimited natural resources, might be seen as an analogue to the commercial optimism (probably unwarranted) Americans displayed at the end of the war. In both international trade and interpersonal relations, these sentimental nationalists looked forward to competitions without losers (except for the British and other conspiratorial rogues). Again and again celebrants were said to "vie with each other to honor the day." Earlier in the Revolutionary era, ladies making broadcloth at a spinning bee would "vie with each other in skill and industry in their profitable employment," even so much as to "vie with the men in contributing to the preservation and prosperity of their country and equally share in the honor of it." Likewise, it was often "all ranks" who seemed to compete for patriotic honors. Whether the competition was between sexes, ranks in society, or just the thirty gentlemen at a Savannah celebration of Washington's birthday, such spectacles made visible the intangible qualities of national virtue while doing away with the specter of interest groups and individualism run amok. The ritually controlled competitive display allowed individuals to display their virtue and simultaneously to subordinate themselves to the public good.[44]

42. David Ramsay, *An Oration on the Advantages of American Independence* . . . (Charleston, S.C., 1778), 6.

43. On commerce as a force that would domesticate (that is, civilize) the world, see Wood, *The Radicalism of the American Revolution*, 217–218.

44. *Pennsylvania Journal*, July 14, 1787; Mary Beth Norton, *Liberty's Daughters: The Revolutionary Experience of American Women, 1750–1800* (Boston, 1980), 167–168;

Washington had earned the undying devotion of the entire country by denying that he had any self-interested desires, except to return to Mount Vernon and rule benevolently over his smaller plantation world. But, in an irony that we no longer miss, the retiring Washington spent his greatest efforts crafting a virtuous public persona. As Washington's progress through towns and cities as general and as president made him a symbol of national virtue, the cult of the nation became the first and perhaps the foremost way for men and women of means to show themselves off without appearing selfish. This was republican sentimentalism nationalized and demilitarized, made public as never before.[45] Rather than truly obliterating the self (or class, for that matter), the display of federal feeling permitted middle- and upper-class individuals to be for themselves and for the whole simultaneously: a new style of virtue.

☆   ☆   ☆

Yet like the paeans to order and sobriety that suppressed disorder and drunkenness, the vaunting of visible patriotic sentiment contained a dark possibility: the risk of misreading. What if individuals meant merely to distinguish themselves? What if they faked federal feeling? Novels and newspapers of the period were filled with rakes who feigned love to the doom of credulous women, counterfeiters of all sorts abounded, and two-faced patriots haunted discussions of good government. In light of the pervasive concern with pretense, it is striking that sensibility remained the measure of character, and faking it the height of perfidy.

Why did Americans in a position of cultural dominance keep their faith in such an unstable merit system? Sensibility, after all, was an unstable system for representing and policing social values. The answer perhaps lies in the crisis of representation itself: the increasing need

---

New-York Journal, Mar. 9, 1788. On sentimental "exchange," see Vincent-Buffault, *History of Tears,* 17–28; David Waldstreicher, " 'Fallen under My Observation': Vision and Virtue in *The Coquette,*" *Early Am. Lit.,* XXVII (1992), 204–218. On commercial optimism, see Cathy D. Matson and Peter S. Onuf, *A Union of Interests: Political and Economic Thought in Revolutionary America* (Lawrence, Kans., 1990).

45. Garry Wills, *Cincinnatus: George Washington and the Enlightenment* (New York, 1984); Barry Schwartz, *George Washington: The Making of an American Symbol* (New York, 1987); Paul K. Longmore, *The Invention of George Washington* (Berkeley, Calif., 1988).

For earlier republican sentimentalism, see Silverman, *Cultural History,* 82–87, 177, 517; and Royster, *Revolutionary People at War,* 87–90.

for some agreed-upon signs of value amid the reconstitution of political discourse, proprietary wealth, and public identities. In the late eighteenth century, identity itself had become increasingly unstable. Highly mobile young people, particularly young men in cities, found that they could make and remake themselves by manipulating appearances. We have come to associate this kind of identity work with success stories like Benjamin Franklin's, but for every Franklin there were probably many rogues like Stephen Burroughs and outright failures like William Moraley.[46] Anonymity was simultaneously a resource for some and a problem for the culture as a whole. Some could rebuild their reputations from scratch, but everyone had to wonder: Which appearances could one trust?

For the larger culture, the rule of sentiment had rewards in that it made fellow feeling wholly compatible with personal aspiration and self-cultivation.[47] Intensely participatory, it expanded the boundaries of the public even as it was a class strategy that excluded the "insensible." Thus it is no accident that, like celebration, sentimental display proceeded in the older public spaces like taverns and the street; new private and semipublic spaces like banquet halls, pleasure gardens, and salons; and the printed materials that circulated in them. The sense of transformative, uplifting possibilities can be seen in a 1786 "Ode to Sensibility."

> From thee proceed those joys refin'd,
> That luxury of the exalted mind,
> Which reading gives—that bliss divine,
> The soul receives from ev'ry line.

.   .   .   .

46. Benjamin Franklin, *The Autobiography* (New York, 1990); Ormond Seavey, *Becoming Benjamin Franklin: The Autobiography and the Life* (University Park, Pa., 1988); Daniel A. Cohen, "Arthur Mervyn and His Elders: The Ambivalence of Youth in the Early Republic," *WMQ*, 3d Ser., XLIII (1986), 362–380; William Moraley, *The Infortunate: The Voyage and Adventures of William Moraley, an Indentured Servant* (1743), ed. Susan E. Klepp and Billy G. Smith (University Park, Pa., 1992); Philip F. Gura, ed., *Memoirs of Stephen Burroughs* (Boston, 1989).

47. See Robert Darnton, "Readers Respond to Rousseau: The Fabrication of Romantic Sensitivity," in Darnton, *The Great Cat Massacre and Other Episodes in French Cultural History* (New York, 1984), 215–252. This is also an important theme in Benjamin Franklin's autobiography, as many modern commentators have noted. See, especially, Seavey, *Becoming Benjamin Franklin*.

Teach me to feel each line they write,
Participate what they indite,
My heart with virtuous joy to glow,
Or taste the luxury of woe.

Ne'er let my soul, with haughty scorn,
The prayer of modest virtue spurn;
Ne'er let my heart, with soul neglect,
Treat modest worth with disrespect—

But let my heart, like wax, receive
Each soft impression thou canst give!
Take all thy pleasures all thy pain
And pity the unfeeling train.[48]

The author of the poem reveals himself or herself and thereby gets to "participate" in the public flow of emotion opened up by "reading." Published in the one-year-old newspaper of backcountry Carlisle, Pennsylvania, pieces like this reveal the excitement of sentimental culture, its promise to expand the sphere of virtue by making true feeling the measure of merit.

Yet the poem also sets up both the "sensible" and the "unfeeling" as objects of a refined gaze that allows the gazer to show pity. As an almanac writer put it, "Vulgar, low expressions, awkward motions and address, vilify, as they imply either a very low turn of mind, or low vocation and low company." According to G. S. Rousseau, "these exterior signs, then, became the new tropes of rank and class." In this new body politic, having the right nerves demonstrated social worth.[49] Interior and

---

48. *Carlisle Gazette*, Mar. 29, 1786.

49. "On Dignity of Manners," in Daniel George, *An Astronomical Diary; or, Almanack, for . . . 1788* (Portsmouth, N.H., 1787); G. S. Rousseau, "Towards a Semiotics of the Nerve: The Social History of Language in a New Key," in Peter Burke and Roy Porter, eds., *Language, Self, and Society: A Social History of Language* (Cambridge, 1991), 211–275, quoted at 226. The display of refined emotion could also be a response to rather different displays by other constituencies—especially the enthusiasm of religious revivals, as Jan Lewis finds for the Virginia gentry's retirement into the cult of sensibility (*Pursuit of Happiness*, 219). On revivals as ritualized display of emotion, see Nathan O. Hatch, *The Democratization of American Christianity* (New Haven, Conn., 1989); Henry Abelove, *The Evangelist of Desire: John Wesley and the Methodists* (Stanford, Calif., 1990); Harry S. Stout, *The Divine Dramatist: George Whitefield and the Rise of Modern Evangelicalism* (Grand Rapids, Mich., 1991).

organic yet transparently visible, sentimental signs and their language were the perfect vehicle for a patriotism that aspired simultaneously to include and to exclude more people, according to natural principles.

Who were the sensible patriots of the 1780s? The epitome of male sensibility seems to have been the members of the Society of the Cincinnati. When they met in Boston on July 4, 1785, "the day was passed with that harmony, festivity and joy, which the meeting of real friends can alone excite.—In friendship formed in dangers, and cemented by mutual misfortunes, there arises a sympathetic pleasure not to be described, and to be conceived only by those who feel it." In William Dunlap's play *The Father; or, American Shandyism* (1789), Colonel Duncas, a member of the Cincinnati, repeatedly engages in emotional scenes of patriotic memory, talking and sobbing at length over fallen friends. By contrast, the newly patriotic Mr. Racket gets ridiculed by his wife for drunkenly celebrating the Constitution and Saint Patrick's Day (and for babbling on at the breakfast table over a newspaper report of ratification).[50]

The very political and economic flux of the 1780s militated against the establishment or recognition of a stable aristocracy. And yet the characteristics of *natural* aristocracy were being more clearly enumerated. A satire of Boston's Sans Souci club finds would-be fops detesting political discussion, accepting former loyalists into their festive circles, and conspiring to outspend the nouveaux riches.[51] With excessive importation ruining the American economy, many signs of luxury and refinement once again came under attack as antitheses of virtue. Good manners had to be redefined. After the war, pronounced John Gardiner in a 1785 Fourth of July oration:

> We soon began to enjoy the blessings of a free, unrestrained trade.
> . . . But elated with success and blinded by prosperity, we too soon

50. *Boston Gazette,* July 11, 1785; Royster, *Revolutionary People at War,* 353; [William Dunlap], *The Father; or, America Shandyism* . . . (New York, 1789); see also Royall Tyler, *The Contrast* (1787), in which the virtuous Colonel Manly is also the most sentimental, and Hannah Webster Foster, *The Coquette* (1797), in which the only truly virtuous and sentimental man is Richman, a general. The names and officer rank of these characters speak volumes for the expected accoutrements of virtue in the post-Revolutionary period.

51. *Sans Souci, Alias Free and Easy; or, An Evening's Peep into a Polite Circle* . . . (Boston, 1785); Wood, ed., *The Rising Glory of America,* 137–153. On the controversy, see Charles Warren, "Samuel Adams and the Sans Souci Club in 1785," Massachusetts Historical Society, *Proceedings,* LX (1927), 318–344.

began to relax in our *manners,* and to adopt the luxury, the follies, the fashions of that nation which so lately we had every reason to detest. . . . Dissipation and extravagance immediately pervaded all orders of our people, and so ridiculous was the triumph of folly among us that even our country-girls in their market-carts, and upon their panniered horses, rode through our streets with their heads deformed with the plumes of the ostrich, and the feathers of other exotick birds.

"Too fondly have we rushed into the arms of Britain, without considering the fatal tendency of our wanton impudence," echoed Jonathan Austin in the next year's oration. Many analysts agreed: America had been feminized, and the women were to blame. Adorning themselves with feathers, their voluntary actions seemed to reverse Revolutionary symbolism, making the Americans into the losers, the geese.[52] This wholesale blaming of the women did not last long. By 1786, no one, particularly respectable men, could imagine that a renascence of virtue could occur without women in a prominent role. The Revolution had allowed women to carve more than a patriotic niche for themselves as prominent boycotters, spectators, manufacturers, rioters, and mourners. Moreover, the new standard of republican wifehood held that female sensibility acted as a spur to male virtue.[53] In his 1787

52. John Gardiner, *An Oration Delivered July 4, 1785* . . . (Boston, [1785]), 33; Jonathan L. Austin, *An Oration, Delivered July 4, 1786* . . . (Boston, [1786]); Jensen, *The New Nation,* 188–189, 291; "On the Degeneracy of the Fair Sex," *Bickerstaff's Boston Almanack for . . . 1785* . . . (Boston, 1784); "Short Queries to Ladies," in Daniel George, *An Almanack for . . . 1786* (Boston, [1785]); "On Female Gamesters," in Daniel Sewall, *An Astronomical Diary; or, Almanac, for . . . 1785* . . . (Portsmouth, N.H., 1784). On the symbolism of feathers, see Ann Fairfax Withington, *Toward a More Perfect Union: Virtue and the Formation of American Republics* (New York, 1992), 225–232.

53. Norton, *Liberty's Daughters;* Linda K. Kerber, *Women of the Republic: Intellect and Ideology in Revolutionary America* (Chapel Hill, N.C., 1980); Kerber, " 'I Have Don . . . Much to Carrey on the Warr': Women and the Shaping of Republican Ideology after the American Revolution," and Alfred F. Young, "The Women of Boston: 'Persons of Consequence' in the Making of the American Revolution, 1765–76," both in Harriet B. Applewhite and Darline G. Levy, eds., *Women and Politics in the Age of the Democratic Revolution* (Ann Arbor, Mich., 1990), 181–257; Barbara Clark Smith, "Food Rioters and the American Revolution," *WMQ,* 3d Ser., LI (1994), 3–38; Kerber, " 'History Can Do It No Justice': Women and the Reinterpretation of the American Revolution," and Laurel Thatcher Ulrich, " 'Daughters of Liberty': Religious Women in Revolutionary New England," in Ronald Hoffman and Peter J.

Fourth of July oration, New Haven lawyer David Daggett lamented: "Patriotism is fled.—The days of 1775, we cannot recall." But hope for republican economy lay with the ladies: "You, my *fair friends,* are possessed of a kind of magical influence over the other sex. . . . It is with you to promote oeconomy and industry, or luxury and extravagance at your pleasure." More than a sign of the feminization of virtue, this was part of a larger effort to domesticate the world. With politics becoming inseparable from a democratized political economy, it is little wonder that the late eighteenth century was a time of such creative instability between public and private spheres.[54]

By the middle 1780s, women were often mentioned in newspapers as attendees of banquets and orations and as spectators at parades. Moreover, they were explicitly noted by men's toasts to "the American Fair"—a gesture that had become de rigueur by 1790. As toasted by their male counterparts, virtuous American women frown on luxury and smile upon virtue; they give their hands only to true patriots. Sometimes they did so only from the peripheries (windows or the evening dinners) of celebration. At the same time, though, these were ideal loci for sentimental exchange, as women could see and be seen without participating in the explicitly political moments of the rituals, such as the toasts. Again, unity in common feeling could transcend even other naturalized distinctions. At the banquet honoring the Fourth of July

---

Albert, eds., *Women in the Age of the American Revolution* (Charlottesville, Va., 1989), 3–42, 211–243; Jan Lewis, "The Republican Wife: Virtue and Seduction in the Early Republic," *WMQ,* 3d Ser., XLIV (1987), 689–710; Bloch, "Gendered Meanings of Virtue," *Signs,* XIII (1987), 37–58. Carolyn Ruth Kyler has found that, in post-Revolutionary conduct books, "the championing of American women—their independence, intelligence and virtue—became a nationalist claim" ("Democracy and Sentiment in the Early American Novel" [Ph.D. diss., State University of New York at Buffalo, 1989], 73).

54. David Daggett, *An Oration, Pronounced in the Brick Meeting House . . . on the Fourth of July, A.D. 1787* (New Haven, Conn., [1787]), 16, 19–20; Jürgen Habermas, *The Structural Transformation of the Public Sphere: An Inquiry into a Category of Bourgeois Society* (1962), trans. Thomas Burger (Cambridge, Mass., 1989); Roger Chartier, *The Cultural Origins of the French Revolution,* trans. Lydia G. Cochrane (Durham, N.C., 1991), 16–36; Dena Goodman, "Public Sphere and the Private Life: Toward a Synthesis of Current Historiographical Approaches to the Old Regime," *History and Theory,* XXXI (1992), 1–20. It should be noted that, whatever the promise of this moment for some women, it was the beginning of the relegation of women to the realm of moral reform, which in turn became the locus of women's public activism.

and the ratification of the Constitution in New Haven, the spectacle of the Great Ship *Constitution* caused "the greatest accord of federal feeling in both sexes."[55]

Given their assumed capacities for sentiment and their ability, even duty, to spur virtue, it is not surprising that some women felt justified in holding their own nationalist celebrations. On the day after the "gentlemen" of Northampton, Massachusetts, celebrated the proclamation of peace in 1783, "a very respectable number of ladies, apprehending that there had not been that attention paid them by the gentlemen, which their exertions and services during the war merited, assembled in the same joyful occasion, when the following toasts were drank."

1. Lady Washington.
2. The Congress.
3. A long continuance to our glorious peace.
4. The Thirteen United States.
5. Success to Independence.
6. May internal disturbances cease.
7. Trade and Commerce throughout the world.
8. Reformation to our husbands.
9. May the gentlemen and the ladies ever unite on joyful occasions.
10. Happiness and prosperity to our families.
11. Reformation to the men in general.
12. May the Protestant religion prevail and flourish through all nations.
13. May reformed husbands ever find obedient wives.[56]

These women intend virtuous reunion with the men—after their "reformation." Similarly, sixty-four ladies of Lansingburgh and Halfmoon, New York, actually paraded in honor of New York's ratification of the Constitution. "Dressed in the utmost neatness and simplicity, without the aid of foreign gewgaws to embellish their persons," they marched

55. *New-Haven Gazette,* July 10, 1788. For examples of toasts, see *Independent Gazetteer* (Philadelphia), Apr. 26, 1783; *Boston Gazette,* July 11, 1786; *Independent Journal* (New York), July 6, 1785, Jan. 17, 1787; *New-Haven Gazette,* Sept. 6, 1787; *New-York Journal,* June 29, 1786, Sept. 25, 1788.

56. See also the satire offered by a "gentleman," which reveals a very close reading of the women's account, and the women's response, which turns the anonymous male satirist into an Indian "savage": *Massachusetts Gazette,* May 27, June 3, 10, 1783; *Independent Gazetteer* (Philadelphia), May 31, June 14, 1783.

through town with the Constitution itself as their banner. On a green outside of town, they were joined by the gentlemen (who had celebrated the day before) for tea and a "country dance." After proceeding back through town, there was more dancing at a private home.[57]

The emergence of women in these genteel celebrations helped an aristocracy desperate to naturalize their social eminence to secure control over public space. As such, it reveals changes in the gendered nature of virtue and how both gender and the ideology of virtue participated in the contemporary reformulation of class. The "reformation" that the Northampton women demanded of their husbands was easily reconciled with the stress on correct manners and sentimental display that already characterized the celebration and that respectable women increasingly claimed as their special attributes. They had only to renounce unrepublican luxury to participate in the newly fashionable festive events. The inclusion of these women even at the margins of celebration was a significant aspect of the republican public sphere, but one that broadcast its own limits: respectability.[58]

Nationalist celebrations proved to be an important venue for a system of visible virtue; that cultural logic, in turn, shaped the contemporary practices and ideologies of nationalism. If women and men with the right sentiments could fully participate in national celebration, others, also contributors to the Revolution, could not.[59] In the politics of con-

57. *New-York Journal*, Sept. 11, 1788; *Federal Herald* (Albany), Aug. 25, 1788. At the Grand Federal Procession in Newark on July 4, 1788, only rain prevented a float of women with spinning wheels from joining the artisans who marched with their wares (*New-York Journal*, July 7, 1788). A piece in the July 2, 1788, *Carlisle Gazette* (reprinted from a New York paper) advertises a "Federal Hat" for ladies. Adorned with thirteen rings and the "federal edifice" itself, it demonstrates female federalism "and that the Federal patriot will ever meet with their approbation."

58. Robert Gross, in Linda K. Kerber et al., "Beyond Roles, Beyond Spheres: Thinking about Gender in the Early Republic," *WMQ*, 3d Ser., XLVI (1989), 574–575; Fredrika J. Teute and David S. Shields, "The Meschianza's Meaning: 'How Will It Sparkle—Page the Future?'" paper presented at the Organization of American Historians annual meeting, Chicago, April 1996. Gross adds that this "emerging elite . . . in international terms, was broadly middle class, though from the point of view of backcountry farmers and urban laborers, it seemed aristocracy or upper class."

59. Linda Kerber notes that post-Revolutionary political culture, like histories subsequently written, had no place for disorderly women. "'History Can Do It No Justice,'" in Hoffman and Albert, eds., *Women in the Age of the American Revolution*, 3–42.

stitutional ratification we can see most vividly the uses of sentimental nationalist celebration, especially in the identification of what and who lay beyond the pale of federal feeling.

INVENTING FEDERALIST AMERICA

Americans in cultural dominance responded to the crisis of the 1780s by asserting their nationalism and by promoting polite standards of celebration. Their performances and published descriptions of patriotic sensibility addressed the problem of virtue by providing new ways of demonstrating membership in the new nation's natural, or republicanized, aristocracy. Yet reliance upon the visible signs of sensibility was part of the very problem of authenticity it was intended to solve. Some of the ways that conservative nationalists defined and fought the crisis of the 1780s would have been unthinkable before the Revolution. While these men and women surely repudiated the crowd actions of the 1760s and 1770s, their intensive uses of the streets and the press drew from the Revolutionary upheavals they desired to contain.

Sentimental patriots of the 1780s sought an aestheticized version of immanent virtue: made genteel, the display of patriotic affiliation and republican identity, which had expanded the field of politics so dramatically in the 1760s, might reform civic life in the 1780s.[60] They relied upon the signs of patriotism yet attempted to rein in the meanings of these signs by subtly altering who could exhibit and evaluate them. The momentum in the 1780s was toward the shrinkage of the political field, but with limits. The Revolution and the older traditions of popular politics behind it would not be so quickly undone. Already seizing the mantle of the nation, proto-Federalists had to proceed in a somewhat public fashion, if only to ratify their own promises of universal

60. The desire for immanent virtue has been seen as a hallmark of the age of democratic revolutions. That it characterized the American 1780s shows that the decade remained a time of Revolutionary possibility as well as one of conservative retrenchment. On immanent virtue and the politicization of personal appearance in the French Revolution, see Hunt, *Politics, Culture, and Class in the French Revolution*, 45–49; Michel Foucault, "The Eye of Power," in Foucault, *Power / Knowledge: Selected Interviews and Other Writings, 1972–1977*, ed. Colin Gordon, trans. Gordon et al. (New York, 1980), 152; Carol Blum, *Rousseau and the Republic of Virtue: The Language of Politics in the French Revolution* (Ithaca, N.Y., 1986); Outram, *The Body and the French Revolution;* Simon Schama, *Citizens: A Chronicle of the French Revolution* (New York, 1989).

regeneration in a virtuous future. This left open the possibility of conflict over, even appropriation of, nationalist celebration by those who
might otherwise have remained spectators.

Thus, I argue that Federalist—that is, nationalist—victory in the
ratification of the Constitution relied not only upon the politics of sentimental patriotism reestablished by elites in the 1780s but also upon
reassertion of truly popular sovereignty by others. The two key groups
were the Antifederalists in several states and the mechanics in the cities.
The Federalists surely won the battle, but not entirely upon their own
terms; the means are surely as significant to the story of the nationalization of American politics as the document that eleven states ratified
in 1787–1788. Seeing ratification as a process might seem to make the
question of the original intent of the founders less relevant. Actually,
it helps us appreciate the changing character of the nationalist movement and the compromises it embodied.[61]

The authors of the Constitution intended to "enlarge the sphere" of
representation in the Republic. The conservative nationalists of the
1780s read the commercial and political localism of the 1780s as profligate vice and, in reaction, called for a larger structure to engineer the
beneficent oversight of a natural aristocracy. The Constitution fulfilled
these intentions in several ways. Most important, it reinvented citizenship as a *national* category, inscribing that identity into its very first
phrase: "We the People of the United States . . ." Drafted by a committee in secret, it makes "the People" both author and audience, erasing
the particular agency of the framers.[62]

Second, the Constitution revised the scale and thus the nature of
political representation in order to secure the election of the right kind
of people. *The Federalist* accomplished this by recasting the *ends* of the
system of representation. For Publius, the goal is not the representation
of the popular will, which is portrayed as irrational passion. Rather, it
is the reconstitution of the body politic so that the body will be gov-

61. I have been influenced here by the formulations in Young, "Framers of the
Constitution," *Radical History Review*, no. 42 (1988), 7–47; and in Matson and Onuf,
A Union of Interests, chap. 6.

62. Wood, "Interests and Disinterestedness," in Beeman et al., eds., *Beyond Confederation*, 69–109; Morgan, *Inventing the People*, 267–306; Warner, *Letters of the Republic*, 97–117.

erned by its highest faculties, rationality and detachment. The public interest (now national and unitary) is an abstraction best discerned by men with the most discerning faculties. Indeed, the Constitution seeks to empower them and the nation they would, in turn, represent.[63]

If the highest Federalist argument demanded rational faculties, what happened to the emotion that seemed so crucial in the evaluation of virtue and the public display of patriotism? The "faculty psychology" that emerges in *The Federalist* is but one version of the broad and contested phenomenon of "sensibility," the eighteenth-century's conflation of opinion and feeling. Writers celebrated the politeness and exalted sentiment of the delegates to "the grand convention" from the convention's first meeting until ratification itself and beyond. Thus Enos Hitchcock made the framers stand in for the essence of the Revolution: "The same patriotism which glowed in the American breast at the commencement of the revolution . . . is renewed in a Convention for devising a more perfect scheme of government."[64] *The Federalist* stresses reason in particular because of the exigencies of the debate: it was easier and even more genteel to paint foes as irrational or improperly passionate than as unfeeling (though others did that as well). For many Federalists, however, the right sentiments came to include the right opinion on the Constitution. And nationalist celebrations and their reportage allowed them to ally those sentiments with the Revolution, the nation, and their personal virtue.

Already on July 4, 1785, the Cincinnati of Newport, Rhode Island, wished that "local attachments be absorbed in the general good." At Georgetown, South Carolina, a year earlier, patriots urged that "Congress be visited with full power to regulate the trade of the American states." Not everyone agreed. The published toasts at Albany in 1786

---

63. Morgan, *Inventing the People*, 277; Howe, "The Political Psychology of *The Federalist*," *WMQ*, 3d Ser., XLIV (1987), 485–509; Gary L. McDowell, "Federalism and Civic Virtue: The Antifederalists and the Constitution," in Robert A. Goldwin and William A. Schambra, eds., *How Federal Is the Constitution?* (Washington, D.C., 1987), 122–144; Wilson Carey McWilliams, "The Anti-Federalists, Representation, and Party," *Northwestern University Law Review*, LXXXIV (1989), 12–38; Sheldon S. Wolin, *The Presence of the Past: Essays on the State and the Constitution* (Baltimore, 1989), 1–16, 120–136.

64. Mullan, *Sentiment and Sociability*, 10; Enos Hitchcock, *An Oration: Delivered July 4, 1788* . . . (Providence, R.I., [1788]), 13. The *Virginia Gazette and Weekly Advertiser* (Richmond) published a poem, "On Dr. Franklin's Shedding a Tear, While Signing the Federal Constitution," Sept. 25, 1788.

saluted: "The *late* army: may that independence, which they fought to establish, be ever defended by all virtuous citizens." Rather than praise military glory or the central government, as other patriotic fetes did that year, these celebrants stressed liberty and virtue in order to reach the magical thirteen:

9. May the Splendor of the American Confederation (like the pillar of fire of old) conduct those who are endangered to the land of liberty.
11. May the Date of American Independency, be the Dawn of Universal Liberty.
13. The Daughters of America!—and may virtue ever continue their distinguishing characteristic.

By contrast, Cincinnati members and public officials in Philadelphia had to add an extra toast in order to wholly fulfill the Federalist agenda:

13. May the Union, Friendship and Happiness of these States be for ever uninterrupted by local prejudices, or local interests.
14. Confidence in our Continental councils, and an Increase of Energy to our Foederal Government.

These proto-Federalists saw their goals as benevolent interventions for the good of the whole. "Interest," once the province of imperially ambitious tories, now exemplified the localism of those who would restore the pre-Revolutionary status quo. Supporters of a stronger federal state, on the other hand, stood for the common good. With decorum, these leaders of cities and states affirmed their status as stewards of the nation. A year later, celebrants in Salem and Providence drank to the Constitutional Convention.[65]

Framing the Constitution in part to save the economy, Federalists naturally claimed to be on the side of progress. "The revolution is but half completed," proclaimed Joel Barlow; the Cincinnati should complete it by promoting a spirit of rational inquiry and giving the people examples of the "conquest of self." The Federalists had another key

65. *Newport Mercury* (R.I.), July 9, 1785; *Columbian Herald,* July 11, 1784; *Pennsylvania Journal,* July 8, 1786. See also *Boston Gazette,* July 9, 1786; *United States Chronicle* (Providence), July 5, 1787; *Salem Mercury,* July 10, 1787; *Carlisle Gazette,* July 11, 1787; *New-Hampshire Gazette,* July 7, 1787; *New-Hampshire Mercury, and the General Advertiser* (Portsmouth), July 5, 1787; *New-Haven Gazette,* July 12, 1787; Alexander, *Selling of the Constitutional Convention,* 106.

supporter of Revolutionary nationalism: the press. Editors and printers were the natural articulators of the buoyant commercial nationalism that went along with the expansion of the public sphere through print culture: they stood to gain subscribers if more people took an interest in extralocal matters. Editors seem to have been disproportionately Federalist in 1787–1788. Just by changing the subject of newspaper discourse from international news and local politics to a national issue that could be acted upon locally, proponents of the Constitution seized the advantage in 1787.[66]

Yet the contest between Federalists and Antifederalists concerned the nature of the republican nation, and the press controversy over ratification itself exemplified different versions of republican ideology. The difficulties that Antifederalists faced in getting into print confirmed their worst fear: an aristocratic conspiracy against liberty and republican government. In Philadelphia, the Antifederalist *Freeman's Journal* reported with horror a Federalist plan to require authors to sign their real names to newspaper contributions.[67] Instead of engineering natural aristocracy, Federalists would naturalize an aristocracy of pretense. Opponents of the Constitution responded to these attempts in the manner of the Revolutionary crowd. When Federalists in Huntingdon County, Pennsylvania, tore down the Antifederalists' posted petitions,

> a number of people of the town of *Standing Stone* collected, and conducted on the backs of old *Scabby* ponies, the EFFIGIES of the principles of the junto, *viz.* John Cannon, Esquire, Member of Council and President of the Court, and Benjamin Elliot, Esq., a member of Convention of that county. The effigies passing near the door of the Court, the honor[able] Mr. Cannon, thinking his dignity wounded,

66. Barlow, *An Oration*, 8–11; James Campbell, *An Oration in Commemoration of Independence* (Philadelphia, 1787); Warner, *Letters of the Republic*, 34–96, 118–150; Albert Furtwangler, *The Authority of Publius: A Reading of the Federalist Papers* (Ithaca, N.Y., 1984), 92–97, 111; Robert Allen Rutland, "The First Great Newspaper Debate: The Constitutional Crisis of 1787–1788," American Antiquarian Society, *Proceedings*, XCVII (1987), 43–58; Alexander, *Selling of the Constitutional Convention*, 215–216, 220–221.

67. Samuel Bryan to Aedanus Burke, in Merrill Jensen, ed., *The Documentary History of the Ratification of the Constitution*, II, *Ratification of the Constitution by the States: Pennsylvania,* microform supplement, document 700a–b; John Lansing, Jr., et al. to Melancton Smith, Mar. 1, 1788, Abraham Yates Papers, box 2, New York Public Library; *Independent Journal* (New York), May 21, 1788; *Freeman's Journal* (Philadelphia), Jan. 23, Mar. 5, 1788.

ordered the Officers of the Court to assist his partisans in apprehending the effigy-men (as they were not numerous) and a number of persons were thrown in jail. Immediately the country took the alarm, assembled and liberated the sons of liberty, so unjustly confined; who passed down the jail steps, under loud huzzahs and repeated acclamations of joy from a large concourse of people; who soon after retired from the town declaring their intention to *duck* the Junto if they repeated their insults.[68]

The Antifederalists stressed that the people were on their side, and in the tradition of whig popular politics the people (defined locally and in their actual persons) expressed themselves ritually, on the streets. Federalists already had an answer to this: the orderly, national, spectacular, and popular celebration.

On February 8, 1788, Boston initiated the newly elaborate and inclusive procession in celebration of Massachusetts's ratification of the Constitution. Afterward, on adoption in the various states, dozens of cities and towns held their own processions, often planned weeks in advance, with local craftsmen marching with banners and floats, behind the Cincinnati, clergymen, professionals, incorporated groups, and other local worthies.[69] Historians have devoted much attention to these Grand Federal Processions (as did contemporaries). But they were only the most impressive examples of the wholesale appropriation of nationalist celebration by Federalists. Ratification pronouncements were read aloud in reenactments of the Declaration of Independence twelve years earlier. The successive dates of ratification in the states provided as many holidays as battles and diplomatic news had during the Revolutionary war, and Federalists seized upon them all to ally their cause with that of the people and the nation.[70] Countless citizens rejoiced spontaneously, and

68. *Freeman's Journal* (Philadelphia), Mar. 18, 1788.

69. *United States Chronicle* (Providence), July 17, 1788, reports that all the other cities had taken the cue from Boston. The most comprehensive accounts of the processions are Whitfield J. Bell, Jr., "The Federal Processions of 1788," *New-York Historical Society Quarterly*, LXVI (1962), 5–39; Loretta Valtz Mannucci, "The Federal Grand Processions of 1787 and 1788," conference paper, Tel Aviv, 1990 (courtesy of Alan Trachtenberg). Mannucci describes how the various processions became increasingly organized from the top down, unlike the more "spontaneous" celebration held in Boston.

70. *Independent Journal* (New York), Feb. 16, 1788; *New-Hampshire Gazette*, May 15, 1788; *Virginia Gazette and Weekly Advertiser*, July 17, 1788; "Diary of Joseph Lewis,"

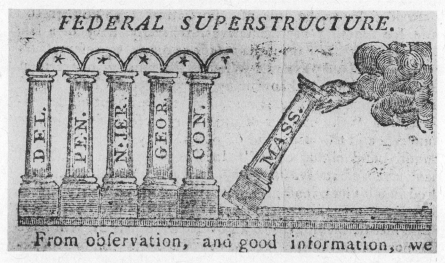

FIGURE 4. The Federal Pillars. Massachusetts Centinel *(Boston)*,
Mar. 1, 1788. Courtesy American Antiquarian Society

then once again at planned spectacles. In ritual renamings, places of
meeting were rechristened for the day (and sometimes permanently) as
Federal Hill or Federal Tavern. Every aspect of patriotic rhetoric and
symbolism (the actual symbols of the nation but also the claims to god-
liness, virtue, rationality, and sensibility) was harnessed to federalism.

"The joy which this event diffused through all ranks of citizens in
this metropolis, was hardly conceivable," insisted an editor in a rather
divided New Hampshire. Describing the "illuminations, bonfires, and
other demonstrations of joy" in Wilmington, North Carolina, after news
of Virginia's ratification arrived, a local writer insisted that "a general
sympathy united all—Hope, *rational hope,* animated every rank and pro-
fession," even though North Carolina itself had not ratified and would
not ratify for another sixteen months.[71] Such assertions of unanimity
should not be read solely as reflections of Federalist majority. They
were also part of the federal construction of unanimity through a will-
ful displacement of dissent. In fact, the most aggressive Federalist uses
of public space and the press occurred in the states most divided over

---

New Jersey Historical Society, *Proceedings,* LXII (1944), 45, 46; Clarkson A. Collins,
ed., "James Brown Diary (1787–1789)," *Rhode Island History,* VI (1947), 99–107.

71. *New Hampshire Gazette,* June 26, 1788; *Wilmington Centinel, and General Advertiser* (N.C.), July 9, 1788.

the merits of the proposed Constitution. In strife-torn Rhode Island, a commentator insisted on the federal purity—and gentility—of his home suburb of East Greenwich:

> It must give pleasure to every friend of liberty to behold this little patriotic village putting on the appearance of Federalism. . . . The conversation of the inhabitants is carried out in a style of Federal purity, and a man may as well expect to make a tour of Europe without any knowledge of the French, as to be distinguished in company without a smattering of the Federal dialect.

Individuality and unity in public? Yes and no.

> Several attempts were made by the Antifederalists of the vicinity to disturb and if possible defeat the arrangements but without effect. The manly, but modest resolution displayed in the behavior of every individual, impressed them with a proper sense of their own insignificance, and drove them to take refuge in the gloom of dreary solitude and obscurity.

Left outside the magic circle of agreement and benevolence, unable to display "the appearance of Federalism," Antifederalists become insignificant, unable to act, selfish, immodest, unmanned. The political other was thus made to disappear. Similarly, a chronicler from Hartford, inscribing his city as sincere and "universally Federal" on his way to invoking divine intent, cast his opponents as deluded visionaries.[72]

Federalist patriots expressed their nationalistic vision by altering the most basic of patriotic rituals: the ceremony of the thirteen toasts. By the 1780s this numerology had become the ubiquitous marker of American nationalism. Masonic meetings, celebrations by printers of Benjamin Franklin's birthday, even the festival that had honored the birth of the dauphin included the ritual of thirteen proclamations, or "sentiments," accompanied by thirteen gun blasts. But after New Hampshire (the ninth state) ratified, most federal celebrations included only *nine* toasts. Lest the meaning of this gesture be missed, a group of Brooklyn celebrants raised their ninth glass in the hope that "continual disappointment and never-dying remorse, pain and poverty

---

72. *United States Chronicle* (Providence), July 17, 1788; *Pennsylvania Packet,* July 25, 1788. On the unmanned as those whose capacity for action had been taken away, see Edward Anthony Rotundo, "Manhood in America: The Northern Middle Class, 1770 to 1920" (Ph.D. diss., Brandeis University, 1982), 46–47.

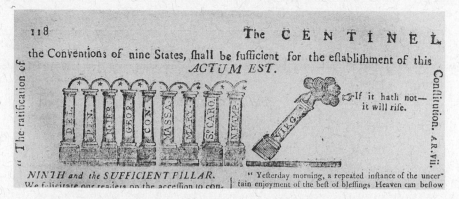

FIGURE 5. The Federal Pillars. Massachusetts Centinel *(Boston)*,
Aug. 2, 1788. Courtesy American Antiquarian Society

[may] ever attend those antifederalists who, through motives of interest, stand opposed to a government, formed for the good of their country." After news spread of Virginia's ratification, toasts numbered ten at such places as Shippensburg, Pennsylvania. At Portsmouth, Virginia, ten rounds were fired, and ten white horses dragged the ship *Federalist*.[73]

Acting late, Antifederalists knew that the Federalists were stealing the show. Federalists' seizure of the primary spaces for symbolic action (really, the spaces for legitimate political action outside the legislatures) did precisely what it was intended to: increase the attractiveness and seeming inevitability of the Constitution, influence ratification in the key states of Massachusetts and New York, and make federalism look more popular than it probably was. Where such celebrations contradicted Antifederalists' sense of the legitimate uses of the streets, they objected strongly and in traditional ways. As a result, most of the riots reported in newspapers during the ratification season (December 1787 to July 1788) originated in controversies over celebrations.

One of the first and best known of these celebration-riots occurred in Carlisle, Pennsylvania. If not directly influential, the Carlisle riots set the stage for similar incidents in Albany, Providence, and New York City. These events do more than show how crucial celebrations were to the Federalist cause. They illustrate the struggle over the meanings of respectability, representation, and popular sovereignty.

Although Pennsylvania had been the second state to ratify, its con-

73. *Worcester Magazine* (Mass.), Feb. 9, 1788; *Pennsylvania Packet*, July 4, 1782, July 15, 18, 19, 20, 21, 1788.

stitutional debates had been nothing if not contentious. Federalist sympathizers in the legislature at Philadelphia had rushed through the
provision calling for a ratifying convention before the fall elections
(though not before enlisting a mob to drag recalcitrant legislators back
to their seats for a quorum). The state convention ratified the Constitution on December 12, but the western parts of the state remained an
antifederal stronghold. Commentators in the press acknowledged that
most inhabitants of Carlisle and the surrounding areas were opposed to
the Constitution. For the Antifederalists of backcountry Pennsylvania,
the Constitution was merely the latest attempt of local elites to establish a deferential politics against the democratic inroads typified by the
radical state constitution of 1776.[74]

Several dozen Carlisle Federalists gathered on December 26 to give
public approbation to the Constitution. A group of Antifederalists,
armed with brickbats and a conviction that three-quarters of the people
did *not* approve of ratification, arrived as the celebratory cannon was
being loaded. Threats were exchanged; neither side budged until the
Federalists said they would fire the cannon no matter who stood in the
way. "Such imperious language was too grating for the cause of freemen," one of the Antis wrote later, and the ensuing brawl "ended in
a total rout of the new federalists." The victors burned an almanac in
which the Constitution was printed and topped the flames with the offending gun.[75]

74. Paul Doutrich, "Pennsylvania: From Revolution to Constitution," in Patrick
T. Conley and John P. Kaminski, eds., *The Constitution and the States: The Role of the
Original Thirteen in the Framing and Adoption of the Federal Constitution* (Madison, Wis.,
1988), 37–53; George J. Graham, Jr., "Pennsylvania: Representation and the Meaning of Republicanism," in Michael Allen Gillespie and Michael Lienesch, eds., *Ratifying the Constitution* (Lawrence, Kans., 1989), 52–70; Jackson Turner Main, *The Antifederalists: Critics of the Constitution, 1781–1788* (Chapel Hill, N.C., 1961), 187–194;
Saul Cornell, "Aristocracy Assailed: The Ideology of Backcountry Anti-Federalism,"
Journal of American History, LXXVI (1989–1990), 1150–1155.

75. *Carlisle Gazette,* Jan. 2, 9, 16, 23, 1788. These accounts and other documents
are conveniently reprinted in Jensen ed., *Documentary History of Ratification,* II, 670–
708, and the microform supplement; see also Cornell's rendering, which differs
slightly from mine, in "Aristocracy Assailed," *JAH,* LXXVI (1989–1990), 1150–1155.
There is no neutral account of these events, despite the claims to objectivity on the
part of at least one of the Federalist commentators. Although it is crucial to establish what happened on some minimum level of fact, *all* the details are potentially
significant—enough so to be fought over in the press by the participants. Perhaps
the most interesting fact about the controversy is the controversy over the facts

The next day the Federalists, armed, reclaimed the town center by reading the state's ratification proclamation "to acclamation" and by firing cannon blasts for the three ratifying states. Some Antifederalists menaced the proceedings, but rather than risk a repeat of the previous day's violence (in which one Major Wilson, a Federalist leader, suffered wounds that might have led to his death a few months later), they met at night for a mock procession. The crowd placed effigies of James Wilson and Thomas McKean (both members of the state supreme court and key supporters of the Constitution) in a cart and consigned both to a bonfire.

The Antifederalists did not get the last word. Pro-Federalist authorities in Carlisle procured a warrant for the rioters and jailed seven who refused bail. The Antis then organized the county militia and circulated a petition for the prisoners' release. An irregularity in the warrant enabled the Federalists to save face, but hundreds of militiamen gathered anyway to execute a legal jailbreak. Marching through town, celebrating the heroic countercelebrants, they sang a song ridiculing aristocrats in retreat, "curls flying / weary steps, and Powdered heads."[76]

All the details and interpretations of this series of events mattered enough to spur quarrels about them in depositions, letters, and newspaper accounts. The first appeared in the *Carlisle Gazette* on January 2. This "impartial observer," who presented himself as an elderly gentleman visitor, stressed the "good order and coolness" of the Federalist rejoicers and described the organizers of the counterprocession as "men perfectly unknown and whose characters were [so] obscure to attract the notice of the citizens of this place, and others who but lately have stripped off the garb of British soldiers."[77]

Outraged, "One of the People" responded in the next issue by portraying the Federalists as the sources of disorder. The celebrants of ratification called no town meeting to gauge popular opinion: "Therefore

---

themselves. Both groups turned the events into a story to serve their own ends and used the press in attempts to convince others. We sometimes take such contests over reality for granted, but Americans in 1788 did not. Although the Federalists did so more effectively, the Antifederalists' use of the press in Carlisle marks a significant advance in their strategy. For Antifederalist leaders' efforts in one state, see Eric Robert Papenfuse, "Unleashing the 'Wildness': The Mobilization of Grassroots Antifederalism in Maryland," *Journal of the Early Republic*, XVI (1996), 73–106.

76. *Carlisle Gazette,* Jan. 23, 1788.

77. *Carlisle Gazette,* Jan. 2, 1788; see also *New-York Journal,* Jan. 15, 1788.

the intended rejoicers were an unhallowed riotous mob." The writer also objected to the old man's bequest to the Federalists of the title "friends of government" and his assertion of their complete innocence in the first day's violence. In fact, while the Federalists' second celebration surpassed the first in arrogance, it signified only its antithesis: "The whole transaction, had the appearance of a funeral ceremony awkwardly performed, but not the least resemblance of rejoicing."[78]

By now, of course, both sides were stretching the truth; yet the precise manner in which each stretched it marked an allegiance to a political struggle with real short- and long-term consequences. These accounts and counteraccounts were read with increasing care and were answered with increasing vituperation. The next attempt, by a Federalist, directly called "One of the People" a liar and compared a contest with him to one between a well-dressed man and a chimney sweep: "Soot and dirt are the only consequences of the victory." But "Another of the people" dressed up his rhetoric anyway, insisting that "every countenance beamed with joy, gladness and happiness" when ratification was read, "except those of a few worthless ragamuffins, who were made drunk for the purpose of burning the effigies." In the next issue, an Antifederalist "SCOURGE" pictured the Federalists as losers in even a scribbling war, having turned from the streets to the courts to the press in their illegitimate quest for hegemony. Some of these very "big men" dared not show their faces in Philadelphia: these Federalists, it seems, were jealous of the recent migrants among the Antifederalists, whose financial credit was better! Both sides, it seems, could play the respectability game. By this time, the editor of the *Gazette* had rejected many pieces on the celebration-riots as too full of invective. Probably he believed that these missives no longer served Carlisle's, the nation's, or his own best interests. In any case, he refused to publish any more.[79]

The events in Carlisle became a reference point for Federalists and Antifederalists all over Pennsylvania and beyond. A correspondent to the New York's *Independent Journal* implicitly compared the jailbreak to Shays's Rebellion, claiming it would result in a loss of executive power and an inability to collect taxes. A sympathetic Antifederalist worried that such incidents of disorder lent credence to Federalist predictions of anarchy. In Philadelphia, leading Antifederalist George Bryan noted with due irony that Federalist "conspirators" in Carlisle feared that

78. *Carlisle Gazette,* Jan. 16, 1788.
79. *Carlisle Gazette,* Jan. 16, 23, 1788.

their houses might be pulled down by the people. For Bryan, mob action could not be pinned wholly on an ungenteel opposition. "Here, in October, we were forced to hold our tongues, lest well dressed ruffians should fall upon us. . . . The common people are latterly too much of our opinion to hurt us. Indeed, none but *gentlemen mobs* have been active in Philadelphia."[80]

Pennsylvania Antifederalists answered Federalist criticisms, but their leaders accepted Federalist standards of respectability and "ordered liberty."[81] Ratifications in the successive states gave the Carlisle Federalists other opportunities to celebrate, which were cited as proof positive of Antifederalism's demise. But to the men and women who attended the jailbreak, what was said in the newspapers might have mattered less than the assertion of the people's right to take to the streets, if necessary, when law lost its legitimacy and the sovereignty of the people was abridged.

In response the Federalists avoided the issue of sovereignty. Accused of celebrating a part of the people as the whole, they claimed, in an unprecedented shift, that celebration was a question of liberty, not subject to town meetings. In doing so they denied not just the obvious intent of celebrations to promote unanimity but also the particular form of nationalist celebration as ratification of *already achieved* popular consensus. Thus they also erased such celebrations' ancient connections to the legitimate—and Revolutionary—crowd action of "the people." While the class-conscious perspective of the Antifederalists pitted "the people" against the would-be patricians, the Federalists denied the salience of class even as they affirmed popular sovereignty and their own propriety in standing for the indivisible, invisible people. Enlarging the scale of the "popular" to mean everything (and thus almost nothing), the Federalists successfully portrayed the Antifederalists as divisive opponents of the nation.

In the Federalist drive for unity through celebration, national unity and the creation of it were the same and self-evident, two sides of the same transparent coin. A Providence Federalist, putting aside the

80. Stephen R. Boyd, *The Politics of Opposition: Antifederalists and the Acceptance of the Constitution* (Millwood, N.Y., 1979), 96; *Independent Journal* (New York), Jan. 23, 1788; *Freeman's Journal* (Philadelphia), Apr. 9, 1788.

81. Cornell, "Aristocracy Assailed," *JAH*, LXXVI (1989–1990), 1148–1172, distinguishes Antifederalist leadership from rank and file in the backcountry. For the Revolutionary consensus as ordered liberty, see Clinton Rossiter, *Seedtime of the Republic: The Origin of the American Tradition of Political Liberty* (New York, 1953), 449.

knotty fact that his state was nowhere near ratifying, justified an upcoming, controversial celebration for the Constitution on the basis that
all nations celebrate great events.

> The establishment of any particular form of government, is a matter
> of sentiment among a free people, and the strength of that govern-
> ment depends on the good opinion people in general have of it; it
> is therefore good policy, and a sure mark of patriotism and public
> virtue, to endeavor as much as possible that all ranks and orders of
> people should be pleased with, and should support it, and nothing
> has a greater tendency to this than for the people of all conditions
> to assemble together, at certain times, to join in the celebration of
> the government under which they live. The intention of such a cele-
> bration is to conciliate and unite, and by no means to offend and
> divide. The man therefore deserves to be execrated and detested,
> by all good men, who would preposterously and wickedly suggest an
> idea, when a public celebration is set foot for the most patriotic and
> beneficial purpose, that [it] is intended thereby to insult the feelings
> of any part, or a member of the community, who at first might not
> have been convinced of the excellence and the advantages of the
> government.[82]

Unlike the Revolutionary celebrations that exiled tories for good, Federalist celebrations came to hold out the promise of regeneration to
Antifederalists. Unrelenting Antis are portrayed as unvirtuous noncitizens, alone and obscure, but as a group they are Americans, and the
hand of fellowship attached to the pointing finger at Federalist celebrations may help explain why Antifederalists were so quickly reconciled
to the national government. The Providence Federalist who suggested
that any attempt to criticize the politics of celebrating the Constitution
was an insult to his "patriotism and public virtue" conceded the importance of popular opinion and its public demonstration. Yet the definition of the celebration's patriotic and beneficial aims preceded public
approval as surely as the writing of the Constitution preceded any popular role in determining its content. To some extent, the Antifederalists
were beaten at a game they had played since the Revolution—the game
of street theater, the embodiment of the people—by opponents who

82. *United States Chronicle* (Providence), June 26, 1788, also in *New-Haven Gazette,*
July 24, 1788.

subtly changed the rules. Or perhaps the rules were the game's most valuable prize.

The Antifederalists played by the rules of popular sovereignty as they understood them. Deeply sensitive to the idea of legitimate crowd action, which allowed for even violent demonstration when the will of the community was ignored, their demonstrations and countercelebrations all took place in states where the Constitution had not yet been ratified or in locales (like Carlisle) known to be popularly antifederal. Abraham Yates, one of the leading New York Antifederalists, reported that tavern patrons in New York City condemned the June 25 ringing of bells there for New Hampshire's ratification as "useless and irritating": though ten states had ratified by that time, the acceptance of the Constitution was hardly certain, since the New York convention had postponed its vote. His Albany correspondent, Abraham Lansing, wrote that, while local Federalists preened over New Hampshire, "they however [have] not proceeded to any public demonstration of Joy on the occasion." Given such tensions, it may not be surprising that the peace lasted only until July 4. On that day in Albany, plans for a joint celebration in the morning gave way by midday to a full-scale street battle, after Federalist militia members marched all over town firing their guns and Antifederalists, in response, burned a copy of the Constitution. One person died, and at least twelve others were wounded in the fracas. Several dozen miles away, in Hudson, New York, some Antifederalists blocked the progress of a parading Federalist artillery company. The commander, wrote a sympathetic observer, "prevented any great mischief, and supported his authority with slightly wounding only one or two of the opposers."[83]

July 4, 1788, saw many Antis celebrating Independence separately from their Federalist neighbors. Yet in other places a nationalist détente had begun to emerge. At Carlisle, both parties held militia parades, orations, and toasts. While the Federalists raised their glasses ten times, they did allow: "If the New Foederal Government is not altogether per-

83. Abraham Yates to John Lansing, June 28, 29, 1788, Lansing to Yates, June 28, 1788, Abraham Yates Papers, box 2; *New-York Journal,* July 14, 1788; *Connecticut Courant,* July 14, 1788; *Norwich Packet,* July 10, 1788; *Newport Herald,* July 17, 1788; *Freeman's Journal* (Philadelphia), July 16, 1788; Linda Grant De Pauw, *The Eleventh Pillar: New York and the Federal Constitution* (Ithaca, N.Y., 1966), 266–268; E. Wilder Spaulding, *New York in the Critical Period, 1783–1789* (New York, 1932), 263; *Hudson Weekly Gazette* (N.Y.), July 8, 1788.

fect, may it speedily receive such amendments as will reconcile it to every citizen who has objected to it from virtuous principles." To admit that Antifederalists could be virtuous was a real concession as well as a strategy to attract moderates, and it had a parallel in the first toast of the Antifederalist company:

1. May the thirteen American states forever remain united, on real federal principles.

At the same time, the Antifederalists defined democracy and true national virtue against "consolidation" and enslavement:

2. May such amendments be speedily framed, and unanimously adopted, as may render the proposed constitution for the United States truly democratical.
8. The virtuous minority of the late convention of Pennsylvania.
12. May the designs of such as endeavor to enslave the citizens of America, prove abortive.
13. May America remain free from tyranny, anarchy, and consolidation.

If the moderate stance of some Antifederalists can be attributed to their class and position of leadership, these very festivities shed light on the varieties of Antifederalist political practice. This celebration was no popular rally, though one might have succeeded. Instead, it is a mirror of orderly Federalist festivity, with only the sentiments (and the attributions of virtue) altered. Similarly, several "gentlemen" in upstate Lansingburgh, New York, who had opposed the Constitution made a point of marching prominently in that town's ratification procession.[84] Some Antifederalists clearly desired a more orderly politics, led by a virtuous minority who took their cue from the majority and who fought in council and in the press, not in the streets.

Country Antifederalists might have seen things differently, but they were beginning to understand that order had its rewards in struggles for patriotic legitimacy. The controversy surrounding July 4 in Rhode Island provides the most vivid evidence. Rhode Island was a stronghold of state rights, paper money, and popular control of government. The Constitution had been submitted to town meeting referendums, where Federalists refused to participate: it lost, 2,711 to 243, and ratification

84. *Carlisle Gazette*, July 9, 1788; Cornell, "Aristocracy Assailed," *JAH*, LXXVI (1989–1990), 1168; *Independent Journal* (New York), Aug. 23, 1788.

did not actually occur until 1790. The seaport towns and the merchants supported the Constitution; farmers inland opposed it, bitterly. After an initial, spontaneous celebration in Providence, on June 24, of New Hampshire's ratification, a group of Providence respectables planned a large joint fete for the Fourth. The Society of the Cincinnati was persuaded to move its meeting from Newport to the state capitol for the event.[85]

When local Antifederalists heard of these plans for a civic spectacle and popular feast on Federal Plain, they organized their own committee. According to the report published in Providence's *United States Chronicle,* the citizens of "the country" became indignant at the city's plot to use a "popular" celebration to win the people over for ratification. More than a thousand citizens assembled in an orderly fashion on the morning of the Fourth and sent a delegation to the organizers of the festival. To forestall violence, the townsmen agreed to celebrate only Independence, not the Constitution, and to fire precisely thirteen gun blasts. The toasts were haggled over for some time, with those who objected to "the rejoicing of two things in one" insisting that the final toasts be not to the "Nine States" but to "The Day." The country then held its own celebration; some of its thirteen toasts are worth quoting in full.

1. Confusion to all usurpers and tyrants throughout the thirteen states.
2. The Old Confederation, with proper amendments.
3. May the sons of freedom in America never submit to a despotic government.
4. May each state retain their sovereignty in the full extent of republican covenants.
8. May we have a well-regulated militia in lieu of standing armies.
13. May merchants and landholders be convinced that their interest depends on the support of each other.

85. John P. Kaminski, "Democracy Run Rampant: Rhode Island in the Confederation," in James Kirby Martin, ed., *The Human Dimensions of Nation Making: Essays on Colonial and Revolutionary America* (Madison, Wis., 1976), 43–76; Patrick T. Conley, "First in War, Last in Peace: Rhode Island and the Constitution, 1786–1790," in Conley and Kaminski, eds., *Constitution and the States,* 268–294; Samuel Danforth Diary, June 24, 1788, American Antiquarian Society, Worcester, Mass.; *Pennsylvania Journal,* July 16, 1788; *Norwich Packet,* July 10, 1788; *Maryland Gazette,* July 24, 1788; *United States Chronicle* (Providence), July 3, 1788.

In response to the country version, the city stressed that there had been no Federalist conspiracy and that their celebration was legal and wholly voluntary: a question of rights. Ridiculing the Antis' rituals, they claimed that the common people had been quickly disillusioned by the whole affair and that in any event there had been only a few hundred, not a thousand, present at the countercelebration.[86]

The inclusion of the latter detail is most revealing. Although the *Chronicle* dutifully printed both committees' renderings and noted as well the separate evening festivities of the Cincinnati (which included nine decidedly Federalist toasts), popular legitimacy was clearly at issue. The Federalist *Providence Gazette,* which initially declined to report at all on the narrowly avoided riot, made sure to highlight that more than five thousand people had attended the city celebration—but also that the thirteenth toast (the only one printed in capital italic letters) had been given, as promised, to *"THE DAY,"* rather than to the Constitution. The very next day, however, news of Virginia's ratification arrived, and Providence Federalists marched all over town, cheering ten times.

Led by several judges (one of whom, William West, later published a painstaking account of his actions), the Antifederalists tried to prevent the equation of federalism with the Revolution, and they got the Federalists to concede that the Fourth of July belonged to them too. But the Federalists did more than reclaim public space on the next day; they also engaged in a lengthy debate over what had actually happened on July 4. The overriding theme of this controversy and of the commentary in out-of-town papers was that (unlike their opponents) Antifederalists like Judge West were not genteel or even respectable. One wag anticipated the sort of reportage that could be expected to appear in the very Federalist *Newport Herald:*

How charming 'twill find in the *Herald* to tell,
That the peasants and cits did in union combine,
The new Constitution to toast in good wine.[87]

86. *Newport Mercury,* July 14, 15, 1788; *Providence Gazette: And Country Journal,* July 5, 12, 1788; *United States Chronicle* (Providence), June 26, July 3, 10, 17, 1788.

87. *Newport Herald,* July 17, 24, 1788; *Independent Chronicle: And the Universal Advertiser* (Boston), July 24, 31, Aug. 7, 1788; *Virginia Gazette and Weekly Advertiser,* Aug. 7, 1788; *Newport Mercury,* July 14, 1788. That gentility was an important theme in Federalist polemic is revealed in the satirical pieces written by Francis Hopkinson, chief organizer and publicist of the Philadephia Grand Federal Procession. See Hopkinson, "A New Roof," in Paul M. Zall, ed., *The Comical Spirit of Seventy-Six:*

The mixture of street politics, print culture, and nationalism remained volatile, and perhaps we should not be surprised that the Federalists, in using these cultural forms so well, did not always live up to their own standards for reason, civility, or order. But these were the standards they originally intended, and the fact that the struggle over ratification did not stay wholly indoors or fully respectable signifies the limits of the conservative nationalist victory in 1788: as the events in Carlisle, Providence, and Albany indicate, the crowd retained a certain legitimacy.[88] Crowds were constitutional because "the people" still insisted on their identity as ordinary folk, distinct from elites, and classlessness remained a rhetorical device deployed situationally, not an achieved reality.

One more example of struggle over celebration may illustrate the shifting meaning and uses of "federal feeling." Thomas Greenleaf, a New York Antifederalist, edited the *New-York Journal.* A scrupulous defender of a free press, he even printed the first numbers of *The Federalist* until readers complained. New York's Grand Federal Procession presented him with a problem, however: New York had not yet ratified, and the intent of the parade was clearly partisan. In his account of the event Greenleaf praised the decorum and peacefulness of the Federalists even as he broke out of the generic constraints of festival reportage in an attempt to deflate federal pretensions.

> It was really laughable to see the variety of phizzes [that is, facial expressions] on this occasion. The poar *antis* generally minded their own business at home; others, who were spectators at an awful distance, looked as sour as the Devil. As for the *Feds,* they rejoiced in different degrees—there was the ha, ha, ha! and the he, he, he!

Noting that the Federal Ship *Hamilton* had fallen over in the launching, damaging the right arm of the statue of Hamilton himself, Green-

---

The Humor of Francis Hopkinson (San Marino, Calif., 1976), 186–194; Hopkinson, "Objections to the Proposed Plan of a Federal Government," in *The Miscellaneous Essays and Occasional Writings of Francis Hopkinson, Esq.,* 3 vols. (Philadelphia, 1792), II, 329; and Hopkinson's satire "Grand Antifederal Procession," in the Hopkinson Family Papers, XIII, esp. 234, Historical Society of Pennsylvania, Philadelphia.

88. On the legitimacy of crowds in the Revolutionary era, see Countryman, *The American Revolution,* 74–79; Gilje, *Road to Mobocracy,* 3–92.

leaf quoted one gentleman as remarking, "There is certainly room for *amendments.*"[89]

Very quickly Greenleaf found himself under fire for his levity. Somewhat apologetically, he maintained that humor "is natural to newspapers." This did not suffice, and on the next Saturday night, when news arrived of New York's ratification, a mob led by a procession organizer broke into his house, destroyed most of his type, and overnight turned his daily into a weekly. A chastened Greenleaf thanked the respectable citizens, some of them Federalists, who had come to his rescue. Whatever the actions of the crowd, he had not been "abandoned by the sentimental and patriotic part of the community."[90]

In objecting to his treatment, Greenleaf found himself caught between sentimental patriotism and popular sovereignty. It is not difficult to imagine his defending the same mechanics who overturned his press as a legitimate crowd representing the popular interest: he became a leading Jeffersonian journalist in the 1790s. Yet he chose to criticize his opponents on their own grounds: the primacy of order, patriotism, and refined sentiments. Thus his implication that the Federalists who attacked his shop were neither sentimental nor patriotic shows us even more vividly the success of the Federalist project. The culturally dominant nationalism of the 1780s was a nationalism of aspirations to order, a nationalism elite in origins but broadened in its practice. It included sentimental performances and their printed representations, whose persuasive possibilities were so great that even Federalists thought them worth rioting over.

During the Revolutionary era, "the mob," according to a despairing Gouverneur Morris, had begun "to think and reason." By contrast, in his ubiquitous account of the Philadelphia Grand Federal Procession, Francis Hopkinson looked around the festive throng and saw in "every countenance . . . the index of a heart glowing with urbanity and rational joy." Likewise, Benjamin Rush, in a letter anonymously appended to Hopkinson's official account, wrote: "Never upon any occasion during the late war did I see such deep seated joy in every countenance."

89. De Pauw, *Eleventh Pillar,* 110–111; Furtwangler, *Authority of Publius,* 21, 48, 82; *New-York Journal,* July 25, 1788. Earlier, Greenleaf had reprinted a satirical piece on the Boston procession: "Philadephia, Feb. 19," *New-York Journal,* Feb. 25, 1788.

90. *New-York Journal,* July 31, Aug. 7, 21, 1788; *New-Haven Gazette,* July 25, 31, 1788. See also Gilje, *Road to Mobocracy,* 97–99; John C. Nerone, *Violence against the Press: Policing the Public Sphere in U.S. History* (New York, 1994), 60–63.

"Every countenance wore an air of *dignity* as well as pleasure."[91] The Grand Federal Processions were so widely replicated precisely because they could bring so many into the stylized order, the new public sphere of the nation whose coin of admission was the display of patriotic sentiments. Recorders of the processions reveled in the supposed disappearance of conflict, describing every participant group and never failing to estimate the numbers of cheering onlookers. Numbers mattered.

The mechanics who formed the bulk of the procession had contributed to this kind of patriotism. Planters in Charleston sat down with mechanics "in a truly republican style." A huge dinner after the Grand Federal Procession in New Haven included "a great number of respectable citizens of various classes." Respectability gained an elasticity that it had lacked at Fourth of July celebrations a few years earlier; it had to. In their own view the artisans had become full participants in the virtuous, orderly, patriotic public.[92]

Nothing more reveals the ambiguous nature of the constitutional compromise than the different messages we hear if we attend to the artisans' own statements. While the "Grand Federal Edifice" might have been intended to keep the people indoors, the mechanics claimed to have raised the columns. Parading with their wares and banners, they gloried in a sense of power that signaled their stake in the commercial economy—and more. Their tributes to the federal union referred to their own ability to join or sunder that union. "Both buildings and rulers are the works of our hands," insisted the Philadelphia bricklayers. The blacksmiths in the procession at York, Pennsylvania, in 1788 proclaimed: "May the Thirteen States be *welded* into the United Empire, by the *hammer* of conciliation, on the *anvil* of peace; and may the man who attempts to *blow the coal* of discord be *burned* by the sparks." The butchers testified: "As the marrow is connected with the bone, or one joint with another, so let us be united, and may no cleaver ever disjoin us."[93]

91. Morris to John Penn, May 20, 1774, in Merrill Jensen, ed., *English Historical Documents: American Colonial Documents to 1776* (New York, 1965), 860–863, vol. IX of David C. Douglas, ed., *English Historical Documents*, cited in Pauline Maier, *The Old Revolutionaries: Political Lives in the Age of Samuel Adams* (New York, 1980), 78; [Francis Hopkinson], *Account of the Grand Federal Procession* . . . [Philadelphia, 1788], 18–20.

92. *Virginia Gazette, and Weekly Advertiser* (Richmond), June 18, 1788; *New-Haven Gazette*, July 10, 1788.

93. [Hopkinson], *Account*, 7; *Independent Journal* (New York), July 23, Aug. 6, 1788; *Pennsylvania Packet*, Aug. 4, 1788.

On the artisans and their parades, see Eric Foner, *Tom Paine and Revolutionary*

Artisan rhetoric drew attention to the constructed, contingent nature of the new constitutional union. Moreover, for these parading working-men, virtue meant something different from what it had for *The Federalist*—a contradiction that we see in the accounts of the Grand Federal Processions. If all the people were one, why would it be necessary to offer particular thanks to the mechanics for maintaining order? The artisans' labor theory of value coexisted uneasily with the assumptions of natural aristocracy. Yet their participation on their own terms in the Federalist processions and the remarkably inclusive nature of those processions suggest that the upheavals of two and a half decades would not be so easily rolled back.

☆   ☆   ☆

The Constitution and the Grand Federal Processions solved the crisis of representation temporarily by embodying the people and permitting a cease-fire in the struggle over the possession of national virtue. The printed accounts of the processions are best read as multivocal texts in which the very existence of different voices offers a temporary resolution to the representational dilemmas of the previous decade. Patriotic identity, of course, is reinscribed as federal, as the unfeeling Antifederalists slink away. The artisans carrying goods restore the commercial republic to solvency on more stable grounds than paper money offers: labor and the things it produces are the sources of wealth as well as a source of patriotic identity for the laborers. And the official, published, disseminated versions of the parade solve the crisis of unruly

America (New York, 1976), 206–209; Sean Wilentz, "Artisan Republican Festivals and the Rise of Class Conflict in New York City, 1788–1837," in Michael H. Frisch and Daniel J. Walkowitz, eds., *Working-Class America: Essays on Labor, Community, and American Society* (Urbana, Ill., 1983), 37–77; Countryman, *The American Revolution,* 214–219, 226–227. Paul A. Gilje has cautioned that the Grand Procession in New York was "an attempt to create or 'invent' tradition by the city's elite" and as such was "only partly successful." The real common people, he suggests, should be sought in "other more extemporaneous types of street theater." See Gilje, "The Common People and the Constitution: Popular Culture in New York City in the Late Eighteenth Century," in Gilje and William Pencak, eds., *New York in the Age of the Constitution, 1775–1800* (Rutherford, N.J., 1992), 48–73, quoted at 54, 63. See also Mannucci, "Federal Grand Processions." Alfred F. Young's work on Boston offers a similar interpretation of artisan politics; see "Mechanics on Parade: Measures of Artisan Consciousness in Boston, 1784–1789," paper presented at the conference "Festive Culture and Public Ritual in Early America," Philadelphia, April 1996.

political discourse. Incorporating the self-representations of banner-carrying participants and describing the true hearts of spectators, it fixes political reality, saving it from future rhetorical inflations.

The struggle for constitutional ratification marked the beginning of the federal union as we know it. Insofar as independence movements usually result in stronger national governments, 1788 fulfilled America's nationalist revolution. Culturally, it was certainly a climax of revolutionary politicization—another, greater Great National Discussion. Closer attention to the streets and the newspapers of the 1780s, though, reveals significant departures from the popular politics of the Revolution. Much more than during the resistance movement, sentimental display trumped traditional crowd action: order was the order of the day. And yet Americans were learning how orderly nationalist rejoicing could express their political differences. The struggle to embody virtue and the nation, to constitute federal feeling, continued. In this sense, as in others, the Revolution had not yet ended.

3

NATIONAL CHARACTERS

The Federalists succeeded in sacralizing the Constitution as the true culmination of the American Revolution. In 1789, Fourth of July orators added the crisis of the 1780s and the foresight of the framers to their recountings of heroic American history.[1] Memorializing the 1780s as a political wandering in the wilderness folded the open-ended nationalism of the Revolution into a conservative return to first principles. At the same time, the ever-rising glory of America seemed finally visible to all. Ideologically speaking, it had to be. Nationalists now faced the task of securing the Revolution (now the past) while making real what the Revolution had made possible: the national future.

That future, for the Federalists, needed to be orderly, national, uplifting, and progressive. It had to restrain unruly expressions of localism, plebeian consciousness, and factionalism, all of which they had implicitly, if not explicitly, delegitimized as divisive and selfish. After ratification, nationalist celebration remained central to the Federalist attempt to carve out "a unitary public sphere": one that admitted the presence while denying the legitimacy of interests deriving from specific social groups. In this new public sphere celebrations provided ways for the upper sorts to display their virtue without admitting to self-interest.[2]

1. Samuel Whitewell, *An Oration Delivered to the Society of the Cincinnati . . . July 4, 1789* (Boston, 1789); Samuel Stillman, *An Oration, Delivered July 4, 1789 . . .* (Boston, 1789); William Rogers, *An Oration, Delivered July 4, 1789 . . .* (Philadelphia, 1789); Edward Gray, *An Oration, Delivered July 5, 1790 . . .* (Boston, 1790).

2. Richard Buel, Jr., *Securing the Revolution: Ideology in American Politics, 1789–1815* (Ithaca, N.Y., 1972); John L. Brooke, "Ancient Lodges and Self-Created Societies: Voluntary Association and the Public Sphere in the Early Republic," in Ronald Hoffman and Peter J. Albert, eds., *Launching the "Extended Republic": The Federalist*

Federalists began by declaring "the commencement of a new era." Rather than waiting for the festivities to begin, John Fenno, the New York arch-Federalist editor of the *Gazette of the United States*, insisted: "From all parts of the Union accounts agree" that 1789's Independence Day "will be celebrated with a degree of hilarity and festivity, hitherto unknown. We have had the *name* of Independence, the *shadow* without the *substance*." For Fenno, the ascendancy of Washington to the new nation's highest office, the triumph over "partial and local regulations," cleared away the gloom that had hung over previous celebrations. Nationhood then had been merely "a *sound*, while the prospect of real *Independence* was receding. . . . This roused us to action, to deliberation, to decision." With a federal Constitution, old scenes of war and "civil discord" would vanish: "A prospect new and splendid dawns upon us." Even Fenno's own editorial congratulation would "excite the most pleasing emotions" and, not incidentally, remind readers to frown upon any "excess and indecency," "rude mirth and hilarity."[3] Predicting what would happen in the national capital and everywhere else in terms of an orderly, national "we," Fenno took the genre of festival reportage itself into the future tense. By expecting and describing national joy, he could help secure its shape and meaning. This was indeed independence.

Fenno's larger innovation, the *Gazette of the United States*, took on this labor of mediating between the new federal government and the rapidly expanding nation. Fenno and his friends in the administration expressed dismay when, two years later, Philip Freneau put out a rival *National Gazette* (also published in the capital city of Philadelphia) to frame political news for the inchoate opposition. Important as both ventures were, they really indicated a wider phenomenon: the creation of a national and nationalistic political culture whose primary medium was print and whose nodal point was the new federal state. Beginning in the early 1790s a profusion of new papers appeared, carrying names like the *Herald of the United States* of Warren, Rhode Island. Carrying as much local news as any other newspaper, Warren's *Herald* also featured congressional debates, laws of the United States, and international af-

Era (Charlottesville, Va., 1996), 317; Gordon S. Wood, "Interests and Disinterestedness in the Making of the Constitution," in Richard Beeman et al. eds., *Beyond Confederation: Origins of the Constitution and American National Identity* (Chapel Hill, N.C., 1987), 69–109.

3. Robert Lewis Diary, July 4, 1789, Lewis Family Papers, Virginia Historical Society, Richmond; *Gazette of the United States* (New York), July 4, 1789.

fairs. The existence of Fenno's and Freneau's sheets might have been less important than the early form of syndication that they infused with new energy. News and texts moved both ways in this information system. Local papers in smaller towns and rural areas carried major essays and documents while providing the urban, coastal papers with enough provincial matter to prove their regional and national coverage.

National citizenship made sense because print culture gave many ordinary men and women access to news about the nation almost daily. Almanacs too carried significant documents like treaties and listed the names of federal officials and congressmen along with state and local public servants. People relied upon such printed materials to know the world and to act in it. The mediation of action and experience by printed texts made the nation seem something more than imaginary.[4]

An extract on newspapers in the fledgling *Kentucky Gazette* (1790) exemplifies this understanding of the relationship between print and public life. As a fragment reprinted in the first issues of the *Otsego Herald* five years later, the form of the piece exemplifies the success of its own message.

> While we are in the world, we must converse with the world; the conversation will in part turn on the news of the day. It is the first subject we begin upon, as a general introduction to everything else. All mankind, indeed, are our brethren, and we are interested, in their pleasures and pains, their sufferings, or their deliverances, throughout the world. Accounts of these should produce in us suitable emotions which would tend to the exercise of different virtues, and the improvement of our tempers. We should accustom ourselves hereby to rejoice with those who rejoice, and mourn with those who mourn.[5]

4. John Tobler, *The South-Carolina and Georgia Almanac, for . . . 1790 . . .* (Charleston, S.C., [1789]); William Waring, *New-Jersey Almanack for . . . 1790 . . .* (Trenton, N.J., [1789]); Benjamin Workman, *The Pennsylvania, Delaware, Maryland, and Virginia Almanack and Ephemeris, for . . . 1790 . . .* (Baltimore, 1789); Robert Andrews, *The Virginia Almanack for . . . 1790 . . .* (Richmond, Va., [1789]); *Bailey's Pocket Almanac, for . . . 1790 . . .* (Philadelphia, [1789]). On the ethic of diffusion and participation in an almost boundless public culture, see Richard D. Brown's essay on William Bentley in Brown, *Knowledge Is Power: The Diffusion of Information in Early America, 1700–1865* (New York, 1989), 197–217; and Michael Warner, *The Letters of the Republic: Publication and the Public Sphere in Eighteenth-Century America* (Cambridge, Mass., 1990), 34–72, 118–175.

5. *Kentucky Gazette* (Louisville), July 12, 1790; *Otsego Herald; or, Western Advertiser* (Cooperstown, N.Y.), Apr. 3, 1795.

Here, anyone who is "in the world" has a responsibility to know the world. Oral conversations in everyday life begin with retellings of printed news from around the globe. To be fully human is to be interested in the "pleasures and pains" of others. Reading the news holds out the promise of individual and international improvement.

Being "in the world," participants in print culture affirm an interest that goes beyond the self but is based upon that self's capacity for affective involvement. And sentimental participation is understood through celebratory practices: "to rejoice with those who rejoice, and mourn with those who mourn." Michael Warner has cited this ethos as evidence of the increasingly "imaginary" quality of public life.[6] But before we mourn or celebrate the rise of distant sympathies, we should consider the practices and events that were the contexts for sympathetic ideas and texts.

The sentimental acts of celebration, which may appear to us distanced, secondhand, and unconnected to real life or politics, seemed at the time to open up a greater sphere of action for more and more citizens. The collective and individual display of political sentiments and affiliation potentially could make good national citizens of every reader and every person, man and woman, who cheered a bonfire or a parade. Moreover, the rise of the nation itself opened a new stage for affective involvement through reading, writing, and celebration. During the 1790s, overseas developments gave Americans much cause for joy and sorrow. Conflicting reactions to revolutions and wars spurred controversy over what should be celebrated and mourned. Yet the sheer proliferation of celebrations and printed accounts of them suggests that more was going on. Celebration and mourning of international events helped Americans make sense of a precarious world in which revolutions and international warfare followed one another in wholly

6. Warner sees the emergence of a national imaginary as a hallmark of the success of republican print culture: ironically, its spread makes citizenship all too imaginary, separating a nationalism of affective involvement from a polity that (in republican theory) would be made up of active participants in public life. See Warner, *Letters of the Republic*, 173–176. In a more idealist and rather uncritical attempt to describe a related process, Thomas L. Haskell looks for the emergence of humanitarian concern for suffering peoples in the spread of a market mentality. See his "Capitalism and the Origins of the Humanitarian Sensibility," parts 1 and 2, with the responses by David Brion Davis and John Ashworth, collected in Thomas Bender, ed., *The Antislavery Debate: Capitalism and Abolitionism as a Problem in Historical Interpretation* (Berkeley, Calif., 1992).

unpredictable succession. The same celebration and publication, street theater and reading, that had constituted Revolutionary nationalism later helped post-Revolutionary patriots to make national sense of the young Republic's most pressing problem: foreign policy.

The complexities of events abroad stymie any simple, retrospective equation of economic interests, ideology, and partisan needs. International war upset the carrying trade—the original spur and source of news—and consumed farmers and artisans as well as merchants. European developments could justify or bankrupt emerging visions of the future, be they agrarian, commercial, or industrial. Revolutions and their fates had implications for the untested forms of republicanism, on which Americans disagreed passionately even as they affirmed a republican national identity. And foreign affairs provided a stage on which the politically aware debated the competing claims of liberty, order, and equality—claims that still had potentially revolutionary meanings for politics at home.

With so much at stake, it did not take long for celebrations of the Fourth of July, Washington's Birthday, and the French Revolution to intervene in political contests. Accounts filled newspapers at the moments of greatest controversy. As the very stuff of a new national political culture, celebrations made it possible for ordinary citizens to act politically between elections.[7] They helped make politics constitute the national culture itself.

At the nexus of this new political culture lay the refashioned national state. Its very stability was an open question, as Federalists so often insisted. For all their paeans to the newness of the new order, the concerns and composition of the political leadership in the 1790s had not changed all that much from the previous decade. Yet the existence of a national state necessarily marked a fundamental shift in the dynamics of nationalism. During the Revolution, the nation could be imagined and embodied on spectacular occasions as the people themselves. The constitutional battles of the 1780s were framed around this question of the people: who counted among them and how to represent their sovereignty.[8] As I have argued, Americans practiced nationalism before

7. See Simon P. Newman, *Parades and the Politics of the Street: Festive Culture in the Early American Republic* (Philadelphia, 1997).

8. Buel, *Securing the Revolution;* William Nisbet Chambers, *Political Parties in a New Nation: The American Experience, 1776–1809* (New York, 1963); Richard H. Kohn, *Eagle and Sword: The Federalists and the Creation of the Military Establishment in America,*

they had a fully developed national state—something that may account for the relatively abstract quality of early and subsequent American nationalism. If so, then the 1790s were a true loss of innocence, and not just because of the emergence of factions on a national level. Parties emerged because the new federal government, its functionaries, and its local allies clothed themselves in the rhetoric and the rituals of the nation. Calling for a new kind of unity, they helped re-form old sorts of division.

Energetic federalism gave new life to the opposition arguments the colonists had drawn upon in fighting the British Empire. To some extent, both sides positioned themselves as inheritors of this whig, or republican, legacy. There was a crucial ideological difference, though, between those who identified with the reigning administration and those who came to see it as a force quite distinct from "the nation." The longest-running, most important debate of the period concerned the relationship of the people—the national polity—to the government. Throughout the decade Federalists claimed to *be* the people's government; any popular intervention between elections, they contended, could only be the carping of disgruntled, self-interested losers or the machinations of "foreigners" who were not really of the people. In 1798 they even passed laws outlawing such activity, prosecuting printers, a congressman, and one unlucky soul who cursed President Adams on his birthday.[9] The war climate that allowed them to, I will argue, only came about through new forms of national-popular mobilization that contradicted the Federalist elite's own dreams of a passive, deferential populace. Their ideally unified nation, once again, rested on a foun-

---

1783–1802 (New York, 1975); Edmund S. Morgan, *Inventing the People: The Rise of Popular Sovereignty in England and America* (New York, 1987), 263–287. James A. Morone argues that the desire for the "collective people" to assume a role in guiding the nation, against "both liberalism and the state," became the republican legacy in American politics. See Morone, *The Democratic Wish: Popular Participation and the Limits of American Government* (New York, 1990), 33–73.

9. John M. Murrin, "The Great Inversion, or Court versus Country: A Comparison of the Revolution Settlements in England (1688–1721) and America (1776–1816)," in J. G. A. Pocock, ed., *Three British Revolutions: 1641, 1688, 1776* (Princeton, N.J., 1980), 368–453; Lance Banning, *The Jeffersonian Persuasion: Evolution of a Party Ideology* (Ithaca, N.Y., 1978), 126–270; Ronald P. Formisano, *The Transformation of Political Culture: Massachusetts Parties, 1790s–1840s* (New York, 1983), 57–83; James Morton Smith, *Freedom's Fetters: The Alien and Sedition Laws and American Civil Liberties* (Ithaca, N.Y., 1956), 270–274.

dation of broadened, contentious participation in public life. The repeated irony of federalism, that its popular successes only furthered its
long-term demise, followed from the Revolution and the struggle for
ratification. Popular partisan mobilization, and the problems it created
for Federalism, long preceded the formal organization of parties.[10]

The opposition had the luxury (or perhaps the burden) of a more
familiar position. Yet the Republicans of the 1790s were not the Antifederalists of 1788. Although continuities of membership and ideology between the two groups were significant, the real change was the
Republican opposition's inevitable acceptance, upon ratification, of
national politics. Antifederalists had fought against ratification in their
states. Democratic-Republicans came to oppose certain administration
measures whether they themselves held power in their home states or
not. As a nationalist movement they too had to find ways to personify
the people and speak for the nation.

From 1792 until 1797 the Republicans made remarkable use of the

10. On a passive populace, see the 1791 Fourth of July address of Edward Bangs,
one of Worcester's premier Federalists, who told his audience that political "jealousy" was not a virtue: it threatened to rock the ship of state. In his discussion,
the pursuit of happiness is a flight from active citizenship. "Secure, that our watch-
men are embarked with us in the same ship, and that while they watch for us, they
watch for their own lives . . . we may turn each one to his private occupation with
dignity, enjoying the independence of our minds, the freedom of our thoughts and
speech, and the fruit of our labours; only taking care, as the times of election come
regularly round, to make a proper choice of our publick servants, and occasionally
amusing ourselves, at leisure hours, with overlooking them in all their proceedings,
by reading the publick printed papers." See Bangs, *An Oration, Delivered at Worcester, on the Fourth of July, 1791* . . . (Worcester, Mass., 1791), 7–12. Six years later in
Worcester, Oliver Fiske tried to persuade the same audience that "a deference to
our rulers, is no other than a respect for ourselves." Partisanship was dangerous because "the rulers and the people are but different modifications of the same mass."
See Fiske, *An Oration, Pronounced at Worcester, on the Anniversary of American Independence* . . . (Worcester, Mass., [1797]), 5–6.

For similar arguments on the demise of federalism but with different periodiza-
tions, see David Hackett Fischer, *The Revolution of American Conservatism: The Federalist Party in the Era of Jeffersonian Democracy* (New York, 1965); Buel, *Securing the Revolution*. On the slow development of parties and the impetus provided by national
politics, see Noble E. Cunningham, Jr., *The Jeffersonian Republicans: The Formation of
a Party Organization, 1789–1801* (Chapel Hill, N.C., 1957); Richard Hofstadter, *The
Idea of a Party System: The Rise of Legitimate Opposition in the United States, 1780–1840*
(Berkeley, Calif., 1969), 40–121.

French Revolution to drive home their criticisms of a nascent aristocracy. Newly inclusive civic feasts dotted the calendar and influenced
even the putatively Federalist celebration of Washington's Birthday. By
mid-decade, toasts at public dinners had become so regular a feature
of public life that a French émigré journalist could describe the Americans as even more obsessed with politics—and print—than his own
countrymen:

> The nomination or retreat of a minister or governor—the anniver-
> sary of an alliance, or the birth of a hero—dear to the nation, is
> the occasion of a public entertainment; at which each one, to mani-
> fest his gratitude, or to make a display of his talents, gives out toasts
> with which the feast is terminated. The day following the printers of
> newspapers do not fail to give a list of them, as also the number of
> cheers which each toast has exerted; from the perusal of which the
> Americans derive as much satisfaction, as a Frenchman would in re-
> counting the number of his *love* intrigues.[11]

All these celebrations and political pronouncements spoke for something, but what? Editors of newspapers relied on toasts as indicators of
public opinion, but they themselves reprinted their favorites and often
satirized those they opposed. As representations of the thoughts of
the people, toasts ideally were spontaneous, but, in practice, were fashioned; their appropriateness was unquestionable in general, yet, in the
particular, was always questioned. Like any utterance, they could raise
doubts even as they allayed them. In this way, cultural forms that Revolutionary patriots had used to resist metropolitan policies now allowed
them to resist each other.

Virtually all decade long, partisans disputed the form and content
of each other's celebrations. The very proliferation of voluntary associations doing the dining, parading, and toasting belied the claims of
any one of them to represent the nation. Yet the very conjunction of
partisan promotion and nationalist display made counterdisplays crucial to political success. More often than not, appeals to the nation and
the drawing of partisan lines were really poles of the same impulse.
Partisan expression served nationalist ends, and nationalist expression
fulfilled partisan needs. None of this sat well with the reigning theories

11. "New-York: March 6 [*Gazette Française*] Republican Toasts," *Federal Intelligencer, and Baltimore Daily Gazette*, Mar. 12, 1795.

of patriotism and politics, but it certainly lent excitement, a "passion," to public life.[12]

Like their contemporaries in France, Americans of the 1790s sought to stem the "the perishability of revolutionary time."[13] Like the French, they fought over the meaning and practice of national citizenship and the true locus of "the people." Like the French, they defined their political enemies as personae non gratae. Perhaps the American Revolution as well as the French "gave birth to a new kind of political community sustained more by rhetorical adrenaline than by organized institutions."[14] Certainly, this seems to be the case when we stress the divisiveness of partisan politics and the weakness of the federal government in the era after constitutional ratification. But the "overinflated expectations" of many post-Revolutionary Americans led them to make festivals—the state's vehicle of uniformity in France—into a place where "rhetorical adrenaline" itself could be replenished and renewed, with real political effects. As a series of attempts to close the gaps between Revolutionary nationalist ideals and the realities of state building, social division, political conflict, economic transformation, and imperial warfare, American national celebrations of the 1790s partook of much of the same logic as French (and British) political culture of the same era, with greatly different consequences, of course. Though Americans too found aristocrats pitted against Jacobins, their revolutionary excesses were neither parallel nor apparent: they lined up in a distinctly American way. If a French comparison reveals as many differences as similari-

12. Marshall Smelser, "The Federalist Period as an Age of Passion," *American Quarterly*, X (1958), 391–419.

13. I borrow this expression and many of my ideas on this topic from David Brion Davis, *The Problem of Slavery in the Age of Revolution, 1770–1823* (Ithaca, N.Y., 1975), 306–326; and Davis, *Revolutions: Reflections on American Equality and Foreign Liberations* (Cambridge, Mass., 1990).

14. Simon Schama, *Citizens: A Chronicle of the French Revolution* (New York, 1989), 906. On the revolutionary festivals in France and the other technologies of the national-popular, see, especially, Mona Ozouf, *Festivals and the French Revolution*, trans. Alan Sheridan (Cambridge, Mass., 1988); Lynn Hunt, *Politics, Culture, and Class in the French Revolution* (Berkeley, Calif., 1984); Emmet Kennedy, *A Cultural History of the French Revolution* (New Haven, Conn., 1989); and Brian C. J. Singer, *Society, Theory, and the French Revolution: Studies in the Revolutionary Imaginary* (New York, 1986). Something of a historiographical consensus has emerged that puts nationalism at the center of the French Revolution. See Geoffrey Best, "Introduction," in Best, ed., *The Permanent Revolution: The French Revolution and Its Legacy, 1789–1989* (Chicago, 1988), 7–9.

ties, it can at least help remind us that, during the 1790s, Americans celebrated the nation in ways that remained, by the standards of the day, Revolutionary.

GEORGE WASHINGTON'S SENTIMENTAL JOURNEYS

It has often been said that Americans did not so much give up their fears of executive power as agree to entrust them to one man. That man, of course, was Washington. The Constitution itself had carried his imprimatur as president of the convention, and even before its release the delegates had fashioned the executive branch with him in mind.

During the first years of the federal Republic a cult of the Constitution was not necessary: a cult of Washington served similar ends, erasing much of the taint of particular interests from the federal experiment.[15] If the Constitution was indeed the culmination of the Revolution, 1788 need not even be seen as a separate venture. The crisis of the 1780s had been merely the latest wandering in the wilderness, brought to the land of plenty by the same saving force. Having Washington as president reinforced assumptions of continuity and consensus.

Before the federal government was long in operation, though, it became clear that Federalist nationalism masked class and regional priorities. At their annual July Fourth meeting in 1789, the Rhode Island Society of the Cincinnati kicked Joseph Arnold out of their fraternity "for making a late tender of the paper currency of that state, to discharge a specie demand." Secretary of the Treasury Alexander Hamilton picked July 4, 1791, to put the stock of the Bank of the United States up for sale. *Dunlap's American Daily Advertiser* of Philadelphia compared the citizens lined up to buy bonds to the patriotic celebrants of Independence Day in various states, "vying with each other" to show "confidence in the public faith." Only a year later, however, an aggrieved Boston taxpayer declared his Independence Day to have been ruined by "a cruel, impolitic INDIAN WAR calculated for no other purpose . . . than to aggrandize a few individuals, who would otherwise sink into their ORIGINAL state." As class and regional critiques of Hamilton's funding system emerged, centrists and nationalists developed their often

15. Ralph Ketcham, *Presidents above Party: The First American Presidency, 1789–1829* (Chapel Hill, N.C., 1984), 69–93. On the slow emergence of the cult of the Constitution, see Michael Kammen, *A Machine That Would Go of Itself: The Constitution in American Culture* (New York, 1986).

conflicting blueprints for a commercial yet agrarian Republic. Many directions seemed possible, especially as the restoration of trade spurred even more speculation in land and goods. One man's property was another man's ideological nightmare. Little wonder that, when toasting the national bank, domestic manufactures, and internal navigation, a group of Bladensburg, Maryland, celebrants expressed relief that Washington had survived an illness and might yet "live for many years."[16]

We know that Washington symbolized the nation and all that was redemptive in it; we know that he was popular beyond any previous possibility of acclaim, at least in part because he spent the better part of his life cultivating the persona of the republican hero. Self-effacing yet ever forthcoming when called upon in the name of the public weal, a military and civic leader who voluntarily relinquished authority, he was precisely the kind of political father required by those of a rebellious generation. With him they could have their resistance and their obedience too.[17] But the cult of Washington also smoothed over the inherent tensions of a "deferential-participant" and *nationalist* politics. Washington united leaders and followers in spectacular exchanges of sentiment that confirmed his own stature while ratifying the judgment of all those who applauded his unparalleled virtues.

During his eastern and southern tours of 1789–1791 the celebration of Washington served the evolving federal state as well as the Grand Federal Processions had served its constitutional establishment. Mobi-

16. *Dunlap's American Daily Advertiser* (Philadelphia), July 6, 19, 1791; *Independent Gazetteer, and Agricultural Repository* (Philadelphia), July 14, 1792; *Salem Mercury* (Mass.), July 14, 1789; John C. Miller, *The Federalist Era, 1789–1801* (New York, 1960), 59; Drew R. McCoy, *The Elusive Republic: Political Economy in Jeffersonian America* (Chapel Hill, N.C., 1980), 136–184; Joyce Appleby, *Capitalism and a New Social Order: The Republican Vision of the 1790s* (New York, 1984); *Albany Gazette*, July 28, 1791.

17. A number of scholars have plumbed the Washington cult for insights into American culture and politics in the late eighteenth century. See Catherine L. Albanese, *Sons of the Fathers: The Civil Religion of the American Revolution* (Philadelphia, 1976), 143–181; Lawrence J. Friedman, *Inventors of the Promised Land* (New York, 1975), 44–77; Jay Fliegelman, *Prodigals and Pilgrims: The American Revolution against Patriarchal Authority, 1750–1800* (New York, 1982), chap. 7; Garry Wills, *Cincinnatus: George Washington and the Enlightenment* (New York, 1984); Barry Schwartz, *George Washington: The Making of an American Symbol* (New York, 1987); Paul K. Longmore, *The Invention of George Washington* (Berkeley, Calif., 1988); Simon P. Newman, "Principles or Men? George Washington and the Political Culture of National Leadership, 1776–1801," *Journal of the Early Republic*, XII (1992), 477–507.

lizing women, young people, and huge, mixed crowds, the opportunity to celebrate Washington's presidency encouraged participation across the lines of class and gender. At the same time, Washington's presence reinforced local authority by giving elites the chance to display their privileged access to his person. Removed from mere politics, Washington gave the nascent federal party the aura of nonpartisanship. By 1793, its style of celebrating his birthday became a matter of great controversy. But even afterward, Washington's presence exerted a centralizing pull in every sense of the word. Union, after all, was what he promoted. And union was a matter of sentiment.

The George Washington handed down to us by scores of biographers is a rather cold fish. The requirements of leadership, we are told, led him to keep his distance. Yet those who met him in other contexts told a different story. Staring into his visage, they saw the very personification of sensibility. Little wonder that they lauded him as "the man who unites all hearts." Diaries as well as newspaper accounts stress the desire of the high and the low to see his face. His fellow Independence Day revelers in Alexandria were not unique in declaring "their happiness by beholding the pleasure that beamed on the countenance of their illustrious and renowned neighbor." By then, Washington had helped teach the better part of the nation to participate in the exchange of federal feeling.[18]

These sentimental exchanges relied upon contemporary understandings of the moral sentiments, in which vision and physiognomy played a central role. Faces reflected character, and seeing such faces formed in the viewer an impression of those virtues (and vices). Seeing Washington's face impressed in his audience's character the sentiments of patriotic union they saw in the hero of the Revolution. In a sense, the obsession with Washington's face replaced the monarchical focus on the king's body, doing so in a way particularly amenable to the requirements of a national print culture. Having smashed the relics of

18. Mary Hewson to Sister, Apr. 22, 1789, Hewson Family Papers, American Philosophical Society, Philadelphia; Diary of Richard W. Venable, June 4, 6, 1791, Virginia Historical Society; Henry Bailey to John Henderson, May 10, 1791, John Henderson Papers, William R. Perkins Library, Duke University, Durham, N.C.; *Virginia Gazette and Alexandria Advertiser*, July 11, 1793. Charles Royster analyzes the sentimental exchanges between Continental army officers, including Washington, in *A Revolutionary People at War: The Continental Army and American Character, 1775–1783* (Chapel Hill, N.C., 1979), 88–90, 353. To some extent, Washington's presidential rituals can be seen as popularized versions of the same process.

royalty (including representations of the king's body), some Americans yearned for a human, not merely constitutional, emblem of naturalized aristocracy to succeed the much-praised Constitutional Convention. This emblem had to be not only visible but also describable in the print medium. More than the common touch, the new, Federalist, American presidency required the sentimental look.[19]

Both Washington's Birthday and his tours adopted the rituals of royalty. As such, they earned the attacks of adherents to rigorous republicanism. But insofar as they remained similar to the King's Birthday and the king's progress, these similarities originated in a particular late-eighteenth-century variety of kingship and a new kind of popular patriotism.[20] Washington's elaborately staged tours were exchanges of nationalist sentiment. Earlier rituals of king and people had traded promises of protection for pledges of obeisance. These post-Revolutionary encounters between the people and the executive confirmed the existence of the nation and the virtue of the participants. On Washington's arrival in New York for his inauguration, just as in the earlier Revolutionary and constitutional celebrations, "every heart" was said to expand with "universal joy": "The aged sire—the venerable matron, the blooming virgin, and the ruddy Youth were all emulous in their plaudits—nay, the lisping infant did not withhold its innocent smile of praise and approbation." None but Washington could inspire such unanimity across social groups. "How *sincere*—and how *expressive* the sentiments of respect and veneration!" exclaimed Fenno's *Gazette of the United States,* devoting as much attention to the audience as to the seeming actor.[21] The sentiments displayed by the populace did more

19. *The Elements of Gesture, Illustrated by Four Elegant Copper-Plates; Together with Rules for Expressing, with Propriety, the Various Passions and Emotions of the Mind* (Philadelphia, 1790); David Waldstreicher, " 'Fallen under My Observation': Vision and Virtue in *The Coquette,"Early American Literature,* XXVII (1992), 204–220; Jay Fliegelman, *Declaring Independence: Jefferson, Natural Language, and the Culture of Performance* (Stanford, Calif., 1993), 31, 58–60.

20. On the emergence of a sentimentalized monarchy and popular patriotism, see, especially, Richard L. Bushman, *King and People in Provincial Massachusetts* (Chapel Hill, N.C., 1985), 241–244; Linda Colley, *Britons: Forging the Nation, 1701– 1837* (New Haven, Conn., 1992), 195–236; Schama, *Citizens,* esp. 155–156; Lynn Hunt, *The Family Romance of the French Revolution* (Berkeley, Calif., 1992), chap. 4; Gordon S. Wood, *The Radicalism of the American Revolution* (New York, 1992), 95–100.

21. See the accounts in John P. Kaminski and Jill Adair McCaughan, eds., *A Great and Good Man: George Washington in the Eyes of His Contemporaries* (Madison, Wis., 1989), esp. 116, 117, 124.

View of the **TRIUMPHAL ARCH**, and the manner of receiving General Washington at Trenton, on his Route to New-York. April 21.ᵗ 1789.

FIGURE 6. *View of the Triumphal Arch, and the Manner of Receiving General Washington at Trenton, on His Route to New York, April 21st, 1789. Columbian Magazine,* III (1789). Courtesy Franklin Collection, Yale University Library

than prove Washington's popularity. They established popular and individual virtue, a clear continuation of the Federalist project.

The form of the Washington receptions on his 1789 and 1791 tours demonstrates the reciprocal nature of the new patriotism. On approaching a town, Washington would leave his carriage and mount his famous white horse. At least a few miles out he would be met by a deputation of militia or local dignitaries, who would then guide him into the state, county, or city. Virtually all the residents of the surrounding areas gathered in town to get a glimpse of the war hero president. Often a full-scale civic procession followed. In the evening Washington attended dinner parties with the local elite, at which the standard thirteen national toasts would be offered.[22]

22. On the tours, see Donald Jackson and Dorothy Twohig, eds., *The Diaries of George Washington* (Charlottesville, Va., 1976–1979), V, 445–497, VI, 96–169; Rufus Wilmot Griswold, *The Republican Court; or, American Society in the Days of Washington,* 2d ed. (New York, 1867), 113–136, 183–202, 329–340; Archibald Henderson, *George Washington's Southern Tour, 1791* (Boston, 1923); Richard Norton Smith, *Patriarch: George Washington and the New American Nation* (Boston, 1993), 87–107; *Newburyport, October 28, 1789: As This Town Is on Friday to Be Honored* (Newburyport, Mass.,

Beyond the universal approval of "the people," the aspects of these rituals most commented upon were the official addresses of civic bodies and the often impromptu responses of Washington. Printed in newspapers all over the country, his replies never failed to express sincere gratitude for the sincere gratitude professed by those who attended him. According to the newspaper reports, the scenes and the sentiments made an impression on everyone, epitomized by Washington's own affective gestures. Consider his legacy to the ladies of Trenton—a short note that was thought touching enough to reprint as a broadside two years later. During the war, Trenton had been the site of one of the Continental forces' major victories. On his way to the inaugural, Washington passed through a triumphal floral arch as young girls in white strewed his path with petals.

> GENERAL WASHINGTON cannot leave this place, without expressing his acknowledgments to the Matrons and Young ladies . . . for the exquisite Sensations he experienced in that affecting moment.— The astonishing contrast between his former and actual situation on the same spot—the elegant Taste with which it was adorned for the present occasion—and the innocent appearance of the *white robed Choir,* who met him with the gratulatory Song, had made such a remembrance, as, he assures them, will never be effaced.

The manner in which Washington refers to himself in the third person here reminds us of the awesome formality and self-discipline that characterized the first president's public performances. Despite (or perhaps *because* of) the formality, however, sentimental unity enables the baring of all breasts, the narration of "exquisite" sentiments, visible virtues, and deep impressions. "His soul was in his eyes,—and the silent tear stole down his venerable cheek," said Samuel Stillman, who retold the story in a July Fourth oration. Formally, a deeply structured if emotional order allowed for the initiative of the women of Trenton. They could come out in public and testify to their patriotism precisely because there was no danger of discord, none of Fenno's "rude mirth and hilarity." Their role in the festive welcome confirmed their gen-

1789), Broadsides Collection, American Antiquarian Society; *By the Committee of Arrangements . . . Salem, October 27, 1789* (Salem Mass., 1789), Broadsides Collection, AAS; *[Order of the Procession] To Be Observed on the Arrival of the President of the United States* (Providence, R.I., 1790); William Bentley, *The Diary of William Bentley, D.D. . . .* (Salem, Mass., 1905–1914), I, 130–131.

dered identities and their natural virtues. Not only the windows during the processions but the evening balls too were unusually crowded with ladies, many of them wearing sashes that read "G.W." From this kind of exchange, no one needed protection. After his inauguration, wrote one observer, Washington told his armed guard that "the affection of his fellow citizens (turning to the crowd) was all the guard he wanted."[23]

Washington himself linked the Revolutionary past to the national future. Old soldiers came out to get reacquainted while their uniformed sons won national manhood from his approving glance. On hearing that the president would pass through their town, fifty-four "youth of note" in Salisbury, North Carolina, formed their own militia company and sent out a sortie of thirteen to meet him at the South Carolina border (more than seventy miles away). The head of that party, Charles Caldwell, remembered being so awestruck that he could not deliver his address of welcome. Yet Washington made a point of complimenting the nineteen-year-old to his fellow "officers" at headquarters. When Caldwell found himself tongue-tied once again at the great man's ritual of departure, Washington acknowledged his escort's deep feelings by bowing and shaking his hand good-bye. "That act, accompanied, as I fancied it to be, by an appearance, in his countenance, of marks of feeling, again completely unmanned and silenced me." Looking back toward his party of fellow dragoneers, he "perceived several of its members, some years older than myself, and noted for their firmness, wiping the moisture from their eyes. . . . When affection is awakened, it is not unmanly for even a soldier to weep."[24] In Caldwell's memory, the young soldiers lost their "firmness" only to establish their patriotism: they were "unmanned" yet "not unmanly." Such sentimental spectacles established bonds of affection, dissolving distance in order to recreate and ratify hierarchy.

23. Kaminski and McCaughan, eds., *A Great and Good Man,* 121; Jackson and Twohig, eds., *Diaries of Washington,* VI, 125, 130, 140, 146; [Alexander Reingale], *A Sonata, Sung by a Number of Young Girls, Dressed in White . . . As General Washington Passed under the Triumphal Arch Raised on the Bridge at Trenton . . .* (Trenton, N.J., 1789); Stillman, *An Oration, Delivered July 4, 1789,* 23; "Robert Mills' Account of President Washington's Visit to Charleston," Miscellaneous Manuscripts—Politics, box 35, South Carolina Historical Society, Charleston; *Western Advertiser and Chambersburg Weekly Newspaper* (Pa.), Aug. 19, 1790; *Federal Herald* (Lansingburgh, N.Y.), Aug. 10, Nov. 9, 1789; letter of Elias Boudinot, quoted in Griswold, *The Republican Court,* 134.

24. Harriot W. Warner, ed., *Autobiography of Charles Caldwell, M.D.* (Philadelphia, 1855), 88–97.

If local elites seeking to establish themselves could gain self-confidence and public credit from proximity to Washington, there were larger and smaller dimensions to this rite of the new nation. As crowd activities of a sort, they contained within them the notion of popular sovereignty. Washington was the nation personified because huge numbers of people agreed that he was. Even in the Federalist version, gratitude to Washington could make anyone a true American. This schema kept the popular in popular politics even as it vitiated what we might call the political. "It is undoubtedly a new and astonishing thing under the sun," noted an often reprinted piece, "that the universal suffrages of a great and virtuous people should centre in one and the same man; for it is evidently a fact, that was every individual *personally* consulted as to the man whom they would elect to fill the office of President of this rising empire, the only reply from Newhampshire to Georgia, would be *Washington*." Thus no one was in a better position to travel about the country wishing to the people of every town "your participation [in] every national advantage."[25]

The popular dimension of the Washington cult suggests the president's centrality within what I will call the ideology of "national character." Instead of using the term as a category of analysis, I will explore its contemporary uses, which expanded dramatically in the mid-1790s. There was a popular dimension to the decade's "politics of character"; I here argue that the practices thereof were an extension or popularization of the cult of "federal feeling" that emerged during the 1780s, when participants joined individual virtue to nationalist sentiment in celebrations. Through celebrations and the controversies that surrounded them, we can see that the politics of character was more than just an elite contest of ritualized challenges and anonymous printed attacks upon each other's character.[26] Rather, the discourse of character and

25. *Cumberland Gazette* (Portland), May 14, 1789, also in Kaminski and McCaughan, eds., *Great and Good Man,* 127; George Washington to the Inhabitants of Georgetown and of Its Vicinity, Apr. 30, 1791, George Washington Papers, South Caroliniana Library, University of South Carolina, Columbia.

26. For the "politics of character" as fought out between national statesmen, see Robert H. Wiebe, *The Opening of American Society: From the Adoption of the Constitution to the Eve of Disunion* (New York, 1984), 35–66; Joanne B. Freeman, "Dueling as Politics: Reinterpreting the Burr-Hamilton Duel," *William and Mary Quarterly,* 3d Ser., LIII (1996), 289–318.

national character informed changing relationships between citizens and structures of power. It was really the groups in the most unstable, ambiguous positions with regard to the national popular political culture—ministers, young men, and middle-class women—who participated most directly in efforts to define and typify the national character.

Parallel to the Federalist identification of the nation with the government, national character compared the nation and the state to the individual. Though national characters like Washington occupied the symbolic center of these debates, the stakes were really far greater than anyone's reputation. Many of the partisan battles of the decade fused or confused the issue of participation in public life with questions of individual and national integrity. Thus it was not only that individual manhood was on the line. The issue is more complicated because the nation was theorized and discussed *in terms of* the individual: that is, the very language used to discuss the national polity involved personifying tropes like "national character." Such comparisons had a long history (consider the metaphor of the "body politic") and did not lack for tangible referents. The United States was a young nation with a new form of government; both nation and state had a reputation, a character, to establish. Projecting an image of unity would help establish that character.

Washington's trips attempted to gauge national character even while contributing to its stability and weight. Touching every state as if to bring it into sympathetic connection, he avoided only Rhode Island (until that state belatedly ratified the Constitution in 1790). Washington could test the national character because his own was so well established. Yet even his own retrospective comment at the end of the southern tour reveals the ambiguities of the project: "The attachment of all classes of citizens to the general government seems to be a pleasing

---

Until recently, "national character" has been a relatively unquestioned concept in scholarly and lay discourse. In its twentieth-century comparative dimension, "national character" tried to describe the differences between national "types" in order to generalize about Americans' individual psychology and their international relations. For examples, see David M. Potter, *People of Plenty: Economic Abundance and the American Character* (Chicago, 1954); Erik Erikson, *Childhood and Society,* 2d ed. (New York, 1963), 283–318; Michael McGiffert, ed., *The Character of Americans: A Book of Readings* (Homewood, Ill., 1964); and the discussions in Philip Gleason, "Identifying Identity: A Semantic History," *Journal of American History,* LXIX (1982–1983), 914–931; and in Rupert Wilkinson, *The Pursuit of American Character* (New York, 1988).

presage of their future happiness and respectability."[27] To deliberately conflate his own popularity with "attachment" to the federal state and to seek in that conflation the spread of a general (individual? collective?) "respectability" was to put a great burden on national unity and its representation. It also encouraged national characters like Washington to define any lack of attachment to the state (or to themselves) as un-American and a failure of character. For the time being, of course, different Americans could interpret the meaning of the festivities differently. But, in the long run, for all his symbolic power, politics moved faster than Washington possibly could in his heroic, sentimental journeys.

"I LIVE HERE IN THE MIDST OF PERPETUAL FETES"

Even as celebrations of Washington helped create a vital center for Federalism, enthusiasm for the French Revolution began to challenge that would-be nationalist consensus. To put it this way, however, presupposes conflicts that developed only gradually, in response to domestic and international events. Until 1793 very few American patriots saw a conflict between toasting the Rights of Man and lauding their own great Revolutionary hero. Even as they downplayed the radicalism of their own Revolution, July Fourth orators also praised the French for their reasonable revolt.

The French, said Philadelphian Robert Porter, were lucky to have a patriot king—and the American blueprint. "France has not only profited by our example, but the Old World bids fair to be regenerated by the New. The renovation of Great Britain herself does not appear far distant." On the eighth anniversary of the evacuation of British troops from New York (November 25, 1791), the Tammany Society toasted "Those heroes of France whose patriotic virtues have caused the Columbian flame to consume the Gallic yoke of despotism." Instead of paying back war debts now a decade old, Americans had given their French allies a more lasting gift: the love of liberty. "We love the French," preached Joseph Eckley before Boston's Ancient and Honorable Artillery Company. "It is the debt of gratitude, for they loved us." He went on to praise the internationalism of the age of democratic nationalist revolutions:

27. Quoted in Griswold, *The Republican Court,* 339.

The time is come when . . . the sons of freedom, in whatever place they dwell, are viewed as *brethren*. We have lived to see the world in mighty motion—combinations forming to relieve the oppressed and set the sons of Afric free . . . and whilst many *are running to and fro, knowledge is increasing.*

The frenetic pace of change (elsewhere and later seen as dangerous) was first interpreted as a harbinger of the coming political millennium. As such, it fitted perfectly the dominant mode of thinking about American history. The Fourth of July might even emerge as "the common jubilee of mankind!"[28]

As David Brion Davis has observed, Americans "had a compelling ideological interest in seeing France transformed." The French Revolution completed the transfer of liberty from old England to young America. Freedom and civilization now moved eastward, reversing the previous course. An approving European gaze confirmed America's own transformation. Even conservative nationalists could join in the French universalist appeal, given America's key role in the new republican world. It would not be the last time that Americans simultaneously sought empire and world peace. Free trade, after all, would civilize the

28. Robert Porter, *An Oration, to Commemorate the Independence of the United States of North-America* . . . (Philadelphia, 1791), 17; see also William Smith, *A Sermon, on Temporal and Spiritual Salvation: Delivered in Christ-Church, Philadelphia* . . . (Philadelphia, 1790); Thomas Crafts, Jr., *An Oration, Pronounced July 4th, 1791* . . . (Boston, [1791]); John Quincy Adams, *An Oration, Pronounced July 4, 1793* . . . (Boston, 1793); John Mercer, *An Oration Delivered on the Fourth of July, 1792* . . . (Richmond, Va., [1792]); Theodore Dwight, *An Oration, Spoken before the Society of the Cincinnati* . . . (Hartford, Conn., 1792).

New York and Boston: New York City Society of Tammany or Columbian Order, Committee of Amusements, Minutes, 1791–1795, 4–5, New York Public Library; Joseph Eckley, *A Sermon, Preached at the Request of the Ancient and Honorable Artillery Company, June 4, 1792: Being the Anniversary of Their Election of Officers* (Boston, 1792), 19; Gray, *An Oration, Delivered July 5, 1790*, 16. Edward Bangs, who had demoted political jealousy to a necessary evil and who depicted newspaper reading as leisure rather than as public vigilance, praised "the Art of Printing" for enlightening the French; see note 10, above.

The best discussions of Francophilic millennialism in the 1790s are Ruth H. Bloch, *Visionary Republic: Millennial Themes in American Thought, 1756–1800* (New York, 1985), 150–201; and Davis, *Revolutions*, chap. 2.

world, enriching everyone. Inspiring this new world order, America could hardly but be a force for regeneration and freedom.[29]

For economic reasons alone American newspapers would have bulged with reports of European events. But the French Revolution had a worth that would not be contained by the cash nexus. Even congressional debates about commercial policy never detached themselves from the Age of Revolution's great social and political question: aristocracy versus equality. By 1792, the new opposition press linked the celebration of July Fourth and the French Revolution; in Philadelphia, a rained-out fireworks display was rescheduled for July 14—Bastille Day. "On this day," suggested Freneau's *National Gazette,* "it is expected, there will, in the future, be a general rejoicing in every part of the United States, *by all* who are Friends to the French Revolution, and consequently *real friends* to the revolution in America." Toasts given at Bastille Day festivals from Charleston to Carlisle proved that "the republican spirit is very fast rising in this country."[30]

By "republican spirit" the *National Gazette* meant much more than republican government. It meant what was expressed in the toasts of a Vermont militia company: "May the American states be long defended from the inundation which is threatened by the increase of aristocrats, who wish for a rich metropolis and a poor peasantry; want a great personage's head on the current coin; and are advocates for keeping shut the doors of the Senate." Bank scandals and an economic slump made Federalist economic nationalists particularly vulnerable to being portrayed as self-interested aristocrats.[31] And the all too real efforts of governing men to raise themselves above public opinion provoked loud and pointed objections.

Such resentments were easily expressible in the new French (and older Anglo-American) language of equality. With the help of an

29. Davis, *Revolutions,* chap. 2. My understanding of the post-Revolutionary paradigm for looking at the world is also influenced by Felix Gilbert, *To the Farewell Address: Ideas of Early American Foreign Policy* (Princeton, N.J., 1961); James H. Hutson, *John Adams and the Diplomacy of the American Revolution* (Lexington, Ky., 1980).

30. *National Gazette* (Philadelphia), July 7, 18, 28, Aug. 1, 1792; *General Advertiser and Political, Commercial, and Literary Journal* (Philadelphia), July 4, 19, 21, 23, Aug. 1, 1792. On the press and the French Revolution, see Donald H. Stewart, *The Opposition Press of the Federalist Period* (Albany, N.Y., 1969); James Tagg, *Benjamin Franklin Bache and the Philadelphia "Aurora"* (Philadelphia, 1991).

31. *National Gazette* (Philadelphia), July 7, 1792; John Zvesper, *Political Philosophy and Rhetoric: A Study of the Origins of American Party Politics* (Cambridge, 1977), 79–83.

increasing number of English and Irish political exiles and French refugees and consuls, nascent Jeffersonians developed a politics of celebration that linked American nationalism to the ideals of an international democratic revolution. Precisely because the extent of America's democratic transformation remained unclear, the French Revolution addressed the insecure achievements of the American Revolution, providing a language for rekindling, or securely ending, that struggle. When the French and British went to war and British ships began to attack American vessels, interest and ideology merged so beautifully that American Francophiles celebrated French military victories as American national holidays. French émigrés and diplomats did honor to the Franco-American alliance, the Fourth of July, and Washington's Birthday with the requisite (by then) fifteen toasts; after the French victory at Valmy, republicans improvised a profusion of "civic feasts." Liberty poles came back into vogue; caps of liberty made the rounds with toasts. The French sansculottes were even elevated to the ranks of the "sanssouliers," the shoeless of Valley Forge.[32]

These celebrations were surely partisan: they helped mobilize the first national opposition party. By 1794, urban Federalists and Republicans celebrated the Fourth of July separately. Yet we lose something of the character of these events if we emphasize only their importance in the creation of partisan subcultures. Like earlier nationalist celebrations, the new civic festivals were attempts to take over public space and create unanimity—often precisely in the act of defining the political other. That is, they aspired to nonpartisanship, defining Francophobia (cum Anglophilia) as outside the circle of true Americanism.

In 1793–1794, much as in 1788, political discourse exploded in

32. *Fête civique célébrée par les patriotes français, américains et hollandais* . . . (Philadelphia, 1795); *Relation de l'anniversaire de la fédération du 14 juillet 1789, célébrée à Charleston* (Charleston, S.C., 1795); *Columbia Gazette* (S.C.), Aug. 1, 1794; Michael L. Kennedy, "A French Jacobin Club in Charleston, South Carolina, 1792–1795," *South Carolina Historical Magazine*, XCI (1990), 17–19; Edward C. Carter II, "A 'Wild Irishman' under Every Federalist's Bed: Naturalization in Philadelphia, 1789–1806," *Pennsylvania Magazine of History and Biography*, XCIV (1970), 331–346; Michael Durey, "Transatlantic Patriotism: Political Exiles and America in the Age of Revolutions," in Clive Elmsley and James Walvin, eds., *Artisans, Peasants, and Proletarians, 1760–1860: Essays Presented to Gwyn A. Williams* (London, 1985), 7–31; *Dunlap and Claypoole's American Daily Advertiser* (Philadelphia), July 6, 8, 1793, July 14, 26, 1794. The best analysis of celebrations of the French Revolution is Newman, *Parades and the Politics of the Street*, chap. 5.

conjunction with innovations in celebration. Toasts were published in unprecedented numbers by the pro-French papers; some printed July Fourth toasts as domestic news well into the month of August. The same forms that revealed the political diversity of cities, however, tended to portray the unity, and probably compromises, in the countryside. The very ubiquity of toasts demonstrated how easily, as a celebrant from Upper Marlboro, Maryland, put it, "the sentiments of the most numerous and the most respectable part of the country are collected and expressed with openness and freedom." This assertion of confidence in the representativeness of published toasts compensated rhetorically for "the smallness of our party" in Upper Marlboro and "enabled the ladies to join in the celebration."[33]

Numerous and respectable in the presence of women: these are familiar juxtapositions. Republican-style national celebration mobilized greater numbers of men and women even as it retained Federalist standards of order, unanimity, and respectability. At a Boston celebration of French victory, "the spirit of real liberty" itself, "uncontaminated with any monarchical or aristocratical sentiments, operated as 'checks and balances' to keep up the order, hilarity, and good humor of the day." The Democratic-Republicans saw themselves above all as true patriots, bearers of Revolutionary legacy. They tapped the antiaristocratic element of Revolutionary ideology, calling each other "citizen" and electing a temporary "president" for the festive day. Their style, however, was also that of 1788, as they joined other "TRUE REPUBLICANS" for "sentimental, patriotic, republican toasts."[34]

American nationalists who sang "Ça ira" and expanded the celebratory calendar were as much in the tradition of revolutionary (that is, Anglo-American) political culture as their Anglophile opponents, and, if we emphasize participation, perhaps more so. Their toasts themselves grew longer and longer, the signs of affiliation (like the Revolutionary cockades they wore) becoming more and more visible. Indeed, the re-

33. *Dunlap and Claypoole's American Daily Advertiser* (Philadelphia), July 26, 1794.

34. *General Advertiser* (Philadelphia), Feb. 12, 1793, "American National Cockade," May 1, 1793; Alfred F. Young, *The Democratic Republicans of New York: The Origins, 1763–1797* (Chapel Hill, N.C., 1967), esp. 356–365, 374–375; Philip S. Foner, ed., *The Democratic-Republican Societies, 1790–1800: A Documentary Sourcebook of Constitutions, Declarations, Addresses, Resolutions, and Toasts* (Westport, Conn., 1976); *Dunlap and Claypoole's American Daily Advertiser* (Philadelphia), July 17, 25, 26, 1794; *Centinel of the North-Western Territory* (Cincinnati), July 18, 1794.

publicans of the 1790s made visibility itself a primary republican virtue.

Republicans had long associated aristocracy with secrecy.[35] Anti-federalists' first criticism of the Constitution had been of the framers' secret meetings. To rigorous republicans, the closed proceedings of the Senate and the guarded secrecy of the Washington cabinet gave ample cause for concern about republicanism's fate in America. Taking pen names like "Mirabeau," "Sidney," and "Equality," they lambasted "lev[e]es, birth-day rejoicings, a seclusion of the first magistrate from the people" as antirepublican. Washington's invitation-only levees, they maintained, were frequented only by fortune hunters; celebrants of his birthday practiced gross sycophancy. "Sidney" suggested that Washington should visit taverns to get the true sentiments of the people.[36] These critics of "monarchical" manners saw a dangerous distance between "We the People" and the federal government. Worse, the Federalists in power seemed to be doing everything they could to widen the breach.

It was this breach that clubs like the Democratic-Republican societies aimed to fill. They based their very existence upon the difference of opinion between the nation and the government.[37] The most important issue on which they differed, of course, was foreign affairs. Given the importance of the French Revolution to so many, this hardly seemed like a narrow base for organization. The Democratic-Republican societies took the French Jacobin clubs as their inspiration,

35. Gordon S. Wood, "Conspiracy and the Paranoid Style: Causality and Deceit in the Eighteenth Century," *WMQ*, 3d Ser., XLIX (1982), 401–441; Hunt, *Family Romance*. An essayist in 1793 complained of those who remain silent in company, accusing them of seeking to profit by not sharing in the openness and frankness. In "our evening clubs, careless of *equality*," such persons "voluntarily become passive and silent subjects, permitting the despot to dictate and decide." Contributing to conversation was, in effect, "a tax you must pay in society." See *Eagle; or Dartmouth Centinel* (Hanover, N.H.), Oct. 21, 1793.

36. *General Advertiser* (Philadelphia), Jan. 21, 31, Feb. 4, 5, 1793; "A Republican," *Greenleaf's New York Journal, and Patriotic Register*, Feb. 18, 1795.

37. Phineas Hedges, *An Oration, Delivered before the Republican Society, of Ulster County, and Other Citizens . . . the 4th of July, 1795* (Goshen, N.Y., 1795), 11–15. On the Democratic-Republican societies, see Eugene Perry Link, *Democratic Republican Societies, 1790–1800* (1940; rpt. New York, 1973); Philip S. Foner, "Introduction," in Foner, ed., *Democratic-Republican Societies: A Documentary Sourcebook*, 3–40; Young, *Democratic-Republicans of New York*, chap. 18; Alan Lee Blau, "New York City and the French Revolution, 1789–1797: A Study of French Revolutionary Influence" (Ph.D. diss., City University of New York, 1973), 266–267, 278, 373–374.

and in many ways, including the profile of their members (professional men as leaders, artisans and middling sorts as followers), that comparison holds. Yet these avid American associationists also had the model of their own Revolutionary committees of correspondence. Organizing public meetings, drafting resolves, planning large-scale celebrations, and holding public dinners, the Democratic-Republican clubs sought to act as intermediaries between a political elite and a larger local citizenry.[38]

What really stands out about the societies that proliferated all over the country between 1793 and 1795 is their use of the press and their nationalism. With published statements, local Democratic societies addressed not only their own towns or counties but also the "citizens of America." Their festivals and meetings produced descriptions of themselves along with requests for the "republican printers" all over the United States to reproduce their toasts and resolves—something that was generally done. Little wonder that these clubs so disturbed the Federalists. Their activities had the potential to reinvent national citizenship on a much more active plane. Moreover, the publication of their resolves threatened to turn the local newspapers into the real loci of national character, making the federal government just another interested party bidding for legitimacy and column space. "Deny the continuance of your confidence to such members of the legislative body as have an interest distinct from that of the people," urged the Republican Society of Wythe County, Virginia. Devoting themselves to the spread of political information, the societies presented themselves as the conduit of the people's voice and, as such, the closest thing to its embodiment. Employing petitions, dinners, and accounts of all of these, theirs was a competing technology of nationalism, visible and local yet always national, that could not be legitimate if the federal government was to remain identified with the people.[39]

38. For an example of Democratic-Republican society members' calling themselves "Jacobin clubs," see *General Advertiser* (Philadelphia), July 5, 1794. The question of influence is ultimately less important than the structural and ideological conundrums that different European regimes shared but that were playing out differently in each country partly because of these nations' often stormy relations with each other. See R. R. Palmer's classic *The Age of the Democratic Revolutions: A Political History of Europe and America, 1760–1800*, 2 vols. (Princeton, N.J., 1959–1964).

39. Republican Society of South Carolina, *Charleston, August, 1793: Fellow Citizens* . . . [Charleston, S.C., 1793]; Minutes of the Democratic Society of Pennsylvania, transcript [1793–1794], Historical Society of Pennsylvania, Philadelphia;

In this context, the famous journey of the new French ambassador Edmond-Charles Genêt from Charleston to Philadelphia no longer appears as the foolish conceit of a rakish, naive diplomat. It was, rather, a striking intervention on the part of those who *received* him. Genêt certainly traveled over land rather than by water in order to sway American opinion against official neutrality and in favor of France. Harry Ammon persuasively argues that Genêt misunderstood his warm reception in a way that was fatal to his mission: the populace and even their leaders could love Genêt to death and still remain officially neutral.[40] The same dichotomy between rhetorical and real policy made it possible for Washington to wish the French well even as he moved toward a treaty with Great Britain. Yet the festivals for Genêt have never really been considered for what they meant to the people who made them happen. Genêt's trip north was the mirror image of Washington's sentimental journeys: it made manifest what was only latent in the president's tours. It enabled "the people" to celebrate themselves and their participation in national politics. It seemed to make ordinary Americans into makers of foreign policy.

If the people came to Washington, Genêt went to the people. Where Washington politely inquired of local informed opinion, Genêt, by his own account, was bombarded by the vox populi. The diplomat never understood the later charge that, after being rebuffed in his search for more material aid from the United States government, he had threatened to "appeal to the people" over the head of the chief magistrate. He did not understand because he had not changed his style since arriving. "In every place the general voice of the people convinced me, in a most sensible manner, of their real sentiments," he wrote to the Philadelphia welcoming committee. Well before he made it to the capital

General Advertiser (Philadelphia), Aug. 1, 1794. Here I disagree in part with James Roger Sharp's assessment of the societies as exemplifying a "grass-roots" localism that opposed the elite brand of national (for Sharp, really sectional) partisanship. It would be just as accurate to say that the Democratic societies were grass-roots nationalists. See Sharp, *American Politics in the Early Republic*, 85–88, 90–91, 112.

40. Harry Ammon, *The Genet Mission* (New York, 1973). Other useful accounts of the mission and its political context include Meade Minnigerode, *Jefferson, Friend of France, 1793: The Career of Edmond Charles Genet* (New York, 1928); Dumas Malone, *Jefferson and the Ordeal of Liberty,* vol. III of *Jefferson and His Time* (Boston, 1962), 90–131; Alexander DeConde, *Entangling Alliance: Politics and Diplomacy under George Washington* (Durham, N.C., 1958); Stanley Elkins and Eric McKitrick, *The Age of Federalism: The Early American Republic, 1788–1800* (New York, 1993), 330–373.

city, Genêt had discovered that Americans shared the same sentimental language that was supposed to be *the* universal language. He won praise for promising to be equally transparent: "An unbounded openness shall be the constant rule of my intercourse with those wise and virtuous men into whose hands you have entrusted the management of your public affairs." He promised to be an emissary of emotion between the French nation and the Americans who addressed him:

> I cannot express how much your address has excited my sensibility.—
> I shall make your sentiments known to my fellow citizens, and no doubt they will receive, with the most lively marks of sensibility the good wishes you have expressed for the success of their arms and the extension of their principles.[41]

Genêt did not exaggerate when he wrote home from Philadelphia: "I live here in the midst of perpetual fetes. I receive addresses from all over the country." The *National Gazette* delighted in the "friendly and polite" manner in which he received Philadelphia's welcoming committee. And, according to a Philadelphia woman who wrote a widely reprinted letter, Genêt "was quite overcome with the affectionate joy that appeared on every face." His arrival made it possible once again to separate the truly affectionate from the false patriots: "It is true that a few disaffected persons did try to check the ardor of the people, but they had the mortification to find all their efforts blasted and were

---

41. *General Advertiser* (Philadelphia), May 17, 1793. Genêt's language was echoed back to him months later by Aedanus Burke, who wrote, "Although your progress was rapid, yet bearing as you did, the public character of your nation, but also that of its Republicanism, this together with the energy of your own spirit by a sort of electrical transmission of kindred impulse, rekindled in us the honest, ardent feelings of 1776." Aedanus Burke to Citizen Genêt, Feb. 16, 1794, in *Washington, Jefferson, and "Citizen" Genet, 1793: A Set of Sevres China* (n.p., n.d.), pamphlet on deposit in the Edmond Charles Genêt Papers, Albany Institute of History and Art. On Genêt's later response to the charge of appealing to the people, see Genêt to Washington, Aug. 24, 1793, in *Washington, Jefferson, and "Citizen" Genet*. On September 18 Genêt wrote to Jefferson: "It was not in my character to speak, as many people do, in one way and act in another—to have an official language and a confidential language" (in Minnigerode, *Jefferson, Friend of France*, 339–340). Compare his evaluation of Washington: "He is extremely reserved, that is his hypocrisy; he is easy to approach, but in reality he is haughty" (209). Whether this was actually true seems less important than the widely shared desires and fears to which such pronouncements responded.

themselves obliged to join the general torrent and affect a cordiality . . . contrary to the feelings of their hearts."[42]

A more official reception a few days later gave citizens and Genêt a chance to perfect this exchange of true sentiment. Genêt asked whether he could offer some "spontaneous effusions of his heart, which, however deficient in point of form, would not be deficient in point of sincerity." Not surprisingly, his peroration "touched the feelings of every auditor": "I will declare openly and freely, for the minister of a republic should have no *secrets,* no intrigue." Genêt professed pure freedom: he did not want to ensnare the Americans in war; he only asked for aid in the French republic's distress. Upon finishing, Genêt went to a window and expressed his joy to the crowd, concluding with the ultimate American celebratory chant: "God save the United States!"[43]

Stealing a page from the Federalists' book, the Jeffersonian leaders and crowds who organized, attended, and then described these events were creating a political culture whose most defining events were spectacular, sentimental, and above all celebratory. "The genuine display of affection for the cause of France, by the citizens, on the arrival of the minister, has once more banished aristocracy, and hailed equality triumphant," insisted "An Old Soldier."

> The bosoms of many hundred freemen beat high with affectionate transport, their souls caught the celestial fire of struggling liberty, and in the enthusiasm of emotion, they communicated their feelings to the worthy and amicable representative of the French nation. What a delicious repast for a mind interested in the cause of humanity!

42. Genêt to Minister of Foreign Affairs, May 31, 1793, in Frederick J. Turner, ed., "Correspondence of the French Ministers to the United States, 1791–1797," *American Historical Association, Annual Report,* 1903 (Washington, D.C., 1904), II, 216; *National Gazette* (Philadelphia), May 18, 1793; *Connecticut Gazette* (New London), June 20, 1793, cited in Claude G. Bowers, *Jefferson and Hamilton: The Struggle for Democracy in America* (Boston, 1925), 219. It is interesting to note that Genêt spoke of his reception as fraternal (the key egalitarian trope of the French Revolution) and occasionally as *paternal* (see his Sept. 5, 1793, letter to William Moultrie in the *Delaware Gazette* [Wilmington], Nov. 23, 1793). If Genêt, whose youth was often noted, did present himself as a son of the American revolutionaries, this can be seen as another way in which he tried but ultimately failed to adopt the terms of the Washington cult, only to become the rebellious son and the prototypical foreign and ideological other.

43. *General Advertiser* (Philadelphia), May 17, 1793.

The exalted feelings experienced by true patriots are compared to a festive meal, at which spectatorship is a political act revealing the true virtue of one "interested in the cause of humanity." In contrast, this writer ridiculed the city merchants' procession to Washington's house with their proneutrality address as "royal folly," an insult to the citizens whose presence alone could make a demonstration of sentiments impressive. The Federalists responded with public meetings endorsing neutrality, but to do so reinforced the role of public opinion in foreign affairs. As the citizens of Savannah observed, just as it had been their privilege to express their opinion of Genêt, so they made it their prerogative to applaud the actions of their president.[44]

In the long run the extension of scrutiny only redoubled the intrigues of foreign and domestic ministers. The Democratic-Republican dream of transparency and sincerity in public life was an ideal whose real referent lay in the opening of politics to public view, the rise of public opinion. Public opinion as an ideal did not depend upon universal or even active participation, but it did leave anyone who invoked it vulnerable to standards of proof (admittedly vague). Where and when had "the people" expressed themselves? Had the nation really spoken? In the 1790s the most popular and participatory political practices, such as public meetings, were inherently the most parochial, the least national. The people could truly be embodied only where they could actually be *seen*. Democratic-Republicans truly believed in "principles not men," but their nationalist rhetoric tended to overstep their relatively egalitarian political practices, which had to remain local even when accompanied by widely reprinted appeals to the nation.

The process suffered from its own transparency. Having appropriated the politics of visible virtue, Republicans too could be accused of vanity. Thus the Federalists' critique of "self-created societies" hit them at their weakest spot. Jesse Appleton, a school instructor who later became president of Bowdoin College, wrote to a friend: "How ever they may arrogate to themselves the appelation of Democratic, is it not plain, beyond contradiction, that their tendency, is aristocratical? For what is aristocracy, but, for a few to engross the power of the whole?" In 1795

44. *National Gazette* (Philadelphia), May 22, 1793; *Southern Centinel, and Gazette of the State* (Augusta), Jan. 30, 1794; *Notice: Citizen Genet, Minister Plenipotentiary . . . Being Shortly Expected in This City . . .* (New York, 1793); Edmond Genêt to John Barber, July 13, 1793, James Nelson Barber Papers, AAS.

Dunlap's Philadelphia paper printed far fewer Fourth of July accounts; some that did appear voiced doubts about the celebratory mode:

> Toasts at public entertainments are said to be indicative of the public sentiment. This is true to a degree; but when two societies composed mostly of the same men, toast each other, it is simply a proof of self-esteem.

Such celebrants, "many of them young and inexperienced persons," forgot that "no partial collection of men, or small portion of them, is the People or Nation."[45] Making a spectacle of the condemnation of aristocracy could make one an aristocrat of sorts.

For all its limitations, what Federalists derided as the "Gallo-American" politics of celebrations, meetings, and petitions served the opposition extremely well. When the execution of Louis XVI or even the Terror brought criticism, republicans pointed to the democratic ideals behind the structures, the liberating cause behind the reigning French government—a move oddly consistent with their approach to politics at home, which viewed policy questions in light of the requirements of revolutionary republican culture. Events like the new French constitution and the (alleged) liberation of the Netherlands proved that the disorders of the Revolution were natural and would pass in time. Ultimately, domestic politics, and its need for nationally as well as locally useful ways to express differences, determined both Jeffersonian and Federalist responses to the French Revolution. How else could diehard Jeffersonian slaveholders have still been toasting the Rights of Man (and Napoleon) in 1797?[46]

45. *Gazette of the United States and Daily Evening Advertiser* (Philadelphia), July 8, 1794; Zvesper, *Political Philosophy and Rhetoric*, 14; Brooke, "Ancient Lodges and Self-Created Societies," in Hoffman and Albert, eds., *Launching the "Extended Republic,"* 273–377; "Of Democratic Societies," *Gazette of the United States,* July 8, 1794; Fisher Ames, "Against Jacobins," in Seth Ames, ed., *Works of Fisher Ames (1854),* ed. W. B. Allen (Indianapolis, Ind., 1983), II, 975; Jesse Appleton to Ebenezer Adams, May 4, 1795. Jesse Appleton Letters, AAS; *Dunlap and Claypoole's American Daily Advertiser* (Philadelphia), July 14, 1794, July 11, 1795.

46. In my reading of newspaper commentary and celebratory orations I have noticed two strategies for dealing with the problem of the Terror from 1794 to 1797. One was to describe it as temporary delirium; the other was to divide the virtuous (though sometimes ignorant) French people from the mistaken government, or from Paris. For an example of the latter, see Joseph Allen, *An Oration, Pronounced*

In 1795, opposition to the Jay Treaty reinvigorated the opposition's celebrations even as debate raged over the patriotism and loyalty of the Democratic societies. "The best celebration of the Fourth of July was to burn Jay's effigy and his treaty," wrote Dr. Nathaniel Ames in his diary, and people from Philadelphia to Fredericksburg agreed. In Charleston a crowd dragged a British flag through the dirt to the tune of "Yankee Doodle." "We last evening witnessed that a mob could exist without a riot," insisted a paper in that city. The treaty would be burned by the public executioner, at the behest of "citizens alarmed with fear for the dignity of the national character." When their predictions of a shameful British alliance emerging from secret proceedings actually came true, Jeffersonians seized the chance to return to 1776—or even 1765. One Philadelphia paper printed a death notice for Mrs. Liberty, the former "consort of America," predicting that the authorities would rejoice while real patriots mourned.[47]

This was only prelude to what happened in Philadelphia that evening and the nationwide commentary it spawned. With "funeral solemnity," approximately five hundred artisans proceeded with an effigy and cart from Kensington to the center of the city and back. The figure of the

---

at Worcester . . . July 4, 1795 (Worcester, Mass., 1795), 9–10; for the former, William [Loughton] Smith, *An Oration, Delivered in St. Philip's Church, before the Inhabitants of Charleston, South-Carolina, on the Fourth of July, 1796* . . . (Charleston, S.C., 1796), 25; Samuel Whiting, *An Oration . . . at Sheffield, July 4th, 1796* (Stockbridge, Mass., 1796), 11–13.

Not until 1798 did most Fourth of July orators distance the American Revolution from the French Revolution. See Charles H. Atherton, *An Oration, Pronounced in the First Parish at Amherst, N. H.* . . . (Amherst, N.H., 1798); Alpheus Moore, *An Oration, Pronounced at Westmoreland* . . . (Walpole, N.H., 1798); Thomas S[tearns] Sparhawk, *An Oration, Delivered at Buckston* . . . (Boston, 1798); Henry William De-Saussure, *An Oration, Prepared, to Be Delivered in St. Philip's Church* . . . (Charleston, S.C., 1798). That year, patently Republican orators avoided the whole topic of France: cf. Geo[rge] Clinton, Jr., *An Oration, Delivered on the Fourth of July, 1798* . . . (New York, 1798). The clergy is a special case, which I will discuss in the next section. The best discussion of American responses to the French Revolution, and one that informs my analysis, is Davis, *Revolutions*, chap. 2.

47. Charles Warren, *Jacobin and Junto; or, Early American Politics as Viewed in the Diary of Dr. Nathaniel Ames, 1758–1822* (Cambridge, Mass., 1932), 59–64; *Dunlap and Claypoole's American Daily Advertiser* (Philadelphia), July 27, 1795; *Federal Intelligencer, and Baltimore Daily Gazette*, July 25, 1795; Rachel N. Klein, *The Unification of a Slave State: The Rise of the Planter Class in the South Carolina Backcountry, 1760–1808* (Chapel Hill, N.C., 1990), 219–220; Stewart, *Opposition Press*, 199–201, 215–221.

former Supreme Court justice and now ambassador Jay carried scales, the side with "British gold" outweighing the one piled with "virtue, liberty, independence." At some point a private militia company ordered the procession to halt; the crowd drove it off with clubs and stones. "Never was a procession more peacefully conducted, no noise, no riot," reported Philadelphia's *Independent Gazetteer.* "The citizens seemed to vie with each other in decorous behaviour."[48]

While seemingly just reenacting the rituals of revolution, these Philadelphians remained at the forefront of popular politics. For weeks editors and correspondents debated whether (and which) city residents had rejoiced or mourned on July Fourth and whether this effigy burning had been orderly or riotous. The extralocal reverberations of these celebrations and anticelebrations in print culture (what a literary critic might call the textualization of politics) does not seem to have reduced anyone's sense of engagement or the relevance of what happened in the streets. If anything, it increased the popularity of popular politics, so much so that Federalists adopted similar strategies, holding meetings and dinners and then reprinting toasts they considered favorable, even when locals mixed praise for John Jay with the cap of liberty and a tribute to the "Republican Trio, America, France and Holland."[49]

Urban-national editors like Fenno and Bache disputed each other's accounts of celebrations, respectively ignored or satirized the recognition of French victories and February 22, and tried to prove the true "federalism" or "republicanism" of the Fourth of July. But we err if we see public life and the nature of celebration solely through their eyes. Polarization and the profusion of symbols spurred confusion and syncretization as well as confirmation of partisan beliefs. Antipartyism exerted a strong centralizing appeal, as did the need to compromise in order to celebrate and publicize convincingly. On July 4, 1796, for example, a group of Marylanders either did not see or deliberately ignored the contradiction in toasting both "true Republicans" and "George Washington: may the day of his nativity be marked in the calendar of time . . . and celebrated to the last ages." Publishers Benjamin

48. *Aurora* (Philadelphia), July 9, 1795 (from *Gazetteer*); *Norwich Packet* (Conn.), July 17, 1795; *Lynchburg and Farmer's Gazette* (Va.), July 25, 1795; Elaine Forman Crane, ed., *The Diary of Elizabeth Drinker* (Boston, 1991), I, 700–701.

49. *Otsego Herald* (Cooperstown, N.Y.), July 17, 24, 1795; *Greenleaf's New York Journal,* July 8, 11, 1795; *Gazette of the United States* (Philadelphia), July 10, 17, 1795; Jacob Hiltzheimer Diaries, July 4, 5, 9, 1795, APS.

Franklin Bache in Philadelphia and Thomas Greenleaf in New York, the entrepreneurs of print and politics who did the most to popularize the French Revolution, brought out republican revolutionary songbooks and calendars; William Cobbett, the British émigré who wrote as Peter Porcupine, brilliantly mocked the whole trend as foreign. Yet the more activity their efforts inspired, the less control these editors exerted over celebrations and their representation.[50]

☆ ☆ ☆

If Federalists prided themselves on their more decorous celebrations and their less moblike meetings, they could not so easily resolve the difficulty in identifying the federal state with nation and the people. More and more, they sought to unify the two by posing both state and nation against class and sectional others (or the two together). Republicans were really an alliance of the unrespectable lower sorts and the truly aristocratic southern slaveholders. These accusations were sometimes difficult for Republicans to answer, since they contained more than a grain of truth. In a strategy that grew out of their attack on the Democratic societies, Federalists also questioned the existence and relevance of local majorities. A writer in Connecticut's *Phenix, or, Windham Herald* insisted that the urban participants in the major anti–Jay Treaty meetings constituted only a small fraction of the total population. An editor of New York's *American Minerva* (probably Noah Webster) preached three theses on this theme:

> The constituted authorities of the country are the only organs of the national will.—What is done by them is an act of the nation as body politic.
>
> The citizens of New-York, Boston, Philadelphia etc. are not the nation.—Their voice is the voice of individuals only.
>
> Every attempt of towns or small bodies of men to influence the

50. [Andrew Beers], *Glori Greenleaf's New-York, Connecticut, and New-Jersey Almanack . . . for . . . 1792* (New York, 1792); *Republican Prayers* (New York, 1796); *Calendrier republicain pour l'an VI* (Philadelphia, [1798]); *The Nightingale of Liberty . . .* (New York, 1797); *The Democratic Songster: Being a Collection of the Newest and Most Admired Republican Songs, Interspersed with Many Originals, to Which Is Added, Some of the Most Admired French Airs* (Baltimore, 1794); Peter Porcupine, *A Bone to Gnaw, for the Democrats . . .* (Philadelphia:, 1795); Porcupine, *History of the American Jacobins, Commonly Denominated Democrats* (Philadelphia, 1796), 13–46; [John Lowell], *The Antigallican; or, The Lover of His Own Country . . .* (Philadelphia, 1797), 17.

representatives of the nation, is an attempt to make a part govern the whole.

A response in Bache's *Aurora* did not deny the first two statements. It objected strongly to the third, noting that this would deny the right of people (not to mention "the people") to express themselves.[51]

In the clamor of voices seeking to represent "the people," America's "rites of assent" remained fruitful sites of contest.[52] The "nation" lay suspended between a millennial ideal with pro-French and egalitarian resonances, and a federal state itself divided among a "neutral" Washington, a pro-British ministry, and an ambiguously situated bicameral legislature. This was a conflict among nationalists who agreed and disagreed. Its temporary resolution began to emerge in a debate over national character itself.

NATIONAL CHARACTER: IDEOLOGY, THEOLOGY, PRACTICE

"National Character" was a way of understanding the relationship between the citizen, or national subject, and the state, or national government. As a concept it already had a long and complex history, including discussions of the "body politic" as well as attempts by travel writers to describe the characteristics of nations and their peoples. Indeed, "national character" brought these intellectual traditions together. Within its aura, individuals could be understood in the light of national culture, and the state could be anthropomorphosed into an individual with a body, a psychology, and a reputation in the world.[53]

If we try too hard to uncover the metaphysics of national identity, we become prisoners of it, as students of national character often have.

51. *Phenix; or, Windham Herald* (Conn.), Aug. 8, 1795; *Aurora; General Advertiser* (Philadelphia), Aug. 1, 1795.

52. For an assessment of the "rites of assent" as spawning conflict only to contain it within an "American ideology," see the essays in Sacvan Bercovitch, *The Rites of Assent: Transformations in the Symbolic Construction of America* (New York, 1993).

53. Richard Helgerson, *Forms of Nationhood: The Elizabethan Writing of England* (Chicago, 1992), 107–191; Lauren Berlant, *The Anatomy of National Fantasy: Hawthorne, Utopia, and Everyday Life* (Chicago, 1991), 3, 20–24. The best way to describe the *use* of "national character" in the 1790s might be to call it an ideologeme, which Fredric Jameson describes as the smallest unit in an ideological struggle, "susceptible to both a conceptual description and a narrative manifestation all at once" (*The Political Unconscious: Narrative as a Socially Symbolic Act* [Ithaca, N.Y., 1981], 87–88).

We lose sight of the histories, global and local, of which the nation is only a part. Here it is less important to theorize some timeless structure of national identity than to uncover its uses in particular moments and movements. In doing so it is helpful to remember that the "the nation" is never just an idea or a thing; it is also a story, an encompassing narrative or set of competing narratives with the potential to crowd out other narratives that may have rather different political implications. National character took its form from contemporary narrative conventions. Thus nationalist ideology suggested not only identification but a script or course of action. At the time of the Revolution, patriots like Thomas Paine compared the rebellious colonies to a child or youth with abusive parents: he needed to rebel, to leave the home, in order to establish a real character.[54] With Independence established, participants all along the political spectrum took it for granted that America was a young nation whose character was still in formation. The Constitution and the success of republicanism abroad held out fine prospects in this nationalist bildungsroman, but the participants could not guarantee that the young (male) innocent would overcome domestic quarrels and the perils of his necessary journeys into the threatening world beyond.

During the Jay Treaty crisis the Democratic-Republicans seized upon the trope of the young man of untried character, fusing it with several celebratory subgenres. A mock funeral notice, "Death of Independence," took up the conventions of the family romance to describe the

54. Thomas Paine, *Common Sense* (1776), ed. Isaac Kramnick (New York, 1976); Edwin G. Burrows and Michael Wallace, "The American Revolution: The Ideology and Psychology of National Liberation," *Perspectives in American History,* VI (1972), 167–306. A large literature interprets the Revolution as the revolt of children or young men. See Stanley Elkins and Eric McKitrick, "The Founding Fathers: Young Men of the Revolution," *Political Science Quarterly,* LXXVI (1961), 181–216; James Kirby Martin, *Men in Rebellion: Higher Governmental Leaders and the Coming of the American Revolution* (New Brunswick, N.J., 1973); Kenneth S. Lynn, *A Divided People* (Westport, Conn., 1977); Peter Shaw, *American Patriots and the Rituals of Revolution* (Cambridge, Mass., 1981); Melvin C. Yazawa, *From Colonies to Commonwealth: Familial Ideology and the Beginnings of the American Republic* (Baltimore, 1985); Peter Charles Hoffer, *Revolution and Regeneration: Life Cycle and the Historical Vision of the Generation of 1776* (Athens, Ga., 1983). Carroll Smith-Rosenberg gives an alternative account of the construction of the national subject against gendered and racial others in "Dis-Covering the Subject of the 'Great Constitutional Discussion,' 1786–1789," *Journal of American History,* LXXIX (1992–1993), 841–873.

danger of a British alliance to the "extraordinary man" born in Philadelphia on July 4, 1776. The infant "Independence" had gained aid from "Gallicus" when his inheritance was disputed by "Britannicus." All eyes upon him, his prospects bade fair, but his debts mounted in early life. Independence's counselors gathered in September 1787 (the date of the Constitutional Convention) and agreed upon a cure, which, after some opposition, was taken. His health and wealth improved. Soon, however, Independence's chief steward of finances (read: Hamilton) conspired to "feed the vanity of INDEPENDENCE," causing his character—his reputation—to decline. "His wife, VIRTUE . . . died about the same time, leaving him one son PATRIOTISM." Lacking virtue, Independence was seduced by "VICE," an emissary from Britannicus's court. The malevolent Britannicus then sent Jay to turn over all his honors and possessions. "Seized with remorse to behold his degraded condition" at the release of the treaty on June 24, 1795, "INDEPENDENCE EXPIRED IN A CONVULSION!!!"[55]

This brief narrative draws on the conventions of both court drama and the sentimental novel. Independence stands in for the (previously deposed) king: his personification equates the male protagonist with the people, the nation, and the state. Yet this is no ordinary tale of seduction. Queen Virtue is a necessity but one noted only in her absence, which turns woman (now Vice) into the seducing agents of a male foreign power. Men are the objects, not the perpetrators, of seduction; conflict returns to a male generational model, bypassing even the popular figure of nation-child as young woman.

Unlike Miss Liberty, who had been buried and brought back to life in protests against the Stamp Act, Independence will not be revived: there is no saving grace or chivalrous Majesty. Only Patriotism, young son of the Revolution, lives on, along with pretenders to the throne: Speculation, Bribery, and Corruption, the offspring of Independence and Vice's unholy "last marriage." In the printed denouement of the

55. "Death of Independence," in *An Emetic For Aristocrats* . . . (Boston, 1795); "Glad Tidings of Great Joy," *North Carolina Centinel and Fayetteville Gazette,* July 25, 1795; "Death of Independence," *Aurora* (Philadelphia) (from *Virginia Gazette*), July 23, 1795. The Republicans of the 1790s did not invent this sort of national allegory. For "MADAM PATRIOTISM," daughter of "Public Virtue," personified as a young woman by the Tories and raped by Faction (that is, the Patriots), see *Royal Gazette* (Charleston, S.C.), Mar. 10, 1781. For female personifications, see also Shirley Samuels, *Romances of the Republic: Women, the Family, and Violence in the Literature of the Early American Nation* (New York, 1996), 3–22.

tale the friends of Patriotism capture Jay and try him for the death of Independence and "treason against the Majesty of the people." This printed text, however, aims toward an embodied, performed coda: the execution of Jay, now a latter-day Lord Bute, in effigy processions on July Fourth. Would readers be patriots in the streets? The future belongs to the young man Patriotism. Now his character remained to be established.

Opposition ritual and rhetoric, then, maintained the vital link between street theater and sentimental culture, a link that allowed for cross-class mobilization. As in the dominant Revolutionary narrative given expression by Paine, America was a young man who could be easily seduced and unmanned by his own sentimental attachments. The very public, visible theater of virtuous citizenship celebrated by the Democratic-Republicans of the 1790s seemed to enhance the dangers (as well as the possibilities) of public life and led, simultaneously, to renewed attempts at blaming such corruptions on fictional female figures and to new appeals to a feminized "virtue." Similarly, novels and narratives of the 1790s stressed the difficulty in determining whether sensible young devotees of republicanism like Arthur Mervyn or Stephen Burroughs would fulfill the promise exemplified by their very openness to education or succumb, like crowds at public punishments, to "mimetic corruption."[56] In this volatile cultural situation, understandings of national character provided the bridge that allowed allegories of the Jay Treaty, or published stories about seduced and seducing young men, to have national political implications.

Opponents of the Jay Treaty insisted that further intercourse with Great Britain would entail a loss of independent manhood. For a moment, neutrality worked to their advantage, and toasts like, "May the U.S. support the character of a free and independent nation," meant keeping a safe distance from the British. Already, however, Federalists recoiled at the seductive "fraternal embrace" of the French, warning the wary of the "French disease." With the help of international events and a blundering, increasingly imperialist French government, Federalists proved better equipped to employ national character not just as

56. Charles Brockden Brown, *Arthur Mervyn; or, Memoirs of the Year 1793*, ed. Warner Berthoff (New York, 1962); Steven Burroughs, *The Memoirs of Stephen Burroughs*, ed. Philip F. Gura (Boston, 1989); Michael Meranze, *Laboratories of Virtue: Punishment, Revolution, and Authority in Philadelphia, 1760–1835* (Chapel Hill, N.C., 1996), 87–127.

rhetoric but as practice to reunite celebrating groups, "the people," and the state. Their celebratory innovations mobilized three key groups to help revive the national character: ministers, young men, and respectable women.

☆ ☆ ☆

Federalist celebrations often had a less-than-affirming character. Their warnings about the licentious side of "liberty" ran against the grain of much millennial sentiment and could not always be easily clothed in Washingtonian glory. In the long run, the Federalists needed more than hero worship, the glorious future, and paeans to order if they were to overcome the class and regional resentments that were drawing many to the opposition. Washington himself provided the beginning of a solution to this problem in his proclamation for a national Day of Thanksgiving in 1795. Citing the need to offer thanks to God, "the great Ruler of Nations," Washington described the prospects of international and domestic peace, linking the forthcoming Jay Treaty to the suppression of the backcountry tax revolts known as the Whiskey Rebellion (see Figure 7).[57] The Thanksgiving of 1795, occurring on February 19 (three days before Washington's birthday) foreshadowed the reappropriation of public space by the Federalists as well as the alliance they would forge against a "seditious," not to mention blasphemous, opposition.

Fast and thanksgiving days were among the oldest ways that Anglo-Americans had negotiated the divide between the temporal and spiritual worlds. Decreed by civil authority but observed in church, they had been especially prevalent in New England, where governors continued them after Independence. Feasts and fasts sought to create unanimity in the body politic and the imagined congregation; anyone not disposed to fasting or rejoicing belonged outside the community of believers. Thus they helped define that community in times of strife. Fasts and thanksgivings were opposite poles on the never completely secular calendar of Anglo-American culture. By decreeing them during the Revolutionary war, Congress had seized authority away from God's chief servant, the king.

57. Buel, *Securing the Revolution,* 168–169; *By the President of the United States of America, a Proclamation . . . to Set Apart and Observe Thursday the Nineteenth Day of February Next . . .* ([Hartford, Conn.], 1795). On the Whiskey Rebellion and the political context of the mid-1790s, see Thomas P. Slaughter, *The Whiskey Rebellion: Frontier Epilogue to the American Revolution* (New York, 1986).

By Authority.

By The President

OF THE UNITED STATES OF AMERICA,

A Proclamation.

WHEN we review the calamities which afflict so many other Nations, the present condition of the *United States* affords much matter of consolation and satisfaction. Our exemption hitherto from foreign war----an increasing prospect of the continuance of that exemption----the great degree of internal tranquillity we have enjoyed----the recent confirmation of that tranquillity, by the suppression of an insurrection which so wantonly threatened it----the happy course of our public affairs in general----the unexampled prosperity of all classes of our Citizens, are circumstances which peculiarly mark our situation with indications of the Divine Benificence towards us. In such a state of things it is, in an especial manner, our duty as a People, with devout reverence and affectionate gratitude, to acknowledge our many and great obligations to ALMIGHTY GOD, and to implore him to continue and confirm the blessings we experience.

Deeply penetrated with this sentiment, I GEORGE WASHINGTON, President of the United States, do recommend to all Religious Societies and Denominations, and to all Persons whomsoever within the United States, to set apart and observe THURSDAY the *Nineteenth* day of *February* next, as a Day of PUBLIC THANKSGIVING and PRAYER ; and on that Day to meet together, and render their sincere and hearty thanks to the Great Ruler of Nations, for the manifold and signal mercies, which distinguish our lot as a nation ; particularly for the possession of Constitutions of Government, which unite, and by their union establish liberty with order----for the preservation of our Peace foreign and domestic----for the seasonable controul which has been given to a spirit of disorder, in the suppression of the late Insurrection----and generally, for the prosperous course of our affairs public and private ; and at the same time, humbly and fervently to beseech the Kind Author of these Blessings, graciously to prolong them to us----to imprint on our hearts a deep and solemn sense of our obligations to Him for them----to teach us rightly to estimate their immense value---to preserve us from the arrogance of prosperity, and from hazarding the advantages we enjoy by delusive pursuits---to dispose us to merit the continuance of his favours, by not abusing them, by our gratitude for them, and by a correspondent conduct as Citizens and as Men---to render this Country more and more a safe and propitious Asylum for the unfortunate of other Countries ---to extend among us true and useful knowledge---to diffuse and establish habits of sobriety, order, morality and piety ; and finally, to impart all the blessings we possess, or ask for ourselves, to the whole Family of Mankind.

In Testimony Whereof, I have caused the SEAL of the UNITED STATES of AMERICA to be affixed to these Presents, and signed the same with my Hand. Done at the city of PHILADELPHIA, the first day of January, one thousand seven hundred and ninety-five, and of the Independence of the United States of America the nineteenth.

Gᵒ: WASHINGTON.

By The President---EDM: RANDOLPH.

FIGURE 7. Washington's Proclamation for a Federal Thanksgiving.
Philadelphia, 1795. Courtesy American Antiquarian Society

Official fasts and thanksgivings had been widely observed, even formulaic, under the Continental Congress. After ratification, however, they became controversial. A November 1789 day of thanks for the Constitution aroused resentment among some members of Congress, and an attempt by Federalists to push through a fast day in late 1792 met with loud objections. A *presidential* proclamation was thus something of a departure: it smacked of royal claims to divine authority. In the margins of an interleaved almanac one diarist noted February 19, 1795, as "The Washington Thanksgiving." Some newspapers objected to Washington's carefully "recommended" day of thanks. Others, though, observed the holiday by not publishing.[58]

Federalist papers made clear what they expected of a day "observed in obedience to a requisition from the president of the union." The ambiguity of gratitude to rulers (for example, Washington) and to God perfectly suited arch-Federalists. "Places of public worship were thronged," reported Fenno, "and the most devout, patriotic, and federal, discourses, were delivered by the respectable Clergy of the several Churches."[59] But why would rabidly anti-British democratic editors like Greenleaf and Bache help spread word of a potentially partisan holiday? Giving thanks at that time enabled Bache and fellow members of the Democratic-Republican societies to distance themselves from the Whiskey rebels. The Jay Treaty had not yet been published; it still seemed possible to favor the French while wishing for peace with England.

Beyond a temporary détente (flanked in many cities that February by opposing celebrations of the French alliance and Washington's Birthday), a more lasting effect of the fast was to return the clergy to an important place in Federalist politics. The last two decades had been a trying time for ministers, particularly those of the mainline denominations. Because of rapid demographic shifts and insufficient funds, many parishes lacked settled ministers. More alarming yet, many traditional clergymen found their flocks attracted to the dynamic preaching of itinerant evangelists. Revivals had a leveling impulse and impact. The

58. W. DeLoss Love, Jr., *The Fast and Thanksgiving Days of New England* (Boston, 1895); Slaughter, *Whiskey Rebellion*, 130. See also Harry S. Stout, "The Life and Death of the Confederate Jeremiad," James A. Gray Lectures, Duke University Divinity School, October 1992; *Albany Gazette*, Feb. 16, 1795; *City Gazette and Daily Advertiser* (Charleston, S.C.), Feb. 19, 1795; *Greenleaf's New-York Journal*, Feb. 18, 1795. Washington's fast day proclamation is in the *Federal Intelligencer* (Baltimore), Jan. 5, 1795, and in virtually all other papers after Jan. 1. The 1795 almanac diary in the Lee Family Papers, AAS, also has the listing of feast dates on the new French calendar torn out, suggesting either special importance to the user or, perhaps, incommensurability with holidays like the fast after 1795.

59. "Thursday, the 19th day of February, 1795, Anticipated," *Federal Intelligencer* (Baltimore), Feb. 18, 1795 (from *Federal Orrerey* [Boston]); *Gazette of the United States*, (Philadelphia), Feb. 16, 21, 1795.

profusion of Protestant denominations, along with the rise of a national political culture, diminished the clergy's former status as principal disseminators of information and learning. Still crucial mediators, more and more they found themselves competing in preaching and in print with rival claimants to public attention.[60]

The clergy had never really lost its prominent role in nationalist celebration. But with the proliferation of celebratory occasions (and of educated young men), more and more orations were being given by old patriots and young professionals (especially lawyers). Often on the Fourth of July the clergy's place was only in the church, to begin the ritual process that had expanded so far beyond its doors. Ironically, ministers' validation of the new American order as the fulfillment of God's plan helped clear the ground for the political culture that marginalized them. If the jeremiad had migrated beyond the clergy's occasional sermons—its very raison d'être being the relationship between God and polity—then clerics need not be indispensable men. Of course, the precise manner in which secular orators dissolved Christianity in millennial nationalism (as opposed to vice versa) often made all the difference to the evangelically inclined. By the late 1780s clerical sermons on nationalist occasions were becoming more and more inventive in reasoning back to the need to thank God for America's present and future glory. In welcoming the savior of our country, asked Joseph Buckminster when Washington visited Portsmouth, New Hampshire, should we not also welcome the savior of the world?[61] Such remon-

60. Stephen A. Marini, "The Religious World of Daniel Shays," and Robert A. Gross, "The Confidence Man and the Preacher: The Cultural Politics of Shays's Rebellion," in Gross, ed., *In Debt to Shays: The Bicentennial of an Agrarian Rebellion* (Charlottesville, Va., 1993), 239–277, 297–320; Nathan O. Hatch, *The Democratization of American Christianity* (New Haven, Conn., 1989), 3–46; Brown, *Knowledge Is Power,* 65–81; Christopher Grasso, *A Speaking Aristocracy: Transforming Public Discourse in Eighteenth-Century Connecticut* (Chapel Hill, 1999), chap. 8.

61. Joseph Buckminster, *A Discourse, Delivered at Portsmouth, New-Hampshire, November 1st, 1789* . . . (Portsmouth, N.H., [1789]); Smith, *A Sermon, on Temporal and Spiritual Salvation.* My understanding of the New England clergy and the institution of their oratory owes much to the work of Harry S. Stout; see Stout, *The New England Soul: Preaching and Religious Culture in Colonial New England* (New York, 1986); and his "Rhetoric and Reality in the Early Republic: The Case of the Federalist Clergy," in Mark A. Noll, ed., *Religion and American Politics* (New York, 1990), 62–76. James M. Banner, Jr., argues for the long-term failure of the Federalist-clerical alliance in *To the Hartford Convention: Federalists and the Origins of Party Politics in Massachusetts, 1789–1815* (New York, 1970), 152–167.

strances were probably effective in getting listeners to remember the Almighty, but they probably also indicate that many needed reminding.

From the point of view of most of the clergy, then, the French Revolution was literally a godsend. International events had ratified their long-term predictions: the millennium was at hand. Many of the published orations of February 19, 1795, even used the occasion to assure doubters that the worst excesses of the French Revolution were over. Others, of course, were beginning to contend that religion itself had lost that revolution. Later, deistic ideas served as a convenient target for the older generation's fears of subversion. But in 1795 deism itself was not really the threat that energized the Federalist clergy; it was rather the combined threat of both revolutions, the American and the French, to the clergy's religious *and* political authority that led ministers to seize upon the fast days to recalibrate the heavens and the earth.[62]

Regardless of their exact stance on France, the sermons of 1795 sought to reverse the erosion of clerical authority. John Andrews did so by positioning Washington as God's chosen servant—an older theme that had new meanings as Federalists claimed the president as their own. Others made a similar move in a more formal fashion. For their exegesis they substituted Washington's own proclamation for a biblical text. These New England preachers remade Washington into their prophet and lawgiver and themselves into servants of a resacralized national state.[63]

It is difficult to say how widespread this kind of preaching was in 1795. Though the newspapers and contemporary diaries indicate a wide observance of the thanksgiving day, nearly all of the published orations

62. Anson Ely Morse, *The Federalist Party in Massachusetts to the Year 1800* (Princeton, N.J., 1909), 86–130; Gary B. Nash, "The American Clergy and the French Revolution," *WMQ*, 3d Ser., XXII (1965), 392–412; Ann Butler Lever, "Vox Populi, Vox Dei: New England and the French Revolution, 1787–1801" (Ph.D. diss., University of North Carolina at Chapel Hill, 1972), 141–210; Bloch, *Visionary Republic*, chaps. 7–9; David Brion Davis, ed., *The Fear of Conspiracy: Images of Un-American Subversion from the Revolution to the Present* (Ithaca, N.Y., 1971), 55–57.

63. John Andrews, *A Sermon, Delivered February 19, 1795* . . . (Newburyport, Mass., [1795]); Thomas Baldwin, *A Sermon, Delivered February 19, 1795* . . . (Boston, 1795); Joseph Dana, *A Sermon, Delivered February 19, 1795* . . . (Newburyport, Mass., 1795); Abiel Holmes, *A Sermon, on the Freedom and Happiness of America; Preached at Cambridge, February 19, 1795* . . . (Boston, 1795); Samuel Kendal, *Sermon, Delivered on the Day of National Thanksgiving* . . . (Boston, 1795); David Osgood, *A Discourse Delivered February 19, 1795* . . . (Boston, [1795]).

hail from New England. Perhaps this concentration has as much to do with the particular political and publishing scene of New England as with the exceptionalism of the New England Protestant clergy. Salem's Reverend William Bentley, a Republican, saw "subscriptions about for the Sermon preached on the last Thanksgiving by Dr. Bernard of this Town. . . . The Clergy are now the Tools of the Federalists, and Thanksgiving Sermons are in the order of the Day."[64] The Reverend Timothy Dickinson of Hollistown, Massachusetts, noted:

> A volley of Political Pamphlets have lately been discharged into the world, chiefly Thanksgiving sermons, last Feb. 19th. . . . I hear of 16 published in this part of New England, and how many more I cannot say. Those which I have seen are political. Now I feel as though ministers have stepped out of their line and preached politics instead of the Gospel; man, presidents and government instead of Christ.

Revealingly, though, Dickinson had resolved the previous autumn not to let "politics" get in the way of God's will:

> [Sept. 5, 1794.] The papers this evening. God is doing great things. The combination against *equal rights* is crumbling away. I mean to speak in favor of Republicanism, for I view it the cause of man.[65]

The real innovation of the Federalist clergy, the one that would be drawn on for the rest of the decade, was less their dabbling in politics than their renewed emphasis upon a nationalist theodicy that no longer relied upon universal regeneration.[66] Instead, they pointed the isolated communicant to God and nation alone. After all, as the Reverend Levi Frisbie put it, "a Nation is considered as a moral and political person." Not coincidentally, ministerial descriptions of the individual's and the nation's thankful feelings closely followed the accounts of federal feel-

64. Bentley, *Diary*, II, 129. Even this qualification of exceptionalism risks tautology, as most mainline clergy were New Englanders, even if only by origin or training. For indications that observance was widespread in interior regions of the South, see *The Diaries of Evan Pugh (1762–1801)* (Florence, S.C. 1993), 356; James Kershaw Diary, Feb. 19, 1795, South Caroliniana Library; Diary of Francis Taylor, Feb. 19, 1795, Manuscripts Collection, Filson Club, Louisville, Kentucky.

65. Thomas A. Dickinson, "Biographical Sketch and Extracts from the Journal of Rev. Timothy Dickinson," Worcester Society of Antiquity, *Proceedings*, VI (1883), 69, 71.

66. See Michael Lienesch, *New Order of the Ages: Time, the Constitution, and the Making of American Political Thought* (Princeton, N.J., 1988), 192–197.

ing we have seen in reportage of patriotic fetes. "Consist[ing] primarily in the internal sentiments and affections of the soul . . . the sense of thankfulness and praise which is kindled in the heart, should . . . ascend up to God in offerings and ascriptions of social adoration, in songs of humble gratitude and joy." If individuals should give thanks, so should "the whole people in their national and collective character and capacity." Inverting the popular Republican accusation of clerical "service" to the Federalist cause, Frisbie compared the rulers of the land to a secular priesthood, who should

> recommend the same conduct, and study to diffuse the same spirit through all the members of the great political body: So that all the constituent parts of it, and consequently the whole, may adore the majesty and mercy of God; may enter his gates with thanksgiving, and his courts with praise.

The problem with popular sovereignty, for Frisbie, was that it made public servants into slaves of men, not servants of God. This resulted from "inattention to the sacred nature of civil Government, and the sacred character of its ministers." God alone, the "Supreme Governor," invested the right of forming government in the people. If they acted rightly, then earthly governors "are ratified by the sanction of divine authority and approbation"—and should be so treated.[67]

Ashbel Green also allied individual "gratitude" (the Federalist word for deference to "constituted authorities") with public thanksgivings, going so far as to involve himself in the vexing problem of the visibility of grace. "It is a law of our constitution, that whatever we sensibly, deeply and habitually feel, we should be prone to express and with difficulty conceal." Such display, of course, was useful: it inspired others. The axiom that "man is a social being" enabled Green to conflate individual and national duties, and both of these with good manners. "We have a *national character* to support in our carriage and demeanour toward Almighty God, a character which he observes, and according to which he will treat us."[68]

67. Levi Frisbie, *A Sermon Delivered February 19, 1795* . . . (Newburyport, Mass., 1795), 21–23.

68. Ashbel Green, *A Sermon, Delivered in the Second Presbyterian Church . . . on the 19th of February, 1795* . . . (Philadelphia, 1795), 12, 16, 17. Green continued this line of inquiry in his 1798 fast sermon to get out of a related theological conundrum. Even though individuals receive their rewards and punishments in the next world, he reasoned, nations exist only in this world. Therefore, only with religion

Already in 1795 the Federalist clergy were beginning to develop a theology for national character. Frisbie did so through a time-honored, almost monarchical political theory that paralleled Federalist attempts to rejustify deference. Green emphasized the same notions of moral sentiments that, during the 1780s, had guaranteed order and uplift through emotional display. Their very rhetorical strategies testify to these sermonizers' deep involvement in contemporary culture but also indicate their relegation, with almost every other culture broker, to the status of middlemen. And like other middlemen (officeholders, journalists, and so forth), they too were open to the charge of being bought and sold. The attempts of clergymen to regain their eminence would engender controversy for decades to come. In the context of 1795, the thanksgiving day sermons point to the justification of, not sacred, but secular authority and an even stronger linkage of the celebrating individual to the independent nation.

Federalist efforts to support politics with religion grew more aggressive during the Quasi War with France. President Adams appointed two national fast days—May 9, 1798, and April 25, 1799—and his second declaration was even more explicitly Christian than the first.[69] "Arts are used to engage the Clergy in the English Interest," noted a disgusted William Bentley. For the 1798 fast Boston's *Columbian Centinel* suggested that, lest the political message of the fast be lost amid devotion, ministers might "read or cause to be read, these papers [of the American diplomats in France], on the National Fast, between the services." And so clergymen all over the Northeast and beyond preached on the theme of the French danger, though not always to the satisfaction of their hearers (as Bentley discovered). Diaries reveal a widespread observance of the fast and an awareness of its controversial meanings. "Only Lacy

---

could nations be happy in the present. See Green, *Obedience to the Laws of God, the Sure and Indispensable Defense of Nations* . . . (Philadelphia, 1798).

On the cultural problem of the visibility of grace, see Edmund S. Morgan, *Visible Saints: The History of a Puritan Idea* (New York, 1963); Colin Campbell, *The Romantic Ethic and the Spirit of Modern Consumerism* (London, 1987).

69. Ashbel Green, by then serving as congressional chaplain, claimed a hand in this. The "religious community of our country" had complained that earlier proclamations were insufficiently Christian; asked for a draft by the president, he "resolved to write one of a more evangelical character." Joseph H. Jones, ed., *The Life of Ashbel Green, V.D.M.* (New York, 1849), 270–271.

Pitts an illnatured Quaker kept open his store," commented a western Pennsylvania churchman, Nathaniel Snowden.[70]

Actually, the 1798 and 1799 fasts were both more energetically observed and more caustically criticized than the fast of 1795. After all, these were not thanksgivings (which more closely resembled celebrations like July Fourth), nor were they sanctioned by Washington (who was no longer president). Some noted the irony of all the hoopla surrounding a supposedly solemn rite. "Fast day, so called," a Burlington, New Jersey, native wrote mockingly in his diary. "Feast day, Many Drank." "This day is appointed by the President for a Fast, Thanksgiving etc.," noted Alexander Anderson, a young New York doctor, "but as my opinion did not exactly tally with those of his excellency, I did not make a holiday of it." One wag declared: "I am not of the opinion, that *in Adams' fall we sinned all.*"[71] In 1799 some Jeffersonian papers even

70. Bentley, *Diary*, II, 266; *Columbian Centinel* (Boston), May 5, 1798; *State Gazette, and New Jersey Advertiser* (Trenton), May 15, 1798; *Columbian Museum and Savannah Advertiser*, May 8, 15, 1798; Increase N. Tarbox, ed., *Diary of Thomas Robbins, D.D., 1796–1854* (Boston, 1886), I, 54; Rev. Jacob Norton Diaries, May 9, 1798, Apr. 25, 1799, William Nutting Diary, May 9, 1798, Apr. 1799, Massachusetts Historical Society, Boston; Nathan Fiske Diary, May 9, 1798, Apr. 25, 1799, Samuel Bridge Diaries, VII, May 9, 1798, Diary of John Cushing, May 9, 1798, Apr. 25, 1799 (typescript), Dwight Foster Journal, May 9, 1798, Foster Family Papers, Nahum Jones Diary, May 9, 1798, AAS; John Anderson, Jr., Diary, May 9, 1798, Henry Laight Diary, May 9, 1798, Apr. 25, 1799, New-York Historical Society; William Ormond, Jr., Journal, May 9, 1798 (typescript), Special Collections Library, Duke University; Elizabeth DeHart Bleecker Diary, Apr. 25, 1799, New York Public Library; Rev. Nathaniel Snowden Diary, III, May 9, 1798, Historical Society of Pennsylvania; James Kershaw Diary, May 9, 1798, Apr. 25, 1799, South Caroliniana Library; Elkanah Jones Diary, May 9, 1798, Apr. 25, 1799, Jones-Goldsmith-Johnson Papers, reel 3, book 2, Nathanael Spencer Diary, May 16, 1798, [Connecticut], Nathanael Spencer Papers, Western Reserve Historical Society, Cleveland, Ohio.

71. *Herald of Liberty* (Washington, Pa.), Apr. 22, 29, 1799; James Craft Diary, I, Apr. 25, 1799, Historical Society of Pennsylvania; copy of Alexander Anderson Diary, May 9, 1798, New-York Historical Society (original at the Columbia College Library); *Centinel of Freedom* (Newark), May 15, 1798. Benjamin Tappan, later an important Jacksonian politician, recalled writing and publishing one of these parodies as one of his first public activities (Donald J. Ratcliffe, ed., "The Autobiography of Benjamin Tappan," *Ohio History*, LXXXV [1976], 121). Bishop James Madison of Virginia used the opportunity to preach against the administration's foreign policy (Charles Crowe, "The War of 'Pure Republicanism' against Federalism, 1794–1801: Bishop James Madison on the American Political Scene," *West Virginia History*, XXIV [1963], 340).

published mock psalms for the fast while attacking the clergymen who warned of a deist conspiracy (the Bavarian Illuminati) as the "New England Illuminati." Along with arguments for freedom of the press they praised the separation of church and state.[72]

By 1798, the clergy had fully joined the battle over what Americans should celebrate. With the Democratic-Republicans pouring ever more invective upon presidential birthday revelers, insisting that the Fourth of July was "the only *legitimate* American festival," the Federalists had clearly retaken the initiative. Their anti-French fast days were erected upon the ruins of opposition festivals, as one Philadelphia minister observed in contrasting the fast days favorably to the "heathenish Calendar" of the French. The obvious partisanship of nearly all these rites did not prevent ministers (or editors) from urging their auditors to "banish all party distinctions from the name of AMERICAN."[73]

With the ideological foundations for Federalist reaction laid by 1795, its practices were tried out over the next four years. Most important, it was a question of mobilizing new constituencies in a way that would obviate the opposition's language of citizens versus aristocrats, in favor of

72. *Centinel of Freedom* (Newark), Apr. 23, 1799; John Knox, Jr., "On the President's Fast," *Aurora* (Philadelphia), Apr. 18, 1799. For an earlier anti-Jeffersonian psalm, see *Impartial Herald: A Periodical Register of the Times* (Suffield, Conn.), May 16, 1798 (originally from the *Independent Chronicle* [Boston]). On the Illuminati controversy, see Vernon Stauffer, *New England and the Bavarian Illuminati,* Columbia Studies in History, Economics, and Public Law, LXXXII, no. 1 (New York, 1918); on the countercharges, see Alan V. Briceland, "The Philadelphia Aurora, the New England Illuminati, and the Election of 1800," *PMHB,* C (1976), 3–36; Davis, ed., *Fear of Conspiracy,* 35–54. These counterconspiratorial charges responded to widespread assertions on the part of the Federalist clergy that deism, anarchy, and Jeffersonian politics were all the same thing. Already on the Fourth of July 1797, Isaac Watts Crane had told his Newark audience: "When . . . you espouse the cause of antifederalism, you espouse the cause of men who are governed by opposition, and who have no steady principles; you launch into an ocean of uncertainty, into a dangerous labyrinth where every thing is confusion. Antifederalists, like deists, find fault with the government, without proposing a better system, and like deists they have a similar diversity of sentiments." Crane, *An Oration Delivered in the Presbyterian Church . . .* (Newark, N.J., 1797), 19.

73. *Centinel of Freedom* (Newark), July 4, 1797; James Abercrombie, *A Sermon, Preached in Christ Church and St. Peter's, Philadelphia: On Wednesday, May 9, 1798 . . .* (Philadelphia, [1798]), 31; William Linn, *A Discourse on National Sins: Delivered May 9, 1798* (New York, 1798), 33.

rhetoric and practices that would shift attention along another axis of identity. Many ministers and others perceived a threat to moral order in "jacobin" scribblings and political activity—but they did not necessarily translate them into the specific identification of Christianity with federalism that articulate Federalists pursued in the late 1790s. Christian identity did provide a broader basis than conservative political theory to justify suppression (symbolic and real) of the opposition.[74] The clergy helped provide the occasions and the language for this decade's Federalist communion. But even preachers were nothing without their flocks. It would take the youngest and the "fairest" of Americans to seal the fissures between the individual, "the people," and the national state.

In 1796 the Federalists were particularly energetic in promoting "sincere, and heartfelt emotions of gratitude" on Washington's Birthday. Not long afterward, the administration's success in getting the Jay Treaty appropriations bill through the House formed a key turning point; for, when the French began to attack American neutral shipping in retaliation for the new, apparently pro-British policy, the opposition found itself in the same political tight spot that Federalists had faced earlier. Urging détente with a hostile power, they could be, and were, attacked as false patriots. The United States now had treaties with both powers; "neutrality" finally walked hand in hand with the support of the administration. "Discord is our fatal foe," proclaimed Daniel Davis in a July Fourth oration that anticipated the themes of Washington's Farewell Address.[75] Federalists were capturing the center in part by shifting the terms of the Republican equation between the French cause and majority rule at home. Now the French were the special interest, plotting against the American people and their government.

74. See Kilborn Whitman, *An Oration, Pronounced at Bridgewater, October 4, 1798, at the Request of the Columbian Society* (Boston, 1798), a fascinating discourse on religion, government, and national character; also Abiel Abbott, *A Discourse, Delivered at North-Coventry, July 4th, 1799* . . . (Hartford, Conn., 1799). For other examples of the dependence of national character on religion, see James Muir, *A Sermon, Delivered at the New North Church . . . May 9th, 1798* (Philadelphia, 1798); Samuel Austin "Fast Sermon, national, April 25 1799," Samuel Austin Papers, AAS.

75. *Gazette of the United States* (Philadelphia), Feb. 22, 24, Mar. 3, 5, 11, 14, 1796; Bentley, *Diary,* II, 173; Buel, *Securing the Revolution,* 114; Daniel Davis, *An Oration, Delivered at Portsmouth, July 4th, 1796* . . . (Portland, Maine, 1796), 19–20.

Suddenly the health of America depended on avoiding the excesses of Bache and Cobbett. "From such papers other nations may consider us a divided people." Even while toasting the Rights of Man ("rightly understood") and an end to conflict with France, the 1797 Independence Day celebrants in Enfield, North Carolina, wished that "there never be a distinction between the government and the people of the United States." In defense, the opposition found itself claiming that it was the Federalists' calls for unity that were in fact divisive. Greenleaf's diagnosis of a British (Federalist) versus an American (Republican) party, foreshadowing the sister republic's deletion from Jeffersonian Fourth of July orations, only papered over the problem of the Republicans' French connection at a time when Federalists were making France the Great American Enemy. The space for legitimate popular opposition was closing fast.[76]

With war looming in June 1798, Congress passed a law calling for a ten-thousand-man reserve army and the mobilization of an eighty-thousand-man militia. As in the 1793–1794 crisis with England, however, eager young men who had spare time and money for uniforms had already been forming private militia groups, meeting regularly and parading on festival days. The militia typified the Revolutionary struggle to locate and personify "the people," for service in the militia was the original act of the virtuous republican citizen. According to tradition, militias consisted of all able-bodied men. In practice, however, military duty was a real burden on working men and distasteful for men of the upper class when they had to stand in ranks with their social inferiors (whom they often preferred to hire as substitutes). During the Revolutionary war, a surfeit of would-be gentlemen clogged the officer ranks while keeping their distance from the rank-and-file yeomen whom republican ideology praised. Meanwhile, military leadership drew its reputation from its civilian basis; standing armies and their careerism were seen as the seedbeds of corruption. In the 1790s hostility to a standing army validated the formation and reformation of volunteer militia companies—often limited to those who had the leisure for regular marching and the money for smart uniforms. At the

76. *Times; Alexandria Advertiser,* Feb. 13, 1798, and An American, "Union," May 28, 1798; *North-Carolina Journal* (Halifax), July 10, 1797; *State Gazette, and New Jersey Advertiser* (Trenton), July 19, 1796, July 11, 1797; *Greenleaf's New York Journal,* April 19, 1797.

same time, the relationship of both the state-run and private militias to federal authority remained unresolved.[77]

Military groups entered enthusiastically into the politics of celebration. With the growth in the number of volunteer companies during 1794–1795 and 1797–1798, more and more accounts of their dinners and toasts appeared in the newspapers. As makers and exemplars of public opinion, militia companies enjoyed significant advantages over the Cincinnati and the Democratic societies. Most simply, there were more of them. And they obviously had gathered for the public weal. Or had they? "I have observed whenever [privately organized] *Independant Companies* have been established, they have ever been engaged in contentions with the Militia," wrote William Bentley in his 1790 diary. "The uniform itself being partial operates to the discouragement of the poorer citizens, and injures that very order of men upon which a country depends for its defence." Presenting a flag to the new Volunteer Greens of Philadelphia in 1794, "a lady" praised the respectable soldiers "whose valour has every excitement that the most intimate relations with the common community, honor, duty, connections, birth, education, and property can inspire."[78]

Militia service remained the poor man's claim to citizenship and the rich man's entrée to honor and advancement well into the nineteenth century. Legally or voluntarily organized, men marching in the streets commanded attention. Two centuries later, with our institutionalized military subculture populated by millions of men and women, newspaper reports of dinners held by volunteer companies, local militia officers, and artisan regulars are apt to look nearly all the same. But we can be sure that contemporaries knew the difference between the ragged regulars and the nattily-turned-out elite. Locally, this difference could have quite specific political meanings. Like other voluntary associations, militia activities helped organize local political movements even as they paraded and trained for national defense. In cities like Baltimore and Philadelphia, partisan affiliation began to replicate class differences in both independent and regular militia companies. Baltimore's Mechanical Volunteers played a crucial role in organizing arti-

77. Royster, *Revolutionary People at War,* 58–95, 320–368; Kohn, *Eagle and Sword,* 91–189; Lawrence Delbert Cress, *Citizens in Arms: The Army and the Militia in American Society to the War of 1812* (Chapel Hill, N.C., 1982), 111–149.

78. Bentley, *Diary,* I, 196; *Gazette of the United States* (Philadelphia), July 8, 1794.

sans for the Republican cause. In the spring of 1794 they mustered almost every day; that year and the next they celebrated George Washington's Birthday with paeans to the French and Tom Paine.[79]

During the middle years of the decade, competing militia groups filled the streets, taverns, and newspaper columns on celebratory occasions, but in 1793–1795 and 1797–1798 shifts in the nation's foreign affairs provided particular opportunities, first, for Democratic-Republicans and, later, for Federalists. When President John Adams left the capital for Braintree upon Congress's recess during the summer and fall of 1797, the new volunteer companies came out in large numbers to celebrate his arrival. These festivities were of course only one among many practices that transferred the presidential aura to Washington's successor. Republicans criticized these "festivals of gratitude" as a loss of republican simplicity, charging that the Federalists' neglect of Vice President Jefferson in their toasts proved that these ceremonies were completely partisan. An "Old Whig" even suggested that Adams should be borne into Philadelphia on the military's shoulders. The *Aurora* had one of its last hurrahs when most of the local militia boycotted the president's return to Philadelphia. "The greatest possible order was observed, not a whisper was heard more than at a funeral," wrote Bache in a classic example of anticelebratory satire. "No gaping multitude to rend the air with their huzzas, no parade of infantry with their martial music, gave disturbance to the regularity and the progress of this procession."[80]

More often, men in uniform found that their service linked them to

79. On the importance of the militia in street life of the nineteenth century, see Susan G. Davis, *Parades and Power: Street Theatre in Nineteenth-Century Philadelphia* (Philadelphia, 1986). On class as a literally organizing principle in the late-eighteenth-century militia, see Steven Rosswurm, *Arms, Country, and Class: The Philadelphia Militia and "Lower Sort" in the American Revolution* (New Brunswick, N.J., 1987); Royster, *Revolutionary People at War*, 58–95; Young, *Democratic Republicans of New York*, 404–405; Klein, *Unification of a Slave State*, 163. On the Baltimore mechanics' companies and their battles with local merchants, see *Maryland Journal* (Baltimore), Feb. 14, 24, 26, 1794; Charles G. Steffen, *The Mechanics of Baltimore: Workers and Politics in the Age of the Revolution* (Urbana, Ill., 1984), 61–62, 146–148, 160–161.

80. Nahum Jones Diary, Aug. 31, 1797, AAS; *Greenleaf's New York Journal,* July 29, 1797; *Gazette of the United States* (Philadelphia), Aug. 22, 1798; *Aurora* (Philadelphia), Nov. 10, 11, 13, 14, 1797. According to Jacob Hiltzheimer, ninety-five militiamen turned out, which was not many for Philadelphia at that time. Elizabeth Drinker also noticed the conspicuous lack of "parade" for Adams. Jacob Hiltzheimer Diary, Nov. 10, 1797, APS; Crane, ed., *Diary of Elizabeth Drinker*, I, 978.

what Federalists called constituted authorities: that is, the Washington and Adams governments. The service of John Anderson, Jr., a young student and later a lawyer in New York, exemplifies these shifting political resonances. On July 4, 1794, the twenty-year-old Anderson walked about with some male and female friends, watching the Independence Day procession while eating some ice cream on the roof of a tall building. The next year he helped paint the American and French flags on silk and later watched the artisans and Republicans parade through town. A few days later he attended a militia muster after getting his notice to turn out. Two years later on the Fourth he went to hear the Democratic oration. In 1798, however, he was out before breakfast on Independence Day in search of a rifle in order to be prepared for his muster. Anderson marched in the sun with his unit for most of the morning and afternoon. His company then dined at a tavern. Completely exhausted, he went home and rested.[81]

The remilitarization of patriotism meant that young men like Anderson finally had a chance to show they had been listening to all those orations: they were indeed faithful sons of the Revolutionary fathers. Earlier in the decade youthful orators had (perhaps less than consciously) linked their own status to the "infant greatness" of America. The emotions of 1776 "remain latent in the bosoms of your children," a young John Quincy Adams assured his audience in 1793. The implicit family romance of the Revolution, according to which the good sons rebelled against a corrupted parent, had its sequel in these festivities of the 1790s, as the "rising sons of freedom" acted as "competitors for the approbation of their worthy sires." Young patriots had long been a fixture at celebrations; even boys sometimes organized to imitate their elders, performing mock maneuvers and after-dinner toasts. With the coming of a post-Revolutionary generation, the youth who had a "character" to establish became an even more potent metaphor for the state of the nation itself.[82]

81. John Anderson, Jr., Diary, July 4, 1794, July 4, 7, 1795, July 4, 1797, July 4, 8, 1798, New-York Historical Society. For a contrary reading of Anderson's diary that stresses the leisure motive and uses him as an example of noninvolvement in public life, see Brown, *Knowledge Is Power*, 131.

82. Joseph Hopkinson oration (Philadelphia), *Times; Alexandria Advertiser*, July 11, 1798; John Quincy Adams, *An Oration*, 13–15; Mercer, *An Oration*; Samuel F[owler] Dickinson, *An Oration, in Celebration of American Independence* . . . (Northampton, Mass., 1797), 18; "Reflections on the Anniversary of American Independence, July 4, 1797," *Salem Gazette* (Mass.), July 14, 1797 (from *Philadelphia Gazette*).

According to contemporary testimony, by 1798 young men wearing the black cockade were said to be "continually brawling about their patriotism, and crying out for war." They displayed their politics and made speeches with the ardor of lifelong listeners to tales of the Revolution. But instead of a rebellious militarism, these young men embraced a loyal, obedient Americanism. Their professions of readiness for battle relied upon spectacles of intergenerational sympathy. The young men addressed as corruptible types in sentimental novels and in published allegories of national character found ways to have their patriotism without another revolution.[83]

Their assertiveness was met joyously by older Federalists. When President Adams had released the documents proving that French diplomats had demanded a cash tribute (the XYZ Affair), supporters organized meetings to express approval of the chief executive's actions, much as they had done following Washington's neutrality proclamation during 1794–1795. This strategy succeeded beyond any previous mobilization, for several reasons. Adams had exhausted all obvious diplomatic alternatives, and there could be little doubt that the French ministry's insistence upon a bribe derived from a weakness they perceived in the American polity. Adams had prepared the public for this failure. Suddenly the Federalists were the champions of publicity. The charge of secrecy now lay at the door of the once open and candid French. With all things revealed, now it was the French and their American champions who seemed to have followed a conspiratorial script. As a result, the XYZ Affair carried a charge that rivaled the Jay Treaty revelation without its more complicated questions of commercial policy. Here citizens gathered to affirm their willingness to defend the nation. And young men took the lead in declaring their attachment to the nation and its current leaders.[84]

On the importance of generations in this era and in general, see Glenn Wallach, *Obedient Sons: The Discourse of Youth and Generations in American Culture, 1630–1860* (Amherst, Mass., 1997).

83. *Times; Alexandria Advertiser,* July 6, 1798; for a similar observation a year later, see *Greenleaf's New York Journal,* July 6, 1799; Steven J. Novak, *The Rights of Youth: American Colleges and Student Revolt, 1798–1815* (Cambridge, Mass., 1977), 39–42.

84. Buel, *Securing the Revolution,* 166–167; Page Smith, *John Adams* (New York, 1962), II, 962–966; Novak, *Rights of Youth,* 44. James Morton Smith sees the XYZ meetings as key in setting the stage for the Alien and Sedition Acts (*Freedom's Fetters,* 16–20). Thus Adams did much to create the war fervor that he later (rightly)

During the late spring and the summer of 1798, addresses to the president and his responses filled the pages of all but the most Jeffersonian newspapers. A volume of 106 of them, published later that year, showcases their diverse origins. They came from all over the country—from cities, towns, counties, state legislatures, even Masonic lodges. More remarkable, perhaps, are the individual responses Adams offered to each group letter. Less generic and more emotional than Washington's, they joined president to citizens through a direct form of address. In these letters Adams (who had often incensed his political enemies by insisting that a healthy republican government had to actually recognize and represent classes and estates) affirmed that he was every man's president. Any constituency could address him and expect a response. And not just a form letter. Adams took on the role of arbiter of American identity. In doing so he also recognized, even thanked, his addressees for affirming his own patriotic services. The addresses are thus best seen as epistolary exchanges that cannot be fully appreciated unless read both ways. They required the president to respond to national citizens even as they affirmed (and even created) local identities.[85]

In 1798, Federalists overcame the seeming attenuation of federal feeling through direct appeals to the commander in chief, who responded most sensibly. To the inhabitants of Arlington and Sudgate in Bennington County, Vermont, Adams wrote:

> If you have no attachments, or exclusive friendship for any foreign nation, you possess the genuine character of true Americans.
> The pledge of yourselves, and dearest enjoyments, to support the

---

took credit for cooling. See Alexander DeConde, *The Quasi-War: The Politics and Diplomacy of the Undeclared War with France, 1797–1801* (New York, 1966).

85. *A Selection of the Patriotic Addresses, to the President of the United States, Together with the President's Answers* (Boston, 1798); *Lancaster Journal* (Pa.), May, 19, 1798; *Georgia Gazette* (Savannah), May 4, 1798; *Carolina Gazette* (Charleston), May 16, 17, June 7, 8, 1798. On classes and interests in Adams's political theory, see Gordon S. Wood, *The Creation of the American Republic, 1776–1787* (Chapel Hill, N.C., 1969), 567–592. When the Harrison County, Virginia, group wrote Adams that "the alarm of war has silenced all essential differences in opinion . . . the day, we trust, is not far distant, when the odious distinction of *aristocrat* and *democrat* will be done away," Adams, in his honest way, insisted that the distinction "would not go away": it "was intended by nature." The best he could offer was the opinion that "the parties ought to be like the sexes, mutually beneficient to each other." *Selection of the Patriotic Addresses,* 313–314.

measures of the government, shews that your ideas are adequate to the national dignity, and that you are worthy to enjoy its independence and sovereignty.

Your prayers for my life and usefulness, are too affecting to me to be enlarged upon.[86]

The weeks-long drama of the meetings, addresses, responses, and their reception, punctuated at every step by publication, was an incredibly potent example of acting locally while thinking nationally. A prolific correspondent, Adams found in the epistolary arts all the charisma he otherwise lacked. The letters that revealed his feelings bolstered *his* national character. In print he looked like a president. Instinctively, Adams made the perusers of newspapers into fellow readers of his enlightening correspondence. Revelations of sentiment, his own and his correspondents', invited every feeling citizen to participate with him in the affective field of patriotism: "Your appeal to my own breast, and your declaration that I shall *there* find your sentiments, I consider as a high compliment." A group of Georgians earned special praise for their distant, unsolicited affection: "An address from the youth of Augusta, so remote from the seat of Government, and where I am personally wholly unknown, is a very high gratification to my feelings. . . . The expression of your confidence in my administration, is the more precious as it was unexpected." "Sentiments more worthy of freemen, and free republicans," he wrote to Portland, "have never appeared." And responding to the message of the Congregational clergy of Massachusetts: "To do justice to its sentiments and language, I could only repeat it sentence by sentence, word for word."[87]

86. *Selection of the Patriotic Addresses,* 12. John William Kuehl notes that the addresses to Adams insisted that Americans "did possess a national character." Elkins and McKitrick write that "the great preoccupation" of Adams's responses "is national unity." See Kuehl, "The Quest for Certainty in an Age of Insecurity: The XYZ Affair and American Nationalism" (Ph.D. diss., University of Wisconsin, 1968), 114; Elkins and McKitrick, *Age of Federalism,* 589.

87. Adams to the Free Masons of the State of Maryland, *Windham Herald* (Conn.), Aug. 30, 1798; John Adams to the Young Men of the City of Augusta in the State of Georgia, Colonial Dames of America Collection, box 10, folder 94, Georgia Historical Society, Savannah; "The People and the Government," *Eastern Herald and Gazette of Maine* (Portland), May 28, 1798; "Devotional Patriotism," *Gazette* (Portland, Maine), June 25, 1798. According to Abigail Adams, the president wrote four or five replies in his own hand every day for more than two months. Quoted in Elkins and McKitrick, *Age of Federalism,* 878 n. 25.

Who was actually present at the meetings and who actually signed the letters are washed out in the printed versions. The vagueness invites the reader to join in and rise with the occasion. "I could not look over the long roll of respectable subscribers," Adams wrote to the Albany memorialists, "without the sentiments of gratitude, esteem and respect." Of course, citizens of Albany probably knew exactly which local politicos were behind such an initiative, but participants could nonetheless position themselves as nonpartisan friends of the nation. Often the meetings to receive Adams's responses drew more people than the gatherings that drew up the letters, possibly because they included women. In practice, it seems, Federalist rites of gratitude to the president enacted their rhetorical invocations of an identity between the people (that counted) and the government. This helps explain why so many participants did not see the addresses as implying deference or as warmed-over monarchy. Displaying gratitude for their leaders did not, as Bache suggested, make them servile; it made them *like* their leaders, full of virtuous sentiments revealed in their words and their actions.[88]

Nowhere was this more true than in the sentimental exchanges between Adams and the groups of young men that in many cases formed themselves precisely to address him. In Philadelphia, fifteen hundred of them marched to the executive mansion to deliver their message. The president met them in full military dress and proclaimed, "No prospect or spectacle could excite a stronger sensibility in my bosom than this which now presents itself before me." Expressing appreciation for the sacrifices of their fathers, the young men promised allegiance to "the religion and the laws" that made up their inheritance. Adams complimented them on the respect they showed for the older generation; but, if his words included anything about order, they were lost on these young Federalists. After leaving the president's house they attacked the print shop of Benjamin Franklin Bache.[89]

At all times the mobilization of young men was encouraged by older politicians: probably there was something very familiar in such public

88. *Albany Centinel,* June 5, 1798; Warren, *Jacobin and Junto,* 77–79. In Newark, the young men voted down a resolution to send Adams a message; the Federalists regrouped and sent one anyway.

89. *Gazette of the United States* (Philadelphia), May 7, 1798; *Selection of the Patriotic Addresses,* 141–142; *Aurora* (Philadelphia), May 9, 1798. Jacob Hiltzheimer described the "young men" who went to address Adams as "volunteers." Hiltzheimer Diary, May 7, 1798, APS.

displays of patriotic sentiment. Unlike 1776, though, "the fathers" now figured as both the present-day state *and* as the latter-day Revolution. Thus in 1798 young men demonstrated their patriotism in rituals of prodigal re-union. Potential revolutionaries, they could rise to maturity by demonstrating to the French "that we are NOT 'a divided People.'" They loudly proclaimed that there was no need for all the noise:

> Our Constitution and laws, by our fathers design'd
> To render us happy—and useful and kind;
> We'll freely support with our lives and estates,
> Without hesitation or lengthy debates.[90]

Federalists noted approvingly, and their opponents noted disparagingly, that the propertied were more than well represented among the signees of patriotic addresses. Yet this imbalance did not lead to a sizable countermovement among Republican-identified young men. In New York they gave up wearing the French cockade, though at Philadelphia fistfights took place in the State House garden between wearers of different revolutionary emblems. On July Fourth a group of William and Mary students burned in effigy a figure of Adams reaching into his bag of "responses" to "royal addresses." But this counterritual was not widely imitated. The liberty-cap-carrying youth of Morristown, New Jersey, only qualified their general military ardor: "The American Youth— May they be united to oppose any foreign invasion, but never lend their aid to enslave their countrymen." Even in arch-Jeffersonian central Virginia, the now obligatory toast to the "The American Youth" wished mildly that "he grow wiser as he grows older."[91]

At Federalist celebrations of July Fourth in 1798, old and young patriots explicitly toasted each other. These could be seen as a long-

90. *Greenfield Gazette; An Impartial Register of the Times* (Mass.), May 14, 1798; *The Launch, a Federal Song* (Newburyport, Mass., 1798), Broadsides Collection, AAS.

91. "Boston, May 5: *From Philadelphia, April 27,*" *Windham Herald* (Conn.), May 10, 1798; Novak, *Rights of Youth*, 44; *Times; Alexandria Advertiser*, Oct. 1, 1798; *Centinel of Freedom* (Newark), July 10, 1798. For a view that stresses the "broad occupational support" for the resolutions, see Thomas M. Ray, "'Not One Cent for Tribute': The Public Addresses and American Popular Reaction to the XYZ Affair," *Journal of the Early Republic*, III (1983), 389–412.

The Sedition Act passed the Senate on July 4; according to at least one source, debate was drowned out by the "martial music" that came in from the streets (Sharp, *American Politics in the Early Republic*, 180).

overdue recognition of generational politics, the addition of a natural constituency to the Federalist cause. No doubt there was a general social problem in the high proportion of young adults at this time, and scholars have been constructing impressive arguments for youth as a central concern in the cultural and gender politics of the early Republic.[92] In the context of politics, however, the mobilization of young men against the specter of "a divided People" shifted attention from one kind of difference (partisanship, with its overtones of class in many places) to another (age). The leading Young Men were Federalists and men of means: but now, instead of proclaiming their respectability or their membership in the merchant or planter elite, they spoke of their youth and their maleness while performing patriotic sentimentalism. Like the mobilization of churchmen and Christians to celebrate new holy days, the young men's festive and martial gatherings blunted the Republicans' class-inflected campaign against aristocrats.

The Federalists in effect challenged the opposition's language of class by declaring it divisive and by pointing instead to religious, generational, and gendered harmonies. How effective this strategy had become is apparent from the widespread shift in celebratory initiative to the Federalist youth in 1798–1799. In Boston, Hartford, New York, Portsmouth, and other cities they celebrated Adams's birthday in October and the dissolution of the old 1778 French treaty in July. "It was kept as a day of joy," noted the somewhat skeptical schoolteacher Nahum Jones in his diary. "Nothing of so much magnitude has occurred since the Declaration of Independence," he wrote, copying the exact words of an account that appeared in newspapers all the way to South Carolina. Arch-Federalists had long dreamed of rewriting the Revolution as secession from France, but this repeated reliance on the trope of Independence may reveal the young celebrants' own desire to have what Paul Ricoeur has called a "first celebration": to be the makers of a commemorated event, not merely vehicles of its memory. If July Fourth and the Declaration signified America's birth, maintained Boston's Thomas Robert Treat Paine, the seventh of July—the date of the treaty repeal—marked the "day of our nation's *manhood*." Rather than overthrowing bad parents, these young men declared their liberation from

92. See, for example, Daniel A. Cohen, "Arthur Mervyn and His Elders: The Ambivalence of Youth in the Early Republic," *WMQ*, 3d Ser., XLIII (1986), 362–380; Cathy N. Davidson, *Revolution and the Word: The Rise of the Novel in America* (New York, 1986), 112–125.

the arms of a French coquette of tellingly ambiguous gender, "whose *touch* is *pollution*—whose *friendship* is *poison*—whose *embrace* is *death.*"[93]

But the "American Youth" and the ministers were not the only key groups that Federalists enthusiastically toasted during the years of the Quasi War. The place of both groups in a reanimated Federalist nationalism depended upon the rhetorical and real presence of many respectable women. Women, of course, were no more exclusively Federalist than young men or ministers. Nor was it only Federalists who saw women as potential allies in the battles for affiliation that characterized popular politics in the 1790s. In 1798, however, women celebrants completed the Federalist ideological alliance of the state, religion, and the nation.

Since the Revolution at least, women had served a key symbolic role for men seeking to construct consensus. Newspaper editors delightedly noted their presence in windows as Washington proceeded through town. Fourth of July orators found particular reasons for women to celebrate: only in America could women "breathe the sacred air of Freedom and nobly unite [their] exertions for the general good." Such appeals to republican womanhood responded to women's presence in the audiences for parades and orations and in public life more generally. Like young men and ministers, women found themselves in an ambiguous situation with respect to public culture during the 1790s. Revolutionary practice had meant for many of them a new awareness of public life, and, like French women of the same era, they quickly

93. William Brown, *An Oration, Spoken at Hartford . . . July 4th, A.D. 1799* (Hartford, Conn., 1799), 21; *Gazette* (Portland), Nov. 5, 1798; *Newburyport Herald* (Mass.), July 6, 1798; *South-Carolina State Gazette, and Timothy's Daily Advertiser* (Charleston), Aug. 14, 15, 1799; *Virginia Federalist* (Richmond), Aug. 24, 1799; *City Gazette and Daily Advertiser* (Charleston), Aug. 9, 1799; "A Card," *Commercial Advertiser* (New York), July 12, 1799; *Salem Gazette* (Mass.), July 12, 1799; *Connecticut Courant* (Hartford), July 22, 1799; Nahum Jones Diary, July 30, 1799, AAS; Paul Ricoeur, *Lectures on Ideology and Utopia,* ed. George H. Taylor (New York, 1986), 261; Thomas Paine, *An Oration, Written at the Request of the Young Men of Boston, and Delivered July 17th, 1799 . . .* (Boston, 1797), 6; Edward St. Loe Livermore, *An Oration, in Commemoration of the Dissolution of the Political Union between the United States of America and France . . .* (Portsmouth, N.H., 1799); "A Card," *Columbian Centinel* (Boston), July 6, 1799. For further reflections on the gender politics of Federalism, see my "Federalism, the Styles of Politics, and the Politics of Style," and Rosemarie Zagarri's "Gender and the First Party System," in Doron Ben-Atar and Barbara Oberg eds., *Federalists Reconsidered* (Charlottesville, Va., 1999).

responded to this experience with new claims of rights, particularly to education, propertyholding, divorce, and, most of all for our purposes, claims for the relevance of their political opinions. By 1793 Americans knew that the republican women of revolutionary France had taken on very public roles in politics; debates about the Rights of Women could be heard in middle-class parlors by mid-decade. At the height of American Francophilia, urban citizens tried out several translations of "citoyenne": Was it "citess"? "Civess"? Toasts to the "world patriotic fair" show that the rigorous egalitarians among the Democratic-Republicans truly appreciated the part that women could play in ratifying a more inclusive definition of popular sovereignty.[94]

Women's appearance in the oppositional rites of the 1790s signified a genuine assertion of popular rule and a revival of the participatory ethos (and sometimes the practices) of the Revolutionary crowd. But in a crucial sense, the Democratic-Republicans' mobilization of women paled before that of the Federalists in 1798 precisely because the former did not bring women out — *as women* — in a way that highlighted, capitalized on, or referred to gender difference. That is, for the Jeffersonians of the 1790s, as for the Revolutionaries of the 1760s–1770s, women did not so much signify "the people" as they acted as part of a truly popular (cross-class and -gender) mobilization. When Republican leaders did talk about women in festive oratory, they spent more time in domesticating them than in seeking their partisan allegiance. As earlier, it was only through their influence upon men that women should truly act as republicans: "The Fair of France and America: May

94. *Greenleaf's New York Journal*, Aug. 29, 1789 (Providence); *Federal Herald* (Lansingburgh, N.Y.), Nov. 9, 1789 (Boston); Joseph Clark, *An Oration, Delivered at Rochester, on the Fourth of July* . . . (Dover, N.H., [1794]), 12; Elias Boudinot, *An Oration, Delivered at Elizabeth-town, New Jersey* . . . (Elizabethtown, N.J., 1793), 23–24; Linda K. Kerber, *Women of the Republic: Intellect and Ideology in Revolutionary America* (Chapel Hill, N.C., 1980), 157–264; Kerber, "The Paradox of Women's Citizenship in the Early Republic: The Case of *Martin vs. Massachusetts,* 1805," *American Historical Review,* XCVIII (1992), 349–355; Mary Kelley, "'Vindicating the Equality of Female Intellect': Women and Authority in the Early Republic," *Prospects,* XVII (1992), 1–27; Newman, *Parades and the Politics of the Street,* chap. 5; Susan Branson, "Politics and Gender: The Political Consciousness of Philadelphia Women in the 1790s" (Ph.D. diss., Northern Illinois University, 1992), 86–124; *National Gazette* (Philadelphia), Aug. 11, 1792 (Charleston); *Virginia Chronicle and Norfolk and Portsmouth General Advertiser,* Jan. 26, 1793; Peter Porcupine [Cobbett], *History of the American Jacobins,* 25.

they each weave a cap of liberty for a husband." Consensual union itself could be used to express what to republicans was a genuinely progressive ethic of marriage, in which the gendered virtues of each sex would enhance those of the other. "The American Fair," toasted one group of pro-French revelers in Alexandria. "May all single Female patriots be speedily called on to testify their civism at the matrimonial altar, and may they experience every happiness in their *United States*."[95]

As authors of sentimental novels portrayed it, even a republican marriage restricted a woman's sphere of action. William Loughton Smith captured the male version of this gender theory in describing how women had advanced the Revolutionary cause: by cheering on the men. "To delight, to civilize, to ameliorate mankind—and to exercise unlimited sway over our obedient hearts, *these are the precious rights* of women!" To act alone or to remain unwed risked a diminution of charms and a decline in respectability. Thus tamed, the Wollstonecraftish slogan could even be turned around to signify female desire for male attention, as in a description of a Litchfield, Connecticut, Independence ball that followed the men-only dining and toasting: "The rights of Women usurped attention, and were politely attended to; so that discord did not dare to open its 'Moused various mouths,' and the night passed pleasantly."[96]

Men's toasts to the American Fair made women's very absence, their disinclination to be present, into proof of their gendered virtue. These toasts performed the crucial cultural work of limiting women's mounting claims to equality and rights. They were defensive; they acknowledged the issue of "the rights of Women" only to deflect attention to the harmonious, nonpartisan aspects of political practice.[97]

95. *National Gazette* (Philadelphia), July 18, 1792; Jan Lewis, "The Republican Wife: Virtue and Seduction in the Early Republic," *WMQ,* 3d Ser., XLIV (1987), 689–721; *Virginia Gazette and Alexandria Advertiser,* July 11, 1793. The most common rhetorical appropriation of this femininity for partisan purposes, shared by both parties, was to toast the "American Fair" with the hope that "their charms be enjoyed only by true Republicans"—or "never . . . bless the Bosom of a Jacobin." See "Denton, Caroline Co., Maryland," *Aurora* (Philadelphia), July 28, 1796; *Columbian Mirror and Alexandria Gazette,* Nov. 15, 1796 (Trenton).

96. Hannah Webster Foster, *The Coquette* (1797), ed. Cathy N. Davidson (New York, 1986); Davidson, *Revolution and the Word,* chap. 6; Smith, *An Oration,* 9; *Gazette of the United States* (Philadelphia), July 24, 1794.

97. The case of New Jersey demonstrates the importance of the partisan dynamic—and the irrelevance of particular party ideologies—to the inclusion or ex-

Nonetheless, in a political culture that mixed rhetoric, ritual, and preparations for battle, gendered symbolism opened a space for actual women. Throughout the 1790s there were signs, in toasts, that men recognized and applauded the power women could exert, publicly, in partisan politics. Celebrants of Washington's Birthday in 1796 in Newburyport, Massachusetts, naturalized the ladies' federalism as patriotism: "As their happiness depends on Federal Union, may their influence be exerted in its support." Yet the possibility that women might rise for the other side made Federalists hesitant, like the Independence Day revelers in Boston that year who toasted "The American Fair: May the serpent of faction never lurk in the paradise of beauty."[98] Women acted as partisans, while neither party's men seemed comfortable with the reality; yet women also signified unity, beyond partisanship at a time when each party defined success as the obliteration of the other group or the ratification of their own claim to stand for the people. So Federalists and Democratic-Republicans politicized women as they politicized everyone else, yet kept them at arm's length.

This remained the case until the Federalists, in 1798, found a complementary place for women, *as women,* in their public drama of national character under siege from without and within. With the coming of the Quasi War, July Fourth toasts began to ask the Fair to inspire male military valor. Moreover, women played a particularly prominent role

───────

clusion of women from politics in the 1790s. Some women of property could and did vote in New Jersey because of the way the Revolutionary state constitution had been written: that is, without specifying that only white males could enjoy the right of suffrage. In 1796 and 1797 women took part in every aspect of several Republican July Fourth celebrations (except the toasts). In Mendham, North Farms, and Caldwell, this included marching in processions with the cap of liberty. In Newark, a special bower was erected for their tea party. The next year, as elsewhere, Federalist women entered the public sphere with a vengeance, along with the rest of the Federalists in New Jersey. Nevertheless, the Republicans of New Jersey did not regard women as a Federalist constituency. At Caldwell, "respectable citizens of both sexes" joined the militia on the green, and sixteen young ladies marched in procession with the cap of liberty. Then as in the coming years, both parties made appeals for women's votes by supporting the "rights of women" when they thought it would benefit them in upcoming elections. *Salem Gazette,* July 15, 1796; *Centinel of Freedom* (Newark), June 28, July 9, 12, Oct. 25, 1797; *State Gazette and New Jersey Advertiser* (Trenton), July 11, 1797; Friedman, *Inventors of the Promised Land,* 122–125; Judith Apter Klinghoffer and Lois Elkis, "'The Petticoat Electors': Women's Suffrage in New Jersey, 1776–1807," *Journal of the Early Republic,* XII (1992), 159–194.

98. *Gazette of the United States* (Philadelphia), Mar. 4, July 12, 1796.

in many towns' 1798 July Fourth celebrations. The ladies of New Mills, New Jersey, proved "no less patriotic and federal than their husbands." Deerfield women gave a fiery toast: "May each Columbian Sister *perceive* and pursue the unfallible *system* of *extinguishing* Jacobinism." The "Patriotic Fair" of Middletown, Connecticut, added six of their own toasts to those of the men and then led them in procession to the liberty tree, atop of which flew the pre-Independence serpent flag, "Unite or Die." When William Cobbett, displaying chauvinist consistency, objected to their demonstrations of opinion, these women responded vigorously in print, suggesting that it was their references to 1776 that the British-born editor found objectionable. In Philadelphia and Princeton, women ignored Cobbett's strictures and wore Federalist "American" cockades, with metal eagle pins, in public. At the New Jersey statehouse in Trenton, women sang "Hail, Columbia" just as the city's three militia companies had done earlier in the day.[99]

That summer witnessed a remarkable revival of women's Revolutionary practice of publicly presenting standards they wove to militia companies. Women's pleas to men to protect them and their homes were hardly new: in urging their young men to enlist and parade instead of asking them out to July Fourth balls, a group of Stockbridge ladies cited the women of ancient Carthage who cut off their hair to make ropes for hanging their enemies. What do appear innovative are the exchanges between the officers and the ladies at the flag ceremonials. After a decade of public addresses and responses that drew on the culture of sentiment to include more men as national citizens and after the recent appropriation of these practices by militarily inclined groups of young men, it is striking that many of the presenters of flags were young, unmarried women and that their speeches to the companies were reprinted in the newspapers. Moreover, as if to complete an alliance, these female speakers connected the protection of the nation with the guarding of their hearts and their religion. As one young woman told a militia captain, "Our love can only be obtained by bravely defending our liberties, the Independence, and the Religion of our Country." "As Christians and as Americans," Charleston's Federal-

---

99. *Gazette of the United States* (Philadelphia), July 10, 11, 14, 1798; *Columbian Museum and Savannah Advertiser,* Aug. 7, 21, 1798; Newman, *Parades and the Politics of the Street,* chap. 5; *Commercial Advertiser* (New York), July 12, 1798; "Spirit of the Ladies," *Gazette* (Portland), July 16, 1798.

ist artillery promised Miss Mary Legare that they would defend the flag of their fathers and the "religious liberty" threatened by the French.[100]

Like many women in the decades to come, the flag-weaving ladies of 1798 demonstrated that religion lay within their sphere. The linkage of "anarchy" to anti-Christianity by the Federalists allowed women momentarily to take center stage in defense of the Christian nation.[101] And like the white-gowned young girls of Trenton who had strewn flowers for Washington, women's practices of nationalism at their most public were also at their most gendered. When helping to tie together Christianity, the nation, and the constituted authorities, they represented, not another group of citizens—women—but rather womanhood itself. For these middle- and upper-class women, "the Rights of Woman" were more than compatible with the institution of a national (male) character. In helping young men to secure their manhood as the very model of citizenship, they also displayed their virtuous womanhood. If anything, the Federalist reconstruction of national unity and active male citizenship required some women's active and gendered assent.

100. *Oracle of Dauphin, and Harrisburgh Advertiser* (Pa.), Aug. 1, 1798 (transcription in file 14465, Fourth of July Celebrations, York County Historical Society, York, Pa.); *City Gazette and Daily Advertiser* (Charleston), Jan. 5, 1799; *Times; Alexandria Advertiser,* Nov. 29, 1798 (from Philadelphia, Aug. 8); "An Address, of the Ladies of Potts-town, Pennsylvania," *Claypoole's American Daily Advertiser* (Philadelphia), July 27, 1798; "Female Patriotism," *Columbian Museum and Savannah Advertiser,* Aug. 14, 1798; "From the Commercial Advertiser: Young Ladies—To Arms!" *Albany Centinel,* July 6, 1798.

101. Young Ruth Henshaw Bascom of Leicester, Massachusetts, had never attended the Worcester Fourth of July celebrations that her father would afterwards recount in detail. But she had attended church on state fast days. On the national fast day of Apr. 25, 1799, she attended meeting and heard a number of songs on "nations"; see Ruth Henshaw Bascom Diary, Apr. 25, 1799, AAS. Martha Ballard of Hallowell, Maine, seems to have had similar experiences; see "Mrs. Ballard's Diary," in Charles Eventon Nash, *The History of Augusta: First Settlements and Early Days as a Town, Including the Diary of Mrs. Martha Moore Ballard (1785 to 1812)* (Augusta, Maine, 1904), 341, 372, 386. Thus if some New England women, as Laurel Thatcher Ulrich argues, found in religion and locale the sources of identity, those religious and local identities were, nonetheless, easily, and increasingly often, politicized and nationalized. See Ulrich, "'Daughters of Liberty': Religious Women in Revolutionary New England," in Ronald Hoffman and Peter J. Albert, eds., *Women in the Age of the American Revolution* (Charlottesville, Va., 1990), 211–243; Ulrich, *A Midwife's Tale: The Life of Martha Ballard, Based on Her Diary, 1785–1812* (New York, 1990), 31–32, 76, 107–108.

Michael Warner has argued that the rise of nationalism initiated (and continues to promote) a disjuncture between actual and merely imaginative participation in public life. This disjuncture permits women to be included in a "national imaginary." "But this symbolic reclassification changed the nature of the nation . . . more than it changed the access of women to the public sphere." With the locations of real politics diverging from those of discourse and imaginative work, "the public of which women were now said to be members was no longer a public in the rigorous sense of republicanism, and membership in it no longer connoted civic action." The language of sentiment, in public life as well as in novels, was part of this shift, domesticating and individualizing the experiences of participation and the very categories by which it was understood. Yet a closer look at the practices of nationalism suggests a still more complex story. Even as the remilitarization of patriotism heightened the individualism in nationalist ideology (as we see in the debate over national character), the crises of the nation-state led to the mobilization of more men and women in very tangible ways, ways that were extremely imaginary and, at the same time, newly participatory.[102] In becoming "patriotic and federal," in enacting national character, at least some young men and women secured their gendered identities, and made political history too.

This kind of nationalist practice held out rewards that were imaginary yet tangible, private yet public. The same may be said for the people we usually refer to as national characters—that is, politicians. For Federalist men in high places, the Quasi War was more the opportunity than the rationale for their attempt to suppress a domestic opposition whose egalitarianism perpetuated the more revolutionary aspects of the American Revolution. They revealed their true colors by intimidating and prosecuting newspaper editors and the raisers of liberty poles. Given that Federalist politicians were so obviously elitist and that their repressive measures met with a successful political response, it is easy to forget that the reactionary nationalism of 1798 succeeded less through legal fiat or disembodied fear than through mobilizing people.[103]

102. Warner, *The Letters of the Republic*, 173–174. For similar interpretations of British patriotism in this era, see Colley, *Britons*, 237–281; Gwyn A. Williams, *Artisans and Sans-Culottes: Popular Movements in France and Britain during the French Revolution*, 2d ed. (London, 1989), xviii.

103. For more on this theme, see Waldstreicher, "Federalism and the Politics of Style," in Ben-Atar and Oberg, eds., *Federalists Reconsidered*.

☆　　☆　　☆

During the 1790s, the Federalists used nationalist celebrations to equate Revolution, nation, and state, but others used them to invent an opposition politics that posed the Revolution against the regime, the nation against the state. Celebrations enabled ordinary citizens to practice national politics but also provided new ways for the not so ordinary to personify the nation. The Federalists got their nationalism and further legitimized their quest for order, but they lost another battle against popular politics. These celebrations, as we will see in the next chapter, became one of the crucial practices of the very partisan subcultures that nobody claimed to want. The Jeffersonians were already reaping the fruits in 1799.

Yet even this admittedly ironic interpretation is a bit too whiggish. In America, as in England, it was the conservatives who defined the nation and a newly empowered state against internal and international threats to national character. American (like British) reactionaries enveloped existing authority with the assumed assent of the people, silencing dissent and sending out armies to pacify the provinces. And in America it was the first ideological Right who, denying that a government can only *represent* and never *be* the nation, unleashed a repressive national state apparatus. If the repression was temporary, the rhetoric and the rituals would reverberate powerfully throughout American history. For all the seeming Frenchness of their sentimental obsessions, perhaps the Americans were still more British than they knew.

ELECTIONS, SECTIONS, AND RACES

4

THE
CELEBRATION
OF POLITICS

During the summer and fall of 1800 Abraham Bishop was a very busy man. In addition to his duties as clerk of the Superior Court of Connecticut and the social obligations entailed by his status as the son of New Haven's mayor, he had been asked to deliver the Phi Beta Kappa oration at Yale's commencement that year. "The choice of subject has always been left to the orator," Bishop would later write. "The society knew that I could not write about broken glass, dried insects, petrifactions, or any such *literary* themes." Instead, he resolved to put his "*one* talent . . . into use."[1] That talent was politics.

For Bishop, a Yale graduate who had traveled extensively abroad in the years before the French Revolution, politics was a matter of organization and communication. It was creating events and spreading word of them; it was spectacle and rhetoric in a plain, accessible style. Getting wind of his plans to attack federalism, the club of scholars and alumni put ads in the newspapers and issued broadsides canceling the speech. Bishop countered with even more publicity. It is hardly an accident that Bishop inaugurated his controversial political career by outraging the Phi Beta Kappa—a body that he accused of selectively forgetting its own political origin and denying its political activities. The oration, which he had had printed in advance and which he gave on the appointed day in a church on the New Haven Green before a curious audience of fifteen hundred, explored the nature of exactly this kind of "political

1. Abraham Bishop, "Appendix," in *Oration Delivered in Wallingford, on the 11th of March 1801, before the Republicans of the State of Connecticut, at Their General Thanksgiving, for the Election of Thomas Jefferson . . .* (New Haven, Conn., 1801), 101.

delusion," by which Federalists inside and outside Yale had made their program appear natural and removed from the taint of politics.[2]

Despite the seeming radicalism of the American Revolution, little had changed in what Federalists proudly called "the land of steady habits": a nearly hereditary elite, supported by an established clergy, ruled the state, aided by deferential habits and restrictive voting regulations. No strong opposition party had emerged in response to local or national issues. Bishop saw a connection between deference to the ruling Federalists and the nationwide repression of 1798. The problem with republicanism in Connecticut, according to Bishop, was that "an habitual confidence in the state representation has been extended to the federal representation." The people were left with no means to affect local or national politics. Indeed, the confusion of the local and the national (and the federal party with the federal government) appeared intentional, a program for deception put into place by the ruling gentry: "The great, wise, and rich men well understand the art of inflaming the public mind and generally present at the outset *the delusive bubble of national glory*." Bishop portrayed a Federalist political elite that was nothing if not active. He lambasted the addresses and responses to President Adams, the clergy's role in the national fasts, and, most of all, the abuse of the opposition party at local and national celebrations:

> The election ball is not well opened, till the republicans are bleeding at every pore. The 4th of July occasions, which you imagined yourselves to have earned, have been wrested from you and they have been perverted into days for chastising the enemies of [the] administration by the odious characters of illuminatists, disorganizers and atheists. . . . Such has been part of the system of tyranny which even before our own eyes has been acted repeatedly on the memorable anniversaries of our independence.

In his first and defining public attack on "well-fed, well-dressed, chariot-rolling, caucus-keeping, levee-revelling federalists," Bishop cinched his argument by exposing the deeds of Federalist "retailers of words and gestures on those anniversaries." He insisted upon the centrality of festive culture, of practical nationalism in the political battles of the day:

2. Ibid., 102; Timothy Phelps to Oliver Wolcott, Sept. 9, 18, 1800, Wolcott MSS, XV, Connecticut Historical Society, Hartford.

battles grounded in the Revolution but that, most recently, had been won by Federalists.[3]

As Gordon S. Wood has observed, Bishop certainly had "a modern understanding of culture." He saw the dangers of hegemony in the "elastic" language of the Constitution insofar as "the men, whose interest it is to stretch it . . . have made themselves the judges" of its meaning. "They know the force and power of every word—the east, west, north and south of every semi-colon and can extract power from every dash or asteris[k]."[4] Whether from his Yale education or his travels abroad, Bishop possessed the same sophistication. Yet he seems to have concluded that counterdiscourse alone would not suffice to rend the Federalists' web of knowledge, language, and power. The entire rationale for his September 1800 oration as an event—its timing, its focus, and its well-planned publicity—lay in the possibility of action: the next week's local and national elections. This was a modern understanding of politics as well.

Bishop's maneuvers were not lost on the objects of his attack. Two of his targets quickly fired off responses to the controversial oration. Noah Webster accused the clerk of the court and his Democratic cronies of spending the summer "riding, writing, reading orations, and distributing nominations and pamphlets." The lawyer and officeholder David Daggett intoned, "You have confessed, Sir, that New Haven was divided by the Democrats into districts.—that men were appointed to operate in these districts." For these up-and-coming members of the state's Federalist establishment, Bishop's "base art of electioneering" (which in the week before the election he took all over New Haven County) tended to "destroy the purity of elections."[5] Bishop's whole point, how-

3. Abraham Bishop, *Connecticut Republicanism: An Oration on the Extent and Power of Political Delusion* . . . (New Haven, Conn., 1800), 11–12, 43, 48.

4. Gordon S. Wood, *The Radicalism of the American Revolution* (New York, 1992), 271–275; Bishop, *Connecticut Republicanism,* 31. Virtually the only extended discussion of Bishop's career is Franklin Bowditch Dexter, "Abraham Bishop of Connecticut, and His Writings," in Dexter, *A Selection from the Miscellaneous Historical Papers of Fifty Years* (New Haven, Conn., 1918), 257–265. For a meditation on similar moments of linguistic awareness in Antifederalist rhetoric, see Saul Cornell, "Early American History in a Postmodern Age," *William and Mary Quarterly,* 3d Ser., L (1993), 337.

5. [Noah Webster], *A Rod for the Fool's Back* (New Haven, Conn., [1800]), 9; Connecticutensis [David Daggett], *Three Letters to Abraham Bishop, Esquire, Containing*

ever, had been that elections were no longer (if they had ever been) pure, if purity meant unaffected by attempts to influence voters. His oration and his electioneering epitomized and even helped initiate the most important shift in the nature of nationalist celebration during the Jeffersonian era. Although the most innovative festivities of the 1790s had been local attempts to participate in the making of national policy, after 1800 celebrants hoped to determine who would become policy makers. American nationalists discovered the ballot and connected it to local action out-of-doors. Party politics would never be the same.

Although it would take eighteen years to change Connecticut's administration, Bishop, as we shall see, kept trying. He acted upon the same need for new kinds of organization that had led William Manning, a self-educated Massachusetts farmer, to pen his unpublished manifesto, "The Key of Liberty" (1797–1799). The parallels between Bishop's and Manning's diagnoses and remedies are striking. To both, the increasing tendency of "the few" to monopolize the institutions of learning and political discourse added up to a national crisis. Manning insisted that a crucial strategic move on the part of "the many" would be to start an "association" organized around its own magazine and discussion groups. A kind of counter–Society of the Cincinnati, Manning's Laboring Society would elect its officers every Fourth of July at 4:00 P.M., the time when most private groups held their festive dinners. Manning also explicitly posed this society against the public exercises of merchants, clergy, "military exhibition," and the cult of Washington. And, like Bishop, Manning saw the potential in harnessing popular energy and print culture to electoral politics. Members of the Laboring Society would pledge to support the government but also to inform themselves about those running for office, produce a monthly magazine and weekly newspaper, and "attend all elections as we can." Integrated nationally but initiated locally, from the ground up, the Laboring Societies would perform the Revolution all over again and redeem the Republic. There was no better place to start than with the national holiday.[6]

Manning has rightly been praised as an example of creative dis-

---

Some Strictures on His Oration . . . (Hartford, Conn., 1800), 33, 34; *Connecticut Journal* (New Haven), Sept. 10, 1800.

6. Michael Merrill and Sean Wilentz, ed., *The Key of Liberty: The Life and Democratic Writings of William Manning, "A Laborer," 1747–1814* (Cambridge, Mass., 1993), 122–123, 161, 168–170, 173, 175–179, 187.

sent from below. His remarkable plan, though not published during his lifetime, shows how "democratization proceeded less from the self-protective sagacity of political elites than from the purposeful thinking and agitation of quite ordinary people." Yet, as Michael Merrill and Sean Wilentz also note, "popular and elite opposition politics unmistakably converged" at the close of the eighteenth century. Its fruits can be seen most vividly in Bishop's remarkable use of print culture and celebrations. For the statewide gathering that he helped organize to celebrate Jefferson's inauguration and to kick off the canvassing season for the spring elections, Bishop produced an almost book-length elaboration of his attack on Federalist politicians and clergymen.[7] His criticism of the "self-stiled friends of order," like his demand for a separation of church and state, certainly came out of a distinctive local situation. But it also boasted of its relevance to the state of the nation.

After 1800 the broad gap between local activity and nationalist ideology came to be filled in new ways by political mavericks like Abraham Bishop. Too often dismissed as demagogues or party hacks, the local officeholders, newspaper editors, and energetic organizers of the first decade of the nineteenth century deserve much of the credit for the democratization of American politics through *electoral* means.[8] Though

7. Michael Merrill and Sean Wilentz, "Introduction: William Manning and the Invention of American Politics," ibid., 1–86, quoted at 76, 85; Bishop, *Oration Delivered at Wallingford;* Richard J. Purcell, *Connecticut in Transition, 1775–1818* (1918; rpt. Middletown, Conn., 1963), 150–152. See also the discussion of Manning in Christopher L. Tomlins, *Law, Labor, and Ideology in the Early American Republic* (Cambridge, Mass., 1993), 1–8. Linda K. Kerber has rightly criticized Merrill and Wilentz for not drawing out Manning's lack of interest in women and blacks; see Kerber, "Embattled Farmer," *Nation,* July 19, 1993, 108–112. Bishop had published an essay in praise of the Saint Domingue revolutionaries, in late 1791; see Arthur Zilversmit, *The First Emancipation: The Abolition of Slavery in the North* (Chicago, 1967), 172; David Brion Davis, *The Problem of Slavery in the Age of Revolution, 1770–1823* (Ithaca, N.Y., 1975), 327. The essay itself is reprinted with a brief introductory essay in Tim Mathewson, "Abraham Bishop, 'The Rights of Black Men,' and the American Reaction to the Haitian Revolution," *Journal of Negro History,* LXVII (1982), 148–154.

8. A similar story was told by Ohio's Benjamin Tappan in his autobiography. The beginning of his career in politics, he recalled, came when two political leaders came to see him in 1801 about traveling around the territory to drum up support for statehood. Unable or unwilling to travel, Tappan instead gave a Fourth of July oration on the subject and had the oration published and distributed all over the Western Reserve. In Tappan's memory there was a definite connection between the

they liked to talk about the "Revolution of 1800" (having themselves invented the term and sponsored celebrations of the event), the real revolution lay in the meetings, canvassing, and pre- and postelection festivals that made local and national politics a continuum, a cyclical, seasonal process that made sense.

When Abraham Bishop decided to have his portrait painted a few years later, he posed with the emblems of his office: the pen and ledger book he used as the newly appointed collector of the Port of New Haven. As in most contemporary portraits of provincial gentlemen, there is no explanation of these devices or any direct reference to the geographical or social setting. This painting, like Bishop himself, was going nowhere; anyone who saw it probably knew the sitter and where he sat. Yet the ledger book is open to a nearly blank page. Bishop, pen in hand, seems to have written only a curious notation: "162" (see Figure 8). This, the tally of electoral votes for Jefferson in the presidential contest of 1804, was apparently Bishop's proudest achievement. Like the Litchfield, Connecticut, newspaper that carried a similar notation on its masthead ("162 vs. 14"), Bishop wanted to be known for his faith in the many over the few, for his links to a national political movement, and for his untiring efforts to bring Connecticut over to the Jeffersonian side.[9] In our pantheon of American democrats who have acted locally but thought nationally, perhaps we might find a space, next to an artist's rendition of the forgotten farmer Manning, for the commissioned portrait of a half-remembered New Haven politician.

Fourth of July event, the publication and distribution of the oration, and electoral success. Donald J. Ratcliffe, ed., "The Autobiography of Benjamin Tappan," *Ohio History*, LXXXV (1976), 136–37.

For a refreshing exception to the denigrating historiography of midlevel political figures, see Kim T. Phillips, "William Duane, Philadelphia's Democratic Republicans, and the Origins of Modern Politics," *Pennsylvania Magazine of History and Biography*, CI (1977), 365–387. The forming of new state constitutions during the 1820s and 1830s, many of which significantly expanded suffrage, would not have occurred had not more and more white men participated in electoral politics after the Revolution; see Chilton Williamson, *American Suffrage: From Property to Democracy, 1760–1860* (Princeton, N.J., 1960), 117–181. For the large growth in voting after 1800 in one state, see Ronald P. Formisano, *The Transformation of Political Culture: Massachusetts Parties, 1790s–1840s* (New York, 1983), 33–54.

9. *Witness* (Litchfield, Conn.), Aug. 14, 1805.

FIGURE 8. Abraham Bishop. *By Ruben Moulthorp, circa 1805.*
Courtesy New Haven Colony Historical Society

Manning, in his anonymity, his ordinariness, and his seemingly instinctual mix of plain and high rhetorical styles, reminds us of what was
most distinctive in Revolutionary ideology. Bishop, in his very profes-
sionalism, prolific activity, and self-conscious plain style, helped define
the actual practice of democratic nationalism for the next century.

1800: A DIFFERENT KIND OF REVOLUTION

The cooling of the Quasi War and the resulting split in Federalist ranks encouraged those who were appalled by the militarism and repression of what would come to be known as '98. The reaction against the American Thermidor started locally. During the summer of 1799, Republicans in Oxford, Pennsylvania, seized upon the form of the patriotic dinner in order to publicize their support for gubernatorial candidate Thomas McKean and to make that contest a referendum on "Republicanism versus Aristocracy." Three months later, after the fall elections in which McKean triumphed, huge celebrations were held all over the state. In Lancaster, 412 people sat at a table with half a ton of meat, much of which was later distributed to hungry spectators. Sixteen toasts linked the Pennsylvania election results to Washington, Adams, Jefferson, and the envoys of peace to France, against the "British faction" who wanted war. After the dinner, a procession gave three cheers at the courthouse, stopping on its way to "salute respectable whigs at their houses." In the working-class district of Kensington in Philadelphia, fifty artisans, some of whom claimed to be out of work because of their political principles, also gathered to toast McKean. A year before the presidential election, they also lifted tankards to "Thomas Jefferson. The man and the next choice of the people." [10]

It may be hard for us today to understand how anyone could credit such an imaginative leap from the local to the national. Told that all politics is really local (or, by the very partitions of our daily newspapers, that national politics is distinctly separable from the local scene), we draw connections only in the months leading up to every second or fourth November, when candidates begin to hitch onto each other's coattails. But at the turn of the nineteenth century, elections were both annual and seasonal. Almost everywhere fall elections followed spring canvasses, the dates of which varied according to local tradition. The effect was something like that of today's presidential primary system, where a succession of local elections creates momentum and excitement while lengthening the statewide and national political seasons.

10. *Aurora; General Advertiser* (Philadelphia), Aug. 13, Nov. 13, 16, 19, 1799; John Bach McMaster, *A History of the People of the United States, from the Revolution to the Civil War* (New York, 1885), II, 448–449. At their 1799 July Fourth celebration, the New York Tammany Society planned a toast to Jefferson and his "success." Society of Tammany or Columbian Order Minutebook, 1799–1808, 28–30, New York Public Library.

The state polls of Pennsylvania in 1799, for example, were seen as a harbinger for the spring legislative election in 1800, which in turn would set the tone for the congressional and presidential contests that would follow in autumn or winter. In years of presidential elections such connections were particularly apparent, since in some states the newly chosen legislators (not the people at large) selected the electors who cast votes for the presidency. Thus legislative elections could be seen as referenda on national issues, just as special "activity and zeal" to elect certain congressmen or local officials could be justified as a response to the successful efforts of the other party six months before.[11]

Within this context, the "Revolution of 1800"—the election of Jefferson and the peaceful transfer of power to what had been the opposition—was a process as much as an event. We lose this sense of process when we speak of 1800 solely as an event, a thunderclap like the shot heard round the world at Lexington or the storming of the Bastille. Obviously, it is the very peacefulness of the Revolution of 1800 that has made it seem so remarkable. Yet this image of tranquillity camouflages the remarkably strenuous electioneering that characterized the long campaign of 1800. By the summer of 1800 the Jeffersonians were reappropriating the Federalist innovations of '98 in their very effort to overthrow Federalist rule. William Duane, successor to Benjamin Franklin Bache as editor of the *Aurora* in Philadelphia, helped organize young Republicans into volunteer militia regiments; they marched prominently in that city on the Fourth of July. "We are to have splendid doings here tomorrow—the only uniform corps here now are the *Republicans*," he wrote excitedly to Ephraim Kirby. "The antirepublicans have sunk before the public opinion. And among them one feast or act of rejoicing is not expected to take place."[12]

11. *Address to the Federal Republicans of the State of New-Jersey* . . . (Trenton, N.J., 1800); *Address to the Citizens of Kent on the Approaching Election* (Wilmington, Del., 1800). The outstanding work on the process of electoral politics in this era is that of Noble E. Cunningham, Jr.: *The Jeffersonian Republicans: The Formation of a Party Organization, 1789–1801* (Chapel Hill, N.C., 1957), 144–261, and *The Jeffersonian Republicans in Power: Party Operations, 1801–1809* (Chapel Hill, N.C., 1963).

12. Daniel Sisson, *The American Revolution of 1800* (New York, 1974); Cunningham, *Jeffersonian Republicans: The Formation;* Carl E. Prince, *New Jersey's Jeffersonian Republicans: The Genesis of an Early Party Machine, 1789–1817* (Chapel Hill, N.C., 1967), chap. 2; *Aurora* (Philadelphia), July 5, 6, 1800; William Duane to Ephraim Kirby, Philadelphia, July 3, 1800, Ephraim Kirby Papers, Special Collections Library, Duke University, Raleigh, N.C. On Duane's role in Philadelphia politics, including

By 1800, any line separating the putatively nonpartisan Fourth of July from other festive politicking had become almost indistinguishable. The reason for rejoicing this year, at this time, was far more significant than any cyclical, transcendent ritual meaning. In Newark, New Jersey, and Alexandria, Virginia, Republicans organized celebrations for the disbanding of the standing army. Rural residents, formerly at a disadvantage because of harvesttime, began to postpone their celebrations of Independence Day, putting their barbecues and parades even closer to fall elections. The only difference between the Chester County Republican Festival in early August 1800 and the fete held there the year before to celebrate McKean's election was the completeness with which the Jeffersonians had assimilated Federalist tactics. In Chester, they brought militia, women, and religion together in a nationalistic campaign against the Federalists and their Alien and Sedition Acts. Mary Cloyd, the wife of the orator of the day, thanked the Republican militia for their "exertions in the cause of Liberty, when it appeared declining, never to revive." The banner Mrs. Cloyd handed over indicates the self-consciousness of this ritual and its participants. It portrays, not an abstract female figure of liberty, but the scene itself: "a female presenting a militia trooper with the colours—round the whole the following motto—'From the Republican Females of Chester County.'"[13]

Marching next to the clergy in the procession, Mary Cloyd and her associates knew very well that they were contesting the Federalists' bid to embody the people and proper gender roles. With a libertarian twist that referred to the Alien and Sedition Acts, they turned around their opponents' claim to have guarded the Revolution against "foreign or domestic usurpation." Orator John Cloyd announced that "the cause of democracy is the cause of God," and Colonel John Bull promised that the ladies' banner would inspire his soldiers "to act consistently with the American character." The same patriot with the unlikely name later served as the secretary of a meeting of Chester County Republicans who resolved to hold a public celebration of their electoral success.[14]

---

his militia activity, see Kim Tousley Phillips, "William Duane, Revolutionary Editor" (Ph.D. diss., University of California, Berkeley, 1968).

13. *Aurora* (Philadelphia), June 19, 23, 1800, "Chester County Republican Festival," Aug. 14, 1800.

14. Ibid., Sept. 3, 1800, Jan. 1, 1801. For accounts of similar flag presentations that stress women's activity but do not note their remarkably partisan nature, see Len Travers, *Celebrating the Fourth: Independence Day and the Rites of Nationalism in*

Although the Republicans adopted Federalist methods in 1800, they infused these forms with different meanings. In making celebrations productive of votes, they turned them into nothing less than enactments of their ideology, which demanded a broadening of suffrage. And like the celebrations of the Revolutionary war period, their festivals did not so much commemorate a past as set a course of action for the future. They did this not just philosophically but also practically, in the prescriptive—and prescripted—aspects of these performances. Celebrations became a form of electioneering: they brought party workers together, identified the candidates, and informed voters about the issues, whether these voters actually attended or simply read the accounts in the newspapers.[15]

The emergence of a distinctive Jeffersonian political culture can be seen in the celebrations of Jefferson's victory in 1801. A new chronology of Revolutionary time, in which Jefferson's election signaled the dawning of a new age, emerged as the first article of faith in the revised Republican political subculture. During the months between Jefferson's apparent election and the day of his inauguration, his supporters repeatedly dramatized their victory as a new birth of liberty, a second American Revolution made possible by the freedom of the ballot. The frontispiece of the mock epic *Jeffersoniad; or, An Echo to the Groans of an Expiring Faction* mimics the almanacs of 1777 in its dating of "March 4, 1801: First Year of the Triumph of Republican Principles" (see Figure 9). Jefferson's ascendancy seemed revolution-

---

the Early Republic (Amherst, Mass., 1997), 137–140; and Laurel Thatcher Ulrich, "'From the Fair to the Brave': Spheres of Womanhood in Federal Maine," in Laura Fecych Sprague, ed., *Agreeable Situations: Society, Commerce, and Art in Southern Maine, 1780–1830* (Kennebunk, Maine, 1987), 222–225.

15. Most students of the Fourth of July have lamented the partisan nature of such rites in the early Republic. Cf. Robert Pettus Hay, "Freedom's Jubilee: One Hundred Years of the Fourth of July, 1776 to 1876" (Ph.D. diss., University of Kentucky, 1967), 44–46; Diana Karter Appelbaum, *The Glorious Fourth: An American Holiday, an American History* (New York, 1989), 35–43. Such patriotic jeremiads miss much of the vitality of these rites and do little to explain the political culture of the period. For useful correctives that capture more of the ambivalence felt by contemporaries over politicization, see Len Travers, "Hurrah for the Fourth: Patriotism, Politics, and Independence Day in Federalist Boston, 1783–1818," Essex Institute, *Historical Collections,* CXXXV (1989), 129–161, and Albrecht Koschnik, "Political Conflict and Public Contest: Rituals of National Celebration in Philadelphia, 1788–1815," *PMHB,* CXVIII (1994), 209–248.

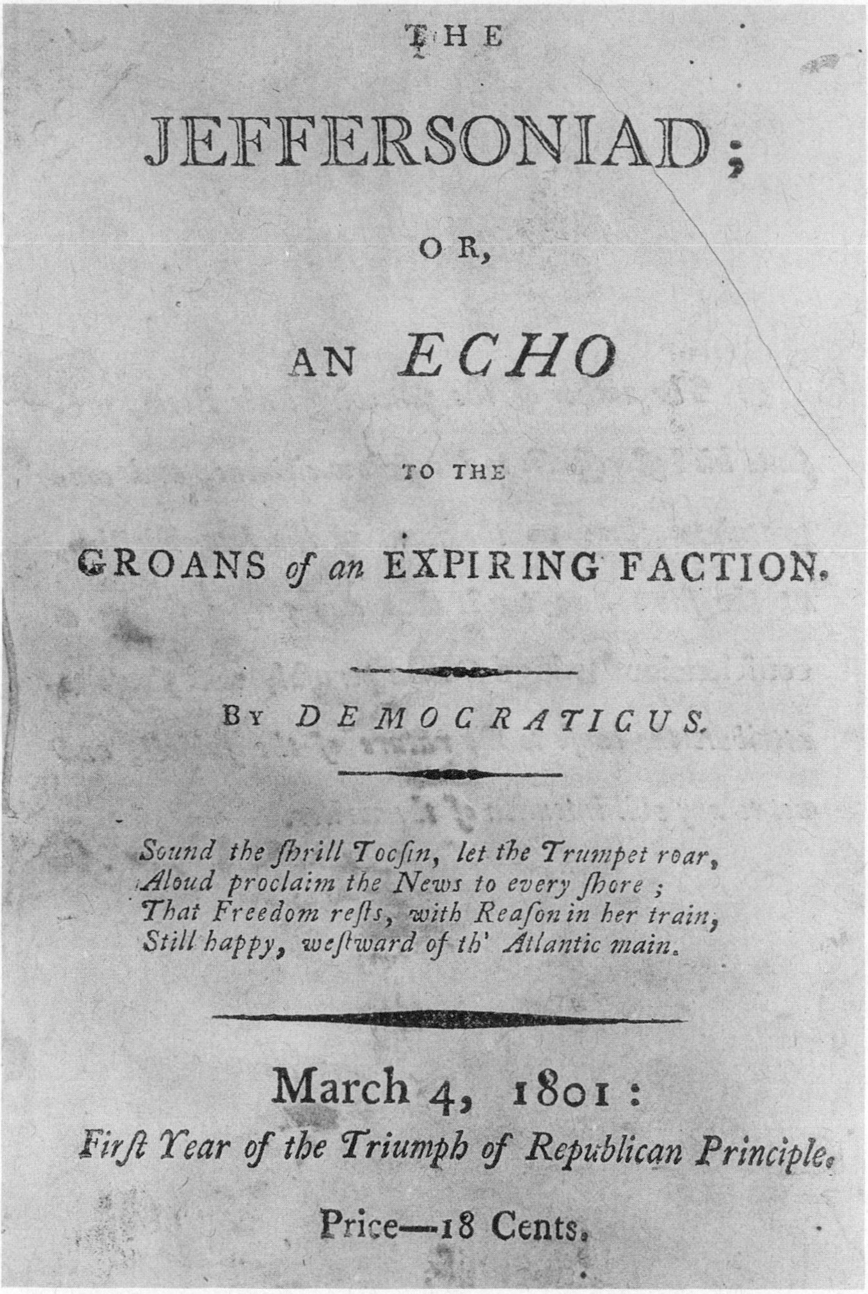

THE

JEFFERSONIAD;

OR,

AN *ECHO*

TO THE

GROANS *of an* EXPIRING FACTION.

By *DEMOCRATICUS.*

Sound the ſhrill Tocſin, let the Trumpet roar,
Aloud proclaim the News to every ſhore ;
That Freedom reſts, with Reaſon in her train,
Still happy, weſtward of th' Atlantic main.

March 4, 1801 :
Firſt Year of the Triumph of Republican Principles

Price—18 Cents.

FIGURE 9. *The Jeffersoniad; or, An Echo to the Groans of an Expiring Faction,*
Frontispiece. Frederickstown, Md., 1801. Courtesy American Antiquarian Society

ary, fully worthy of the languages of popular sovereignty and sentimental patriotism. Kentuckian James Brown wrote to his brother in Connecticut:

> No language can convey a correct idea of the general joy diffused among the citizens of this state by the unexpected but complete triumph of republicanism in the election of the Patriots Burr and Jefferson.—Every face announces a heart overflowing with satisfaction bordering on rapture.—What a change! What a glorious revolution in the situation of parties!!! That we, that the people of Kentucky, that the republicans over the Union, who were termed a *faction,* the enemies of the Constitution, the foes of regular government, should now "changing style" be called the majority, the friends of the constitution, the friends of regular government, the *Federalists* of America, is a change almost too great to be credited.[16]

Finally, the voting process had dovetailed with the "rapture" of the national-popular will fulfilled: politics as the direct enactment of popular feeling, and celebration as the local ratification of the electoral process. The system, it seemed, had worked.

Active partisans gave credit where credit was due. In Killingworth, Connecticut, they recreated the long delay in the counting of the electoral ballots (due to the Federalist scheme to preserve the Jefferson-Burr tie in electoral votes and thus throw the election into the House of Representatives) by toasting first the "eight republican states" that had originally cast in favor of Jefferson, then waiting thirty-six minutes (for the number of ballots) to fire two guns and toast Maryland and Vermont, then delaying another thirty-six minutes to toast Delaware and South Carolina. Finally, only after sundown, did they raise glasses to the people of the recalcitrant Federalist states. The folk artist Lewis Miller

16. "Pageant Exhibited in Virginia, on the Election of Mr. Jefferson," *National Intelligencer and Washington Advertiser,* Mar. 6, 1801; "Jefferson and Liberty," in *The Democratic Songster: Being a Collection of New Republican Songs* (Baltimore, 1801); John J. Hawkins, *The People's March* (Philadelphia, 1801); "The Triumph of Truth and Liberty," "The Jubilee," in *The Republican Harmonist: Being a Collection of Republican, Patriotic, and Sentimental Songs, Odes, Sonnets . . . with a Collection of Toasts and Sentiments,* 2d ed. (Boston, 1801), 9–13, 27–29; [J. Horatio] Nichols, *Jefferson and Liberty; or, Celebration of the Fourth of March: A Patriotic Tragedy . . .* (n.p., 1801); Democraticus, *The Jeffersoniad . . .* [Fredericktown, Md., 1801], frontispiece; James Brown to John Brown, Lexington, Ky., Jan. 8, 1801, John M. Brown and Preston M. Brown Papers, box 1, folder 26, Sterling Memorial Library, Yale University, New Haven, Conn.

captured his fellow inhabitants of York, Pennsylvania, holding a "black cockade funeral," burying the emblems of Federalism as patriots had buried King George to begin the new republican era (see Figure 10). After all, the Federalists had acted rather too much like tories. Inauguration day orators started a trend by listing the tyrannies of the Federal reign in the king-accusing syntax of the Declaration of Independence: "They have. . . . They have. . . ." March 4, 1801, signified nothing less than a "political redemption," an "emancipation." Jeffersonian partisans repeatedly announced, "The reign of terror is no more."[17] The Revolution of 1800 was conceived and carried out as a national revolution, a second Declaration of Independence, and in its aftermath it was described and celebrated in exactly that way, as another Fourth of July.

And they had the author of the Declaration to prove it. Jefferson knew as well as his predecessors that style is substance, and he delighted supporters all over the country with his studied refusal of ostentation. With the ritual exchanges of 1798 in mind, the president-elect told a group of Baltimore citizens who had met to address him that he generally disliked such formal addresses. The new *National Intelligencer* seized upon this careful gesture and asked all American citizens to respect the "chaste republican character" of Jefferson by "repress[ing] the indulgence of their feelings, wherever the public good requires it." Jefferson and his followers drew these distinctions so regularly that we might call this aspect of their discourse a form of ritualized antiritualism. They feelingly, ostentatiously, and loquaciously refrained from expressing their feelings. When a Frenchman dared to write about the "Etiquette of the Court of the U.S.," President Jefferson fired off an anonymous response to the *Aurora:* "There is no 'court of the U.S.' since the 4th of Mar. 1801," he insisted. "That day buried levees, birthdays, royal parades, and the arrogation of precedence in society by certain self-

17. *Bee* (New London, Conn.), Mar. 4, 1801; Lewis Miller, *Sketches and Chronicles: The Reflections of a Nineteenth Century Pennsylvania German Folk Artist* (York, Pa., [1966]), 30, 76; Ebenezer Wheelock, *An Oration Delivered at Middlebury, before a Large and Respectable Collection of Republican Citizens, Assembled on the Day of the Inauguration of Thomas Jefferson* . . . (Bennington, Vt., 1801), 6–7; Bishop, *Oration Delivered at Wallingford,* 7, 96, 97; Alexander Wilson, *Oration, on the Power and Value of National Liberty, Delivered to a Large Assembly of Citizens, at Milestown, Pennsylvania, on Wednesday, March 4, 1801* (Philadelphia, 1801), 23; "Jefferson and Liberty," in *The American Republican Harmonist; or, A Collection of Songs and Odes, Written in America, on American Subjects and Principles* . . . (Philadelphia, 1803), 78–81; *Albany Register,* Mar. 8, 1803.

FIGURE 10. Funeral Procession of the Black Cockade.
By Lewis Miller. Courtesy Historical Society of York County

stiled friends of order, but truly stiled friends of privileged orders."
Jefferson's deliberate abdication of Washington's "monarchical" style
did not prevent the Republicans from linking the new president to the
preeminent national hero, whose death (and extended obsequies) had
only increased his nonpartisan potential.[18] In one song, Jefferson's pen
joins Washington's sword to make the nation free. If anything, Jefferson's hard times during the 1790s prove his rightful place:

Tho' slandered by a tory band
He's still the guardian of the land,

18. *National Intelligencer* (Washington), Mar. 2, 1801, "Thoughts on Addresses,"
Mar. 16, 1801; Thomas Jefferson to *Aurora* (Philadelphia), Feb. 13, 1804, in Dumas
Malone, *Jefferson the President: First Term, 1801–1805* (Boston, 1970), vol. IV of *Jefferson and His Time*, 499–500. Of course, both Jefferson and Samuel Harrison Smith
(editor of the *Intelligencer*) made a distinction between "any expression of the sentiments and desires of any number or association of citizens on any particular or
important occasion, when such expression may be an act of high and indispensable duty" and "those adulatory and congratulatory productions, which have lately
flourished so luxuriantly in this country" ("Thoughts on Addresses"). Cunningham discusses President Jefferson's fascinating relationship with the press—he disavowed interest but read the papers fastidiously and wrote a number of important
pieces for publication—in *Jeffersonian Republicans in Power*, 253–265.

For the linking of Jefferson to Washington: Michael Fortune, *Jefferson and Liberty: A New Song* . . . (Philadelphia, [1801]); Abijah Davis, *An Oration, Delivered at
Port-Elizabeth, State of New Jersey, on the 21st Day of March, 1801* (Philadelphia, 1801),
12–13; Stanley Griswold, *Overcoming Evil with Good: A Sermon, Delivered at Wallingford,
Connecticut, March 11, 1801* . . . (Hartford, Conn., 1801), 35–36. For later examples,
see Daniel Waldo Lincoln, *An Oration Pronounced at Worcester,* . . . *July 4, 1805* (Worcester, Mass., 1805); Nathaniel Cogswell, *An Oration, Delivered before the Republican
Citizens of Newburyport* . . . *Fourth of July, 1808* (Newburyport, Mass., 1808), 10.

Like WASHINGTON, his labors prove
His skill and patriotic love.[19]

Washington and the Revolution he had supposedly led could be absorbed into the new cult of Jefferson.

During the next several years, Republicans in many communities celebrated the anniversary of Jefferson's inauguration, the fourth of March. Like the earlier Federalist-sponsored celebrations of Washington's birthday, these late-winter rites centered on the persona of the national leader and included paeans to his manifold virtues and wise policies. Nevertheless, Jeffersonians insisted that they were not creating another cult of personality. This was not the anniversary of Jefferson the individual; it commemorated Jefferson's election to the presidency. Even though the fourth of March was really the anniversary of the third president's inauguration and therefore more akin to a king's coronation day than to anything else, Jefferson's partisans described it as the day that they—the people—had put him into office. As a variant of the popular song "Jefferson and Liberty" put it, "Election is Liberty's race, / By which noble charter our freedom we cherish / At the helm of the nation then Jefferson place."[20]

Like the increasingly separate and partisan Fourth of July celebrations, the fourth of March enabled the Republicans to show off their strength (and faith) in numbers. William Bentley, Salem's renowned minister and a dedicated Jeffersonian, counted participants at these events as avidly as he recorded the caucus meetings of both parties. In many places these festivals served as ad hoc meetings for party organizers. Newspaper announcements, broadsides, and other sources reveal striking overlap in the membership of Jeffersonian March fourth, July Fourth, and electioneering committees. The Republicans of Providence asked celebrants to arrive a full two hours before dinner, "in order that . . . they may have time to indulge themselves in conversing upon those ample topics of felicitation which have been furnished by the present administration." Republican organizers in Virginia issued long statements introducing their festive plans and published them in the papers, much as they did when nominating candidates for office. Not surpris-

19. "Jefferson, Freedom, and Glory," in [*3 Songs*] (n.p., 1801), Broadside Collection, American Antiquarian Society, Worcester, Mass. See also John Leland, *A Stroke at the Branch* (Hartford, Conn., 1801), 11–13; "Song, for the Fourth of July" and "Independence," in *The National Songster* . . . (Philadelphia, 1808), 69–70, 136–137.

20. "Jefferson and Liberty," in *The Democratic Songster* (1801).

ingly, the states with the widest-spread and best-organized Jeffersonian committees, such as Connecticut, Massachusetts, Pennsylvania, and Virginia, also produced the most and the best-attended March fourth celebrations. For these Jeffersonians, success in getting more people to celebrate made the point that, if only more people voted, nothing like '98 need ever happen again. Thus, even in planter-dominated Virginia, their toasts supported a wide suffrage: "The people of Virginia— not the freeholders exclusively." At Richmond in 1803, more than a hundred artisans gathered at an arms manufactory on March fourth to toast "the restoration of the principles of our revolution."[21]

There was always another, next election to win, and thus the necessity of a vigilant popular activity that, if successful, would make the achievement all new again. Congressional acts striking down odious federal legislation spurred new celebrations of old freedoms, as in the repeal of various internal taxes and the judiciary law on June 30, 1802. Republicans in Hartford wadded a cannon with copies of the overturned acts and threw in a few Federalist newspapers for tinder. At Chillicothe, Ohio, Jeffersonians held an old-fashioned bonfire, ceremoniously burning a copy of the *Gazette of the United States* that contained the text of the offensive tax law. "Guns and bells announce Regeneration of U.S. in Jefferson's reelection," wrote Nathanael Ames in his diary.[22] Making the holiday customary and linking it to the Revolution did not make it old hat; if anything, it completed the Republicans' appropriation of American nationalism and the entire "republican" legacy. To them, the remarkable transformation of 1800 ratified the fusion of "republican" and nation, precisely as proconstitutionalists validated the term "federal" as the equivalent of "national" after 1788. Formerly saddled with the label "antifederal" (an ambiguous term that conflated critics of the Constitution in 1788 with those who opposed the Federalist ad-

21. William Bentley, *The Diary of William Bentley, D.D.* . . . (Salem, Mass., 1905–1914), esp. II, 14, 15, 17, 22, 30, 32, 77–78, 85; "Journal of Ephraim Bateman of Fairfield Township, Cumberland County," *Vineland Historical Magazine*, XIV (1929), 113, 160; "Republican Festival," *Providence Phoenix*, Mar. 3, 1804; *Petersburg Republican* (Va.), Feb. 22, 1803; *Virginia Express* (Fredericksburg), Mar. 12, 1804; *Petersburg Intelligencer* (Va.), Mar. 7, 1804; *Examiner* (Richmond), Mar. 9, 1803. For analyses of the relative organization in the states, see Cunningham, *Jeffersonian Republicans in Power*, 125–202.

22. *Bee* (New London), Mar. 24, 1802; *Aurora* (Philadelphia), July 2, 14, 21, 1802; *Kline's Carlisle Weekly Gazette* (Pa.), July 7, 1802; *Scioto Gazette* (Chillicothe, Ohio), July 30, 1802; Nathanael Ames Diary, *Dedham Historical Register*, XIII (1902), 80.

ministration afterwards), the Republicans now cast their opponents as "anti-republican" zealots craven enough to oppose a "republican" government elected by a national act of the sovereign people.

Describing their celebrations, supporters of Jefferson exploited the ambiguities of their identity as "the republican citizens." After one of Duane's beloved Philadelphia militia units paraded on March fourth in 1802, it retired "to partake of those pleasures which the exertions of republicans in combatting a host of internal foes, abetted by external influence, so well entitle them." In Worcester, March fourth was "welcomed by *all* true republicans." Like many Federalists, Ruth Henshaw of Leicester, Massachusetts, reacted against this angrily in her diary by changing the celebrating party's name, and thus its identity: "The re[p]ublicans, or Democrats, or Jacobins celebrated the birthday of Jefferson's."[23] Nevertheless, on March fourth as well as on July Fourth, Jeffersonians acted out their philosophical republicanism as well as their partisan Republicanism. They were having their nationalism and their partisanship too.

And why not? The Revolution belonged at least as much to them as to the Federalists, who, in their view, had abrogated their hard-won liberties, funded a standing army, sought a fusion of church and state, brought them to the brink of war, and nearly sold out the country to the British. On both anniversaries the Jeffersonians refined and recited their own narrative of American history, in which the reign of Adams served as the dark days of despotism, the tyrannical past that had engendered the second American Revolution. They claimed the Constitution and even Washington's presidency as their own, and sometimes even exonerated (or "drew a veil over") John Adams himself by blaming a conspiring aristocracy who had filled federal offices during the 1790s and who, acting upon their diabolical hostility to all things republican, had tried to maneuver America into war with France.[24]

23. "Speech on the Anniversary of Mr. Jefferson's Election," *Enquirer* (Richmond), May 9, 1804; *Aurora* (Philadelphia), Mar. 5, 1802; *National Aegis* (Worcester, Mass.), rpt. in *American Citizen* (New York), Mar. 16, 1803; Ruth Henshaw Bascom Diary, Mar. 4, 1803, AAS.

24. "Fourth March," *Western Spy, and Hamilton Gazette* (Cincinnati), Apr. 6, 1803; John Foster, *An Oration, Delivered . . . on the Fifth Day of July, 1802* . . . (Stonington, Conn., 1802); Tunis Wortman, *An Address, to the Republican Citizens of New York, on the Inauguration of Thomas Jefferson* . . . (New York, 1801); Benjamin Hemstead, *An Oration, Delivered at Groton, on . . . July Fourth, 1805* (Norwich, Conn., 1805); Joseph Gleason, Jr., *An Oration Pronounced on the Thirtieth Anniversary of Independence, before*

In this political and ideological contest, which continued to make sense as the hemispheric struggle between England and France lurched on, partisan warfare appeared to continue both the battles of the Revolution and the international struggle of liberty against despotism. The muster of actual troops to serve Federalism in 1798 and the subsequent raising of Republican militia companies simply gave corporeal reality to the military metaphors increasingly used to describe political life in general and electioneering maneuvers in particular.[25] Savannah Republicans were urged to call a meeting and "rally under their standard" for the upcoming fall elections. Federalist Fourth of July orators called upon hearers to "attend the enemy on the heights." An 1807 broadside compared the New York elections to the Revolution: "Every Shot's a vote, and every vote kills a TORY!" Samuel Brazer, an active Worcester County Republican, ended his stirring March fourth oration of 1807 by reminding his listeners of their election-day orders:

> *On the first Monday of APRIL,* let no *minor engagement,* no *enticement,* and no *threat,* induce a single Republican to be absent from his post! Nor confine yourself to the performance of your individual duties!

---

the *Young Democratic Republicans of the Town of Boston* . . . (Boston, 1806); Elias Glover, *An Oration, Delivered at the Court-House in Cincinnati, on the Fourth of July, 1806* (Cincinnati, Ohio, 1806); Samuel Brazer, Jr., *An Oration, Pronounced at Lancaster, July 4, 1806* . . . (Worcester, Mass., 1806); Ebenezer French, *An Oration, Pronounced before the Republican Inhabitants, of Portland, on the Fourth of July, 1806* . . . (Portland, Maine, 1806); Levi Lincoln, *An Oration Pronounced at Brookfield, (Mass.) . . . Fourth of July, 1807* . . . (Worcester, Mass., [1807]).

25. Richard Buel, Jr., *Securing the Revolution: Ideology in American Politics, 1789–1815* (Ithaca, N.Y., 1972). On military language, see, for example, "The Republican Legion," in *American Republican Harmonist,* 77; and Fisher Ames's comment on the "Jacobin mode of waging war," spurred by his hearing of March 4 celebrations: Ames to Christopher Gore, Feb. 24, 1803, in Seth Ames, ed., *Works of Fisher Ames* (Boston, 1854), I, 320–321. William Bentley (*Diary,* II, 346–347) noted the trope of partisan battle as an amusing departure in August 1800: "In the [Salem] Register. . . . The parties were represented with great humour as prepared for action. Their position, strength and movements were determined." Jean H. Baker has noted this aspect of partisan ritual in "The Ceremonies of Politics: Nineteenth-Century Rituals of National Affirmation," in William J. Cooper et al., eds., *A Master's Due: Essays in Honor of David Herbert Donald* (Baton Rouge, La., 1985), esp. 174–176; and in her *Affairs of Party: The Political Culture of the Northern Democrats in the Mid-Nineteenth Century* (Ithaca, N.Y., 1983), 287–291, 297. See also Robert H. Wiebe, *The Opening of American Society: From the Adoption of the Constitution to the Eve of Disunion* (New York, 1984), 101–105; and, most amusingly, Washington Irving's *Salmagundi* (1807).

Senator James Hillhouse saw plans for a festival in New Haven as nothing less than "a declaration of open hostility to the morality, Order, and Steady Habits of Conn[ecticut]" that would "develop the Views of the [Jeffersonian] party to every Man who can read." Even the election of Salem's town officers earned a broadside clarion call to guard the Revolution: "TO YOUR TENTS, O! ISRAEL!"[26]

If elections were wars, then every celebration was a battle, and every oration or newspaper essay a strategic move or at least a well-timed volley. A reveler at a Philadelphia Tammany celebration recognized as much when he toasted "Republican warfare—*goose quills* instead of bayonets and bullets—shedding of *ink* instead of bloodshed."[27] Little wonder, then, that each side kept such a careful watch over the other's actions: they hoped to unearth any attempts to steal a march in these seasonal exercises of spectacle and publicity. Historians have too often treated these campaigns as the quaint scribblings of latter-day ideologues or (worse) as partisan sullying of "patriotic" (and therefore somehow apolitical) rites. Such appraisals only repeat the complaints of the Federalists, many of whom sought to escape responsibility for the rise of partisanship. To see partisan nationalist festivals as somehow lacking in true national spirit is to miss completely the meaning and significance of these rites. In their festive activities and newspaper missives each party sought to make *its* respective practices epitomize the true national and Revolutionary perspective, to spur citizens to act as self-evidently good Americans would act at election time.

Post-1800 electioneering methods, such as caucusing and the distribution of printed ballots, were quite innovative, but perhaps none was more so than the linkage of biennial elections to the tradition of nationalist celebration. Like nationalism itself, this sort of innovation

26. *Southern Patriot* (Savannah), Sept. 1, 1806; William Hunter, *An Oration, Delivered in Trinity-Church, Newport, on the Fourth of July, 1801* (Newport, R.I., 1801), 31. For similar examples, see Thomas P. Grosvenor, *An Oration, Delivered at the Town of Claverack, on the Fourth of July, 1801* (Hudson, N.Y., [1801]); Gaius Conant, *An Oration Pronounced at Franklin on the Fourth of July, 1803* . . . (Providence, R.I., 1803); *The Last Day* (n.p., 1807), Broadsides Collection, New York State Library, Albany; Samuel Brazer, Jr., *Address Pronounced at Hatfield, on the 4th of March 1807, in Commemoration of the Inauguration of Thomas Jefferson, as President of the United States* (Northampton, Mass., 1807), 15; James Hillhouse to Simeon Baldwin, Feb. 17, 1803, in Simeon E. Baldwin, ed., *Life and Letters of Simeon Baldwin* (New Haven, Conn., n.d.), 437; *To Your Tents, O! Israel!* [Salem, Mass., 1806].

27. *Aurora* (Philadelphia), May 15, 1805.

succeeds by its very bows to tradition. In this case, it was the Federalists who were more than a little disingenuous (or we might say more charitably, provincial) in claiming that all the electioneering, with the festive yet embattled atmosphere it lent to poll days, departed from traditional practice.[28] As students of Anglo-American politics have discovered, the pure, unmediated election was a fantasy of republican theory. Throughout the eighteenth century, candidates and voters had increasingly cajoled, seduced, treated, threatened, and harangued each other all the way to the ballot box. Perhaps the Jeffersonian Republicans deserve credit rather than blame for helping to keep elections on a public calendar that had always consisted of various kinds of "mixed" meetings, exchanges of deference and condescension, and moments of communal (or at least partisan) rejoicing. The era we date from Jefferson's election initiated a long-term rise in voter turnout; not a little of this growth in participation can be ascribed to the Jeffersonians' combination of national politics with the oldest and most widely practiced occasions for street theater: election days. A Connecticut minister traveling in South Carolina wrote worriedly that all the dinners given, free drinks exchanged, and "swearing, cursing and threatening" led the ignorant "to believe the national welfare was at stake and would be determined by the issue of this back-woods election."[29]

28. On nationalism, innovation; and tradition, see Tom Nairn, *The Break-up of Britain: Crisis and Neo-Nationalism* (London, 1977), and *The Enchanted Glass: Britain and Its Monarchy* (London, 1988). On tradition's "invention" as typical of later-nineteenth-century nationalism in Europe, see Eric Hobsbawm and Terence Ranger, eds., *The Invention of Tradition* (Cambridge, 1983); and Hobsbawm, *Nations and Nationalism since 1780: Programme, Myth, Reality* (New York, 1990).

David Hackett Fischer, in *The Revolution of American Conservatism: The Federalist Party in the Era of Jeffersonian Democracy* (New York, 1965), describes Federalists' protest against and simultaneous embrace of electioneering in terms of a generational split: older Federalists refused to dirty their hands with such methods while younger Federalists gradually proved just as creative as their opponents. Richard Buel rightly objects that "this assumes that before 1800 the Federalists were as innocent of political technique as they claimed to be" (*Securing the Revolution*, 243).

29. Charles S. Sydnor, *American Revolutionaries in the Making: Political Practices in Washington's Virginia* (New York, 1962; orig. publ. as *Gentlemen Freeholders: . . .* [Chapel Hill, N.C., 1952]), 21–59; Edmund S. Morgan, *Inventing the People: The Rise of Popular Sovereignty in England and America* (New York, 1988), 174–207; Frank O'Gorman, "Campaign Rituals and Ceremonies: The Social Meaning of Elections in England, 1780–1860," *Past and Present*, no. 135 (May 1992), 79–115; Formisano, *Transformation of Political Culture*, 136–150; Richard R. Beeman, "Deference, Repub-

Politicians who organized for elections and the Fourth of July did not see themselves as corrupters of the purity of the polls or as demagogues who despoiled patriotic holidays; they saw themselves as saving polls and festivals from inefficacy and irrelevance—or subversion. Abraham Bishop's quest for republicanism in Connecticut provides a vivid example. The overwhelmingly Federalist legislature of the state had reacted to the Republicans' ambitious 1800 campaign by passing a "stand-up" election law: voters would be required to publicly proclaim their votes at the autumn elections. Connecticut remained the most Federal state in the Union, but Bishop's fortunes were rising nonetheless. Over the objections of local merchants, President Jefferson appointed Bishop's father, the eighty-year-old mayor of New Haven and a respected nonpartisan figure, to the lucrative post of collector of customs. The son succeeded to the post two years later. This first of national political plums freed Bishop from the patronage of his political opponents. As his letters reveal, he wrote regularly for the Republican press and devoted time and money to the distribution of political books and pamphlets all over the state.[30]

After two successful March fourth celebrations in Wallingford, Bishop helped bring the inauguration festivities home to New Haven in 1803. Five weeks in advance he personally penned the announcement of a "Republican Festival" for Hartford's *American Mercury*. This

---

licanism, and the Emergence of Popular Politics in Eighteenth-Century America," *WMQ*, 3d Ser., XLIX (1992), 401–430; Alan Taylor, " 'The Art of Hook and Snivey': Political Culture in Upstate New York during the 1790s," *Journal of American History*, LXXIX (1992–1993), 1371–1396; J. Franklin Jameson, ed., "Diary of Edward Hooker, 1805–1808," American Historical Association, *Annual Report*, 1896 (Washington, D.C., 1897), I, 900.

30. William F. Willingham, "Grass Roots Politics in Windham, Connecticut during the Jeffersonian Era," *Journal of the Early Republic*, I (1981), 130–136; Purcell, *Connecticut in Transition*, 139; "Remonstrance, of the Merchants of New Haven," *Connecticut Journal* (New Haven), July 29, 1801; Bishop to Ephraim Kirby, May 25, Dec. 9, 1801, Aug. 23, 1802, Feb. 23, 1803, Ephraim Kirby Papers, Duke University; Abraham Bishop to Elisha Babcock, Jan. 10, 1803, Feb. 4, 1803, Babcock Papers, Connecticut Historical Society, Hartford. For further background on Connecticut politics I have relied on Norman Levaun Stamps, "Political Parties in Connecticut, 1789–1819" (Ph.D. diss., Yale University, 1950); Edmund B. Thomas, Jr., "Politics in the Land of Steady Habits: Connecticut's First Political Party System, 1789–1820" (Ph.D. diss., Clark University, 1972); Stephen R. Grossbart, "The Revolutionary Transformation: Politics, Religion, and Economy in Connecticut, 1765–1818," MS, courtesy of author.

anonymously published missive minced few words in listing the reason for celebrating "our deliverance from aristocracy": "It is that the facts should be known, and that this knowledge should operate in our elections." Not long after, a Bishop-authored circular letter, addressed to Republican organizers all over the state, found its way into the Federalist papers, put forth as an example of the outrageous Republican conspiracy to electioneer. "We shall meet not only to rejoice," Bishop had written on behalf of a committee, "but we shall meet *to unite in measures,* which shall yield further occasions of joy at the next anniversary." Local Republican leaders were urged to promote the circulation of Babcock's *Mercury* and to get everyone to attend the spring elections. In what might have amounted to the first party convention, they were also invited to come to New Haven the day before the festivities.[31]

Publishing the circular letter and penning satire after satire, Federalists treated this episode as the exposé to end all exposés. Bishop exploited it as an opportunity for still more publicity. He cheerfully admitted being the author of the circular; he even claimed to have intended it for publication. The controversy only drew more attention to the event. Although an evening ball seems not to have come off, by most accounts Bishop managed an exciting affair, from the reading of Jefferson's inaugural address, through the seventeen-cannon salute that echoed twice during the day, to the evening fireworks. The popular millennialist preacher David Austin put in an appearance and praised the Jeffersonian gospel of popular suffrage as God's plan. At least a thousand marched in the procession at New Haven, and fifty women in Wallingford held a parallel feast, toasting their children, their "Republican Sisters Throughout the Union," March fourth, and the *Mercury,* their favorite newspaper.[32]

Bishop and his colleagues made this annual celebration a movable

31. Bishop to Babcock, Feb. 4, 1803, Babcock Papers; *American Mercury* (Hartford), Feb. 10, 24, Mar. 3, 1803; *Connecticut Journal* (New Haven), Feb. 24, 1803.

32. See the accounts in the *American Mercury* (Hartford), Mar. 17, 1803; Samuel Farmer Jarvis Diary, Mar. 9, 1803, Yale Miscellaneous Diaries Collection, Sterling Memorial Library, Yale University; [David Austin], *Republican Festival, Proclamation, and New Jerusalem . . .* (New Haven, Conn., 1803). On Austin, see Ruth H. Bloch, *Visionary Republic: Millennial Themes in American Thought, 1756–1800* (New York, 1985), 138–141, 165–167; and Jack McLaughlin, ed., *To His Excellency Thomas Jefferson: Letters to a President* (New York, 1991), 40–48. Thomas Paine put in a guest appearance at the festival; see William L. Philie, *Change and Tradition: New Haven, Connecticut, 1780–1830* (New York, 1989), 39–40.

feast. In 1804, they met in Hartford, the state capital, the day after the Federalists' solemn General Election Day rites (when the clergy traditionally came to town to witness the investing of state officers, and churchmen joined statesmen for an evening feast at the taxpayers' expense). Bishop once again gave an oration that served as party platform, paean to the administration, defense of Connecticut Republicans, and call to action: "Our rejoicing . . . should stimulate to exertion," he insisted. "In his confined sphere of action each may do much for himself and the general cause; and a single vote may decide the fate of a nation."[33] Given the evident proliferation of both celebratory and electoral activity in this era, it seems fair to say that many took Bishop quite seriously.

The Federalists certainly did. By 1803 they were publishing as many pamphlets and Fourth of July orations as the Jeffersonians, replying at length to every missive sent out by a decidedly handicapped Republican press. *The Sixth of August; or, The Litchfield Festival,* a pamphlet response to an 1806 celebration, drew upon the old Federalist theme of a conspiracy of demagogues seeking to take over the government for the purpose of aggrandizing themselves. Like the French they so admired, Connecticut's Jacobins used festivals "to revolutionize the State." The author makes a convincing case that the private meetings and top-down organization of the Connecticut Republicans make them something less than democratic: they preach rotation in office but don't practice it with respect to the federal appointments they actually hold. A proper response, he suggests, is attendance at the freemen's meetings: "Say not that there will be enough without me."[34]

---

33. Bishop, *Oration, in Honor of the Election of President Jefferson, and the Peaceful Acquisition of Louisiana, Delivered at the National Festival, in Hartford, on the 11th of May, 1804* (New Haven, Conn., 1804), 21. On General Election Day rites in Connecticut, see Purcell, *Connecticut in Transition,* 122–123; for Massachusetts in the same period, see Formisano, *Transformation of Political Culture,* 86–87.

34. [Tapping Reeve], *The Sixth of August; or, The Litchfield Festival: An Address to the People of Connecticut* (Hartford, Conn., 1806). On Federalist publishing of pamphlets, see [Richard Alsop], *To the Freemen of Connecticut* (n.p., 1803); Uriah Tracy, *To the Freemen of Connecticut* ("6th September 1803")(Litchfield, Conn., 1803); Joseph Backus et al. to David Daggett, Oct. 30, 1804, David Daggett Papers, General Correspondence, box 1, folder 16, Sterling Memorial Library, Yale University; "Abraham Bishop," *Wasp* (Hudson, N.Y.), Sept. 9, 1802; "Review, of Abraham Bishop's Last Oration," *Balance, and Columbian Repository* (Hudson, N.Y.), July 3, 1803, 210–211, 219, 226–227.

If the Federalists defined "glorious resistance" to Republican festivals as high voter turnout, then the Republicans had truly chosen the field of battle. Nowhere did they appreciate this better than in Connecticut, where public rituals had served as party forums for as long as anyone could remember. Everyone regretted it; nobody could afford to cease and desist. As one Jeffersonian orator put it the same year, "*Election—Thanksgiving—fast-day,* and *federal 4th of July sermons,* are considered as so many engines, made subservient to electioneering purposes." He could only conclude, "Therefore, march to the proxies."[35] For better or worse, future American revolutions would consist of the victories of parties in elections.

NATIONALISM AS PARTISAN ANTIPARTISANSHIP

Parties without acknowledged partisanship: this was the paradox of American politics in the maturing "first party system." Even after the election of 1800, partisanship remained mostly an accusation, not a widely legitimized (much less theorized) practice. At the same time, though, both parties engaged in recognizably partisan activities, such as organizing for elections and getting out the vote. In the longer scope of American political history, this era has seemed to be a transitional moment between the deferential political culture of the colonial period and the rise of party institutions during the Jacksonian era. Ronald P. Formisano captured the transitional nature of this political culture by inventing for it a hybrid term: "deferential-participant." In the early Republic, older figures who retained an aura of patriotism and probity from their Revolutionary service advanced the "politics of the revolutionary center": a politics that embodied both an older tradition of deference to established leaders as well as a republican ideal of virtuous activity or participation.[36]

Yet to define political life by its center can lead us to gloss over the

35. Consider Sterry, *An Address to the Republican Citizens, Delivered at Norwich, (Con.) on the 4th July 1806* (Norwich, Conn., 1806).

36. Formisano, *Transformation of Political Culture,* 3–83. It is important to note that some partisans had already begun to justify partisan politics as good citizenship. The editors of the *Georgia Republican and State Intelligencer* (Savannah), for example, proclaimed in their first issue, "When the nation is divided into parties . . . justice cannot be equally balanced between them and it is the duty of every citizen to take a side" (Nov. 24, 1802).

productive tensions, the negotiations, the active politicking, and the simultaneous denial of partisanship that were the most salient and obvious features of politics at the turn of the nineteenth century. By taking the sharpest edges off local partisan activities, nationalism helped engender the very thing it was supposed to oppose. In the Fourth of July, the March fourth festivals, and similar rituals lay the origins of the boisterous partisan cultures of the later nineteenth century. In acting as partisans, the Democrats and Whigs of Lincoln's time felt like and even learned to be Americans. For the partisans of the early nineteenth century the converse is also true: they became partisans through their rites of nationhood. As a result, nationalist celebrations of the early Republic displayed a vitality and creativity that they have long since lost. Rather than spoiling the party with the cant of parties, Republican and Federalist celebrations lent the "ritual process" a range of contested meanings that the traditional anthropological concept of ritual, with its bias in favor of integration and resolution, can hardly accommodate.[37]

If the Fourth of July was ever a site of creative meaning-making and political action, it was during the heyday of the first party system. But how could rituals of national unity allow space for partisan battles? The local nature of electoral contests, within a nationalist political culture, enabled partisanship and nationalist ideology to work both ways. Since nonpartisan desire and partisan reality intersected locally and nationally, local partisan activity in the form of competing celebrations could be justified by a larger goal of national unanimity, whether defined as support for the Jefferson administration or as a return to Federal principles. At the same time, local unanimity, in a single celebration with even a slightly partisan cast, could be interpreted geographically in terms of national partisan divisions. Even to the most active partisans, party means ultimately served nationalist ends. If there is a patriotic world we have lost, it is not some pristine communal Fourth of July removed from the stink of party politics. Rather, it is the remarkable practices that Jeffersonian Americans developed in order to have their partisanship with their nationalism, their *communitas* with their campaigning: to be local citizens and national subjects.

In appreciating the practices of partisan politics we should not under-

37. Baker, *Affairs of Party*, 10, 71–107. For the newer view of "ritual as a busy intersection . . . a place where a number of distinct social practices intersect," see Renato Rosaldo, *Culture and Truth: The Remaking of Social Analysis*, 2d ed. (Boston, 1992), xvii–xviii, 17.

estimate the vehemence and effectiveness of antipartisanship, the belief that parties were undesirable and possibly dangerous. On the Fourth of July, the nation's best orators performed rhetorical handstands to keep up the appearance of local and national unity. "We have called by different names brethren of the same principle. We are all republicans, we are all federalists"—Jefferson's inaugural assertion dissolved policy differences into ideological consensus and inspired many hopeful echoes. One could always blame "a few *unprincipled demagogues,* of both *political parties.*" At the same time, antipartisanship was consistently articulated, not as an ideal in itself, but as a necessity for *national* progress. Since national progress or recovery could also be achieved through partisan victory, political discourse could be quite partisan even at its most professedly nonpartisan (really antipartisan) moments. Jefferson's conjunction of Republican and Federalist soon fused into new hybrid party labels that were as much about strategy and trajectory as they were about compromise. Jeffersonians proposed that all should become "Republican Federalists" while Federalists tried to reinvent themselves and everyone else as "Federal Republicans."[38]

We must distinguish, then, between antipartisanship and nonpartisanship. As an ideology and a practice, nonpartisanship is only possible when some political actions can be conceived of as removed from structures of partisan wrangling. During the 1790s, however, thanks to the Republican antiaristocratic politics of style and the Federalist repression of "Jacobinism," partisan causes had been equated with virtually everything, including dress, manners, and religion. Nonpartisan ideals did not address such a partisan political reality. An antipartisan stance, however, could work if one identified one's own party, not as a party, but as the real nation—whether by virtue of that party's numbers or its superiority. Nationalists, then, did not have to be nonpartisan. To

38. Richard Hofstadter, *The Idea of a Party System: The Rise of Legitimate Opposition in the United States, 1780–1840* (Berkeley, Calif., 1969), 122–169; Thomas Jefferson, "First Inaugural Address," in Merrill D. Peterson, ed., *The Portable Thomas Jefferson* (New York, 1975), 291–292; James Kennedy, *An Oration, Delivered in St. Philip's Church . . . in Commemoration of American Independence* (Charleston, S.C., [1801]), 37–38; George I. Eacker, *An Oration, Delivered at the Request of the Officers of the Brigade . . . Fourth of July, 1801 . . .* (New York, 1801); James Wilson, *An Oration, Delivered at Providence . . . Fourth of July, 1804* (Providence, R.I., 1804); Joseph Bartlett, *An Oration, Delivered at Biddeford, on the Fourth of July, 1805* (Saco, Maine, 1805), 8–9; Richard Evans, *An Oration, Delivered . . . Fourth July, 1805* (Portsmouth, N.H., 1805).

act politically, they could not be. Instead, they denied the other party's legitimacy and the partisanship of their own party.

Some orators, in classic antiparty style, broke the first rule of non-partisanship by blaming the rise of party wholly on their opponents. The best path to a Washingtonian unanimity, insisted one avowed anti-partisan, was vigilance against the Republicans and their heresies.[39] Likewise, A "Song, Composed for the 4th of March, 1801" asks Jeffer-sonian celebrants to "join hand in hand—Party Spirit we'll rout; / Attention! ye Feds, to the Right face About." One man's malevolent party, it seems, was another man's solution to political division. Feder-alists especially insisted that the vice of demagoguery came with other Jeffersonian innovations, direct from France. Alden Bradford, the July Fourth orator at Wiscasset, Massachusetts, in 1804, beseeched his audi-ence to "check the violence of party emanations," the "infidelity" and "vile spirit of calumny" that threatened "the triumph of political truth and federal republicanism."[40] Antipartisan appeals clothed the worst kinds of partisan cant.

At the same time, appeals to harmony stood alongside celebrations of party victory, especially for the party in power. Jeffersonian songsters strove to make Jefferson's elevation to the presidency into the precon-dition for an end to "party toasts." Where the old "Hail, Columbia" sung in 1798 had pledged eternal war against "rude foe[s]" at home and abroad, the Republicans' "New Hail Columbia" sang in an Ameri-can golden age helped along by celebratory abstinence:

All party toasts we here disclaim
Which joined with wine the soul inflame
    And prove the source of civil broils.

.   .   .   .

39. John Wentworth, *An Oration, Delivered at Portsmouth, New-Hampshire, on the Fourth of July, 1804* (Portsmouth, N.H., 1804); John Danforth Dunbar, *An Oration, Pronounced on the 4th July, 1805, at Pembroke; at the Request of a Convention of Republicans, from Various Parts of the County of Plymouth* (Boston, 1805); John William Caldwell, *Oration, Pronounced at Worcester, (Mass.) July 4, 1803* (Worcester, Mass., 1803). This perspective might have been the most "Washingtonian" of all, since as president Washington had attacked his critics as an illegitimate faction while encasing his own increasingly partisan administration in the rhetoric and symbols of national unity.

40. *American Roast Beef* (n.p., 1801), Broadsides Collection, New York Public Library; [Ezra Sampson], *The Sham-Patriot Unmasked* (Hudson, N.Y., 1802); Alden Bradford, *An Oration, Pronounced at Wiscasset, on the Fourth of July, 1804* . . . (Wiscas-set, Mass., 1804), 16.

Let us this day, that made us free,
Devote to social harmony.
    So rapidly our states increase,
    cherish'd by freedom, nurs'd in peace,
If bumpers to each state we take,
Uproar might all our country shake.[41]

This popular rendition then went on to reserve a single toast for Thomas Jefferson, "revered" alongside the immortal Washington. At a Petersburg, Virginia, July Fourth festival, planned in the hope that "party distinctions will be entirely obliterated," such "national songs" leavened the intervals between toasts to "The Spirit of Republicanism," "The Memory of French liberty," and "The State of New Hampshire— May the work of regeneration progress." The nationwide celebrations held in early 1804 for the acquisition of Louisiana shared the same strategy: to persuade all to laud the existence and the accomplishments of the Republican administration as a national blessing.[42]

Indeed, on the Fourth of July the Jeffersonians presented the Revolution itself as their own achievement. Audiences were reminded that President Adams and his government "were not actuated by the principles of the revolution."[43] The Republican committee of arrangements for their 1803 celebration in Boston issued a special ticket to Major General William Heath, a Revolutionary war hero who resided in Roxbury: "The pleasing prospect of a pleasant day, we trust, will encourage you to join in company with those Republicans, who wish to preserve those genuine principles that led to our glorious Revolution, in which you have born so active and honorable a part." As they fared better and better at the polls, the Republicans claimed the Fourth of July as essentially *their* holiday. Reading the Declaration aloud at Republican celebrations reinforced this conceit: after all, the Republican president was its author. Federalists understood the effects of this conflation very

41. "New Hail Columbia," in *The Carolina Harmonist* . . . (Charleston, S.C., 1803), 78. See also John Wentworth, *Patriotic Odes: Composed for the National Jubilee, July 4th, 1804* (Portsmouth, N.H., 1804).

42. *Petersburg Intelligencer* (Va.), July 3, 6, 1804.

43. Benjamin Hobart, *An Oration, Pronounced July 4, 1805, at Abington* . . . (Boston, 1805), 11–13. William A. Fales reminded his listeners in the western Massachusetts town of Lenox to respect all heroes of the Revolution, even though some "have forgotten the principles of '75" (*An Oration Pronounced at Lenox, July 4th, 1807* . . . [Pittsfield, Mass., 1807], 21–22).

well; but, whenever they objected to the reading of the Declaration (sometimes on the grounds of a diplomatic need to encourage more friendly attitudes toward England), Jeffersonians had a field day. Before the 1802 celebration in Albany, a special session of the city council met to overturn the committee's plans to dispense with the reading of the Declaration; the story made the rounds of the Republican papers. In 1808, the *Democrat* of Boston printed a special "Declaration of Dependence" upon Great Britain for the use of its Federalist opponents.[44]

What was true for the Declaration was true for the celebration as a whole. For Republicans, the Federalists (who were really tories) simply could not appropriately commemorate Independence. "The language of that day was, *we the people,* etc. Now the language of these men are, *we the noble, chosen, privileged few,*" insisted Christopher Manwaring, an active Connecticut politician. "If they [the Federalists] pay any attention to this day, by way of *celebration,* their pretensions are *evidently hypocritical.*" When frustrated Federal editors suggested that the Fourth had become nothing but a drunken orgy, their counterparts pounced: "The celebration of this day revives in the hearts of all true Americans, a strong attachment to liberty, and a detestation of tyrants. . . . This is the true reason why objections are made to the annual exhibition of that sentiment of republicanism, by whose powerful authority America was emancipated from Britain." Who but a "*good royalist*" would slander or ignore the Fourth?[45]

While true republican Americans celebrated, Federalists could be doing only the opposite. "Sorrow and disappointment was marked in

44. Nathaniel Noyes to William Heath (with ticket), July 3, 1803, William Heath Papers, AAS; *National Intelligencer* (Washington), July 7, 1806; *American Citizen and General Advertiser* (New York), July 15, 1802 (from *Rhode Island Republican*), July 17, 1802, July 20, 21, 1805; *New-York Evening Post,* July 6, 1804; *New-York Herald,* July 7, 1805; *Morning Chronicle* (New York), July 11, 1804; "American Independence," *Witness* (Litchfield, Conn.), July 2, 1806; "Celebration at Simsbury," *American Mercury* (Hartford), July 17, 1806; "Federalism Unmasked" (from *Albany Register*), *Providence Phoenix,* July 27, 1802; *Aurora* (Philadelphia), July 18, 1808 (from *Democrat* [Boston]). See also Philip F. Detweiler, "The Changing Reputation of the Declaration of Independence: The First Fifty Years," *WMQ,* 3d Ser., XIX (1962), 557–574.

45. Christopher Manwaring, *Republicanism and Aristocracy Contrasted; or, The Steady Habits of Connecticut, Inconsistent with, and Opposed to the Principles of The American Revolution: Exhibited in an Oration, Delivered at New-London (Con.), July 4th, 1804* . . . (Norwich, Conn., [1804]), 9; *American Citizen* (New York), July 5, 1800, July 8, 1801. For a similar remark, see Hobart, *An Oration,* 14–15.

their countenances, and to them it seemed as though their hearts were clothed in sackcloth and ashes, as on some day of general mourning." The cult of sentiment continued to inform the discernment of political sensibilities. If politics remained a matter of sympathy, of deep feeling, its public performance allowed insights into character. It fused individual and collective identity, ratifying personal worth in light of communal display, whether of the majority or (increasingly for Federalists) a virtuous remnant. The fashioning of patriotic partisan identity required political others who lacked virtue and, most of all, sincerity. When news arrived of Delaware Republican Caesar Rodney's senatorial victory over the Federalist James Bayard, "universal gladness cheered the countenances and pervaded the hearts of all, except for a few of the *'friends to order'* . . . who generally sicken at the voice of the people whenever that voice is expressed *contrary* to *their* views." Even where Federalists patently galvanized their forces in the same manner, Republicans insisted that they could only have "*pretended* to celebrate the day."[46]

How did Federalists respond to these attacks on their legitimacy and their patriotism? Actually, both sides remained thoroughly immersed in the two-sided cultural logic of celebration and execration in which Revolutionary nationalism had been fashioned. In the eyes of each party, the other simply could not truly celebrate. Partisans did not ignore or easily dismiss their opponents' parades, orations, toasts, and commentary; to the contrary, they obsessively attacked them in speech, in letters, and, most especially, in print. Since Federalists were doing less of the celebrating in these years, Federalist newspapers regularly featured stinging responses to Republican festivals and toasts; and when the Republicans were not kind enough to provide good material for satire, Federalists dissected the entire process anyway by publishing mock accounts of celebrations and then directing all the Jeffersonian papers to reprint them. Like their briefs against the festivals for the French Revolution a decade earlier, Federalist satire portrayed Jeffersonian celebrants as inherently inebriated, rowdy, and senseless. Far from being orderly expressions of virtuous sentiments, they were the worst kinds of crowd action. The Louisiana Purchase fetes in the cities constituted "a becoming concourse of mob majesty." Participants in

46. *Aurora* (Philadelphia), July 5, 1800; *Republican* (Petersburg, Va.), Oct. 21, 1802; *American Mercury* (Hartford), July 11, 1805.

the Litchfield Republican festival of 1806 earned the closest thing to a Federalist compliment by being "less noisy, turbulent and riotous, than could be expected."[47]

Federalist anticelebratory writing, like most good satire, sought to define the identity of its subjects.[48] But this was more than just good strategy. Federalists continued to be horrified by the efforts of those they called "democrats" to bring more and more people into politics. The wrong people were celebrating; how could they but celebrate wrongly? Again and again Federalists like Timothy Swan decried the mixed crowds at Jeffersonian festivals:

> The Demos held their feast at Elisha Kents they sent invitations to the neighbouring towns for help and invited all the little boys here to join them, telling them that their Eating and drinking should cost them nothing—numbers you know is all they want, no matter whether black or white, by information I have Rec[eive]d I believe they had a motley Crew. They will undoubtedly give their celebration a brilliant Colouring in Babcocks paper—False colouring is their trade, and truth is rank poison to them.[49]

For Swan, there was a clear connection between the true identities, or color, of Republican celebrants and their celebratory styles: a connection paralleled by the relationship between Republican publicity and its "colouring," or content. Similarly, Swan's allies in Connecticut portrayed Abraham Bishop as a whoremonger for his recruitment of women to attend the 1803 New Haven revel. Drinking throughout his delivery of a mock oration, the fictionalized Bishop tells female listeners: "Prepare for the exercises of the day and of the *evening*. . . . For you are reserved the *delightful entertainments* of the evening." A brilliant mock-prophetic account of the New Haven festival entitled "Chronicles

47. *Connecticut Courant* (Hartford), July 13, 1802 (from *American Telegraphe* [Bridgeport]); "Patriotic Song," *New York Herald,* July 31, 1802 (from *New England Palladium* [Boston]); "Democratic Proclamation: By the State-Manager," *Berkshire Reporter* (Pittsfield, Mass.), June 11, 1808; "Democratic Carousal" (from *New-York Spectator*), *Litchfield Monitor* (Conn.) May 16, 1804, "From the Frederick-Town Herald," June 20, 1804, Aug. 13, 1806.

48. Linda K. Kerber, *Federalists in Dissent: Imagery and Ideology in Jeffersonian America* (Ithaca, N.Y., 1970), 11.

49. Timothy Swan to Luthe[r] Allen, July 6, 1803, Timothy Swan Papers, AAS. For an example of a similar complaint in Cincinnati in 1800, see *Western Spy* (Cincinnati), Aug. 13, 1800.

of King Thomas [Jefferson]. Chapter X" proclaimed that "of devout women there were not one" who responded to the festive proclamation of the evil Abraham. "Old men and boys, and no man knew whence they came, nevertheless they all cried with one voice, 'we will rejoice.'"[50]

These latter-day Connecticut wits improved upon a kind of literary blackface: fake letters in black dialect, supposedly addressed by black writers to black audiences, that described their interest or participation in Republican festivals.[51] Often, as if to seal an argument about the Republicans' complete inversion of the natural order of things, these fictional missives appeared in the newspapers *after* every other aspect of the Jeffersonian celebration, particularly the class and gender of the other participants, had been ridiculed. In one of these pieces, the most culturally invisible of potential spectators—black women—become key participants in the festival, but only to point out their lack of virtue: "All de *brack* Ladie will be invite to de *pribate houses,* where dere will be de fine fun—Masse *Heidigger* will prepare ebery Ting for de brack Ladie, he and de oders be berry great friends to de Liberty of de brack woman." The Connecticut Jeffersonians and their followers here threaten to turn American into African festivity, "just like in Guinea":

50. *Connecticut Courant,* Mar. 2, 1803, "Circular" (from *Connecticut Gazette*), Mar. 9, 1803; *Monitor* (Litchfield, Conn.), Feb. 2, 9, 16, Mar. 9, 1803, May 23, 1804.

51. Shane White has noted similar moments in newspapers and almanacs of the late eighteenth and early nineteenth century and also sees in them the antecedents of blackface. See White, *Somewhat More Independent: The End of Slavery in New York City, 1770–1810* (Athens, Ga., 1991), 68–73, 188; White, "'It Was a Proud Day': African Americans, Festivals, and Parades in the North, 1741–1834," *JAH,* LXXXI (1994–1995), 25–27. For the best-known example, see Hugh Henry Brackenridge, *Modern Chivalry* (1792), ed. Claude M. Newlin (New York, 1962), II, 115–116, in which a black man addresses the American Philosophical Society in black English. What makes the particular fictions of black speech I discuss here different may be their portrayal of black dialect as a written, as well as a spoken, language. These pieces depict blacks in the act of spreading the word, or the meaning, of celebrations—in effect, broadening participation by their own efforts; they also presume that blacks see participation in celebrations as liberating.

On the forms of blackface in the nineteenth century and its relation to political culture, see Baker, *Affairs of Party,* 213–243; Alexander Saxton, *The Rise and Fall of the White Republic: Class Politics and Mass Culture in Nineteenth-Century America* (London, 1990), 165–182; David R. Roediger, *The Wages of Whiteness: Race and the Making of the American Working Class* (London, 1991), 95–114; Eric Lott, *Love and Theft: Blackface Minstrelsy and the American Working Class* (New York, 1993).

De brack Shentlemen will fetch de fiddle to play de Hornpipe—
while de brack Ladie go into de *pribate Houses*—and *Abram Wyshop*
will beat on he fader's head with de drum stick, the marsale [Mar-
seilles] Hymn, and make sound like de Drum.

This faux proclamation "To All Good People of Color" carried the sig-
nature of "Prince Cuffee," a common name for the Negro governors
who had led Negro Election Day in New England.[52]

Even as they turned Bishop's innovative partisan rites into an example of local color, these satires drew attention to the real possibility
of free black citizenship. After the celebration in question, a Middletown paper printed a fake letter from a free black named "Pompey," in
which the narrator relates how he told John Heyleger, the Republican
organizer, that he is "a fre man in gude Publican tu." Heyleger responds
by shaking his hand and asking why he didn't bring more friends to the
festival, since "de fre Brak man was gude as de Wite man an kurd vot de
sam." They agree that most blacks, though Republicans, did not know
that they would be allowed to attend the white celebration. Reporting
on what he saw and did at the festival, Pompey admits that he could
not understand half of what the orator had said—but predicts that he
and friend "Prins" can read it when it appears in the papers. What
he did hear, though, persuades him to vote for "Mr. Kliby" (Ephraim
Kirby, a Republican congressional candidate) in the elections. At the
festive dinner Pompey drinks a great deal and has a run-in with an
Irish-American sailor, who calls him a "Brak son-of-a-bitch." Pompey
responds again by informing his fellow reveler that he is a free man and
a good Republican.[53]

52. *Monitor* (Litchfield, Conn.), Feb. 9, 1803. On Negro Election Day, see Melvin
Wade, " 'Shining in Borrowed Plumage': Affirmation of Community in the Black
Coronation Festivals of New England, ca. 1750–1850," in Robert Blair St. George,
ed., *Material Life in America, 1600–1860* (Boston, 1988), 171–181; William D. Pier-
sen, *Black Yankees: The Development of an Afro-American Subculture in Eighteenth-Century
New England* (Amherst, Mass., 1988), 113–140.

53. "Copy of a Letter from a Black Gentleman to His Friend in the City," *Middle-
sex Gazette* (Middletown, Conn.), Mar. 14, 1803. In Philadephia, Federalist wags
suggested that blacks would be the next recruits for Democrat William Duane's militia. In Troy, New York, Federalists satirized the Republican-dominated Tammany
Society by publishing mock announcements for black (and then native American
and canine) Tammany chapters and their festivals. See *Spirit of the Press* (Philadelphia), I, no. 17 (October, 1806); *Tickler* (Philadelphia), July 19, Aug. 23, Oct. 25,
Nov. 8, 1809.

Black participation on an equal footing epitomized the loss of virtue that Federalists decried. Republican descriptions of Federalist non-celebrants of the Fourth of July elaborated an important, if obvious, fact: Federalists were in mourning for their golden age.[54] The elaboration of mourning, however, was not merely an expression of the Federalist persuasion. It was also a strategic response to the celebratory activity of the Jeffersonians, a cautionary warning of national decline. Federalists *performed* the melancholy ascribed to them by their opponents, turning it into a matter of pride. On July 4, 1801, the schoolteacher Nahum Jones saw in the newspaper a "Monumental inscription of the Talents and resources of the Federal Administration of the Government of the United States; Washington and Adams, Presidents." A young Richmond lady wrote to a suitor: "On the Day that we received intelligence of the election of Jefferson, the *cannons* kept up an incessant fire—and at night the Capitol was most splendidly Illuminated, as also all the Democratic Houses in Town. But we poor *Dejected, Disappointed,* Federalists, remained in entire darkness.—We even closed the shutters next the Town, to make it appear as gloomy as possible." By these symbolic actions and rhetorical turns Elizabeth Gamble and her family turned electoral defeat into moral victory, constructing for themselves a political identity as the nation's virtuous remnant:

> Those *criers out* for "Liberty and the Rights of Man," even talked of compelling the Federalists, at least to put on the semblance of Joy, on the Fourth of March.—While [the Federalists'] Patriotic Hearts, were sinking within them, to see their Countrymen so Infatuated.—and their loved Country, verging on its *ruin.*
>
> But I fancy they thought better of it—They found it would not be so easy a matter to Trample on the rights of Noble, Firm, and United Freemen.[55]

This anticelebratory strategy continued to be employed by the Federalists throughout their long winter of dissent. With the controversial

54. Linda Kerber discusses this "Augustan" aspect of Federalist ideology in *Federalists in Dissent,* 1–22. For a good example of Federalist nostalgia for the 1790s, see Isaac C. Bates, *An Oration, Pronounced at Northampton, July 4, 1805* . . . (Northampton, Mass., 1805).

55. Nahum Jones Diary, July 4, 1801, AAS; Elizabeth Washington (Gamble) Wirt to Thomas Bayly, Mar. 11–12, 1801, Virginia Historical Society, Richmond. I would like to thank Anya Jabour for the latter reference and for generously sending me a transcript of this letter.

attempts by Jefferson to abolish federal courts and to challenge the tenure of his predecessor's "midnight judges," Federalist papers printed funeral arrangements for the corpse of American Justice (with the Constitution as the chief mourner). An 1806 song for Independence Day called on all good Federalists both to feel their melancholy and to "suppress each fear, / The rising sigh, th' indignant tear," not in the name of national unity, but for the sake of "FEDERAL PRIDE."[56]

After the Revolution of 1800, and especially during the Embargo crisis in 1806–1808, some suggested that shame and "mournful songs" were the order of the day for both the June anniversary of the Embargo and the Fourth of July. Under earlier presidents, "the day [the Fourth] was celebrated as a real Jubilee. In fact we *have* been free and independent, but alas! it has dwindled to a name." In Newburyport, on the anniversary of the Embargo, sailors with crepe on their arms marched to muffled drums while flags flew at half-mast and minute guns, "signs of extreme distress," were fired. Such announcements were often printed with the black borders befitting a newspaper on a "DAY OF MOURNING."[57]

The opposition pursued its performative nostalgia in funeral exercises for two of their greatest partisans and patriots, Alexander Hamilton and Fisher Ames. Both of these spectacles attempted to recreate the nonpartisan yet unmistakably Federalist aura of the Washington obsequies that had swept the nation during the first months of 1800.[58] When Hamilton died, Federalists in Albany, New York City, Philadelphia,

56. J. M. Sewall, *Songs for the Celebration of American Independence, 1806*, Broadsides Collection, New-York Historical Society.

57. *Republican; or, Anti-Democrat* (Baltimore), July 5, 19, 1802 (from *Columbian Centinel*); "Burlington," *New-York Herald,* July 17, 1802; *New-York Commercial Advertiser,* July 5, 1806, July 5, 1808; *Song, for the First Anniversary of the 'Terrapine Aera'* (n.p., n.d.), Broadsides Collection, New York Public Library; "Independence," *Berkshire Reporter* (Pittsfield), July 4, 1807; *True American and Commercial Advertiser* (Philadelphia), Dec. 30, 1808, Jan. 2, 1809. The repeal of the Embargo, of course, inspired celebration; see *To the Federal Republican Citizens of Albany and Colonie* (Albany, N.Y., 1809).

58. Fischer, *Revolution of American Conservatism*, 104–105. On the Washington funerals and their diffusion, see Richard D. Brown, *Knowledge Is Power: The Diffusion of Information in Early America, 1700–1865* (New York, 1989), 253–257. For a possible exception to the rule that funerals for party statesmen were Federalist affairs, see William Bentley's comments on the aftermath of Jacob Crowninshield's death in Salem: Bentley, *Diary*, III, 355.

Charleston, Salem, New York, Wilmington, North Carolina, and other places held public meetings and resolved that citizens should wear crepe for thirty days in recognition of the "great national loss." As in the case of George Washington's funeral, Hamilton's obsequies were a perfect venue for the ostensibly nonpartisan political participation of women. They published dirges and elegies and appeared in mourning attire and in doing so helped present the deaths of these Federalist statesmen as a deeply felt loss to the sentimentalized national family.[59] Four years later, when the arch-Federalist former senator Fisher Ames passed away, his champions took the body from Ames's home in Dedham all the way to Boston in a huge procession, much to the dismay of Ames's brother, a committed Jeffersonian. These obsequies are best seen as a continuation of a Federalist cult of leadership that attempted to dissolve all partisanship in a genuine aristocracy of virtue.[60] Unfortunately for Federalists, Hamilton and Ames were not George Washington; the

59. *New-York Evening Post,* July 16, 1804; *Northern Post* (Salem, N.Y.), Aug. 2, 1804; *Charleston Courier* (S.C.), Aug. 3, 1804; *Wilmington Gazette* (N.C.), Aug. 7, 1804; John M'Donald, *A Sermon, on the Premature and Lamented Death of General Alexander Hamilton* (Albany, N.Y., 1804); *A Poem on the Death of Genl. Alexander Hamilton: By a Young Lady of Baltimore* (Baltimore, [1804]); Sally Ripley Diary, Jan. 9, Feb. 22, 1800, AAS; Elizabeth De Hart Bleecker Diary, Dec. 29, 1799, Feb. 22, 1800, New York Public Library; J[ohn] M[itchell] Mason, *An Oration, Commemorative of the Late Major-General Alexander Hamilton . . .* (New York, 1804); Eliphalet Nott, *A Discourse, Delivered in the North Dutch Church, in the City of Albany, Occasioned by the Ever to Be Lamented Death of General Alexander Hamilton . . .* (Albany, N.Y., 1804); Hez[ekia]h N. Woodruff, *The Danger of Ambition Considered, in a Sermon, Preached at Scipio, N.Y. Lord's Day, August 12, 1804; Occasioned by the Death of General Alexander Hamilton . . .* (Albany, N.Y., 1804); Harrison G[ray] Otis, *Eulogy on Gen. Alexander Hamilton, Pronounced at the Request of the Citizens of Boston, July 26, 1804* (Boston, 1804). Some avowed Republicans joined in the mourning for Hamilton; see Clara, "The Grave of Hamilton," *American Citizen* (New York), July 21, 1804; *Enquirer* (Richmond), July 21, 1804. (Clara's tone is so personal as to suggest that she, a New Yorker, probably did know Hamilton.) Others sharply criticized the proceedings, insisting that Hamilton's death in a duel was a loss for his family and the federal interest, not for the country. Cf. "Death of General Hamilton," *American Mercury* (Hartford), July 26, 1804; Anthony Pasquin [pseud.], *The Hamiltoniad; or, An Extinguisher for the Royal Faction of New England . . .* (Boston, 1804).

60. Charles Warren, *Jacobin and Junto; or, Early American Politics as Viewed in the Diary of Dr. Nathaniel Ames, 1758–1822* (Cambridge, Mass., 1931), 222–224. On the Federalists and leadership, see Simon P. Newman, "Principles or Men? George Washington and the Political Culture of National Leadership, 1776–1801," *Journal of the Early Republic,* XII (1992), 477–508.

more nonpartisan they were made to appear in eulogies, the less benefit accrued to surviving partisans.

While Federalists might have wished for more entombments, the
party needed something more regular than the all-too-occasional
funeral for a passing hero. They found it in the cult of Washington's memory. Celebrations of Washington's Birthday continued in
some places, especially where Jeffersonians actively celebrated their
own hero's ascent to the nation's highest office on March 4. For the first
several years after his decease, Washington's Birthday (February 22) was
recognized by a feast held for Federalist congressmen and officeholders
at Washington, D.C. An account of this gathering and the toasts given
appeared annually in Federalist newspapers and served as something of
a counter to the inauguration fetes of the Jeffersonians, held less than
two weeks later.[61]

Gradually the Washington feasts were taken over by a new voluntary
association, the Washington Benevolent Society. Founded at Alexandria in 1801, it became popular after 1807, when a younger generation
of Federalists found that its public rituals could be put to the same
uses as July Fourth and March fourth: party organizing and electioneering. The Boston Washingtonians divided their city into twelve wards.
The Philadelphia Washington Association fined its members fifty cents
"for non-performance of duties at elections." In addition to parading
on February 22 and July 4, the Massachusetts Washington societies
held their annual meeting on April 30—the anniversary of Washington's 1789 inauguration. Members received printed identification cards
along with a personal copy of Washington's Farewell Address.[62]

61. Elizabeth Gamble to Thomas Bayly, Mar. 11–12, 1801, Virginia Historical
Society; Simeon Baldwin to Elizabeth Baldwin, Washington, Feb. 22, 1805, Baldwin
Family Papers, 1st Ser., box 8, folder 116, Sterling Memorial Library, Yale Univer-
sity; *New York Herald,* Mar. 3, 1802, Mar. 3, 1804; *Providence Gazette,* Mar. 19, 1803,
Mar. 10, 1804; *Berkeley and Jefferson Intelligencer* (Martinsburg, Va.), Mar. 2, 1804.

62. *Constitution of the Washington Society, Instituted the 28th of January, 1801* (n.p.,
1801); *The Constitution of the Washington Society of Maryland* (Baltimore, 1810); *The
Constitution and Laws of the Washington Association of Philadelphia* (Philadelphia, 1811),
10; *The Constitution of the Washington Benevolent Society of the Town of Charlton, in the
County of Saratoga* (Albany, N.Y., 1811); Washington Benevolent Society of Massachusetts Journal, Washington Benevolent Society Records, Massachusetts Historical
Society, Boston; Worcester County, Mass., Washington Benevolent Society Records,
I, AAS; *Order of Performances for the First Celebration of the Washington Benevolent Society
of Massachusetts, April 30, 1812* (n.p., 1812). Many of the imprints of Washington's

Like the old Democratic-Republican societies of the 1790s, the Washington societies proclaimed their primary interest to be the national welfare. The initiation rites of the Worcester Society (1812) read like a party platform joined to a Federalist Fourth of July oration. While Washington had stood at the helm, the nation had prospered. "But, since that period, we believe our Constitution has been violated, political sentiment has been corrupted. . . . The members of this society have thought it necessary to associate themselves for the purpose of inculcating and maintaining the true principles of Government." After hearing this speech, inductees were asked:

Are you attached to the U.S. Constitution?
Will you seek to have Government conducted under Washington's principles?
Will you vote so?

Washington Benevolents never called themselves Federalists: the name of Washington served the same, ideal ends, simultaneously vague and specific. The societies were nationalist and nonpartisan in promise, local and partisan in practice. The national past (the myth of Washington), combined with the glorious future to be rewon in elections, justified the peculiarly antipartisan partisanship of the present. Not surprisingly, in the same year they codified their organization the Worcester County Washingtonians held a huge, centralized, election-oriented Fourth of July in Worcester.[63]

Like the town and country Republicans who were meeting to plan partisan strategy and Fourth of July celebrations, the Washington societies practiced national patriotism and local politics simultaneously.[64]

Farewell Address reproduced in the Readex *Early American Imprints* series contain copies of membership cards.

The most useful studies of the Washington societies are Dixon Ryan Fox, *The Decline of Aristocracy in the Politics of New York* (New York, 1919), 89–99; Fischer, *Revolution of American Conservatism*, 111–128.

63. Worcester County Washington Benevolent Society Records, I, AAS; Edward D. Bangs to Nathaniel Howe, June 15, 1812, Bangs Family Papers, AAS.

64. For examples of rural Republican activity, see the various petitions, orations, meeting and celebration notices, and toasts in the Hoosick County, New York, Papers, MSS, New-York Historical Society; George Lathem to Lewis Malone Ayer, May 16, 1803, Lewis Malone Ayer Papers, South Caroliniana Library, Columbia, S.C.

The requirements of national citizenship could be adapted and expanded to create effective as well as evocative links between local and national spheres of public life. Though the Jeffersonians seized the moment in 1800 and continued to be less ambivalent about what they were doing, Federalist critics of the Jeffersonian order had much more than a niche in the partisan politics of celebration.

CELEBRATORY POLITICS AS THE
EARLY REPUBLIC'S PUBLIC SPHERE

We have seen how both parties tried to have their nationalism and their partisanship too. Whatever contradictions haunted events like the partisan Fourth of July were productive; they engendered both nationalism and party affiliation rather than sapping one to feed the other. Retrospective criticisms of rabid partisan rhetoric, politicized rituals, or narrow electioneering fail to account for the intentions of partisans and the role of celebrations in the post-Revolutionary era. Although nationalist (and classical republican) ideology discouraged the pursuits of partisanship, nationalist celebration nonetheless made possible and perhaps even legitimated certain kinds of party organizing. This productive tension continued half a century later, when parties had come to be taken for granted. "The ceremonies of politics," such as ratification meetings and election-eve parades, came to serve as "rituals of national affirmation," educating white men to be sentimental patriots and, at the same time, active partisans.[65]

What, then, was the ultimate content or meaning of these nationalist partisan political cultures? All discussions of political culture that assume democratization to be a good thing (mine included) tend to be haunted by two issues: the quantity of actual participation and the quality of that participation. Did a broadened polity translate into a decline in the quality of political engagement? Along similar lines, the most sophisticated students of nationalism suggest that it tends to a decidedly "imaginary" participation in public life: the "national subject" resides in an all-too-comfortably passive (even domesticated, or non-public) position. Was this true of the early Republic?[66]

65. Baker, "The Ceremonies of Politics," in Cooper et al., eds., Master's Due, 162–178.

66. Benedict Anderson, Imagined Communities: Reflections on the Origins and Spread of Nationalism, rev. ed. (London, 1991); Michael Warner, "The Mass Public and the

Theories of "the public sphere" offer another perspective from which to assay the emergence of a partisan and nationalist political culture in the United States. According to Jürgen Habermas, the bourgeois public sphere arose in eighteenth-century European countries as a counterpart to the growing state and its bureaucratic apparatus. Crystallized in coffeehouses, clubs, and salons and by the new products of a secular print culture discussed in them, the public sphere existed for the express purpose of "rational-critical" discussion of "public" matters, particularly the actions of the expanding nation-state. In Habermas's account, however, there is a damning paradox in the "structural transformation," or broadening, of the public sphere during the next century. The entrance of more and more people into the "bourgeois" public sphere "brought degeneration in the quality of discourse." This history of the public sphere is ironic. Quantity displaced quality: the price of democratization, or widening of the public sphere, was a decrease in active, thoughtful, and critical debate in public life.[67]

Mass Subject," in Craig Calhoun, ed., *Habermas and the Public Sphere* (Cambridge, Mass., 1992), 377–401; Lauren Berlant, "The Theory of Infantile Citizenship," *Public Culture*, XI (1993), 395–410.

For a relatively optimistic assessment of the rise of popular politics in the 1790s, see Simon P. Newman, *Parades and the Politics of the Street: Festive Culture in the Early American Republic* (Philadelphia, 1997); for a pessimistic account of the succession of attempts to institutionalize popular power in American history, see James A. Morone, *The Democratic Wish: Popular Participation and the Limits of American Government* (New York, 1990). In *The Opening of American Society* (New York, 1984), part I, and in *Self-Rule: A Cultural History of American Democracy* (Chicago, 1995), esp. 21–38, Robert H. Wiebe maintains that politics in the early Republic was wholly unlike that of the Jacksonian period. An especially fine corrective to this view is Alan Taylor, *William Cooper's Town: Power and Persuasion on the Frontier of the Early American Republic* (New York, 1995), 141–291.

67. Jürgen Habermas, *The Structural Transformation of the Public Sphere: An Inquiry into a Category of Bourgeois Society* (1962), trans. Thomas Burger (Cambridge, Mass., 1989); Craig Calhoun, "Introduction: Habermas and the Public Sphere," in Calhoun, ed., *Habermas and the Public Sphere*, 3, 23. Habermas has accepted many of the criticisms that have been launched at his trajectory of decline and his neglect of other possible public spheres. See his "Further Reflections on the Public Sphere," in Calhoun, ed., *Habermas and the Public Sphere*, 424–430, 438. See also John L. Brooke, "Ancient Lodges and Self-Created Societies: Voluntary Association and the Public Sphere in the Early Republic," in Ronald Hoffman and Peter J. Albert, eds., *Launching the "Extended Republic": The Federalist Era* (Charlottesville, Va., 1996), 273–377.

I call particular attention to Habermas's narrative of decline because it parallels a disturbing tendency in writing on eighteenth- and
nineteenth-century American politics and culture. Where philosopher-
sociologists like Habermas and Richard Sennett idealize the genteel
and orderly public cultures of eighteenth-century Europe, political
theorists portray the American founding, and late-eighteenth-century
America generally, as a golden age of reasoned political discourse. The
ideal features of the American polity are supposed to have been chis-
eled by the rugged minds of the founders in the agora of their letters,
their essays, and their constitutional conventions; all else is the ravages
of history, a fall from grace into the mire of practical politics. Since
this milieu of "the thinking revolutionary" looks so very different from
the boisterous, ritualistic mass politics of the mid-nineteenth century,
even the most knowledgeable writers treat the two as wholly different
worlds. As a result, the period of transition—the early Republic—has
been left almost unexplored. Moreover, with the epochs separated into
neatly marked-off centuries, nineteenth-century popular politics has
also come to be seen somewhat nostalgically by historians, though for
very different reasons: its remarkable record in winning the allegiances
of people and in getting them out to vote.[68]

The realities of public life in the early Republic complicate this
tendency to portray the period by its loss of what came before (the
founders and their rationality) or its lack of what came after (popular

68. Richard Sennett, *The Fall of Public Man* (New York, 1978); and see Ralph
Lerner, *The Thinking Revolutionary: Principle and Practice in the New Republic* (Ithaca,
N.Y., 1987), for one among many possible examples in delineating a golden age.
For criticisms of Habermas's model of civil and rational discourse and his account
of European history, see Nancy Fraser, "What's Critical about Critical Theory? The
Case of Habermas," in her *Unruly Practices: Power, Discourse, and Gender in Contem-
porary Social Theory* (Minneapolis, Minn., 1989), 113–143; Fraser, "Rethinking the
Public Sphere: A Contribution to the Critique of Actually Existing Democracy," and
Geoff Eley, "Nations, Publics, and Political Cultures: Placing Habermas in the Nine-
teenth Century," in Calhoun ed., *Habermas and the Public Sphere*, 109–142, 289–339.
For balanced, if appreciative, assessments of nineteenth-century popular poli-
tics, see Baker, *Affairs of Party;* Michael E. McGerr, *The Decline of Popular Politics: The
American North, 1865–1928* (New York, 1986), 3–41; Wiebe, *Self-Rule.* On the nos-
talgic tendency in the scholarship, see Richard L. McCormick, *The Party Period and
Public Policy: American Politics from the Age of Jackson to the Progressive Era* (New York,
1986), 130–133; Michael Schudson, "Was There Ever a Public Sphere? If So, When?
Reflections on the American Case," in Calhoun, ed., *Habermas and the Public Sphere*,
157–161.

politics and its rituals). The era's mix of public debate and ritual assent contained features that have been championed both by those who mourn the loss of eighteenth-century rationalism and, on the other hand, by those who recall the excitement of nineteenth-century ceremony. If not a golden age of American politics, the period should at least be seen as a fertile, not a barren, middle ground. What made this middle ground possible were precisely those aspects of the public sphere that theorists, political scientists, and historians all tend to overlook: the relationships between local and national publics and the crystallization of those relationships in celebrations and celebratory publicity. Local partisans developed communal rituals with an eye toward a national public sphere. Their celebrations of national holidays required and engendered oral and printed debate over national politics. As a result, they practiced partisan division and nationalist reunion on two planes simultaneously. The local and political basis of nationalist practice made it possible for the citizens of the early Republic to engage in substantive debate *and* in communal ritual.

The mutual dependence of rationality and ritual may be seen in local competitions over the Fourth of July. Explicitly partisan and intentionally nonpartisan celebrations both required negotiations among groups in order to inspire the requisite demonstrations of assent. Ritual incantation and attempts at persuasion, while in some sense the same thing, in another sense actually depended upon each other. The most popular forms of the celebration, the toasts and the oration, display this marriage of debate and declamation. For example, party leaders submitted the toasts in advance, subject to revision by a committee; surviving lists of July Fourth toasts are often filled with cross-outs and emendations. When John Steele brought seventeen toasts to a meeting in Salisbury, North Carolina, only six were accepted without corrections. A group of Virginians celebrating the Fourth in 1800 retained a toast praising "All, who fought, all, who laboured for, and all, who wished success to, American liberty and Independence—high and low, rich and poor," but they did without what had originally followed: "for a good republican is 'no respecter of persons.'" Little wonder that attempts of festival organizers "to effect a union of all parties" often "proved fruitless"! The effort to do so, however, surely provoked substantial conversations about what people really believed and what they wanted to say—to publicize—in a particular context. The composing, revising, hearing, and cheering of toasts unavoidably engaged with political alternatives, the ultimate goal being to establish a clear choice among them. Yet de-

TOASTS,

FOR FOURTH JULY 1804.

1st. THE DAY WE CELEBRATE---May this, and every revolving fourth of July, inspire us with the spirit of 76.

2d. THE UNITED STATES---May those who administer our Government, learn wisdom, and fidelity, from the example of their predecessors.

3d. THE MEMORY OF WASHINGTON---The historic page, proud of its treasure, shall convey his name to latest times, while the affections of a grateful country, shall guard, and immortalize the trust.

4th. THE STATE OF CONNECTICUT---firm and unshaken, in the correct principles of Federalism, may the administration of her government, never be intrusted to disorganizers.

5th. HIS EXCELLENCY JONATHAN TRUMBULL, Governor of the State of Connecticut---May we bestow the reward which his merit deserves.

6th. LT. GOVERNOR TREADWELL, the HON COUNCIL, with the other constituted authorities of the State of Connecticut---We admire talents, integrity and virtue.

7th. THE CLERGY---As they are the patrons of learning, virtue and good order, may the admirers of these, ever be their friends.

8th. THE MEMORY OF THOSE HEROES & STATESMEN, who by their exertions achieved our Independence.

9th. THE JUDICIARY OF THE UNITED STATES---May they never sacrifice their independence to Virginia's usurpation.

10th. THE NAVY OF THE UNITED STATES---The guardian of commerce, may it flourish in its true element, and the honor of this establishment be bestowed where due.

11th. AGRICULTURE, COMMERCE, and MANUFACTURES---Dependant on each other, may neither branch be ever destroyed by the visionary wanderings of a meer speculatist.

12th. HIS EXCELLENCY JOHN T. GILMAN, Governor of the State of New-Hampshire---While we admire his independence, may we cherish similar efforts to resist the encroachments of southern despotism.

13th. OUR FIRE SIDES AND ALTARS---As we received them from our ancestors, may we transmit them inviolate to our posterity.

14th, OUR GALLANT TARS---May those who are in bondage be soon redeemed, and not suffered by our administration to remain in captivity, from principles of modern economy.

15th. THE PRESS---Free as air, in disseminating truth, and only shackled from lies, and scandal.

16th. One more AMENDMENT to the NATIONAL CONSTITUTION---More free votes, and less slavish ones.

17th. THE AMERICAN FAIR---May their smiles ever be withheld from the disciples of Godwin.

FIGURE 11. *Toasts, for Fourth July 1804.*
Courtesy American Antiquarian Society

spite the wish for closure, toast making was a continuing process. When toasts were reprinted in newspapers and could be compared, they often provoked a second round of discussion, with reprintings serving as celebratory assent, rebuttals (and toasts at the next holiday) as creative counterritual.[69]

The same may be said of orations, which flourished anew with the punctuation of public life by print.[70] After 1800, more and more secular celebratory orations were published in newspapers or as pamphlets; as we shall see, partisan competition made the anniversary speech a subtle and contested business. More than ever, oratory became a political as well as literary art, one that led would-be orators to seek advice and even instruction. Once again, Abraham Bishop provides us with a glimpse behind the scenes of celebratory politics and culture. Writing to his brother-in-law one summer, Bishop noted that a certain event had been postponed; could he give an oration? Bishop then went on to recommend what the oration should look like. "It will be necessary to steer clear of the wide field of national politics. Our concerns are local." The Connecticut party leader then offered a sketch for an oration that would deftly link the local and national political situations.

69. John Steele to Nathaniel Macon, Salisbury, Sept. 12, 1803, in Kemp P. Battle, ed., *Letters of Nathaniel Macon, John Steele, and William Barry Grove,* James Sprunt Historical Monographs, no. 3 (Chapel Hill, N.C., 1902), 39–44; Jameson, ed., "Diary of Edward Hooker," AHA, *Annual Report,* 1896, 904–905; "Toasts for the 4th of July, 1800," Misc. MSS, Virginia Historical Society; "Fourth of July Toasts, Schoharie, New York, 1803," MS, New York State Library, Albany. For examples of criticisms of toasts, see *Friends of America, Look at the Insolence of Federalists* (New York, n.d.), Broadsides Collection, New-York Historical Society; *Western Spy* (Cincinnati), Aug. 6, 13, 1800; *Georgia Republican* (Savannah), Apr. 7, 1803; *Scioto Gazette* (Chillicothe, Ohio), July 30, 1804; *Repertory* (Boston), July 16, 1810.

70. Barnet Baskerville contends that newspapers extended the influence of oratory after 1820, in *The People's Voice: The Orator in American Society* (Lexington, Ky. 1979), 33. Ann Fabian's forthcoming work on amateur authorship suggests that, in the early nineteenth century, print often regulated, or commented on, oral performances or stories spread by word of mouth. Thomas Leonard, in turn, observes that newspapers themselves were very often read aloud, in public. See Fabian, "From the Mouths of Murderers," MS; Thomas C. Leonard, *News for All: America's Coming-of-Age with the Press* (New York, 1995), 3–32. For important insights into the place of oral culture in the Revolutionary and post-Revolutionary eras, see Harry S. Stout, "Religion, Communications, and the Origins of the American Revolution," *WMQ,* 3d Ser., XXXIV (1977), 519–541; and Jay Fliegelman, *Declaring Independence: Jefferson, Natural Language, and the Culture of Performance* (Stanford, Calif., 1993).

I would propose 1st

To take your stand in the Great measures of the present administration, as occasions of joy, Let them be *chiefly* recited.

2d From this stand take a view of the little faction of 14 against 162. Comment on its rise, progress and present condition — under this head name precisely the reason of a few aristocratic clergy, lawyers and rich merchants appointing, with a set of interests and feelings, distinct from the body of the people, shew how inconsistent federalism has been with religion, even with its own professions.

3d.   Having exhibited federalism as it was and is, conclude by shewing how cordially the friends of revolution ought to abhor it as an unprincipled system — and insist on the vast importance of republican freemen attending universally at freemen's meetings.[71]

Bishop's letter can be seen as evidence of a top-down party bureaucracy, the capture of "free," or truly public, discourse by a political elite that does half the talking and writes the rest of the scripts. But such an interpretation does not account for the substantial debate that these exercises sparked. The pages of partisan newspapers continually reveal that Federalists and Republicans listened and talked to each other. Had they not, they could not and would not have gone to the trouble of ridiculing each other's language.

Americans of the early Republic displayed a healthy skepticism about representations and a savvy awareness of the power of words in the construction of reality. For example, consider this assertion, introducing a critique of the Federalists as "impostors," or false representations of true federalism: *"Words* are not always the signs of *Things;* for things, and words too, change their meaning and character." In diaries, private letters, and the columns of newspapers, partisans deconstructed each other's language because they knew that such pictures of the world had a large part in the making of political reality. If their elaborations and denunciations of each other's rhetoric now seem picayune, if not ridiculous, perhaps we have lost their almost instinctual sense of an intimate connection between ordinary speech and modes of citizenship. Anyone

71. Abraham Bishop to Jonathan Law, Aug. 8, 180[5 or 6], Abraham Bishop Letterbook, Miscellaneous Manuscripts Collection, Sterling Memorial Library, Yale University. For a similar, if less explicitly partisan or locally oriented, set of directions, see Robert Fulton to Joel Barlow, June 23, 1809, Miscellaneous Manuscripts Collection, New-York Historical Society, with the oration actually delivered by Barlow at Washington.

who proclaimed a toast, cheered one, or discussed it was a participant in both ceremony and criticism. Even an English visitor, arguably from a very similar political culture, noticed that the Americans' "*habits of quotation, imitation and parody*" were most prominently exercised in the wake of celebratory occasions.[72]

By 1810, certainly, many took it for granted that a Fourth of July orator would rejoice in his "political friends" and "investigate the conduct of political enemies." In this context, attempts to reach détente with intentionally vague, "unmeaning toasts" could be seen as the most dangerous of all symbolic sleights of hand. "The different celebrations of the 4 July attract notice," wrote the Reverend William Bentley, no lover of partisan fury. "The competition is evident. . . . The toasts were not of an equivocal nature, and inspire the firmness necessary." Leverett Saltonstall, a young lawyer from the same town but of the opposite political loyalties, saw the same events the next year as portents of decline. "To what a height has party spirit arrived in this country," he asked, when "the event which equally concerns all should be celebrated distinctly by different parties, and each avoid the other as pestilential. . . . Tho' the 4th of July be celebrated with noise and pomp and every demonstration of joy, still the aged patriot of N. England must sigh when he looks back to '76."[73]

This was the old Federalist stance of nostalgia, taken up in the face of insurgent Jeffersonian activity and electoral success. Four years later, Saltonstall had learned to sing a different tune. "You have undoubtedly

72. Edward Augustus Kendall, *Travels through the Northern Parts of the United States, in the Year 1807 and 1808* (New York, 1809), I, 156–161, quoted at 160; "From the Aurora: Words the Signs of Things," *Palladium* (Frankfort, Ky.), July 18, 1807.

On speech and citizenship: Nina Eliasoph observes that deportment, tone, and attitude can constitute political statements even when they avoid, or distance themselves from, the "political." By this performative notion of communication, the "rational" stance of an objective critic is fully as rhetorical—and potentially as ritualized—as the stance and discourse of a participant in a parade. See Eliasoph, "Political Culture and the Presentation of a Public Self: A Study of the Public Sphere in the Spirit of Erving Goffman," *Theory and Society,* XIX (1990), 465–494.

73. Rollin C. Mallary, *An Oration, Pronounced at the Republican Celebration of Our National Independence, at Poultney, (Vt.) July 4, 1810* (Rutland, Vt., 1810), 5; "Hartford," *American Mercury* (Hartford), July 10, 1806; Bentley, *Diary,* III, 32; Leverett Saltonstall Diary, July 4, 1804, in Robert E. Moody, ed., *The Saltonstall Papers, 1607–1815* (Massachusetts Historical Society, *Collections,* LXXX–LXXXI [Boston, 1972–1974), II, 205–206.

heard of my delivering an oration here on the 4th inst.," he wrote to his father.

> It was very federal, but not virulent. My own party appear pleased, and the other whom I did not wish to please, are displeased. Had I been very moderate and only tinged it with federalism, the demo's would have misrepresented it, and it would not have made warm friends among the feds.

The difficulty of controlling the political resonances of words, along with the very situational and local nature of Saltonstall's speech, made him reluctant to publish it, despite pressure from fellow Federalists. His oration had been meant for those "warmed by the occasion"; he feared it would be too partisan even for his own brother. Still, he had no regrets: "An oration of doubtful politics would please nobody in Salem."[74]

And not just in Salem. Daniel Mulford, a schoolmaster who had moved to Georgia from Morristown, New Jersey, wrote to his brother after reading in his hometown paper that "Whelpley was to deliver an oration" on the Fourth of July. "If he gives another 'milk and water' dish," the Republican Mulford commented, "he ought to be silenced as a politician." Mulford did not yet know that, "to the astonishment and confusion of the Demos," Federalists in Morristown had packed the Republicans' meeting (announced in the paper) to choose an orator and an arrangements committee. They picked Whelpley, who fell ill shortly before the Fourth; Whelpley's own nephew wrote to Mulford that Whelpley's oration would be given verbatim by a substitute, "I suppose . . . to the disgust of many."[75] What might seem conciliatory, a "'milk and water' dish," was an act of partisan aggression to others. It was hard to separate pablum patriotism from partisan harangues, because most orators were performing both simultaneously—introducing an element of doubt that only increased the scrutiny of spoken words and festive forms.

74. Leverett Saltonstall to Nathaniel Saltonstall, July 9, 19, 1808, in Moody, ed., *Saltonstall Papers,* II, 447–448. One diarist wrote that Saltonstall's oration "gave most too high strokes to be be stomached." Bentley, who did not attend, heard soon enough to record in his diary that day that the oration had been "in the genuine style of party." "Diary of Archelaus Putnam of New Mills," Danvers Historical Society, *Historical Collections,* V (1917), 67; Bentley, *Diary,* III, 370.

75. Daniel Mulford to Levi Mulford, July 6, 1809, William Whelpley to Daniel Mulford, July 3, 1809, Daniel Mulford Papers, book I, Georgia Historical Society, Savannah.

For answers to the great questions left by the American Revolution—who the people were, what their character was, what they believed—people looked, between elections, to the festivals and printed commentary that sought to persuade everyone how to act on election day. In Charleston, a group of young Jeffersonians opened this large can of worms in 1809, when they questioned whether the Federalist-dominated Revolution Society should be allowed, through its annual orations, to represent the true opinions of Charlestonians. They founded an alternative organization, the Seventy-six Association, which proceeded to sponsor orations annually on July Fourth and March fourth. Very quickly the columns of a new, self-described democratic, radical newspaper filled with attacks on the Seventy-sixers as conservative "lawyers" who showed their true elitism by constitutionally excluding the foreign-born (that is, the Irish) from their number. The controversy continued for weeks, with critics suggesting quite baldly that the aim of the new society was to tell "the people" what to think—not to empower them against federal hegemony, but rather to prevent their gaining a more active role in the public life.[76]

Americans were seeing grave implications in *who* spoke in public on festive occasions as well as in *what* was said. They were engaging in debate over the very shape and nature of their public sphere. Some published orations of the decade after 1800 bear the markings of these controversies: prefatory notes explain that they would not have been published at all if they had not been "misrepresented." These battles over what was said and heard suggest the need to reconsider the nature and purpose of such addresses and the critiques they inspired. Fourth of July oratory was already being satirized and dismissed as trite, but citizens of the early Republic did so out of a sense of anger or disappointment rather than disinvestment. Attacked or applauded, Fourth of July orations were provocative topics of conversation, occasions to make sense of national history and local politics.[77] Justifying its criticism

76. Marc D. Kaplanoff, "Making the South Solid: Politics and the Structure of Society in South Carolina, 1790–1815" (Ph.D. diss., University of Cambridge, 1979), 234; *Times* (Charleston, S.C.), July 22, Aug. 4, 5, 7, 10, 1809; *Strength of the People* (Charleston, S.C.), July 25, Aug. 12, 15, 17, Sept. 26, 1809. The Seventy-six Association survived; the *Strength of the People* folded a year later.

77. John Rogers, "Notice Prefatory," in *An Oration, Pronounced at Camton, New-Hampshire, on the Fourth of July, 1803* (Concord, N.H., 1803); Ebenezer Belknap Morse, "Apology," in *An Oration, Pronounced at Westborough (Mass.) on July 4th, 1804 . . .* (Worcester, Mass., 1804); Aaron Hall Putnam, *An Oration, Pronounced*

of John W. Mulligan's effort (criticism first made by a group of listeners who had walked out), the *American Citizen* of New York reminded its readers that only the previous year "the character of the oration" had been attacked by the other party "before it was composed, the subject ridiculed, and the composition slandered." Samuel Harrison Smith, editor of Washington's influential *National Intelligencer,* even attempted to typologize Republican versus Federalist orations.[78] Partisans needed few lessons in the functions of criticism.

Local political competition seems to have increased the centrality of the oration in the bricolage of symbolic actions that characterized these holidays. Though party orations did differ, all obeyed the rules of the genre by telling the story of Revolution, invoking sentiment, and appealing for national unity. As a result, the past, present, and future were all at stake in the rival Fourth of July orations and celebrations. In 1808, the Federalists of Worcester County tried to retake Independence Day with a countywide celebration at Barre. Emboldened by widespread opposition to Jefferson's embargo, these partisans "openly avowed" in Isaiah Thomas's friendly *Massachusetts Spy* "that one of the objects of the intended celebration is to consolidate the strength of the friends of the Constitution, and to rally round the standard of our liberties, the followers of WASHINGTON and ADAMS!" While inhabitants of the town of Bolton, on the other side of the county, advertised a nonpartisan celebration, Worcester Republicans quickly mobilized to pull in their supporters to Worcester town on Independence Day. A broadside they sent out to "their Republican brethren" directed attention to the newspapers for arrangements and asked each town to report on the "probable numbers" who would attend.[79]

July 4th, 1805 . . . (Charlestown, Mass., 1805), 2; Bradford, *Oration, Pronounced at Wiscasset,* 5n; Joshua Cushman, *An Oration, Pronounced at Wiscasset, on the Fourth of July, 1808* . . . (Wiscasset, Mass., 1808); Jabez D. Hammond, "Preface," in *An Oration Delivered on the Glorious Tenth of June, 1809, in . . . Otsego, at a Celebration of the Revocation of the British Orders in Council, and . . . the Repeal of the Non-Intercourse Law as It Respected Great Britain* (Otsego, N.Y., 1809), 3; David Allen, *An Oration Delivered in the Brick Church in Lansingburgh, July 4th, 1809* (Lansingburgh, N.Y., 1809), 2; Samuel Brazer, Jr., *An Oration, Pronounced at Springfield* . . . (Springfield, Mass., 1809), 3–4.

78. *American Citizen* (New York), July 7, 1804; *New-York Commercial Advertiser,* July 5, 1805; *National Intelligencer* (Washington), Aug. 14, 1805.

79. "Celebration at Barre," *Thomas's Massachusetts Spy; or, The Worcester Gazette,* June 22, 1808; "To the Republicans of the County of Worcester!!!" *National Aegis* (Worcester), June 29, 1808; *Worcester, June 20, 1808; Sir,* (Worcester, Mass., 1808).

The battle over Independence Day in Worcester began during the third week in June; thanks to the newspapers, it would continue for many days after the Fourth of July. The Republican *National Aegis* called on all Worcester "Tories" to attend their party caucus at Barre; true "democrats" would ignore the Federalists and celebrate in Worcester town. Like the Connecticut Federalists who had ripped Abraham Bishop years before, the busy Republicans who wrote for the *Aegis* provided exposés of Federalist preparations. They particularly charged Francis Blake, manager of the Barre celebration, with ghostwriting a partisan oration for his nephew, Joseph Caldwell. By contrast, the "excellent, nervous, and truly *Republican*" oration at Worcester achieved verisimilitude: "It was indeed a vivid display of the sentiments of the *Orator* and his *audience;* altho it had not been subjected to a previous revision and modification." Actually, as a member of the *Aegis* staff who was also a celebration organizer noted in a private letter, a number of "Tories" had "left the Meeting-house during the services." After reading the attack in the *Aegis,* an outraged Caldwell and Blake came to the paper's office and threatened the editor with a whip, causing a crowd to gather. While physical violence was avoided, Bangs concluded gleefully that both Federalists "shall receive a pretty severe *flogging* in our paper."[80]

While print could always seem inauthentic, a consciously constructed afterthought, it gained spontaneity through the productive tension with oratory and street theater. Both strove for precision and for true feeling and gained verisimilitude through contrast with the performances of the other party. Thus the politics of celebration spurred newspaper wars; newspaper wars set the stage for and then reviewed celebrations. None of this would have been possible, or necessary, without the reciprocal influences of national issues and local elections. Leaders of both parties were active in founding and sustaining sympathetic newspapers, and the appearance of a competing paper in a town or county signaled that literal and literary fireworks would soon commence. After the establishment of a Republican paper in Federalist-dominated Providence, local Jeffersonians celebrated March fourth with a dinner. Federalists responded by parading Tom Paine in effigy and "insulting and hooting at every person not of their sect" in the streets and in front of

80. "Attention!—Tories," "A Hint," June 29, 1808, *National Aegis* (Worcester), July 6, 13, 20, 1808; Edward D. Bangs to Nathaniel Howe, July 7, 1808, Bangs Family Papers, AAS.

their homes. The editor of the Federalist *Providence Gazette* apparently approved, sparking still more objections in the Republican *Providence Phoenix*. A year later, the *Gazette* praised the town-appointed Fourth of July oration as "replete with political wisdom. . . . The names of *Federalist* and *Republican* were buried in that of *American*." To the *Phoenix*, however, the oration epitomized "the *true federal cant*" and had been illegitimately edited for its appearance in the press. For a month, "critics upon critics" argued the partisan and nonpartisan merits of the speech.[81] The context was local, the subjects national; and the discourse, if not always "rational" or "civil," was, at the very least, rigorously critical.

The events in Providence in 1803–1804, like those in Worcester during the summer of 1808, are only especially vivid examples of the expansion and intensification of political debate that occurred when newspapers multiplied and celebrations divided by party. As the near-altercation in the *Aegis* office in Worcester shows, newspaper editors emerged as key mediators in this nexus of public space, oratory, and print culture. Often given pride of place in the very celebrations they publicized (Republicans widely toasted William Duane), they could also run afoul of the local politics of class when their satire offended the honor of Federalist elites. On a number of occasions Federalists (primarily young men) violently assaulted Republican publishers who ridiculed their behavior at celebrations. These incidents differed from the press destructions of the Revolutionary era, which had been led by gentlemen but expressed communal outrage. Rather, these incidents of harassment and outright assault were personal, directed against the authors of allegedly libelous paragraphs. In the most famous incident (which itself spurred a pamphlet war), the Boston lawyer Thomas Selfridge, a Federalist, shot Charles Austin dead in the street after his father Benjamin Austin criticized Selfridge in his *Independent Chronicle* for his role in a dispute over the tavern bill for a July Fourth celebration. After Selfridge won acquittal on the grounds of self-defense, Republican crowds burned him in effigy, repeating the exercise on March fourth. The Federalist papers then made their own meaning out of the crowd's actions, insisting, as one observer noted in his diary, that the effigy actually represented, not Selfridge, but Thomas Jefferson.[82]

81. "Republican Rejoicings," Mar. 5, 1803, *Providence Phoenix*, Mar. 12, 19, 1803, July 7, 18, 25, Aug. 1, 1804; *Providence Gazette*, Mar. 5, 1803, July 7, 28, Aug. 4, 11, 1804.

82. Warren, *Jacobin and Junto*, 187–214; Bentley, *Diary*, III, 245, 266, 269–270, 274–275; Ethan Allen Greenwood Diary, Greenwood Papers, Mar. 4, 1808, AAS.

When the editor of Trenton's *True American* prodded the Federalists for their laxity in recognizing July Fourth, only to spoof their revel at city hall as drunken and "riotous," thirty of his subjects appeared at the paper's office, dragged editor James J. Wilson outside, and pummeled him severely. "The majority were students of Law, Physick etc.," noted a Federalist paper with disgust. In this case of group libel, some doubted whether the politics of Federalist hooligans was really so personal. A letter to Newark's *Centinel of Freedom* suggested that the true motive of the attack had been to "[pull] down the only republican press now in Trenton, and then proceed to suppress and overcome the republicans at the ensuing election."[83]

Both sides objected so strenuously to what they saw as misrepresentations because they knew that street performances, meetinghouse speeches, and newspaper descriptions all shaped public perceptions and reputations. A large part of the Federalist attack on the Litchfield festival of 1806 lay in the accusation that it had been planned to draw attention to the case of Selleck Osborn, an editor of Litchfield's *Witness* who was awaiting trial for the libel of a Federalist judge. One critic even suggested that the date (August 6 rather than July 4) had been picked, not to "accommodate the farmers," but to mark the first anniversary of Osborn's newspaper. Whatever their original plans, the Republicans flamboyantly offered a prayer for Osborn's liberty and marched in procession past his jail cell. No one knew the stakes better than Osborn himself. A week before the celebration, he warned readers from his cell that Federalists would try to sabotage the festival. They might be daring enough to spike the cannon or "steal the bell tongue," as they had done at Plymouth, Massachusetts, the year before. They might publish "another *negro* letter, full of obscene allusions." They might even turn

---

For an interesting example of a Republican printer and his political activities, see Carl E. Prince, "John Israel: Printer and Politician on the Pennsylvania Frontier, 1798–1805," *PMHB*, XCI (1967), 46–55. Israel, the target of an anti-Semitic campaign on the part of the Federalist *Pittsburgh Gazette,* headed a Republican militia company and "served as vice-president of the assemblage at the town's annual Fourth of July celebration."

83. "Trenton," *Commercial Advertiser* (New York), July 13, 1803; *Aurora* (Philadelphia), July 14, 21, 27, 1803; *True American* (Trenton, N.J.), July 18, 25, Aug. 1, 1803; *Trenton Federalist,* July 11, 18, 25, Aug. 1, 1803; "Federal Outrage," *Federal Republican* (Elizabeth Town, N.J.), July 26, Aug. 2, 1803; *Centinel of Freedom* (Newark), Aug. 2, 1803. The editor of the *Centinel* maintained that a Federalist mob had almost done the same thing to him in 1798 (July 19, 1803).

fiction into fact, literary blackface into actual performance, "and hire negroes and vagabonds who are in their service to join the procession, to throw ridicule on it."[84]

Here we have come full circle: reality not only seems composed of ritual, but ritual and reality take their cues from partisan rhetoric. This moment is especially revealing, not because of its hall-of-mirrors quality, but because of what that quality may imply about the breadth and caliber of participation in the early national polity. According to the Federalist satire examined earlier, Republicans solicited free black participation in some of their Connecticut festivals because of Republicans' concern for numbers and the possibility of black votes. Yet while white Jeffersonians certainly possessed an ideological predisposition toward the widening of the public sphere as constituted by parading, reading, and voting, this predisposition only temporarily crossed racial lines. The definition of the public sphere endorsed by Osborn and his allies might have been protoliberal in its concern for the rights of citizens, but it still depended on an earlier, racialized, and gendered republican notion of a citizenship grounded in personal independence—their difference from those who, like most African Americans (whether slave or free) could be said to be in "service." Attacking Federalists for *their* cynical uses of African Americans at election times (whether as performers of imaginary blackface routines or as actual voters), Republicans too portrayed blacks as degraded, dependent, and unworthy of citizenship.[85] This was precisely the way Federalists continued to describe the mass of Jeffersonian working-class supporters. In a republican rhetoric replete with class inflections, each party depicted blacks in the service of the other. To Federalists, black participation in festi-

84. *Connecticut Courant* (Hartford), Aug. 13, 20, 1806; *Litchfield Monitor* (Conn.), July 23, 30, 1806; *Witness* (Litchfield, Conn.), July 30, Aug. 6, 13, 1806. Connecticut Republicans succeeded in making Osborn a national cause célèbre: "Federal Persecution," *Enquirer* (Richmond), Aug. 5, 8, 1806; *Charleston Courier*, Aug. 15, Oct. 11, 1806; *National Intelligencer* (Washington), Aug. 13, 1806 (from *Norfolk Herald*), Aug. 27, 1806. Osborn later became editor of the *Democrat* (Boston) as well as other papers and served as an officer in the militia and U.S. Army (*Columbian Phoenix* [Providence], July 23, 1808); Willa G. Cramton, "Selleck Osborn: A Republican Editor in Federalist Delaware, 1816–1822," *Delaware History*, XII (1969), 198–219.

85. For examples outside Connecticut, see *American Citizen* (New York), Nov. 25, 1807; *Centinel of Freedom* (Newark), Aug. 2, 1803. The latter piece, the same one that accuses Federalists of trying to destroy the Republican press, accuses Federalists of "admitting black people and slaves" into the courts.

vals and elections epitomized the low-class origins, and demagoguery, of the Jeffersonians. Yet these same Jeffersonians constructed their republican virtue atop the symbolic foundation of an underclass—a black underclass.

Fully aware that voting and the Fourth of July might have liberatory meanings to African Americans, each party cynically used them for its own immediate purposes and hypocritically decried such uses when the other party did the same. Here we see the limits of celebratory politics as the early Republic's public sphere: The same structure of electoral competition that periodically encouraged one party to put aside its racism immediately provoked the other side to exploit racial bigotry. Here, debate in print and competition in celebration worked against true democratization of the public sphere. For both the Federalists and the Republican editor Osborn, the bigotry took the form of a printed exposé: the rhetorical and ritual building blocks of political celebration were drawn in black hues, exposed as mere invention, as insincere, as unreal. These literary exposés took the poetics of anticelebration— the critical inversion of the political other's celebration—to its logical extreme, through which the other is read out of the polity. By equating conspiratorial Federalists (or Republicans) with blacks, both blacks and the other party are shown to be devoid of independence and of sincere devotion to the common weal. The recurrence of the printed attack on the political other's celebration in the case of racial politics shows that the public sphere (as constituted by the practices of celebration, printed discourse, and electoral politics) tended to police its own standards of inclusion. A good part of the debate and the ritual in that public sphere concerned precisely these issues of participation. In a sense, the debate itself functioned as a ritual of exclusion.

Did blacks actually participate in the Connecticut Republican celebrations? Or were Federalists merely using them as a symbol, the visible mark of the degradation of public life by their opponents? White racist satires consistently suggested that blacks took more than a little interest in what went on in the streets and the newspapers at times of nationalist festivity. A 1793 cartoon that ridicules a Democratic-Republican club celebration includes a black man who, when asked, "What you think of all this," replies: "tink! Fine ting Broder bockrah our turn nex" (see Figure 12).[86] It is no accident that such thinking could refer simulta-

86. *A Peep into the Antifederal Club* (New York, 1793). During the controversy over the Sedition Act, when a group of New York Federalists made their slaves put up a

FIGURE 12. *A Peep into the Antifederal Club.* Philadelphia, 1793.
Courtesy Library Company of Philadelphia

neously to the expansion of political participation at home and to the
revolutionary overthrow of slavery in Saint Domingue. The "turn" that
free blacks took toward antislavery activism and a specifically African
American nationalism—a turn that itself both criticized and adapted
the celebratory practices of American nationalism—will be the subject
of another chapter. For now, it is enough to note that the place of African Americans in American political culture would depend on their
own efforts as well as on the structures of partisan competition in the
nationalist public sphere.

If blacks took center stage in the public sphere only in moments
of extreme partisan warfare, women, after 1800, became key partici-

liberty pole to mock the Republicans' pole-raising protests, the blacks decorated it
with a sign that read, "FREEDOM TO AFRICANS." Donald H. Stewart, *The Opposition
Press of the Federalist Period* (Albany, N.Y., 1969), 346.

pants in the simultaneous struggles for partisan victory and nonpartisan nationalism. In some areas, women occupied such prominent places in processions that their presence did not even attract special notice. In their diaries, middling and elite women revealed an active interest in celebrations, including the ones they did not attend.[87] Yet, despite a few early Jeffersonian attempts to turn out the women as the Federalists had done in 1798–1799, the large number of ladies who marched in parades and listened to orations almost never attended the moment of highest partisanship and greatest political importance: the toasting ritual. Even when they were guests at the festive dinner, they left just before the toasts.

Many women took an active interest in politics; for traditionally-minded men, far too many. But, while men found ways to have their partisanship and their nationalism too, women increasingly had to settle for the latter, at a remove. Uncomfortable with their partisanship and the politicization of women that partisanship encouraged, men continued to rely upon the ideal of republican motherhood to explain women's political activity and their own solicitation of that activity. The contradictions of a public sphere that joined local political action to long-range, nationalist ideology were, by 1800, already encouraging a differentiation of these labors along gender lines. Generic male toasts to the "ladies," given in their official absence, told them to "be the nurses of Heroes, Patriots and Statesmen." Revealingly, the very ritual of these holidays, from procession or oration to the return procession or evening ball, usually began and ended with women at their most prominent. Spatially, however, even these women (often dressed in white) were led and surrounded by men. Even their partisanship, where admitted, could exist only in relationship to men, and in antici-

87. John Howe to Stephen Child, July 16, 1805, Miscellaneous MSS Collection, Connecticut Historical Society; Mary Guion Downes Diary, July 1804, transcript, New-York Historical Society; Ruth Henshaw Bascom Diary, AAS; Rebecca Noyes Diary, July 5, 1802, Connecticut Historical Society; Candace Roberts Diary, July 5, 1802, July 4, 1806, transcript, Connecticut Historical Society; Sally Ripley Diary, Jan. 9, Feb. 21, July 4, 1800, Mar. 3, 1801, AAS; *Diary of Sarah Connell Ayer* (Portland, Maine, 1910), 51, 69, 78, 108; Nancy Avery White Diary, I, July 4, 1808, July 4, 1809, II, Aug. 20, 1812, White-Forbes Family Diaries, AAS; Adeline Marble Diary, July 4, 1820, Susan Bishop Marble Diary, July 4, 1820, box 54, Day Family Papers, Sterling Memorial Library, Yale University; Clarence Cook, ed., *A Girl's Life Eighty Years Ago: Selections from the Letters of Eliza Southgate Bowne* (1887; rpt. Williamstown, Mass., 1970), 161, 169.

pation of an end to partisanship as in the often repeated toast, "May they *all* breed republicans—and may they breed *all* republicans."[88]

Such toasts reveal a competition for women's attachments: they make maternity a metaphor for politics. They also defuse the language of partisanship by making it possible to understand female political activity, not as partisan, but instead as just another way of being a mother. This containing strategy on the part of Federalist and Jeffersonian men was merely the obverse of their tendency to accuse politicized females of being "public women" in the older, illicit sense, like the women ridiculed as prostitutes after Abraham Bishop and his colleagues invited them to the Connecticut Republican festival in 1803. White women could still signify disorder, unreason, the lack of (male) virtue. But women in white simultaneously signified peace, a feminized virtue, liberty, and nationality.

Republicans as well as Federalists used women to heighten their claim upon the nation and its future and to naturalize (and thus depoliticize) the partial, partisan aspects of any such claim. Partisanship and patriotism went hand in hand when men decried the rise of partisanship and invoked women's influence as the path back to the pure republicanism of the Revolution. In toasting "The Ladies of Muddy River; who have a taste for independence," the Kentucky men who formed the "Muddy River Democratical, Didactick Society" suggested that such women, like themselves, were not partisan but rather followed in the true spirit of 1776. "Party spirit slept," insisted a newspaper account, when, at Pawlet, Vermont, in 1811, "17 young ladies in uniform, representing the states" marched and sang an ode in the Fourth of July parade, after the militia troops; the rest of the town's "Ladies in general" and the "Matrons, in black" brought up the rear of the procession, in between the "Military Strangers, in uniform" and the "Citizens at Large." A volunteer toast praised: "The 17 Young Female *Representatives*

88. *Aurora* (Philadelphia), July 11, 1803; Samuel Farmer Jarvis Diary, Mar. 7, 1803, Sterling Memorial Library, Yale University; "Independence," in Jonathan Grout, *An Oration, Delivered in Heath, on the Anniversary of American Independence . . .* (Greenfield, Mass., 1803), 3–4; *Anniversary of American Independence, Farmington, July 4th, 1800* (Farmington, Conn., 1800), Broadsides Collection, Beinecke Library, Yale University; "Youngston Ohio," *Aurora* (Philadelphia), July 19, 1805; Linda K. Kerber, *Women of the Republic: Intellect and Ideology in Revolutionary America* (Chapel Hill, N.C., 1980), 185–231, 265–288; Paula Baker, "The Domestication of Politics: Women and American Political Society, 1780–1920," *American Historical Review,* LXXXIX (1984), 620–647; Ryan, *Women in Public.*

in Uniform. Emblems of innocence and purity—the only sure basis of all republics: when thus represented, our rights and liberties are safe."[89]

Male liberties were indeed safe, in part because women had been represented, though not truly included, in the public sphere. Women, recruited as spectators and participants in festivals, had become symbols of a unified electorate at a time when any such unity could only be temporary, and in fact mythical: a desire for nationalist consensus in a polity rife with ideological, sectional, and class differences. In a political culture that mixed appeals to partisan action with encomia to national unity, women helped make that unity possible. Their real, substantial, and effective participation usually consisted of doing so in partisan guise. But their partisanship could never be explicitly acknowledged; it was instead encased in the feminine signs they wore on their bodies and that increasingly stood for the nation itself. This is the legacy not only of 1776 but of 1788 and 1798, when the Federalists called on women, dressed in white, to declare their cause to be the true national one and successfully (though temporarily) routed their opponents in doing so. By 1800, when Mary Cloyd joined her husband in organizing the Chester County Republican Festival, women had secured their place as the foremost partisans against partisanship, the quintessential nationalists whose very disinterest in party, cemented by the very shape of their occasional but critical partisan gestures, signified their patriotic virtue—and their lack of citizenship.[90]

89. David Everett, *An Oration, Pronounced at Amherst, New-Hampshire, July 4, 1804* (Amherst, N.H., 1804), 5–7, 19–21, 23–36; *Mirror* (Russellville, Ky.), July 7, 1808; *News-Letter* (Bennington, Vt.), July 16, 1811.

90. In his broad overview of the use of women in the iconography of early America, John Higham observes, "Female symbols provided the chief allegorical device for evoking both the general principles and the specific, indigenous roots of the early American republic" ("Indian Princess and Roman Goddess: The First Female Symbols of America," American Antiquarian Society, *Proceedings*, C [1990], 45–79, quoted at 79). See also Elizabeth McClung Fleming, "Symbols of the Young Nation, 1765–1790," in William Vincent Shannon et al., *Symbols and Aspirations, 1776–1976* (Cleveland, Ohio, 1976), 25–41; Lester C. Olson, *Emblems of American Community in the Revolutionary Era* (Washington, D.C., 1991). On women's representing noncitizens in the early Republic, see Jan Lewis, " 'Of Every Age Sex and Condition': The Representation of Women in the Constitution," *Journal of the Early Republic,* XV (1995), 359–388.

☆ ☆ ☆

Another way to appreciate the significance of this gendering of nationalism and partisanship is to examine the ways in which women of opposing parties appropriated nationalist celebratory forms to proclaim women's rights. Could women successfully employ the Fourth of July tradition on behalf of women's interests? In 1796, a number of ladies met in an arbor outside York, Pennsylvania, for tea and a group of toasts, which they sent to the local Federalist paper:

1. The day we celebrate—may it always return with equal prosperity.
2. The Inhabitants of the United States—may they possess and practice the virtue of gratitude.
3. The Constituted authorities—may they be reverenced in place of equality.
4. The Man to whom, under Providence, we owe the celebration of this day.
5. Repentance to all political sinners.
6. Forgiveness to all political penitents.
7. The American Fair—may they never approve or favor the addresses of pretended patriots.
8. The Rights of Women.[91]

Offering union in patriotism, these Federalist women used religious language—repentance, forgiveness—to banish partisanship, even as they gave four strongly Federalist (proadministration) toasts and identified opposition partisans as nonpatriots. Obviously, they were no fans of "equality," even if they found something liberating in the potential of declaring their rights. But only in national union defined against divisive "politics" could these Federalist women locate these "rights."

Jeffersonian women were more likely to use the languages of revolutionary republicanism and universalism, even to the point of claiming women's rights as equal rights, but they were no more able to do so within the structure of partisan politics than Federalist women. Mary Cloyd and her fellow "Republican Females of Chester County," after all, relied upon the ambiguity of the term "Republican," a word that, like "federal," could as easily translate as "national" or "American." The fifty "ladies" in Wallingford, Connecticut, who could not attend 1803's

91. *Lancaster Journal* (Pa.), July 15, 1796; for a similar example, see the Chillicothe, Ohio, Federalist ladies' celebration in the *Scioto Gazette,* July 9, 1804.

big Jeffersonian election festival in New Haven, performed the same delicate but necessary rhetorical feat when they met at a private house and gave celebratory toasts. Daring to toast the "4th of March, 1801" and the region's premier Jeffersonian newspaper (to which they sent their account), they remembered to cast their politics as patriotic, and properly feminine: "Our Republican Sisters Throughout the Union — May their hearts or their hands never be given to the enemies of our freedom."[92]

Neither Federalist nor Democratic-Republican women could simultaneously participate in popular politics and act to change women's place in the public sphere, because a certain version of true womanhood undergirded the very mode of participation that was available to them. The converse also proved true: when attempting to expand the reach of women's republicanism, or women's rights, they could not simultaneously participate in politics as partisans. When a few Republicans did link women's rights to the tradition of nationalist celebration, their partisanship, even in its distinctly patriotic mode, dropped away. A New York woman who took the pseudonym of Clara reported a decidedly liberationist Fourth of July celebration to a Jeffersonian paper at the same time that other Jeffersonians, like those in Pennsylvania and Connecticut, were using Independence Day to forecast — and mobilize for — their liberation from federalism in the upcoming elections. But aside from adopting the Jeffersonian rhetoric of liberty, Clara made no mention of the partisan cause; if anything, she insisted upon the difference, even superiority, of the ladies' celebration from those of partisan men.

> We too, wishing to acknowledge no other lords or masters, but our own husbands, met on the 4th of July, to celebrate, in our own way, the glorious and ever memorable day. This is perhaps the first instance in our country of the like meeting, and for that reason you may be induced to take notice of it in your republican sheet. I expect our toasts, if not as *warm* as the others will be found as patriotic as they are expressive of the genuine sentiments of our hearts. We have

92. *American Mercury* (Hartford), Mar. 17, 1803. Rosemarie Zagarri observes that Federalists' particular hostility to women's rights arose from their hostility to all rights talk. Democratic-Republicans, on the other hand, had to develop special (and spurious) rationales for not extending the rights of citizenship to women. See Zagarri, "The Rights of Man and Woman in Post-Revolutionary America," paper delivered at the meeting of the Society for Historians of the Early American Republic, Cincinnati, July 1995.

resolved to meet next year on the like occasion, and expect to have a considerable accession to our number. The example, for the ladies, you know, are fond of novelty, may possibly be imitated throughout the union. With all confidence to the gentlemen, we have allowed them the precedence, conceiving that our *toasts* would not grow the *cooler* for laying a few days on the shelf. As a brother, I embrace you on behalf of the sisterhood, and am, yours, etc. etc.

CLARA

Celebration holds out the promise of a national sisterhood, organized and promoted in the same way that nationalist and partisan publics had been institutionalized: through public performances and printed publicity. But female difference is foregrounded by the rhetoric of sentimental patriotism, set against the fires of male (partisan) toasting rites. In the "Ladies Toasts" given at the event, the assertion of women's rights, following upon men's, in the very first toast ("Our fathers, husbands, and brothers, who fought for the rights of man, and thereby secured those of women"), is quickly mitigated by assertion of a love that conquers all differences, except those of gender.

> The female republicans of France—May they have it in their power
>   to reward the conquering heroes of their regenerated country.
> A speedy downfall to tyrants, but the tyrant love.
> Love for Love.
> The Graces—May the fair sex never be without them.
> May all national quarrels end like our's, in amity and the renewing
>   of love.
> May all chains be soon broken in our country, but those of love. . . .
> May our daughters never smile on the enemies of America.
> May those who fight the ties of wedlock, never experience the
>   sweets of love.
> Sentiment without coquetry, and attachment without interest.
> The rights of women—may they never be curtailed.[93]

93. *American Citizen* (New York), July 10, 1800. For other writings on celebratory occasions by Clara, see "Song for the Fourth of July," *Morning Chronicle* (New York), July 4, 1802; "Ode," *American Citizen,* July 4, 1804, "The Grave of Hamilton," July 21, 1804. The last piece is a decidedly nonpartisan (and personal) appreciation of the late Federalist leader, at a time when many Jeffersonians refused to mourn. See note 59, above.

Nor do we see even the tried and true endorsement of real "republicans," which on this occasion is left for the men. Women have become experts in the arts of love, in the cooling of "national quarrels." In this feminized version of liberty, love, understood as a form of self-discipline, reduces the dangers of both natural (and potentially anarchic) individual rights and the restraining (potentially tyrannical) power of the nation-state.[94] Creating a sisterhood in favor of the rights of women, Clara and her peers did no more to challenge the gendered relationship of sentimental patriotism to partisan politics than the more religiously-minded Federalist women had a few years before.

In the aftermath of that same turn-of-the century Fourth of July, an anonymous man or woman in Connecticut published an oration in the decidedly Jeffersonian *American Mercury* of Hartford. Its author declared that the men of the Revolution—the founding fathers—had been praised too much: only the egalitarian principles of the Declaration of Independence, and not the establishment of the American nation, deserved real celebration. From this beginning the writer went on to attack the denial of naturalization to immigrants, and then, at greater length, slavery, hoping that "this day" would inspire "Ethiop" as it had inspired democrats around the world. Finally, the writer asserted that "those principles of freedom, which embrace only half mankind, are only *half systems*. . . . Our daughters are the same relations to us as our sons; we owe them the same duties, they have the same science, and are equally competent to their attainments. The contrary idea originated in the same abuse of power, as monarchy and slavery."[95]

94. James Jasinski, "The Feminization of Liberty, Domesticated Virtue, and the Reconstitution of Power and Authority in Early American Political Discourse," *Quarterly Journal of Speech*, LXXIX (1993), 146–164, esp. 157.

95. "An Oration Delivered by a Citizen of the United States, on the Fourth of July," *American Mercury* (Hartford), July 10, 1800. Some internal evidence and the claim of citizenship in the title seem to indicate that the author was a man, but the writer could have been passing as male—a common enough practice. The matter was not resolved eight years later when the oration was reprinted as *An Oration Delivered on the Fourth Day of July 1800, by a Citizen of the United States, to Which Is Added the Female Advocate, Written by a Lady* (Springfield, Mass., 1808). On *The Female Advocate*, an essay favoring women's rights first published in New Haven in 1801, see Mary Kelley, "'Vindicating the Equality of Female Intellect': Women and Authority in the Early Republic," *Prospects*, XVII (1992), 11–12, 14. For a contemporary toast to "Women; an equal participation of right to our fair sisters," see "Republican Celebrations," *Bee* (New London), Mar. 18, 1801.

This ringing affirmation of American Revolutionary equality did make its way into the newspaper. Revealingly, though, the speech was presented anonymously, so that we do not know whether it was written by a man or a woman. It certainly resonated with the Jeffersonian rhetoric of the *Mercury:* in 1800 only Democratic Republicans were praising the Declaration or recalling the American Revolution as an inspiration to revolutionaries worldwide. Nevertheless, its forceful defense of immigrants, antislavery, and women's rights was made without any reference to the partisan battles raging at the time or the sex of the author. The oration and its author participated in public life in ways that might still inspire, but not in contemporary "politics" as constituted by the system of elections, party publications, and celebrations. That this piece of oratory rose above the partisan squabbles of the day to contest that very system as exclusionary shows how limiting that political system truly was. But its disembodied presentation should also remind us of the ways in which these limitations themselves came to be a gendered phenomenon.[96]

The celebrating women of the early Republic certainly acted politically, but the fact that they were usually not acknowledged to be doing so and the fact that we have completely overlooked the significance of their partisan political activity shows that they remained prisoners of the Revolution's unfinished business, its dream-work: not just the dream of equality, but also the dream of consensus; not just the dream of rights, but also the dream of uplift, of a populace made virtuous and "respectable." Little wonder, then, that during the next economic and diplomatic crisis an Ohio woman called upon women to rise up and conquer "the stubborness of party zeal" with "women's tears."

96. For the promise of disembodied membership that American identity offers, see especially Warner, *The Letters of the Republic;* Warner, "The Mass Public and the Mass Subject," in Calhoun, ed., *Habermas and the Public Sphere,* 377–401; Lauren Berlant, *The Anatomy of National Fantasy: Hawthorne, Utopia, and Everyday Life* (Chicago, 1991); Berlant, "Theory of Infantile Citizenship," *Public Culture,* XI (1993), 395–410; and Anne Norton, "Engendering Another American Identity," in Frederick M. Dolan and Thomas L. Dumm, eds., *Rhetorical Republic: Governing Representations in American Politics* (Amherst, Mass., 1993), 125–142. As Robyn Wiegman has observed, modern, disembodied citizenship seems to require the visible embodiment of women and racialized others: see *American Anatomies: Theorizing Race and Gender* (Durham, N.C., 1995), 6.

The eloquence of tears then, yes tears in torrents, and all the pathos of sighs and lamentation, shall be lavish'd on this occasion, to win and reconcile the opposition, else all is lost. . . . Let it then be woman's part to quell the opposition, disarming Fed. and Rep. and Demo. and reconciling man to man, and man to rule, and save the land from pending woe; know ye, then, our country and her honor sav'd; the glory of the deed is woman's.

Woman's spectacular tears act as a universal solvent, returning the nation to its ideal state of rest in political sameness and gender difference: "Let men be brothers; women sisters, and all Fredonians." Or, as another writer who took on a woman's voice put it during the politically and regionally divisive War of 1812:

Among the men what dire divisions rise,
For *union* one—and one *no* union cries;
Shame on the sex which such disput[e] began,
Ladies are all for UNION, *to a man*.[97]

Trapped by their own nationalism and that of American men, women could not be "political" in the same contradictory but efficacious ways as those men. Their effective expansion of nationalism and containment of partisanship helped obscure the contradictions of a male-dominated, competitive, nationalist political culture. In doing so, however, they also broadened their own influence and importance in the post-Revolutionary public sphere. The price that women paid—that they would continue to pay as they went public in the nineteenth century—was the price of their extraordinary engendering: the heightening of their gendered difference whenever they entered the male-dominated public sphere.[98]

97. "Daughters of Fredonia," *Western Sun* (Vincennes, Ind.), Mar. 18, 1809; "Friends of the Union," *Missouri Gazette and Illinois Advertiser* (Saint Louis), July 2, 1814. Fredonia, like Columbia, was a female name for America.

98. See, for example, the "Female Oration" given by a Miss Cole at Marlborough, Vermont, in 1822 and reprinted in Baltimore and Hartford newspapers (*American Mercury*, Aug. 5, 1822). On the paradoxes of women's struggles for citizenship, see Nancy F. Cott, *The Bonds of Womanhood: "Women's Sphere" in New England, 1780–1835* (New Haven, Conn., 1977), 5, 199–206; Ryan, *Women in Public*; Linda K. Kerber, "The Paradox of Women's Citizenship in the Early Republic: The Case of *Martin vs. Massachusetts*, 1805," *AHR*, XCVIII (1992), 349–378; Joan

☆ ☆ ☆

If the Jeffersonian moment truly witnessed an important expansion of the public sphere, it lay in the activities of the white workingmen who used the rituals of republican nationhood to assert their class-inflected identities as virtuous, independent, productive citizens. "There was a grand democrat procession in Town on the 4th of July," wrote a student at Saint Mary's College in Baltimore. "All the farmers, tanners, black-smiths, shoemakers, etc. were there that were in Town; they marched all threw Town and afterwards they went to a grand feast in Howard's park." Mechanics' societies celebrated their own anniversaries in Fourth of July style, always giving the requisite number of national toasts. In such "artisan republican festivals," New York's artisans "blended American republicanism with the ideal of 'the Trade.'" It should be added that in Jefferson's time the importance of these rituals grew as elections became more and more contested. When New York artisans marched as "republicans," they encased within their revolutionary republican identities their affiliation with *partisan* Republicans. The mechanics of Lewiston (Mifflin County), Pennsylvania toasted themselves and their political party on the Fourth in 1805:

> 7. The independent mechanic, who nobly thinks for himself without giving fear to any; and detestation and contempt, to the double faces who carry water on both shoulders, their actions speak not the language of this day, neither ought they to celebrate it.

These artisans employed a trade metaphor for a political situation, a common trope that dated back to the remarkable banners of 1788's Grand Federal Processions and probably before. The referent, however, was partisan. The "double faces who carry water on both shoulders," figured here as deficient in solidarity and independence, are the two-faced Pennsylvania "Quids" who bolted the Republicans to form a third-party movement. The Lewiston artisans' vision of virtuous independence insisted upon the importance of the workingman's vote within the party system: "May the farmers and mechanics of the union duly consider their weight in society, and convince the world of their political hon-

---

Wallach Scott, *Only Paradoxes to Offer: French Feminists and the Rights of Man* (Cambridge, Mass., 1996).

esty, as well as of their great majority."[99] Their political identities were artisan, nationalist, *and* partisan.

The manly firmness and independence that made partisan voters of farmers and mechanics was precisely what free blacks and white women supposedly lacked. In some of the very same cities where mechanics' numbers gained them power in local politics, free blacks could vote too. Before long, however, blacks who attempted to celebrate the Fourth of July found themselves ejected from the parks and the streets.[100] The racial battle for public space in early-nineteenth-century cities is beyond the scope of this study, as are the many ways women found to participate in public life.[101] Yet the codification of citizenship as the prerogative of voting might have helped to mark the public sphere as "political" in its gendered and racialized sense. It also meant that, even for the self-identified working class, the claim to republican citizenship would be a quintessentially middling claim in its reliance upon upper (aristocratic, conspiratorial) and lower (racialized, manipulated) classes whose lack of virtue contrasted with good republican claims to citizenship. On celebratory occasions, white women ratified these claims

99. William White Hall to Edward Hall, July 10, 1809, case 64, James A. Montgomery Collection, Historical Society of Pennsylvania, Philadelphia; Sean Wilentz, *Chants Democratic: New York City and the Rise of the American Working Class, 1788–1850* (New York, 1984), 87–97, 180, 183, quoted at 93; Wilentz, "Artisan Republican Festivals and the Rise of Class Consciousness in New York City, 1788–1837," in Michael H. Frisch and Daniel J. Walkowitz, eds., *Working-Class America: Essays on Labor, Community, and American Society* (Urbana, Ill., 1983), 37–77; Howard B. Rock, ed., *The New York City Artisan, 1789–1825: A Documentary History* (Albany, N.Y., 1989), 3–19; *Aurora* (Philadelphia), July 22, 1805. On partisanship in Pennsylvania during this period, see Sanford W. Higginbotham, *The Keystone in the Democratic Arch: Pennsylvania Politics, 1800–1816* (Harrisburg, Pa., 1952).

100. Fox, *Decline of Aristocracy*, 269–270n; Gary B. Nash, *Forging Freedom: The Making of Philadelphia's Black Community, 1720–1840* (Cambridge, Mass., 1988), 177; Paul A. Gilje, *The Road to Mobocracy: Popular Disorder in New York City, 1763–1834* (Chapel Hill, N.C., 1987), 159–163; White, *Somewhat More Independent*, 207–209; White, "'It Was a Proud Day,'" *JAH*, LXXXI (1994–1995), 13–50.

101. For elite women and politics after 1800, see Fredrika J. Teute, "Roman Matron on the Banks of Tiber Creek: Margaret Bayard Smith and the Politicization of Spheres in the Nation's Capital," in Donald R. Kennon, ed., *A Republic for the Ages* (Charlottesville, Va., 1999); Elizabeth R. Varon, "Tippecanoe and the Ladies Too: White Women and Party Politics in Antebellum Virginia," *JAH*, LXXXII (1995–1996), 494–521.

in their persons, by embodying respectability and the separation from racialized others. If the indeterminate definition of "the people" who celebrated in the streets of the 1770s, 1780s, and 1790s had held the promises of democracy and equality in its very vagueness, the triumph of partisanship helped make the identities (or, as Timothy Swan had put it, "colouring") of real public men quite clear.

Partisan practice clarified the meanings and goals of nationalism, but not without ultimately narrowing the political. Finally, perhaps, the Revolution was over. "It is high time that societies for the emancipation of white slaves were established in New England," wrote Bishop in 1800, comparing the "invisible slavery" of white men in Federalist Connecticut to the material bondage of "a Southern slave." "Connecticut is a conquered country; it is high time for the white slaves to rise in mass, not with arms, but with their votes in their hands," he declared a few years later in the headnote to an important series of newspaper essays. In these telling moments Bishop reversed the tropes of slavery and revolution he had employed in his own antislavery essay of 1791. Where a decade earlier blacks had picked up the torch of the democratic revolutions and applied it to the condition of slavery, now the protest against slavery provided a model for an apparently more pressing domestic political struggle, once again cast as the true revolution. That Bishop, speaking of slavery and revolution, could so easily exchange referent for metaphor reveals the truly unstable, egalitarian potential of Revolutionary rhetoric. But changing the subject changed the whole thrust of the message—especially when even the unfreedom of blacks was, despite the gradual nature of emancipation in New England, restricted to the South, and when legitimate resistance, white or black, was limited to organizing for elections.[102]

102. Bishop, "Rights of Black Men," in Mathewson, "Abraham Bishop," *Journal of Negro History*, LXVII (1982), 150–154; Bishop, *Connecticut Republicanism*, iv; [Bishop], "To the Porpoises of Connecticut," *American Mercury* (Hartford), Mar. 31, Apr. 14, 1803. Bishop mentions his authorship of the Porpoises series in a letter to Elisha Babcock, Feb. 4, 1803, Babcock Papers, Connecticut Historical Society. For Bishop's antislavery essay, see the works cited in note 7, above. Quite probably Bishop was making an ironic comment on New England Federalists' enthusiasm for antislavery and their commitment to liberty in far-off locales like Haiti and the American South (see Chapter 5). But his shift in focus at this time speaks volumes about the limitations of the movement for political democratization he so

The irony of political bondage in free territory might also have been applied to the African Americans whom Bishop must have seen on the streets of New Haven every day. Whether or not Bishop actually encouraged free blacks and white women to participate in Connecticut's Republican celebrations (as the Federalists would charge), the larger national political culture that gained strength from Bishop's efforts systematically evaded the issue of whether enslaved Africans could be free, and even whether, once legally free, women or African Americans could be citizens of the Republic they were helping to build. For a long time to come, slaves, free blacks, and women too would remain in bondage to a partisan electoral system and a public sphere that were not of their own making. Sadly, it is no accident that, when Abraham Bishop and his fellow Jeffersonians finally won their campaign for a new state constitution in 1818, that constitution explicitly gave the vote to white men only.[103] In the future that Abraham Bishop and parading workers helped to create, when white men celebrated politics, they celebrated themselves.

eloquently and effectively supported. For the process by which New Englanders absolved themselves of responsibility for American slavery, see Joanne Pope Melish, "Disowning Slavery: Gradual Emancipation and the Cultural Construction of Race in New England, 1780–1860" (Ph.D. diss., Brown University, 1996).

103. Roediger, *The Wages of Whiteness*, 57. The Federalist-dominated legislature had first voted to ban blacks from voting in 1814 (James Truslow Adams, "Disenfranchisement of Negroes in New England," *AHR*, XXX [1924–1925], 545). On the black community in New Haven at this time, see Robert Austin Warner, *New Haven Negroes: A Social History* (1940; rpt. New York, 1969), 5–11.

5

REGIONALISM, NATIONALISM, AND THE GEOPOLITICS OF CELEBRATION

If the politics of celebration encouraged citizens of the early Republic to think nationally while acting locally, they also learned how to negotiate their regional differences while celebrating their Americanism. Festive culture had a local, face-to-face politics, but it had a geopolitics as well. Generally refering to relations between empires, regions, or continents in a "world-system" of nation-states, a geopolitical analysis can also address the competing regions of a large and expanding federal republic like the early United States. The divergence of the commercial republic identified with Hamilton from the agrarian republic envisioned by Jefferson only begins to suggest the magnitude of evolving east-west and north-south polarities in the new nation's political economy. Meanwhile, the West continued to be fought over and enlarged. The vague borders of British America had been a major contested issue before the American Revolution, as European colonists, native American tribes, and imperial officials struggled for control of the trans-Appalachian and Great Lakes regions. The future of these lands and their several peoples remained negotiable through the War of 1812.[1]

---

1. See, especially, Immanuel Wallerstein, *Geopolitics and Geoculture: Essays on the Changing World System* (New York, 1991); Richard White, *The Middle Ground: Indians, Empires, and Republics in the Great Lakes Region, 1660–1815* (New York, 1991); Gregory Evans Dowd, *A Spirited Resistance: The North American Indian Struggle for Unity, 1745–1815* (Baltimore, 1992). For an extremely helpful geographical overview of early American history, see D. W. Meinig, *The Shaping of America: A Geographical Perspective*

The colonial ambitions of France, England, and Spain, the Napoleonic Wars, and native American resistance to expansion made the frontiers of American settlement vulnerable not only to raids but also to temptation, should their white inhabitants feel insufficiently protected or represented by the United States federal government. At the same time, conflicting visions of western development affected the way easterners, north and south, viewed each other: their different interests, hardly latent in the making of the Federal Constitution, became all the more manifest in the following decades. In each region, American national identity had to be balanced with regional interests and the possibilities for interregional partisan affiliations.[2]

The context for these balancing acts was the same as for the development of national partisan subcultures: indeed, the forging of regional political identities cannot be understood apart from the emergence of party politics. In the early Republic both parties broadcast their own patriotic nonpartisanship while projecting the specter of factionalism onto their opponents. This dynamic lent a partisan and nationalist cast to the most local political contests. A similar logic operated between the regions of the expanding nation. This chapter explores the remarkably nationalist regionalisms that emerged during the two and a half decades after the ratification of the Constitution. Nationalism provided the context for the development of regionalism; and the emergence of New England, southern, and western regionalisms helps explain the patterns of assent and dissent in domestic politics during the War of 1812. The emergence of nationalist (and partisan) versions of regional-

---

on *Five Hundred Years of History,* I, *Atlantic America, 1492–1800* (New Haven, Conn., 1986), and II, *Continental America, 1800–1867* (New Haven, Conn., 1993).

2. The work of Peter S. Onuf has been central to the reconstruction of this too often neglected aspect of early national history. See Onuf, *The Origins of the Federal Republic: Jurisdictional Controversies in the United States, 1775–1787* (Philadelphia, 1983); Onuf, *Statehood and Union: A History of the Northwest Ordinance* (Bloomington, Ind., 1987); Onuf, "Federalism, Republicanism, and the Origins of American Sectionalism," in Edward L. Ayers et al., *All over the Map: Rethinking American Regions* (Baltimore, 1996), 11–37.

Stephen Aron makes the case for the formative importance of the trans-Appalachian West in the shaping of western history, in "Lessons in Conquest: Towards a Greater Western History," *Pacific Historical Review,* LXIII (1994), 125–147; for a review of the literature, see also Andrew R. L. Cayton and Peter S. Onuf, *The Midwest and the Nation: Rethinking the History of an American Region* (Bloomington, Ind., 1990).

ism also foreshadows the modes of sectional protest that shaped American politics through the Civil War.[3]

What is regionalism? Like nationalism, we seem to know it when we see it: that deep-seated attachment to a particular state or section of the country, be it the South, the West, New England, or portions thereof. Yet it is important to remember that regions can take on political meaning only in a larger (imperial, continental, or national) context. Missing the forest for the proverbial trees, studies of regionalism tend to replicate the nationalist or regionalist rhetoric through which Americans came to define political reality in the nineteenth century. Looking for the organic growth of sectional identity, attachment to the union, or the absence of either, scholars have often made regionalism and nationalism mutually exclusive phenomena. Under such assumptions, a regional perspective detracts from a nationalist one, and mature nationalism subsumes fugitive expressions of regional identity. But it need not be so. Indeed, in the early national era, regionalism as often as not actually contributed to nationalism, even if how it did so ultimately weakened the federal union.

In his justly acclaimed essay "The Historian's Use of Nationalism and Vice Versa" (1963), David M. Potter noted that nationalism and regionalism do not necessarily conflict: during the Civil War era, for example, the South faced a contradiction between regionalist and nationalist interests and ideologies while the North remained able to conflate the two.[4] Potter's observation reminds us of the situational nature of both nationalist and regionalist expression. Both are ideologies mobilized for particular ends, ends that can be regionalist, nationalist, or regionalist *and* nationalist simultaneously. Extending Potter's insight, we might say that, for any region, a combination of political and economic alignments, with sufficient control or influence over the federal government, can create an ideal situation, in which that regional political subculture can conflate regional and national goals.

Naturally, regions whose predilections matched those of the federal

3. A similar argument is presented in Ayers and Peter S. Onuf, "Introduction," in Ayers et al., *All over the Map*, 1–10.

4. David M. Potter, *History and American Society: Essays of David M. Potter*, ed. Don E. Fehrenbacher (New York, 1973), 90–92. See also Merle Curti, *The Roots of American Loyalty* (New York, 1946), 47.

government or at least were recognized by it displayed more devotion to "the concept of a perpetual union." In a rapidly growing United States, however, citizens east, west, north, and south knew (if not always consciously) that any such declaration was situational, contingent. Such understandings did not signal any lack of nationalism. Yet neither can adherence be traced to the absence or insignificance of regionalism. Rather, because both the nation and its regions were in such flux, one day's happy identification of region and nation could be the next day's intractable political dilemma.[5]

The situational nature of regionalist expressions did not make them any less potent. Rather, they became even more important to partisan politics. As Pierre Bourdieu has written, "Regionalist discourse is a *performative discourse* which aims to impose as legitimate a new definition of the frontiers and to get people to know and recognize the *region* that is thus delimited in opposition to the dominant definition."[6] The dynamic that Bourdieu defines in terms of center and periphery (or core and region) was especially characteristic of the early American Republic, where three regions triangulated within the brace of nationalist ideology.

We need to recognize the rhetorical aspect of ordinary people and political leaders speaking in regionalist and nationalist accents: they were not necessarily expressing their innermost sense of identity. Partisan identities, tangible and expressible in local political activity, *were* important to white male (and sometimes female) self-definitions in the

5. Kenneth M. Stampp, "The Concept of a Perpetual Union," in Stampp, *The Imperiled Union: Essays on the Background of the Civil War* (New York, 1980), 3–36, argues generally for the very halting emergence of devotion to the federal government as an end in itself but implicitly conflates devotion to the state with nationalism; for a similar analysis, see John M. Murrin, "A Roof without Walls: The Dilemma of American National Identity," in Richard Beeman et al., eds., *Beyond Confederation: Origins of the Constitution and American National Identity* (Chapel Hill, N.C., 1987), 333–348. For a critique of this tendency in the scholarship, see Wilbur Zelinsky, *Nation into State: The Shifting Symbolic Foundations of American Nationalism* (Chapel Hill, N.C., 1989). For similar observations regarding the coexistence of nationalism and sectionalism, see Meinig, *Atlantic America*, 406, 444; Robert F. Durden, *The Self-Inflicted Wound: Southern Politics in the Nineteenth Century* (Lexington, Ky., 1985), 2.

6. Pierre Bourdieu, "Identity and Representation: Elements for a Critical Reflection on the Idea of Region," in Bourdieu, *Language and Symbolic Power*, ed. John B. Thompson, trans. Gino Raymond and Matthew Adamson (Cambridge, Mass., 1991), 221, 223.

early Republic. Articulations of regional identity, however, were more sporadic, in part because their very utterance could betray the loss of that happy conflation of region and nation. Usually a response to a temporary or persisting political crisis, regionalist expression was more of a top-down phenomenon, as statesmen developed subtle geopolitical strategies in response to other regions and other parties.

Hence the particularly performative nature of regionalist discourse. In early national America, "struggles over classifications" took place on celebratory occasions, in celebratory forms. It is no accident that such declarations most often took the form of toasts: those scripted, applauded, and printed watchwords of early American politics by which groups, locatable by place if not always by party, took stances in response to recent news and the pronouncements of other, similar gatherings. Such toasts were often written and rewritten by elites who sought to mediate between the people of their locales and those of larger regional and national areas.[7] And one of the crucial ways in which they did so was by publishing their toasts. Southerners, New Englanders, and westerners read accounts of each other's toasts and oratory in the newspapers and commented on each other in turn at their own celebrations. Given the local nature of celebrations and, presumably, regional loyalties, it may be surprising to see how much of the work of regionalism was done in what had become nationalist forms and forums. If we recall, though, that each variety of regionalism depended on the existence of the nation and other regions to give it meaning, we can begin to see regionalism and nationalism in creative tension—tensions that would shape regional and national histories.

Diehard unionists and recalcitrant sectionalists alike used nationalist festivity and its system of publicity to mobilize constituencies and to affect national politics. Increasingly, party and region came to overlap, so that partisan and regionalist discourses reinforced one another. Celebrations served as the site for an important cultural dialogue that mixed appeals to national unity with demands for partisan-regional solidarity in the face of hostile other regions or a not-so-friendly federal

7. Peter Onuf has noted the particular role of leadership in such arenas as movements for statehood in the territories as well as their telling use of the rhetoric of the Revolution to justify their claims for national inclusion (*Statehood and Union*, 87). Sectionalism emerged, as Onuf writes, as "a top-down phenomenon, the result of ad-hoc alliances among state leaders who discovered common interests as they sought to promote or obstruct the exercise of central governmental power" ("Origins of American Sectionalism," in Ayers et al., *All over the Map*, 21–22).

administration. Acknowledging potential trouble, political actors did their best to resolve the seeming contradiction of nationalist regionalism: they aspired to make their regionalism express their Americanism. Particularly in toasts, the talismans of this American geopolitics, New England Federalists constructed their Americanness in contrast to the deviant foreignness of Southern "Jacobins." Likewise, Southern Republicans argued for their normative Americanness in contrast to parochial "Federalism of the Boston stamp."[8] Westerners asserted their loyalty and ultimately their centrality to an expanding nation: their seeming eccentricity, they insisted, signified the true cutting edge of American identity. Attempting to solidify regional or national hegemony, each section used the others as ally or enemy to win over the ever-shifting middle, both persons and regions. In celebrations and the accompanying public prints, Americans worked out three distinct nationalist regionalisms as part of their continuing efforts to define the present, create the future, and celebrate both.

NEW ENGLAND AS AMERICA

By the end of the eighteenth century, New Englanders had a long tradition of national regionalism. From the Puritans of the 1630s to the Boston rebels of the 1760s, even when New Englanders did not see themselves as America writ small, they at least defined themselves as its saving remnant. The myth of the errand into the wilderness persisted. Into the nineteenth century, latter-day Puritans could still see the emergence of an American empire as a direct continuation of their original project.[9]

Yet by the mid-1790s it had become clear that New England was losing political power in the nation as a whole. Eastern areas remained nearly stable in population while the natural and imported increase was forging southward and westward into less densely settled regions. The increase in the number of states was decreasing the proportion of senators and representatives who championed New England interests

8. "Federalism of the Boston Stamp!!" *Telegraph* (Georgetown, Ky.) (from the *Enquirer* [Richmond]), Sept. 29, 1813.

9. Perry Miller, *Errand into the Wilderness* (Cambridge, Mass., 1956), 1–15; Sacvan Bercovitch, *The Puritan Origins of the American Self* (New Haven, Conn., 1975); Bercovitch, "The Ritual of Consensus," in Bercovitch, *The Rites of Assent: Transformations in the Symbolic Construction of America* (New York, 1993), 85.

in Philadelphia and then Washington. Thanks to the Napoleonic Wars, Yankee farmers and merchants flourished during the decade after ratification; but international conflict also led to controversies over national policy, like Jefferson's embargo, that highlighted the distinctiveness of Yankee political economy. Nationally, New England Federalists were on the defensive after 1800, when a series of Virginia Republicans occupied the presidency, and they found themselves increasingly challenged by "democrats" at home.[10]

Tellingly, the rearticulation of New England regionalism began in an attack upon southern distinctiveness. New England Federalists projected the growing internal opposition to their political dominance at home into the nether regions, making the southern planter the emblem of a national threat: hypocritical support for democracy and the French Revolution. Who were those "feudal barons, who reign over a thousand negroes," to talk of aristocracy in government?[11] The partisan critique of southern slavery meshed with rising antislavery activity in the North, but Federalists held no patent on antislavery notions in New England. The critique in this instance was part of a strategy to conflate party and region: to symbolically place all the nation's sins (including the Republican opposition) "mostly in the southern and middle states." Actually, such expressions made only a limited contribution to antislavery, because they were not meant to end slavery: they were meant to discredit southern Jeffersonians and their allies. The New England attack on southern slaveholding often centered on the three-fifths clause of the Constitution (by which 60 percent of slaves were counted in apportionment of presidential electors and seats in the House of Representatives, increasing white southern power in the federal government). Nothing in their pronouncements suggests that Federalists thought that south-

10. James Truslow Adams, *New England in the Republic, 1776–1850* (1926; rpt. Gloucester, Mass., 1960), 186–211.

11. "Communications," *Gazette of the United States* (Philadelphia) (from *Columbian Centinel* [Boston]), Jan. 15, 1796. For similar examples, see Daniel Davis, *An Oration, Delivered at Portland, July 4th, 1796* . . . (Portland, Maine, [1796]), 16; "Remarks on the 'Feast of Reason' at New-York," *Gazette of the United States,* July 18, 1797. For the importance of the theme of New England regionalism in Federalist ideology, see David Hackett Fischer, *The Revolution of American Conservatism: The Federalist Party in the Era of Jeffersonian Democracy* (New York, 1965), 159; James M. Banner, Jr., *To the Hartford Convention: The Federalists and the Origins of Party Politics in Massachusetts, 1789–1815* (New York, 1970), 99–109; Linda K. Kerber, *Federalists in Dissent: Imagery and Ideology in Jeffersonian America* (Ithaca, N.Y., 1971), 23–66.

ern slaves—or, for that matter, free blacks north or south—should exercise the vote. Thus the participants at a Forefathers' Day feast in Boston toasted, "Our Sister Virginia—when she changes three fifths of her Ethiopian skin we will respect her as the head of our White family."[12]

If the rise of the Republicans fearsomely paralleled the demographic growth of the South, the acquisition of the Louisiana Territory in 1803 threatened to further reduce New England's power in the nation. Orators wasted little time in blaming the South, and Virginia in particular, for a scheme that would lead to New England's subjection and, eventually, western secession. George Washington Stanley insisted that any "inhabitants of New England" who celebrated such an event could no longer be "in principle New-Englandmen." On the Fourth of July prominent Federalists accused Virginia of "trying to divide the northern from the southern states" and seeking to "increase the number of her *slaves* among the *freemen* of New England." In 1804, a profusion of toasts urged New Englanders to "resist the encroachment of Southern despotism." Campaigns to alter the three-fifths clause or delay the admittance of new states to the union were said to illuminate the Constitution by a "steady Northern light."[13]

12. John Hubbard, *An Oration, Pronounced at Walpole . . . July 4th, 1799* (Walpole, N.H., 1799), 10. On the relation of antislavery to New England federalism, see Benjamin W. Labaree, *Patriots and Partisans: The Merchants of Newburyport, 1764–1815* (1962; rpt. New York, 1975), 126–127; Banner, *To the Hartford Convention*, 107–108; David Brion Davis, *The Problem of Slavery in the Age of Revolution, 1770–1823* (Ithaca, N.Y., 1975), 339–342. For an attempt to give federalism the credit for antislavery that ignores the profound racism of New England Federalists, see Paul Finkelman, "The Problem of Slavery in the Age of Federalism," in Doron Ben-Atar and Barbara Oberg, eds., *Federalists Reconsidered* (Charlottesville, Va., 1999). For an interpretation of federalism and antislavery closer to my own, see Andrew Siegel, "The Public Philosophy of Connecticut Federalism," in the same volume; and Larry E. Tise, *Proslavery: A History of the Defense of Slavery in America, 1701–1840* (Athens, Ga., 1987), 217, 229–237.

For a classic statement on slave representation, see [Sereno Edwards Dwight], *Slave Representation* (New Haven, Conn., 1812). The toast, which dates from 1803, is cited from Worcester's *Aegis* in William Bentley, *The Diary of William Bentley, D.D. . . .* (Salem, Mass., 1905–1914), III, 4; it was also picked up from the *Aegis* by the *Wilmington Gazette*, Mar. 10, 1803. This Jeffersonian North Carolina paper proclaimed that real Americans would be made furious by reading such a toast.

13. Stephen Longfellow, *An Oration, Pronounced July 4th 1804 . . .* (Portland, Maine, 1804), 16; Junius Smith, *An Oration, Pronounced at Hartford, before the Society of the Cincinnati . . . July 4th, 1804* (Hartford, Conn., 1804), 17–20; George W[ashing-

For the next decade, New England Federalists cultivated a vision of a loyal but aggrieved northern America. The geographical contours of this region remained purposefully ambiguous, as these Federalists hoped to bring eastern or seaport areas, particularly New York, into their northern or eastern political fold. The image of the feudal landlord or aristocratic tyrant, surrounded by his real (black) and political (Republican) servants, helped opponents of Jefferson to rewrite the "Revolution of 1800" as the first act of an era that they hoped would conclude with their own second American Revolution. "The People of the Northern States" were toasted by the Connecticut Cincinnati in 1804: "Descended from Freemen, they will never be governed by Southern Slaves."[14]

The Embargo controversy helped the Federalists to flesh out this picture with an international dimension. Southerners were "Frenchified enemies to commerce," and New England Republicans mere functionaries of the French interest. In this atmosphere, disunion, unspeakable to nationalists, could be openly discussed or even proposed, because its cause was always the actions of the conspiring, foreign-influenced other party. Disunion was really a defense of New England (and America) against narrow regionalists who cloaked their southern agenda in nationalism. Republican papers carried article after article on the "Essex Junto," who favored a northern confederacy. Federalists replied with exposés of the "Virginia Junto," who caused the bad blood in the first place.[15]

ton] Stanley, *An Oration, Delivered at Wallingford, August 8th, 1805: In Commemoration of the Independence of the United States* (New Haven, Conn., 1805), 11; Spencer Pratt, *An Oration, Pronounced at Norridgwock, on the Fourth Day of July, 1805* (Augusta, Maine, 1805), 13; James Dean Hopkins, *An Oration Pronounced before the Inhabitants of Portland, July 4th, 1805* . . . (Portland, Maine, 1805), 24; *Toasts, for Fourth July 1804* (Norwich, Conn., 1804).

14. John Lowell, *The New-England Patriot: Being a Candid Comparison of the Conduct of the Washington and Jefferson Administrations* . . . (Boston, 1810), 142; A Friend to Freedom, *Southern Oppression: An Address to the People of the Eastern States, Developing the Causes of Their Oppression* (New York, 1813); *Connecticut Courant* (Hartford), July 11, 1804. This understanding culminated later in abolitionist and Republican views of the southern "slave power." See David Brion Davis, *The Slave Power Conspiracy and the Paranoid Style* (Baton Rouge, La., 1969); Eric Foner, *Free Soil, Free Labor, Free Men: The Ideology of the Republican Party before the Civil War* (New York, 1970), 40–72.

15. Nathaniel Ames Diary, Feb. 21, 1809, in Charles Warren, *Jacobin and Junto; or, Early American Politics as Viewed in the Diary of Dr. Nathaniel Ames, 1758–1822*

FIGURE 13. Republican Governor Hancock's Ball for Boston's African Americans.
From Richard Alsop, The Echo, and Other Poems *(New York, 1807). Courtesy Beinecke
Rare Book and Manuscript Library, Yale University*

Although the machinations of real Essex secessionists amounted to
little, northeastern Massachusetts emerged nonetheless as the mythic
center of New England, if only because it revived the celebration of
the Pilgrims' landing at Plymouth and Puritan Forefathers' Day in Boston. On these occasions, similar in form to General Election Day rites,
Federalist preachers reminded all who came of the superior virtues of
New England's founding generation.[16] If the "myth of New England ex-

(Cambridge, Mass., 1931), 233; Margaret Law Callcott, ed., *Mistress of Riversdale:
The Plantation Letters of Rosalie Stier Calvert, 1795–1821* (Baltimore, 1991), 197, 203;
"Alteration of the Constitution," *Columbian Centinel and Massachusetts Federalist* (Boston), Feb. 22, 1804. In 1800, Republicans had already turned Federalist attacks on
the influence of the Bavarian Illuminati into a critique of the "New England Illuminati." On the construction of the "Myth of the Essex Junto" by Republicans, see
David Hackett Fischer's essay of that title in E. James Ferguson, ed., *National Unity
on Trial, 1781–1816* (New York, 1970), 93–127.

16. Albert Matthews, "The Term Pilgrim Fathers and Early Celebrations of Forefathers' Day," Colonial Society of Massachusetts, *Transactions,* XVII (1913–1914),
293–391; John Allyn, *A Sermon, Delivered at Plimouth, December 22, 1801* (Boston,

clusiveness" developed and disseminated through these festivals was a provincial myth, it also asserted its righteous Americanness and for this reason served New England's Federalists well. It helped them relocate declension geopolitically, justifying their resistance to the federal government as the godly actions of a saving remnant.[17]

When the Republican-dominated Congress, led by southern and western War Hawks, voted to commence hostilities against England in 1812, Massachusetts governor Caleb Strong lost little time in declaring a statewide fast for July 23. In his official message Strong beseeched God to "inspire the President and Congress, and the Government of Great Britain, with just and pacific sentiments." Pointing to England as the "bulwark of [our] religion" and the source of American patrimony, Strong asked every citizen to pray against an American alliance with the infidel, France.[18]

This fast on July 23, also observed in Connecticut, set the tone for

---

1802); Abiel Abbott, *A Discourse Delivered at Plymouth December 22, 1809, at the Celebration of the 188th Anniversary of the Landing of Our Forefathers in that Place* (Boston, 1810). New England gentlemen in New York founded a New England Society that also held its anniversary on December 22 ("Anniversary of the N.E. Society," *New-York Herald,* Dec. 28, 1808). According to one student of the figure of the forefathers in literature, "The first decade of the nineteenth century was a coming of age for the Pilgrim fathers"; see Mark L. Sargent, "Rekindled Fires: Jamestown and Plymouth in American Literature, 1785–1863" (Ph.D. diss., Claremont Graduate School, 1985), 102. For a discussion of the role of these festivals in the 1820s and an interpretation of New England sectionalism that complements my own for a later period, see Harlow Elizabeth Walker Sheidley, "Sectional Nationalism: The Politics and Culture of the Massachusetts Conservative Elite, 1815–1836" (Ph.D. diss., University of Connecticut, 1990), esp. chap. 6.

17. Samuel Leonard, *The Substance of a Discourse, Delivered at Poultney, Vermont . . . Fourth of July, 1804 . . .* (Salem, Mass., 1804); Samuel Austin, *The Apology of Patriots; or, The Heresy of the Friends of Washington and Peace Policy Defended: A Sermon, Preached in Worcester . . . August 20, 1812* (Worcester, Mass., 1812); Jeremiah Evarts, *An Oration, Delivered in Charlestown, (Mass.) on the Fourth of July, 1812* (Charleston, S.C., 1812); Benjamin Whitwell, *An Oration, Pronounced July 4, 1814, at the Request of the Selectmen of the Town of Boston . . .* (Boston, 1814). On the myth, see Banner, *To the Hartford Convention;* Harry S. Stout, "Rhetoric and Reality in the Early Republic: The Case of the Federalist Clergy," in Mark A. Noll, ed., *Religion and American Politics* (New York, 1990), 62–76.

18. W. De Loss Love, Jr., *The Fast and Thanksgiving Days of New England* (Boston, 1895), 391–392; William Gribbin, *The Churches Militant: The War of 1812 and American Religion* (New Haven, Conn., 1973), 19–20.

the remarkably sectional dissent of the New England Federalists during the War of 1812. Seizing upon the form of the fast day as avidly as they had in the late 1790s, sacred and secular officials alike described a true New England that resisted the war effort out of tradition and a belief in their region's superior Christianity. "The Puritans of New England must not, will not, cannot be dragged into this execrable war," intoned Elijah Parish in the best-known of the 1812 fast sermons. "You must change the radical traits of your character, you must cease to be New England men, before you can exhibit this tame, African, slavish deportment." Throughout the war, these Federalists portrayed Republicans not only as southern and western in orientation and as morally and racially contaminated by a slavish dependence on slaves but also as Frenchified "infidels." "Fast Day, appointed by our excellent Governor Strong," wrote a leading citizen of Brookline in his diary: "that the People may atone for their sins in electing over them rulers, without Honesty or Knowledge, men neither fearing God or who have any love for their country." [19]

Federalist leaders combined this revival of New England Christian identity with a claim to the heritage of the American Revolution. A widely published song of 1812 presents the New England "fathers" as the planters of liberty in America. Their eighteenth-century sons defended these liberties against the British and the French; this tradition gave Americans the right to stay out of Europe's interminable wars. But then the Madison administration had dropped the country back into the "quicksand" of imperial struggles:

> They might know, witless dunces, the method at once, is
>   To give up the helm to *New-England*—
> .   .   .   .
> Our true Northern notions would settle commotions,
>   And teach them respect to *New-England*.[20]

19. William Westmore Diary, July 21, 1812, Historical Society of Pennsylvania, Philadelphia; Thaddeus Larned Journal, July 23, 1812, Larned Family Papers, Historical Society of Pennsylvania; E[lijah] Parish, *A Protest against the War: A Discourse Delivered at Byfield, Fast Day, July 23, 1812* (Newburyport, Mass., 1812), 13, 20; Samuel Walker, *A Sermon, Delivered before the Second Society in Danvers, January 12, 1815, Being the Day Appointed for National Humiliation and Prayer* (Salem, Mass., 1815), 19–20; "Extracts From the Diary of Benjamin Goddard of Brookline, 1812–1821," Brookline Historical Society, *Proceedings*, IX (1911), 26.

20. "New England: A Song," *Columbian Centinel* (Boston), July 29, 1812, reprinted

In 1812 Federalists still hoped for an electoral solution to the problem of the war; this preelection song rallied the faithful to the polls. Yet the "them" here seems intentionally ambiguous: is it Europe, or the floundering Republican administration, that must learn "respect to *New England*"? In the next stanza, the Republican rulers themselves are again the culprits. Having left the northern coasts unprotected, they seem to revel in the decline of New England and in its possible invasion by the enemy. Nevertheless, "these buckskins will find, the Yankee's inclin'd / To stick to the RIGHTS OF NEW ENGLAND." After this defense of ancient, local liberties that antedate yet inform the American national Revolution, the song concludes with a promise to join loyally in wartime defense:

> But since War is declar'd, let us all be prepar'd,
>   For the dangers that threaten our dear land;
> With a STRONG to parade us, who'er may invade us,
>   We'll fight for the RIGHTS of *New-England—*
>   We'll die or live free in *New-England—*
>   In the shade of the TREE of *New-England—*
> And the NATION shall know, who is truly their foe,
> Is also the foe of NEW ENGLAND!

"Our dear land," it turns out, may suffer "dangers" from any number of invaders, perhaps including the federal government. New England must be defended, but can be only from within New England itself, under the original liberty tree. Although it is finally admitted the "the nation" is more than New England, the last appeal is one of self-definition through opposition. The real enemies of America are those who oppose New England's "RIGHTS."

Placing themselves simultaneously in the lineage of the Puritans and the founding fathers, New England Federalists constructed a mythic South and West that possessed no real claims to the legacy of the Revolution. It should be stressed, though, that the Federalists did so in a manner no less authentic than the Republicans' own version of the War of 1812 as a struggle to reestablish the (once again unstable) "national character." Theirs was the conservative American Revolution, the one limited to the restoration of ancient (British) rights and privileges. The Massachusetts Federalists consistently stressed New England's British

---

as "The Key of Sedition" in *The American Patriotic Song-Book* . . . (Philadelphia, 1813), 34.

heritage, ethnic homogeneity, and leadership of the Revolution. On the floor of the House of Representatives and in an often reprinted Washington Benevolent Society oration, Josiah Quincy charged that the "original compact" of the nation had been abridged by the extension of equal representation to "Frenchmen, Spaniards . . . Creoles and Negroes."[21] In a truly reactionary derivation of political citizenship, intellectuals and politicians like Quincy traced American rights, not to nature, but to genealogy, prefiguring a century of racial Anglo-Saxonism that would continue to validate its intellectual pedigree in New England. "Our adversaries accuse us of foreign partiality, we love no country like our own," insisted Benjamin Whitwell in Boston's official July Fourth oration in 1814.

> We are attached to the union, being all members of one body, of which Virginia assumes to be the head, but we know that NEW-ENGLAND is the heart; their sons have no certificates of French citizenship to divide their love. She has no patriots by adoption. . . . Her sons trace their descent from ancestors, whose institutions they preserve and whose memory they venerate. She requires no mixture of the best nations on earth in her political composition, let the head, and the heart, and the arm be purely American.[22]

"Ancestors," in these New England festivals of national memory, meant Puritans and revolutionaries. Latter-day patriots did not have to resist Old England at all, since the new tyrants lay among the partisans of the new France.

The isolation of New England during the war only strengthened the ideological link between the defense of liberty and New England tradition. Federalists in other states gladly lauded Massachusetts as the leader of this latter-day rebellion in toasts like one given at Fairhaven, Vermont, on July 4, 1813: "The Commonwealth of Massachusetts—The

---

21. Steven Watts, *The Republic Reborn: War and the Making of Liberal America, 1790–1820* (Baltimore, 1987); Banner, *To the Hartford Convention*, chap. 3; Josiah Quincy, *An Oration Delivered before the Washington Benevolent Society of Massachusetts, on the Thirtieth Day of April, 1813* . . . (Boston, 1813), 25.

22. Whitwell, *An Oration, Pronounced July 4, 1814*, 18. On the Federalists' retreat into ascriptive norms of citizenship, see Rogers M. Smith, "Constructing American National Citizenship: Strategies of the Federalists," in Ben-Atar and Oberg, eds., *Federalists Reconsidered*. For later varieties of racial Anglo-Saxonism, see Reginald Horsman, *Race and Manifest Destiny: The Origins of American Racial Anglo-Saxonism* (Cambridge, Mass., 1981).

cradle of American liberty; she still nurses its defenders." Those Massachusetts legislators who supported attempts to foil the enlistment of federal troops in New England "evinced a spirit worthy of *Freemen*, but dreadful to tyrants."[23] Resistance to war was defense of the Revolution, and Federalists who sang celebratory odes participated in national renewal:

> Rouse to action every power,
> Now's the dire, decisive hour,
> True to freedom's high command,
> Independence bids you stand.

Indeed, the "clamorous patriots of Virginia, Kentucky and Tennessee," according to one orator, not only had no real interest in the maritime issues that had supposedly led to war; they were also the authors of the Whiskey Rebellion and the Virginia and Kentucky Resolutions of 1799. When the national capital was in the hands of truly disloyal men, it could not be disloyal to protest those who would ruin the Atlantic trade and expose the seaports to attack in order to augment territories more than a thousand miles away. The New Englanders who toasted four of their fellow Yankee states went on to raise their glass to "The state of Louisiana—The fifth wheel of a Waggon!" No expansive union worthy of the name could depend on the patriotism of these southern and western former rebels and their supporters. Active opposition to the war would ultimately "convince your rulers, that there exists, at least in New England, a redeeming spirit, able and willing to save the country."[24]

To think of the New Englanders who participated in these rituals

23. "Fairhaven Celebration," *Vermont Mirror* (Middlebury), July 28, 1813; "Address of the Franklin County Washington Benevolent Society, Assembled at St. Albans, on the 22d February, 1814, for the Celebration of the Birth of Washington," *Washingtonian* (Windsor, Vt.), Mar. 21, 1814. John L. Brooke describes the Worcester County Federalists of this era as ideologically "Harringtonian": they focused on the safeguarding of ancient liberties (*The Heart of the Commonwealth: Society and Political Culture in Worcester County, Massachusetts, 1713–1861* [New York, 1989], 262–263).

24. "Ode," in Asa Lyon, *An Oration, Delivered before the Washington Benevolent Society of the County of Grand-Isle* . . . (Plattsburgh, N.Y., 1812), 18–20; *Connecticut Courant* (Hartford), Aug. 3, 1813; "July Toasts—Selected," *Bennington News-Letter* (Vt.), Aug. 17, 1813; George Washington Stanley, *An Oration, Delivered at Wallingford, April 4, 1814: In Celebration of the Late Glorious Events in Europe; Which Have Resulted in the Overthrow of the Tyrant of France* . . . (New Haven, Conn., 1814), 30–31.

as either tools of a conservative elite or as hopelessly provincial sectionalists would be merely to repeat the accusations of the dominant party.[25] Every bit as much as the Republicans who demonized *them* as the new tories, New England Federalists spent the War of 1812 ritually reenacting the American Revolution. Like the Democratic-Republican opposition of the 1790s, they posited the true Revolution, and the real America, against false patriots and the illegitimate state. The irony that during the 1790s their party had declared similar practices to be illegitimate and disloyal—even passing laws to that effect—seems to have been lost on most of them. Their real contribution was the sectional dimension they added to the continuing politics of Revolutionary virtue: a politics they knew by reflex if not by descent, having heard it in countless rehearsals of Revolutionary history, at decades of national celebrations.

The sectional nationalism of the New England opposition was so secure that it enabled them to do something that shocked other sections of the country: they celebrated the victories in the European theater of the nation's official enemy. Of course, many Anglophiles had long rooted for Great Britain in its struggle against Napoleonic tyranny. The defeat of one combatant in the Continental war did in fact hold out the possibility of international peace. But it also made it likely that Britain would be freed to shift its strength to its western front—which it soon did, sacking Washington and other coastal sites.

In spite of howling denunciations by Republicans all over the country, Federalists continued to revive the spirit of '98, making their war the war against French infidels and their domestic supporters. Newspapers all over New England gave prime space to orations by Robert Goodloe Harper and Gouverneur Morris that praised Britain's victori-

25. Including those of President Madison himself. He tried to set up the war through the "revelation" of the possibly fraudulent and not especially revealing John Henry letters, which centered on a British plot to induce New England to secede. For a reading of this event and interpretation of wartime politics that is very (perhaps overly) sympathetic to the Federalists, see Donald R. Hickey, *The War of 1812: A Forgotten Conflict* (Urbana, Ill., 1989), esp. 37–39. Banner and Fischer note the popular nature of opposition to the war in Massachusetts; see Fischer, "Myth of the Essex Junto," in Ferguson, ed., *National Unity on Trial*, 120; and Banner, *To the Hartford Convention*, chap. 8. See also Roger H. Brown, *The Republic in Peril: 1812* (New York, 1964), 98–99; Samuel Eliot Morison, "Dissent in the War of 1812," in Morison, Frederick Merk, and Frank Freidel, *Dissent in Three American Wars* (Cambridge, Mass., 1970), 1–31.

ous effort (and also, in Morris's case, the restoration of the Bourbon monarchy) as "the cause of mankind." At one of the first of these festivals, held at Boston in honor of the French retreat from Russia, the presiding minister read from a scriptural prophecy concerning a "King of the South" who would "exult himself even above God." The toasts carried parallel messages about European and American geopolitics. Where Russia had overcome the tyranny of the South, and had even preserved the freedom of southern Europe, the "commonwealth of Massachusetts" might play a similar role: "May the fire of its patriotism, like the flames of *Moscow,* expel what is French, and burr Southward and Westward, until it consumes all but native influence." [26]

The real work of New England Federalist dissent lay securely in its nationalist forms: it would have been unthinkable without the prior experience of Francophobic, anti-Republican mobilization during the Quasi War of 1797–1799. It had little to do with actual secession schemes, but everything to do with resistance to Republican party hegemony. The New England Federalists developed their regionalism in so conservative an idiom, and used it so harshly to bludgeon their Republican opponents at home, that it is easy to miss its nationalist and popular dimensions. Celebrating themselves as sons of the Revolution and the true Americans, these Yankees set a pattern for regional, partisan, and nationalist dissent that would later be taken up by the very region they proclaimed to be most un-American: the slaveholding South.[27] At the same time, theirs was a particularly nationalist form of sectionalism. It was disloyal, if loyalty is defined as devotion to the national will expressed in law or federal policy. Ideologically, however, New England Federalists never gave up their claim to embody the nation, no matter what came out of Washington. For the time being, southerners, westerners, and those New Englanders under their sway were simply the national enemy. This enmity made it possible for regionalism to be a nationalist form of dissent.

26. Zebulon R. Shipherd, *An Oration, Delivered before the Washington Benevolent Society at Poultney, on the 4th of July, 1814 . . . with an Adress . . . by Chauncey Langdon, A.M.* (Middlebury, Vt., 1814), 10, 23; "Resolutions," in Rejoice Newton, *An Oration, Delivered at Worcester, Mass., on the Fourth of July, 1814* (Worcester, Mass., 1814); *Portsmouth Oracle* (N.H.), June 26, 1813; *Washingtonian* (Windsor, Vt.), July 28, 1814; "Solemnities and Festival, in Honor of the Russians," *Columbian Centinel* (Boston), Mar. 27, 1813.

27. For a similar strategy on the part of the Confederacy during the Civil War, see Drew Gilpin Faust, *The Creation of Confederate Nationalism: Ideology and Identity in the Civil War South* (Baton Rouge, La., 1988), esp. 14.

AMERICA GOING SOUTH

Thus the sectional perspective of New England Federalists drew from and did not really contradict their nationalism. But the emergence of this political style also helped New England's Jeffersonian Republicans, after 1800, to solidify their own version of the continuing American Revolution. The "hue and cry about Virginia influence and Virginia domination," insisted Republican orators, proved that Federalists did not really have the interests of the whole nation at heart. From this perspective, the New England Federalists were the true partisans and sectionalists. After all, such sectional complaints had not been heard during the Revolution, Republicans asserted (wrongly); Washington himself had warned against such jealousies. "The name of Washington cannot be employed by the Opposition as he was pointedly opposed to Separation of the States," noted William Bentley in his diary on Washington's Birthday, 1810.[28]

The most trenchant criticisms of New England Federalist festivity came out of New England itself. Yankee Republicans satirized Boston "cossack dinners" and orators who "called the people in the wilderness bad people, that they wanted to cut up the Union, and verily to blame the people of New England for the sacrilege." One burlesque of Governor Strong's Fast Day mocked pretensions of New England virtue in typical Yankee fashion: "Be Massachusetts, Lord, they care / And grant us faith and riches, / May we as zealous be in pray'r, / As when we hung the witches." Printed in key newspapers like the *Aurora*, such pieces were then republished in newspapers all over the country.[29] New

28. Nathaniel Coleman, *An Oration, Delivered at Chesterfield. . . . on the Fourth of July, 1804* (Northampton, Mass., 1804), 13; Joshua Cushman, *An Oration, Pronounced at Augusta, (Maine) on the Fourth of July, 1807* . . . (Augusta, Maine, 1807), 19–20; Joseph E. Sprague, *An Oration, Delivered at Salem, on the Fourth of July, 1810* ([Salem, Mass.], 1810), 7–8; Edward D. Bangs, *An Oration, Pronounced at Sutton . . . July 5th, 1813* . . . (Boston, 1813), 10–12; David Kidder, *An Oration, Pronounced at Bloomfield (Me.) July 4th, 1814* (Hallowell, Maine, 1814), 12–13; Bentley, *Diary*, III, 500. According to William J. Cooper, Jr., "Republicans had stained Federalists with the brush of antisouthernism" in the 1790s as well; see *Liberty and Slavery: Southern Politics to 1860* (New York, 1983), 113.

29. *The Fourth Book of the "Washington Benevolents"* . . . ([Boston, 1814]), 11; *The Strong Fast; or, Hypocrisy in the Suds: A Hymn for the Occasion* (Boston, 1812). For examples of reprintings in southern papers, see "From the Aurora," *Carolina Gazette* (Charleston), June 1, 1803; "Virginia Influence," *Virginia Express* (Fredericksburg), July 16, 1803; "From the Republican Farmer," *Wilmington Gazette* (N.C.), Jan. 31,

England Republicans praised their "brethren of the South and West" who suffered the abuse of their Anglophilic northern neighbors; southern and western Republicans returned the favor by toasting the valiant efforts of New England's Jeffersonian minorities to win back their states to "first principles." During the 1790s, the figure of the young man seeking to establish his character had emerged as a trope for the young nation demonstrating its independence. New England, by contrast, "resembles some antiquated fair one, who sees those who were infants, when she was in full bloom and influence, usurp her dominion."

> She endeavors to prop her sinking reputation, by defaming her competitors. She accuses Miss Ohio of being awkward and indolent; Miss Kentucky of having no religion, and drinking Whiskey; Miss Georgia of living among Negroes, and chewing tobacco. She declares, that they ought not be admitted into *genteel* company, and she will not permit it![30]

For Jeffersonians, such effeminate, aristocratic, old-fashioned behavior was the real cause of disunionist sentiment. To be upper-class and a woman was to be unpatriotic. Real Americans were young, male, aggressive and of diverse backgrounds, unified by their desire to defend the nation.

By the War of 1812, twelve years of Republican rule had reinforced the cross-regional partisan alliance that had made the Revolution of 1800 possible. One of the very first celebrations of Jefferson's victory, in Pennsylvania, included toasts to the "Southern Planters" and to the "State of Virginia, and their twenty-one [electoral] votes." To Republicans north and south, the West offered a resolution for regional conflict. For this reason, Jeffersonians in both regions celebrated the Louisiana Purchase as the greatest national event since the ratification of the Constitution. Rather than stretching the nation beyond its natu-

---

1804; "Federal Hypocrisy Stripped of Its Mask" and "Reflections on Rebellion," *Morning Herald* (New Bern, N.C.), Nov. 11, 1808, Feb. 16, 1809; "Hartford Convention," *Western American* (Williamsburg, Ohio), Jan. 14, 1815.

30. Kidder, *An Oration*, 13; *Times* (Charleston, S.C.), May 14, 1804; *Enquirer* (Richmond, Va.), July 15, 1806; "Locust Grove, Scott County," *Kentucky Gazette and General Advertiser* (Lexington), July 19, 1803; *Mississippi Herald and Natchez Gazette*, Jan. 18, 1805; R[ollin] C[arolus] Mallary, *An Oration, Addressed to Republicans, Delivered at Poultney, Vermont, July 4, 1814* (Rutland, Vt., 1814), 13.

ral bounds (as New England Federalists charged), Louisiana would cement "the union of the states."[31]

Expansion was a basic component of Jeffersonian republicanism: more land, it was thought, would solve a multitude of social ills, including the emergence of a landless underclass. In orations given at celebrations, the Virginians Ferdinando Fairfax and Chapman Johnson proposed that the new territory might even solve the problem of slavery, by providing a colony for ex-slaves. This "upper south dream" of a yeoman white republic did not last for very long.[32] For a time, though, certain factors made the dream seem viable. Rapid population shifts took place in the southwestern areas of white settlement during the first two decades of the nineteenth century. Many southeastern political leaders speculated in western lands and had relatives who left Virginia or South Carolina to seek opportunity in Kentucky, Tennessee, and the vast Louisiana Territory. More and more over the course of this period, southerners toasted their "western brethren" with familial terms of endearment that had literal as well as political meanings.[33]

But it was actually antisouthern attacks by New England Federalists

31. "Greensburgh, Jan. 3, Republican Festival," *Aurora; General Advertiser* (Philadelphia), Jan, 13, 1801, "Celebration," May 14, 1804; "A Public Dinner," *Augusta Chronicle* (Ga.), Feb. 11, 1804; "Halifax Court House," *Virginia Argus* (Richmond), July 21–28, 1804.

32. Michael H. Hunt, *Ideology and U.S. Foreign Policy* (New Haven, Conn., 1987), 29–30; Robert W. Tucker and David C. Hendrickson, *Empire of Liberty: The Statecraft of Thomas Jefferson* (New York, 1990); Chapman Johnson, *An Oration, on the Late Treaty with France, by Which Louisiana Was Acquired: Delivered in Staunton on the Third of March, 1804* (Staunton, Va., 1804), 10; Ferdinando Fairfax, *Oration Delivered in Charlestown, in Virginia, on the Fourth of July, 1805* (Washington, D.C., 1808). On Fairfax and the context of early colonization efforts generally, see Winthrop D. Jordan, *White over Black: American Attitudes toward the Negro, 1550–1812* (Chapel Hill, N.C., 1968), 551–554, 565; Douglas R. Egerton, " 'Its Origin Is Not a Little Curious': A New Look at the American Colonization Society," *Journal of the Early Republic*, V (1985), 466–467; Egerton, *Gabriel's Rebellion: The Virginia Slave Conspiracies of 1800 and 1802* (Chapel Hill, N.C., 1993). For the "upper south dream" of slavery's conditional termination, see William W. Freehling, *The Road to Disunion*, I, *Secessionists at Bay, 1776–1854* (New York, 1990), 121–161.

33. Thomas P. Abernethy, *The South in the New Nation, 1789–1819* (Baton Rouge, La., 1961); *Virginia Argus* (Richmond), Feb. 25, 1804; *Republican and Savannah Evening Ledger* (Ga.), May 2, 1812; Marion Nelson Winship, "Power in Motion in the Trans-Appalachian West: The Case of Thomas Worthington," paper presented at the meeting of the Society for Historians of the Early American Republic, Chapel Hill, N.C., July 1993.

that provoked a distinctive southern nationalism, not solidarity with the West. During the 1780s there had been little sense of the South as a coherent region; Virginia itself was seen as a middle, not a southern, state. For the time being, the most worrisome regional differences were those between East and West, often within the states as much as between them. Even the emergence of the question of the navigation of the Mississippi, which did provoke an awareness of a geopolitical divergence that would put the South and West on one side and New England on the other, did not quickly translate into a sense of southern identity. Crucial debates over slavery in the First Congress apparently did little to change this. A writer who lamented "Partial Attachments to Country" in the *Georgia Gazette* three years after ratification cited New Englanders as the sole possessors of a separate regional identity in the new nation. Why didn't elite southerners, whose political interests were already manifestly different from those of their New England counterparts, articulate a regional identity before 1800? In part, because there was no political reason to. Before 1800 the Republican party had already forged a "common identity" with the South. "The south accepted the party as its representative and protector. . . . Most southerners discerned little distinction between the Republican party and the nation or between their own interest and the national interest."[34] The confluence of southern, Republican, and national prerogatives smoothed under successive Virginia presidents, to be interrupted only by the Missouri Crisis in 1819–1821.

Beginning in 1803, southerners responded to the charge of Virginia domination by accusing New Englanders of fomenting disunion. At Fourth of July celebrations in Virginia it became standard to toast Virginian patriotism and to question the loyalty of Massachusetts. A group of mariners gave specific nautical directions to northern windbags:

> 8. *About ship lads*—Massachusetts; may no jealousies ever divide the union.

34. Jack P. Greene, "The Constitution of 1787 and the Question of Southern Distinctiveness," in Greene, *Imperatives, Behaviors, and Identities: Essays in Early American Cultural History* (Charlottesville, Va., 1992), 327–347; "On Partial Attachments to Country" (from *Georgia Gazette* [Savannah]), *National Gazette* (Philadelphia), July 7, 1792; Thomas P. Slaughter, *The Whiskey Rebellion: Frontier Epilogue to the American Revolution* (New York, 1986); Cooper, *Liberty and Slavery*, 96, 113, 120. As Cooper notes, it is striking that the most self-consciously Virginian of politicians, John Taylor and John Randolph, failed to win many of their peers over to the third-party "Quid" movement.

11. *It blows hard my brave lads*—New England; may the Northern regions never be too cold for the spirits of Warren, Allyn, Wooster, Green and Sullivan.

Massachusetts had clearly departed from the examples of its heroes; she had better imitate "the State of Virginia . . . the first to propose . . . the last to surrender American Independence." Like the New Englanders they criticized, southerners too rewrote the family romance of national character according to a revised geography. Citizens of far-away Pinckneyville, Mississippi Territory, who resented "bullying from the North" against their admission to the union, suggested that Massachusetts, "like an old maid," should "try the blessings of a *single state*." Boston appeared as "the cradle of monarchy" to a July Fourth reveler in Mecklenburg County, Virginia, who wished that "the infant she has long reared, die for want of suck, and never be raised for a king in America."[35]

And as with New England's patriots, Virginians too used nationalist celebrations to lay claim to the Revolutionary heritage, constructing for themselves a longer lineage that mimicked, even as it contested, New England typology. In May 1807, an editor of the *Apollo* from Fredericksburg proposed a "GRAND NATIONAL JUBILEE" to commemorate the two-hundredth anniversary of the arrival at Jamestown of "the forefathers of Virginia, and it may be said the founders of North-America." His proposal, specifically addressed to Virginians, decried the absence of annual homage to ancestors in the Old Dominion in light of New England's tradition of Forefathers' Day. A Richmond native made it a point of honor: "Shall Virginians surrender the palm to their brethren of the N. England states, who have instituted the feast of Pilgrims? Shall *they* celebrate the landing of their forefathers at Plymouth; and shall the landing at Jamestown be completely neglected?" At the same time that Virginians should celebrate the day as the hallmark of their particular (that is, regional) "national existence," the holiday was proposed as a national—American—jubilee. "No occasion is better calcu-

35. "Vindication of Virginia," *Enquirer* (Richmond, Va.), June 13, 20, 1804, "Republican Feast," Mar. 11, and July 5, 1808, July 16, 1814; *Virginia Argus* (Richmond), July 13, 1804; *Georgia Journal* (Milledgeville), July 11, 1810; "Charleston, Oct. 18," *Morning Herald* (New Bern, N.C.), Nov. 18, 1808; *Time Piece* (St. Francisville, La.), July 11, 1811.

lated to produce the true American spirit. We shall meet at Jamestown as Americans."[36]

On May 13, 1807, two thousand people descended on the ruins of Jamestown. According to the official account, at least thirty-two ships recreated the landing of the original settlers. Afterward, the passengers made their way, as "pilgrims," to the graves of the first Virginians. The event narrated Virginia history as a teleology of liberty and national greatness. Perched atop a crypt, Bishop James Madison, a staunch Republican, set the tone with his invocation to prayer: "It was here, O God, it was on this chosen ground, that thou didst first lay the sure foundations of political happiness." The orators of the day traced an unbroken history from Columbus to Pocahontas and John Smith through Indian wars to the American Revolution. The "moral and political consequences" of Jamestown (and the defeat of Virginia's "tawny inhabitants") were nothing less than the making of America, the greatest nation on earth. The resort to origins permitted Virginians also to claim an original relationship to the American Revolution—a notion that so gripped the Williamsburg contingent at the festival that upon their return to the old colonial capital they celebrated the May fifteenth anniversary of Virginia's 1776 resolution on Independence.[37]

Accounts of the festival at Jamestown appeared in papers all over the South, and the genealogy of American nationality presented there found its way into many an oration. For years to come, toasts to "the Virginia Convention" linked southern virtue to national glory. It is no coincidence that a southern myth of American origins emerged just as New Englanders were refining their own pedigree in the realm of cultural politics.[38] Both sections were using the tradition of national

36. *Virginia Argus* (Richmond), May 6, 1807; "Communication: Grand National Jubilee," *Enquirer* (Richmond, Va.), May 8, 1807. According to Wesley Frank Craven, this festival was inspired by John Daly Burk's history of Virginia, which insisted that Virginians' historical commitment to liberty rivaled that of New England; see *The Legend of the Founding Fathers* (1956; rpt. Ithaca, N.Y., 1965), 84–86.

37. *Enquirer* (Richmond, Va.), May 19, 1807; "National Jubilee" (from *Norfolk Herald*), *Raleigh Register and North-Carolina State Gazette*, May 28, 1807; *Report of the Proceedings of the Late Jubilee at James-Town, in Commemoration of the 13th May, the Second Centesimal Anniversary of the Settlement of Virginia* (Petersburg, Va., 1807), 14, 16–35.

38. *Raleigh Register* (N.C.), May 28, 1807; *Western World* (Frankfort, Ky.), May 21, 1807; "Jubilee Oration," *National Intelligencer and Washington Advertiser,* June 3, 1807; "Jubilee at James Town," *Berkeley and Jefferson Intelligencer* (Martinsburg, Va.), June 5, 1807; *Times* (Charleston, S.C.), July 1, 4, 1807; *Miller's Weekly Messenger* (Pendleton, S.C.), July 9, 1807, "Oration . . . Delivered by Thomas Holland," July 30, 1807;

celebration for regional and partisan ends, loudly insisting upon their own Americanness and Revolutionary identity while questioning the motives of the other region.

Ultimately, it is less important to identify who invented or first developed nationalist regionalism than to understand the dynamic that engendered both nationalist and regionalist expression, depending always upon the shifting geopolitical context. For these activities also served partisan ends, as one of the Jamestown orators knew when he urged his fellow Virginians to be "the high priests of Republicanism." For the first two decades of the nineteenth century, southern Republicans had the immense luxury of a comfortable fit among nationalist, regionalist, and partisan expression. Circumstances like the victories of Jefferson, Madison, and Monroe in presidential elections gave them reasons to boast that true patriotism made its home on their doorsteps. On old and new national holidays they defined geopolitical reality to their regional and partisan advantage without in any way sacrificing the nationalist tradition. Indeed, nationalism was the prerequisite for their regionalist performances. When President Andrew Jackson did battle in toasts with southern states rights advocates at the famous Jefferson Day dinner of 1830, with the former toasting "Union" and the latter celebrating the revolutionary "liberties" of nullification, both sides continued the dialogue of regionalism and nationalism that took shape at the beginning of the century.[39]

WEST MEETS EAST

With the rise of North-South antagonism during the first half of the nineteenth century, the West became the battleground for the fate of the nation. Would America's sprawling wilderness be an empire for

---

"The Fourth of July," *Raleigh Register* (N.C.), Aug. 6, 1807; Wm. H[olland] Wilmer, *A Sermon: Delivered in St. Paul's Church, on the Fourth of July, 1813* (Alexandria, Va., 1813); *Enquirer* (Richmond, Va.), Mar. 18, 1811. On New England and the southern myth, see, especially, William R. Taylor, *Cavalier and Yankee: The Old South and American National Character* (New York, 1963), pt. 1.

39. William W. Freehling, *Prelude to Civil War: The Nullification Controversy in South Carolina, 1816–1836* (New York, 1965), 192. For a fascinating example of this give-and-take and the crucial role of toasts during the Nullification crisis, see William Drayton, *An Oration Delivered . . . Monday, July 4th, 1831, by the Hon. William Drayton, to Which Is Annexed, an Account of the Celebration of the 55th Anniversary of American Independence, by the Union and States Rights Party* (Charleston, S.C., 1831), which contains 126 volunteer toasts given at the occasion.

slavery? Would compromises and balancing acts allow the union to endure half-slave and half-free? From the Missouri Crisis to the Kansas-Nebraska Act, from debates over internal improvements and Indian removals to the Civil War itself, the ever-shifting frontier signified the outer limits of American nationality and yet, simultaneously, the course of the American future. As competing regional ideals of "national character" developed, the West stood as foil and fulfillment of northerners' and southerners' national dreams.[40]

"Those who inhabit the hinterlands become the most evident examples of ambiguous nationality," writes the political theorist Anne Norton. Depending on the context—the relative security of the frontier, the changing needs of those at the center—frontiersmen can be portrayed as "the national par excellence" or, conversely, as "the exemplars of anti-national traits."[41] Fully aware of their own liminality, frontier inhabitants themselves create this dynamic in dialogue with those at the center. They claim their difference from those at the center, complain of mistreatment, and boast of their superiority.

These oral metaphors for frontier political action (claiming, complaining, boasting) capture an essential aspect of frontier political practice and provide a clue to the special role that celebrations and celebratory forms played in the definition of the West in early national America. Although scholars have noted the "oral aggression" of the frontier stance (as epitomized by Davy Crockett's feats of eating and talking) and the consumption of frontier images by easterners, they have missed how western political leaders, participants in a national and nationalizing political culture, relied upon printed manifestations of their oral prowess.[42] Celebratory toasts served as a two-way mirror in which westerners expressed themselves for local audiences with the full knowledge that their pronouncements would be reprinted and re-

40. On the north-south cultural conflict, see Taylor, *Cavalier and Yankee;* for the significance of the West, see the classic account by Henry Nash Smith, *Virgin Land: The American West as Symbol and Myth* (1950; New York, 1970).

41. Anne Norton, *Reflections on Political Identity* (Baltimore, 1988), 57, 61, 63. Like Norton, I use the masculine advisedly: it is generally the frontier male who is deployed as a symbol.

42. Frances Lea McCurdy, *Stump, Bar, and Pulpit: Speechmaking on the Missouri Frontier* (Columbia, Mo., 1969); David Crockett, *Narrative of the Life of David Crockett of the State of Tennessee* (1834; Lincoln, Nebr., 1987); Norton, *Political Identity*, 60–61; Carroll Smith-Rosenberg, *Disorderly Conduct: Visions of Gender in Victorian America* (New York, 1985), 90–108.

deployed back east in newspaper accounts. Westerners used celebrations and print with remarkable success to negotiate their nationality in the face of Indian warfare, secession plots, and their own objectification by easterners of every stripe and latitude.

The problematic of frontier nationalism became apparent even before the thirteen states were securely in American hands. *The Narrative of the Life and Captivity of Colonel Ethan Allen* (1779), a crucial text of the American Revolution, supports Norton's claim for the importance of border discourse (and discourse about the borders) in the continual reformation of political identities. Allen penned his wartime best-seller in an effort to defend his reputation after a tumultuous and controversial career in the Continental army. As leader of the Green Mountain Boys, he claimed to have led the frontiersmen's surprise attack on Fort Ticonderoga, a crucial early victory for the patriots. Subsequent disputes over rank, however, and his erratic behavior as a prisoner of war had made Allen (one of the "mushroom patriots" created by the Revolution) into a symbol of the fragility of Revolutionary virtue and loyalty.[43]

As a result, Allen's text is a rehearsal and revision of his patriotic performances at the margins of Revolutionary American identity. He begins the *Narrative* by linking his "sincere passion for liberty" to his manhood. Mature manhood signifies a particular kind of citizenship based on knowledge and passion:

> The history of nations doomed to perpetual slavery, in consequence of yielding up to tyrants their natural born liberties, I read with a sort of philosophical horror; so that the first systematical and bloody attempt at Lexington, to enslave America, thoroughly electrified my mind, and fully determined me to take part with my country.

Allen immediately allies himself with his audience as a fellow reader of patriotic prints. Indeed, the first lines of the book already make the *Narrative* into a republican prooftext through which the reader follows in the footsteps of Allen himself, coming into manhood by reading history. Allen stands already as the epitome of the cause, not just a wit-

43. Ethan Allen, *The Narrative of Colonel Ethan Allen* (1779; rpt. Cambridge, Mass., 1989); Charles Royster, *A Revolutionary People at War: The Continental Army and American Character, 1775–1783* (Chapel Hill, N.C., 1979), 6, 259. Allen's narrative was excerpted in newspapers and almanacs, for example, *Russell's American Almanack, for . . . 1780* (Danvers, Mass., 1779).

ness to the creation of America but the embodiment of the intertwined Revolutionary processes of republicanization and Americanization. Far from being an erratic man of the margins, Allen, like his audience, is a fellow reader of news from Lexington who completes a circuit of outsiders turned Revolutionary insiders, of silent readers turned speaking patriots, by presenting his own electrifying story.[44]

Displacing the problem of authority by identifying with his readers, Allen whisks us away, before the end of the first paragraph, to Fort Ticonderoga and his inspiring speech to his troops. The most dramatic moments in the *Narrative,* in fact, are direct quotations of Allen himself, as when he demands that the British surrender "In the name of the great Jehovah and the Continental Congress." Before he undertakes another mission, Allen already participates in two celebrations, both times giving "loyal Congress healths." This convention of toast giving reappears periodically as the very model of genteel, orderly, civil speech, in contrast to the "extravagant language" that Allen himself employs so expertly in contact with the enemy. Allen's oral prowess, in short, differs in kind depending upon whom he is talking with. With his civilized colleagues he speaks the language of patriotic sentiment. At the bestial enemy he brays like a man of the wilds.[45]

Before long Allen is captured during an attempt to seize part of Canada. His text then becomes a captivity narrative, but with a difference: it turns the British into the "savages." The redcoats are savage in part because they ally themselves with the Indians but mostly because they fail to treat Allen with the respect due an officer of his rank. This personification of the struggle for national identity (to win official recognition and recognition as an officer) leads Allen to the very acts of verbal extravagance and subterfuge that epitomize his eccentricity at home. Sent to England in chains while still disguised as a Canadian, he

44. Allen, *Narrative,* 5. In the introduction Allen also creates a contrast between patriots and those "who read the history of the cruelties of this war with the same careless indifferency, as they do the pages of the Roman history" (*Narrative,* 1).

45. Allen, *Narrative,* 7, 8, 11, 28. Michael A. Bellesiles writes that, by the time of his arrival in the Green Mountains, "Allen had elaborated this strategy of frontier swagger into an art form and a highly effective political tactic." At the same time that he "appeared everywhere in the Green Mountains" in person or by reputation, he also published defenses of his fellow settlers in New England newspapers and as separate pamphlets. Bellesiles, *Revolutionary Outlaws: Ethan Allen and the Struggle for Independence on the Early American Frontier* (Charlottesville, Va., 1993), 89–90, 96–97, 99.

insists that he is a "full blooded Yankee" and "expatiate[s] on American freedom" from behind bars to large audiences. On parole in British-occupied New York, he finds it "political in some measure to act the madman" in public while in private he toasts Washington's victories with his fellow officers. Finally exchanged for "a British officer of rank and importance in their army," Allen returns to Bennington to be feted with guns and toasts: "thirteen for the United States, and one for young Vermont."[46]

Allen's *Narrative* drew upon and contributed to several key strategies in the invention of American identity. As a member of the colonial elite, a creole, his lineage and his status are in doubt, so he seeks respectability according to the standards of armed gentility even as he takes up arms against the empire. In his account, decorum, politeness, and traditional festivity are adopted by American patriots and denied by the very British nationals who, at their best, had embodied them. Yet the narrative also expresses the particular ambivalence of frontier identity—a sort of double liminality in this context. Allen's own potentially savage status, as a mountain man, epitomizes his Americanness to an outside (British) audience while it simultaneously undermines his claims to participate in the official, genteel Americanness of the Continental Congress and the Continental army. The extra gunshot to Vermont, of but not yet in the "United States," reveals Allen's potential excess and eccentricity. Allen is the sort of patriot who elicits delight and fear in alternate, abundant measures. He concludes self-consciously with "loyal healths to the rising states of America" and ends his narrative "with the same loyal spirit," because by its very strenuous, performative nature his border patriotism undercuts its own stability.[47]

The *Narrative* typifies the especially performative nature of frontier nationalism. At the same time, its importance in the Revolutionary struggle lay at least as much in its printedness as in its own uncompromising insistence upon the importance of oral exchanges. The reproduction of the *Narrative* in almanacs and periodicals and as a best-selling pamphlet inaugurated a tradition by which Americans in more settled areas came to know the frontier through the printed texts that

46. Allen, *Narrative,* 43, 44, 78, 93–94, 124. The pro-statehood Vermonters continued to fire fourteen cannon and to make toasts like, "May the rights of Vermont be established by the American Independence." *Independent Gazetteer; or, the Chronicle of Freedom* (Philadelphia), May 31, 1783.

47. Allen, *Narrative,* 124.

publicized the frontiersman's Americanism.[48] In the matrix of celebration and publication, westerners performed their loyalty and their
liminality, but the tension was resolved only when printed accounts succeeded in making a virtue of their liminality itself. As an orally trans-
mitted, active force, frontier regionalism and nationalism remained in-
cendiary and explosive, however inspiring and patriotic their venue.
Only within the calmer boundaries of printed exchange did western
identity begin to be a unifying national force, a successfully nationalist
regionalism.

☆   ☆   ☆

The first fifty settlers of "New Connecticut" passed through the wilds of
upstate New York, over the Alleghenies and into the Western Reserve,
arriving in the new territory on the Fourth of July 1796. After stowing
their baggage and pitching their tents, General Moses Cleaveland and
his party of surveyors went to the beach and fired a "federal salute" of
fifteen rounds and "then the 16th in honor of New Connecticut." Then
they "gave three cheers and christened the place Fort Independence."
All fifty settlers, women and children included, then drank from "two
pails of grog," toasting the president, "the State of New Connecticut,"
the Connecticut Land Company, and the rapid population of their
settlement. "I believe there never was anything of the kind done with
more sincerity," wrote one of the participants in a letter home. General
Cleaveland himself felt that his charges "retired in remarkable good
order." Having left the purview of the official United States, the settlers
of the Western Reserve celebrated themselves back into its orbit, by invoking and following its rules for decorous yet innovative festivity.[49]

All over the early West, frontiersmen performed similar festive rituals when they entered the territory or when their territory entered the
union. They celebrated the American nation to convince themselves
and others that, despite their presence on the extremities of the United
States, they were just as American as the first patriots of 1776. To show
themselves, they performed the rites; to show others, they produced
textual equivalents. Shortly after Fort Detroit came under American

48. Richard Slotkin, *Regeneration through Violence: The Mythology of the American
Frontier* (Middletown, Conn., 1973), chaps. 8–10.

49. "Extract from the Journal of General Moses Cleaveland," Moses Cleaveland
Papers, John Milton Holley to Luther Holley, Aug. 12, 1796, John Milton Holley
Papers, Western Reserve Historical Society, Cleveland, Ohio.

rule, in 1797, the military attachments paraded in honor of George Washington's Birthday. The curé of Detroit sang a special mass for the occasion and gave a sermon praising the great American hero, which the military officers had translated and sent to the capital. Whether at Washington County, Pennsylvania, in 1786, Cincinnati in 1794, Natchitoches in 1804, Saint Charles, Missouri, in 1808, or Baton Rouge in 1811, frontierspeople celebrated the Fourth of July and had accounts of their doings printed in their fledgling newspapers, even though it often took weeks for those accounts to appear.[50]

These new westerners had good reasons for their assertive celebrations and publications. They knew that easterners viewed the volatile frontier with varying degrees of pride and worry, thanks to backcountry tax revolts, Indian wars, and separatist movements from Ethan Allen's Vermont to the stillborn state of Franklin in western North Carolina. These concerns grew as the size of American territory doubled with the Louisiana Purchase. Even those disposed to celebrate the fruits of expansion spoke of their "western brethren" in a manner that alerted any careful listener to potential dangers. "Louisiana. May its attachment to the Union grow with its growth," read one Lexington, Virginia, toast printed soon after Louisiana's transfer into American hands. In Pendleton County, South Carolina, on the previous Fourth of July, Republicans tried to diminish the alarming specter of frontier political protest. Westerners, they hoped, would be of "one body" with easterners "when necessary."[51]

The acquisition of territory, however, only expanded the field of play for daring, potentially disloyal speculators like William Blount, James Wilkinson, and Aaron Burr. The year 1807 found Republican orators once again assuring their audiences (and themselves), whatever the designs of men like Burr, "We have no reason, no cause to suspect our western brethren of entertaining a spirit of disunion." Vermont Federalists were much more direct about their fears, which in numerous

50. F. Clever Bald, *Detroit's First American Decade, 1796 to 1805* (Ann Arbor, Mich., 1948), 101–102; *Pittsburgh Gazette*, Aug. 19, 1786; *Centinel of the North-Western Territory* (Cincinnati), July 13, 1794; *Mississippi Herald and Natchez City Gazette*, Aug. 24, 1804; *Missouri Gazette* (Saint Louis), Aug. 2, 1808; *Louisiana Gazette and New Orleans Advertiser,* July 15, 1811.

51. Slaughter, *Whiskey Rebellion*, 47–60; *Virginia Telegraphe; or, Rockbridge Courier* (Lexington), July 10, 1804; "Pendleton District, July 8," *Carolina Gazette* (Charleston), Aug. 11, 1803.

toasts functioned as an accusation: "The Western Territory—May they never be so blinded to their own interest as to think of a separation from their Atlantic brethren."[52]

Westerners responded to these eastern fears by using celebrations to distance themselves publicly from conspirators like Wilkinson and Burr. These demonstrations received due notice in the eastern (especially southern) newspapers. At the young town of Columbia, Ohio, Fourth of July celebrants lifted their glasses to the president, the governor, and their fellow "citizens of the North-West territory" in the hope that they would "never become the dupes of design or intrigue." Citizens of Frankfort, Kentucky, burned an effigy of "A Western American," the author of a newspaper article advocating disunion in the wake of the closure of New Orleans to American Mississippi River traffic in 1802–1803. Nashville residents did the same with Aaron Burr in 1807. After the Burr affair, revelers in Dayton, Ohio, linked their loyalty to their perspective on western conspiracies: "The State of Ohio, the youngest member of the Federal family: May she be foremost to suppress insurrections, or chastise foreign intolerance." And at a dinner for twelve hundred near Nashville in 1810, one of the official toasts blessed "the union of the states" while wishing "a speedy dissolution to the *traitors* who have, or may attempt to dissolve it."[53]

"The Western Country—Infamy attend the wretch who would separate us from the Union": toasts such as this proclaimed a western identity that, as in New England and the South, was simultaneously regionalist and nationalist. Yet there was more to the western unionists' vigorous festivity than the mere demonstration of loyalty. Western

52. Andrew R. L. Cayton, "'When Shall We Cease to Have Judases?': The Blount Conspiracy and the Limits of the 'Extended Republic,'" in Ronald Hoffman and Peter J. Albert, eds., *Launching the "Extended Republic": The Federalist Era* (Charlottesville, Va., 1996), 156–189; "The Fourth of July," *Raleigh Register* (N.C.), Aug. 6, 1807; Hosea Ballou, *An Oration, Pronounced in the Meeting-House in Hartland, on the Fourth of July, 1807* (Randolph, Vt., 1807), 14.

53. *Western Spy, and Hamilton Gazette* (Cincinnati), July 8, 1801; "Fallacy of the N.Y. Herald," *Virginia Telegraphe* (Lexington), Apr. 9, 1803; "Frankfort, April 14," *Georgia Republican and State Intelligencer* (Savannah), May 19, 1803; William Taylor Barry to Dr. John Barry, Jan. 27, 1807, William Taylor Barry Papers, Filson Club, Louisville, Ky.; *Liberty Hall and Cincinnati Mercury*, July 28, 1807; "Fourth of July 1810," *Review* (Nashville), July 6, 1810. For similar examples in Kentucky, see *Western World* (Frankfort), Sept. 10, 1807; *Mirror* (Russellville), July 9, 1807; "Festivity," *Political Theatre* (Lancaster), Dec. 10, 1808.

orators and toastmakers expressed all of their translocal political positions on the same occasions and in the same manner as easterners, but their toasting, with the appearance of their toasts in newspapers, had an added dimension. While certainly attuned to local and national partisanship, "the voice of the people" displayed at these western celebrations was particularly designed for eastern consumption in print.

This was not the original idea behind the rise of print culture on the trans-Appalachian frontier. The initial impetus for the emergence of the press in the West was often to aid the workings of territorial government: the first newspaper in the Ohio region (*Centinel of the North-Western Territory* in Cincinnati, 1793) made one of its central goals the dissemination of the proceedings of the federal Congress. Print, like law, would move from east to west. But western needs did not run in one direction, and the mistrust was mutual. In an early issue of the *Centinel* a subscriber bitterly complained about that paper's printing of a report on the pacific disposition of local Indians, claiming that such publications, spread all over the country, did irreparable damage to western interests. Nine years later, the editor of Frankfort's *Guardian of Freedom* furiously protested a New Jersey paper's interpretation of the large numbers of robberies, rapes, and murders in the frontier state as evidence of Kentucky's submission to "Democracy" and infidelity. Westerners needed the right information to move from west to east.[54]

Professions of national loyalty and partisan allegiance took shape in the context of an interregional, east-to-west and west-to-east system of communication. In 1811, for example, Cincinnati's *Liberty Hall* got information about the Southwest via the *Baltimore Whig*. The nationalization of politics with the rise of an eastern-based federal government made savvy westerners quite sensitive to the impressions and perceptions of themselves held back east and the consequences of negative portrayals. One historian has even suggested that the Burr conspiracy itself was a product of newspaper speculation, spurred by easterners'

54. "Chillicothe, July 9," *Scioto Gazette* (Chillicothe, Ohio), July 9, 1803; "The Printer . . . to the Public," Nov. 9, 1793, "To the Printer," Feb. 15, 1794, *Centinel of the North-Western Territory* (Cincinnati); Francis S. Philbrick, *The Rise of the West, 1754–1830* (New York, 1965), 366; "From the Newark Gazette," *Guardian of Freedom* (Frankfort, Ky.), Jan. 1, 1802. For the role of the state in the establishment of newspapers, see Mary Kupiec Cayton, "The Economics of Printing and the Establishment of Printed Discourse in the Ohio Valley, 1786–1810," paper presented at the meeting of the Society for Historians of the Early American Republic, Chapel Hill, N.C., July 23, 1993.

obsessive concern with western loyalty: "What a 'conspiracy'! Not only the people of the West but those of the East were watching its production."[55]

Even as westerners grew adept at expressing loyalty to the nation, a sense of separate western interests emerged. Before Ohio and Kentucky won statehood, newspapers in these territories printed lists of toasts that promised obeisance even as they complained of neglect. The toasts for the first publicized July Fourth celebration in Kentucky (1788), for example, had expressed approval of the as yet unratified federal Constitution. At the same time, celebrants proclaimed the existence of a coherent "Western World" that could flourish independently on its own terms—even, if necessary, separately:

1st. The United States of America.

2nd. The Western world, perpetual Union, on principles of equality, or amiable Separation.

3rd. The Illustrious GEORGE WASHINGTON Esq., may his services be remembered.

4th. The Navigation of the Mississippi, at any price but that of Liberty.

5th. Harmony with Spain, and a reciprocity of good offices.

6th. Our brethren at Muskingum, and prosperity to their Establishments.

7th. May the Savage enemies of America, be chastened by Arms, and the jobbing system of Treaties be exploded.

8th. The Convention of Virginia. . . .

9th. Energetic Government, on Federal principles.

10th. Tryal by Jury, Liberty of the Press, and no standing Army.

11th. May the Atlantic States be just, the Western States be free, and both be happy.

12th. The memory of departed Heroes and Patriots.

13th. No paper Money; no Tender Laws, and no Legislative interference in private Contests.

14th. The Commonwealth of Kentucke, the fourteenth luminary in the American Constellation, may she reflect upon the original States, the wisdom she has borrowed from them.

55. Meinig, *Atlantic America*, 400–402; "From the Baltimore Whig: The Western World," *Liberty Hall* (Cincinnati), Nov. 20, 1811; Philbrick, *Rise of the West*, 234–252, quoted at 240–241.

The second and eleventh toasts divide the American world, leaving open the possibility of an "amiable Separation." Intervening sentiments set forth both western sectional and Federalist partisan political wishes. The last toast, though, sets the star of Kentucky within the national firmament, suggesting that at the present moment the original thirteen could set their lights by watching their most distant neighbor. Likewise, at the height of the Quasi War, a group of Cincinnatians celebrated "The Western people—ready to support the government of their choice, and determined not to survive it." And at an 1808 fete held by Kentucky's Muddy River Democratical, Didactick Society, toasts to the United States, Washington, and Jefferson cushioned an explicit warning: the "Federal Government . . . let it not transgress its assigned boundary."[56]

The most repeated western Fourth of July demands (earlier, for navigation of the Mississippi River; later, for statehood) elicited mixed responses back east.[57] They could be seen as the just rights of a people who wanted to be prosperous and politically free—or as the premature and dangerous demands of frontier yahoos whose erratic behavior might upset the balance of power on the continent, not to mention in Congress. The Louisiana Purchase complicated matters further by increasing the number of marginal settlements and foreigners under

56. Andrew R. L. Cayton, " 'Separate Interests' and the Nation State: The Washington Administration and the Origins of Regionalism in the Trans-Appalachian West," *Journal of American History*, LXXIX (1992–1993), 39–67; Aristedes, "To the Inhabitants of Western America," and "To the Citizens of Western America," *Kentucky Gazette* (Lexington), Jan. 4, 1794, Sept. 20, 1797, and July 5, 1788, July 25, 1798; *Mirror* (Russellville, Ky.), July 7, 1808. As Robert Pettus Hay observes, the dual nature of these celebrations, in which Kentuckians asserted their loyalty *and* petitioned for redress, continued throughout the period; see "A Jubilee for Freemen: The Fourth of July in Frontier Kentucky, 1788–1816," Kentucky Historical Society, *Register*, LXIV (1966), 169–195.

57. For examples of toasts advocating navigation of the Mississippi, see "Lexington, (Ky.)," *Georgia: The Augusta Chronicle and Gazette of the State*, May 7, 1803; "Columbia, July 4th, 1800," *Western Spy* (Cincinnati), July 9, 1800; *Knoxville Gazette* (Tenn.), Feb. 17, 1796. For toasts advocating statehood, see, for example, *Palladium: A Literary and Political Weekly Repository* (Frankfort, Ky.), May 26, 1803 (Shelbyville, Louisiana Territory); *Mississippi Messenger* (Natchez), Feb. 25, July 14, 1808; *Louisiana Gazette* (Saint Louis), July 12, Aug. 2, 1810; "Kaskaskia, July 15," *Western Sun* (Vincennes, Ind.), July 23, 1808 (Indiana Territory); *Louisiana Gazette* (New Orleans), July 5, 15, 1811.

United States jurisdiction and further polarizing the raging debate over development between New Englanders and Southerners, Federalists and Jeffersonian Republicans. Because of their positions on the geographical borders of the nation, western political pronouncements could almost always be read both ways: as promises or as protests, as boasts of national loyalty or as threats to undo the national revolution, to use the tools of 1776 to perform their own declaration of independence. After all, as one Ohioan insisted before his home region achieved statehood, "the present government of this territory has been not improperly called colonial." Addressing an audience at Wakefield, Mississippi Territory, on the Fourth of July in 1806, Harry Toulmin observed, "The situation of this part of the American territory, bears indeed, too near a resemblance to the state of things in which the colonists were stimulated to resistance against the mother country not to call into action some portion of the spirit of seventy-six." Yet the lack of national incorporation did not prevent frontierspeople from claiming national rights; in this sense, statehood movements were themselves a nationalizing force. Ohioans who sought representation in Congress used the Fourth of July to hail the coming day "when the citizens of this territory shall be re-instituted in their ancient and native rights." The law that finally granted statehood provided an occasion to rehearse the original celebrations of Independence, using the same sentimental language of sparkling eyes and beaming faces that had publicized local patriotism and virtue since the Revolution itself.[58]

The more doubtful the nationalization of a frontier region, the greater the lengths to which its inhabitants went to demonstrate their patriotism in public and in print. This was especially true in the former domains of France and Spain. On July, 4, 1804, in Natchitoches, forty gentlemen heard the Declaration of Independence read in French as

58. "To the Citizens of the North-Western Territory, No. 1," *Scioto Gazette* (Chillicothe, Ohio), Feb. 12, 1801; Toulmin, "An Address to the People of Tombigbee at Wakefield, on the 4th of July, 1806," *Mississippi Messenger* (Natchez), Aug. 12, 1806; *Western Spy* (Cincinnati), July 9, 1800; Andrew R. L. Cayton, *The Frontier Republic: Ideology and Politics in the Ohio Country, 1780–1825* (Kent, Ohio, 1986), 76. For similar examples in Indiana, see "Patriotic Effusions," *Missouri Gazette* (Saint Louis), July 26, 1808; *Western Sun* (Vincennes, Ind.), July 8, 1809. On statehood movements as a nationalizing force, see Cayton and Onuf, *The Midwest and the Nation*, 21; Andrew R. L. Cayton, "Radicals in the 'Western World': The Federalist Conquest of Trans-Appalachian North America," in Ben-Atar and Oberg, eds., *Federalists Reconsidered.*

well as English: the Frenchmen present reacted "with pleasure and astonishment." Afterward, they toasted the principles of July 4, 1776, Washington, Jefferson, Governor William C. C. Claiborne and General James Wilkinson, the vice president and Congress ("May they be more friendly to our rights as they know more of us"), and "The memory of de Soto and deSalle the discoverers of Louisiana." According to the account published in the *Mississippi Herald and Natchez City Gazette,* the celebration's "importance consists in its shewing that the inhabitants of Louisiana are willing, or may readily be brought to adopt as their own, those national customs practiced in those states who bore the burthen in the heat of the day."[59]

The correct mode of celebration could help determine the shape of the geopolitical future. No one realized this better than the pro-American and Francophone residents of polyglot New Orleans. For Claiborne, the newly appointed governor of the territory, the "acclamation of thousands" at the ceremonial unfurling of the American flag in New Orleans proved the future loyalty of the inhabitants, even though a French observer heard mainly "uneasy silence," and cheers from only "a certain group of spectators." Jeffersonian papers in the East took proud notice of this event, reporting no dissenting note. Yet it could not remain so easy, and during the first year of American rule Claiborne sprinkled his reports to Secretary of State James Madison with references to controversies surrounding national festivities. New Orleans already had a tradition of public balls—a French creole tradition that would not be so easily translated or assimilated into an Anglo-American model. In January 1804 at least two incidents marred the winter festive season as American and French officers came to blows over whose national songs would be played by the band.[60]

59. "From a Correspondent, Natchitoches, July 5, 1804," *Mississippi Herald and Natchez City Gazette,* Aug. 24, 1804.

60. Rowland Dunbar, ed., *Official Letter Books of W. C. C. Claiborne, 1801–1816,* 6 vols. (Jackson, Miss., 1917), I, 304–307, 323, 331; C. C. Robin, *Voyage to Louisiana* (1807), trans. Stuart O. Landry, Jr. (New Orleans, La., 1966), 66; "From the National Intelligencer," *Wilmington Gazette* (N.C.), Feb. 21, 1804; Clarence E. Carter and John Porter Bloom, eds., *The Territorial Papers of the United States,* 27 vols. (Washington, D.C., 1934–1969), IX, 180–181; George Dargo, *Jefferson's Louisiana: Politics and the Clash of Legal Traditions* (Cambridge, Mass., 1975), 27–28; Samuel Kinser, *Carnival, American Style: Mardi Gras at New Orleans and Mobile* (Chicago, 1990), 24–29. A similar incident was narrowly averted on the next Bastille Day (Dunbar, ed., *Letter Books of Claiborne,* II, 249).

Traditionally, the governor had regulated the public balls of New Orleans, but Claiborne, knowing how easily he could offend, did not hesitate to hand this hot potato over to the mayor. In spite of Claiborne's caution, revelry soon became controversial anyway. A group of 140 inhabitants of New Orleans drew up a widely publicized petition to the Congress in which they protested their delayed incorporation as a state, the division of the territory into two units, and the suppression of the African slave trade. "We passed under your jurisdiction with a joy bordering on enthusiasm," the memorialists noted, appealing to the Declaration, the Constitution, and taxation without representation: "We invoke the principles of your revolution." With the locals going over his head, Claiborne also found himself visited by a delegation of free blacks, whose militia company had been present at the flag ceremony of December 20 but had been excluded, not surprisingly, from the proslavery citizens meeting. They expressed their "lively joy that the Sovereignty of the Country is at length united with that of the American Republic" and asked also to continue as a full-fledged citizen militia.[61]

What was the solution to this babel of patriotic performance? More national celebration. Whereas the French in New Orleans turned out for Bastille Day in 1804 and Spaniards lauded their King's Birthday (with an appearance by Claiborne), pro-American forces celebrated the first anniversary of the Treaty of Paris (April 30, 1803), with Claiborne, according to the new English-language paper, in the role of Washington: "The cheerful and animatory deportment of the Governor during the whole of the Festival, excited the plaudits of every beholder." Impressed with the possibilities, Claiborne looked forward to "the 4th of July, which will be celebrated in this city with great Pomp." "I think it may have a good Political tendency, and I shall therefore spare *neither trouble nor expence.*" Indeed, on the Fourth in New Orleans a High Mass was held, and orations were given in both English and French. Claiborne's official translator (and one of the proslavery memorialists),

61. Dunbar, ed., *Letter Books of Claiborne,* I, 355, II, 217–218, 233, 234–235; *Mémoire présenté au Congres des Etats-Unis d'Amérique par les habitants de la Louisiane* (New Orleans, La., 1804); *Memorial Presented by the Inhabitants of Louisiana to the Congress of the United States* (Washington, D.C., 1804), quoted at 4, 20; Carter and Bloom, eds., *Territorial Papers of the United States,* IX, 174–175. The proslavery petition provoked a pointed response from Thomas Paine, apparently first published in the *Aurora:* see "To the French Inhabitants of Louisiana," *Louisiana Gazette* (New Orleans), Nov. 2, 1804.

Pierre Derbigny, gave the latter speech, which echoed the terms of eastern Republican celebrations of the Purchase. He hailed the transition to American rule as "our political emancipation" and had the oration printed in both languages. Meanwhile, Claiborne thanked one of the local printers for refusing to print a proposal for a meeting of the free people of color, recognized the mulatto militia, and successfully dissuaded black leaders from holding a public protest. Blacks' efforts probably had some effect: thanks to Claiborne's brokering as well, the proslavery whites stopped agitating for renewal of the slave trade.[62]

Claiborne and his supporters seem to have succeeded in using nationalist festivity to promote loyalty at home and confidence abroad. For several years, the Americanizing inhabitants of New Orleans celebrated the anniversaries of the treaty and of the official transfer of the territory as well as Washington's Birthday and the Fourth of July. On the first anniversary of the official transfer from France to the United States, the editor of the *Orleans Gazette* expertly performed the ritual of anticipating, enacting, and then describing nationalist sentiment. Yet he did so with specific reference to the "calumnies" of those who (quite sensibly) doubted the new territory's loyalty and republicanism:

> This day, this auspicious day, has repelled the charges with effect, and has done us justice in the eyes of our country and the world. Every heart beat with joy, and every countenance beamed patriotism and courage.—It was difficult to determine, whether joy for the event, or devotion to government, preponderated; so strong were they expressed in every face, that certain index to the heart. Frenchmen, Spaniards, and Americans, joined heartily together, and vied only in showing their love of liberty and order.

With political competition rechanneled into productive sentimental exchange—in the same language used since the 1770s to describe the

62. *Louisiana Gazette* (New Orleans), Nov. 9, 1804; "New Orleans, May 4," *Georgia Republican* (Savannah), July 10, 1804; "An Oration Delivered at the Principal in This City, on the 4th July, 1804, by P. Derbigny, Translated From the French," *Union* (New Orleans), July 11, 1804; Dunbar, ed., *Letter Books of Claiborne*, II, 158, 234–235, 236, 237, 239, 244; Carter and Bloom, eds., *Territorial Papers of the United States*, IX, 261, 304–305, 312; Donald E. Everett, "Emigres and Militiamen: Free Persons of Color in New Orleans, 1803–1815," *Journal of Negro History*, XXXVIII (1953), 377–402. Derbigny's speech is reprinted as it appeared in the *Telegraphe* (New Orleans), bilingually, in *Louisiana Historical Quarterly*, I, (1899), 292–302.

interactions of men and women and of people of different classes at celebrations—the blessings of the future could be considered secure:

> Fellow citizens, this day has confounded your enemies—the good tidings of your patriotism will be conveyed to Congress in due time— and thus obtaining correct intelligence of your principles and devotion, you will be rewarded by being introduced into the second grade of government.[63]

Six years later, when American residents of West Florida rebelled against Spanish rule and declared themselves an independent republic, they too tried to gain recognition for their patriotism, and for the legitimacy of their rebellion, with published accounts of their July Fourth celebrations. "The joy which fills every American heart this day, is as strongly felt in Florida, as in Richmond, Philadelphia, or Boston," wrote an enthusiastic editor in Saint Francisville. And because of the jurisdictional rivalry with Louisiana (it was unclear whether West Florida should be part of the soon-to-be-created state of Louisiana, given status of a separate territory, or not recognized at all), West Florida's Americanism would be validated by contrast with New Orleans: "Here is soul, is feeling, while west of the Mississippi, is only observable a cold apathy, a glorious silence, unworthy of Americans and freemen. It is true that in the city of New-Orleans, there are those who respect the day— but to the great mass of the population, it is a day of mourning rather than joy."[64]

The connections between celebration, publication, acts of reading, and the demonstration of national affiliation by those on the frontier were vividly and candidly discussed in a remarkable series of letters published in a New Orleans paper under the name of Gilbert Hurlstone in early 1805.[65] Much like Ethan Allen, Hurlstone presents himself in the first person as an ordinary man awakened to politics by the printed word. Under the rule of the Spanish monarch, he maintains, he has lived a double life. "Out of doors, with the people, I used to talk of his Catholic Majesty, call him our *common father;* speak loud in praise of monarchy, abuse republics, and wish the United States the devil. At

63. *Louisiana Gazette* (New Orleans), Dec. 22, 1804, Feb. 26, April 30, Dec. 24, 1805, Feb. 25, May 2, July 7, Dec. 23, 1806; *Orleans Gazette; and Commercial Advertiser* (New Orleans), May 3, July 5, 1806; *Orleans Gazette, for the Country*, Dec. 22, 1804.

64. *Time Piece* (St. Francisville, La.), July 4, 1811.

65. "To the Editor," "Letter I," "Letter II," *Orleans Gazette, for the Country* (New Orleans), Feb. 9, 1805.

home, I used to talk with my wife, and lament that we had a king, that we could not speak as we pleased, to every body, and read and print every thing." He had read the French-language paper by day, and at night he educated himself for republicanism with Voltaire and Roman history. All this changed overnight, we learn, when the Americans took hold of the territory. In what he calls a "drunken frolic," he signs subscriptions for both Anglophone papers.

In this first, introductory installment of a three-part series of letters, Hurlstone constructs his former self under monarchy as a duplicitous citizen and, of necessity, a dependent reader. His description of insincere speech parallels Ethan Allen's account of his public madness in British captivity. For a free American citizen, however, it is not enough to toast the authorities sincerely: " 'Now,' says I to myself, 'I will print, and be an author.' " Hurlstone's path to authorship, partially blocked by his suddenly apolitical wife, is smoothed by a professional man, a doctor who validates his literary talent. Patronized and freed from his private condition, he writes this very letter to the editor, rending and re-fusing his formerly divided world by displaying *in print* the very transformation he would gain *through* printed publicity.[66] Tellingly, the first things he authorizes are his own spontaneous acts of national celebration and his desire to immerse himself in print.

As Hurlstone tells it in this parable of national citizenship, he is utterly revolutionized by the new fusion of his public and private, his celebratory and literary lives. The proof is in his new habits of rejoicing and his eagerness to publicize them. Suddenly he would tell us his whole life story ("My name is GILBERT HURLSTONE . . ."), including his dubious patrimony as the son of a Revolutionary war deserter. Political confessions like this one pave the way for Hurlstone, like Allen, to persuade others to do likewise. And persuade he does. "Letter I," the next piece, narrates mainly his own acts of speech on the day of the American flag raising. Having purified (and publicized) his home by roaring into it, "We are now free, and I'll become an author," Hurlstone proceeds to yell out the benefits of American rule and to toast liberty and the American officials Governor Claiborne and General Wilkinson. His

66. For a similar tendency in Benjamin Franklin's autobiography and other writings, see Michael Warner, *The Letters of the Republic: Publication and the Public Sphere in Eighteenth-Century America* (Cambridge, Mass., 1990), 73–96; Larzer Ziff, *Writing in the New Nation: Prose, Print, and Politics in the Early United States* (New Haven, Conn., 1991), 83–106.

neighbors arrive to confirm that everyone else is rejoicing. The series ends, however, on a mixed note. Hurlstone describes a dream he has had of a free people with a free government, "a paradise" that suddenly, for no apparent reason, turns into a nightmarish scene of tyranny. He asks the editor of the *Gazette*, and by implication the reader, for an interpretation. In the last letter, he presents alternate interpretations of the dream. His own version divides the scenes of the dream spatially: Louisiana is the heaven, and neighboring Florida, still under Spanish rule, is hell. His anti-American neighbor "Shylock," however, construes the bipolarity as one of time rather than of space. Louisiana had been free, but will soon suffer as never before.

Hurlstone's story about celebration, publication, and national identity testifies to the continual spread of nationalist practices to the very peripheries of the nation itself. These practices survived and flourished at the borderlands, not because of some primordial loyalty, but because of their usefulness in the territorial political situation. Hurlstone's imaginative rendering of national dream-work, even as it seeks to resolve the question of loyalty, also points to the amount of persuasion left to be done. Now securely American, New Orleans remains the frontier, even if disloyalty (and misinterpretation) can be projected onto a Jewish neighbor. It is the process of interpretation—the practice of national citizenship through persuasive acts of reading, writing, and celebration—that is most confidently affirmed. Just by inviting readers to interpret his national dreams, Hurlstone secures his own patriotism. Like many a border nationalist, he understood the relationship between nationalist imaginings and the practice of frontier politics.

The Hurlstone letters' experiment with print, remarkable as it is for its success and its excess, is merely an individual example, a local manifestation of larger developments in the construction of interlocking regional, national, and partisan identities.[67] The way in which Americans

67. Yet Hurlstone appears to have inspired others. One David Millinger of Natchez quoted Hurlstone ("We are now free, and everybody may write and print what he pleases") to justify the publication of the toasts from a Republican March fourth celebration "at the Mechanical and Republican Hall at the home of James Martin's." These toasts had been refused by the other Natchez paper, probably because of their radicalism: "May villainous land speculators in the Mississippi Territory be unmasked so that they may appear plain to a common observer, and scouted from the territory for robbing the needy of their might and increase[ing] the wretchedness of the wretched by cheating the poor out of their old Spanish

east and west came to hold celebrations for the acquisition of Louisiana in 1803–1804 is another example of this larger process. On one level, as indicated earlier, the Louisiana rites were only part of a series of Republican attempts to ratify their version of recent history: Jefferson's election as the Revolution of 1800. Yet the Louisiana festivals also had a sectional dimension that cannot be reduced to partisanship alone, no matter how well they served the Jeffersonians. Rather, the dynamic at work in these celebrations tells us much about the regional dimensions of partisanship and the increasingly partisan aura of regionalism in the early Republic.

The first formal festival in honor of the cession of territory from France seems to have been held at Lexington, Kentucky. Lexingtonians celebrated the promise of Louisiana to all the people of the West; the account published in the *Kentucky Gazette* claimed that "differences of political opinion were forgotten." Toasts included "Our present administration," the state of Ohio, free navigation of the Mississippi, and "The People of Kentucky—whom no injuries nor inflammatory addresses could excite to insurrection."[68] For Kentucky Republicans at least, Louisiana was an opportunity to conflate local and national desires where they met, in the realm of region.

The account of this festival, first published in the local paper, appeared two weeks later in *Kline's Carlisle Weekly Gazette,* a midway stop in the west-east communication system. A week later it was picked up by the Washington-based *National Intelligencer,* which printed the text as proof of western loyalty and Jeffersonianism: "The following account of the celebration in Kentucky . . . evinces the patriotism, republicanism, and steadfast adherence of our western friends to those principles and measures on which the welfare of all America depends." After local celebrations of the Louisiana acquisition dotted the calendar that fall, the same Carlisle paper proposed a nationwide festival to be held following the date when the United States took official possession of the Territory. The handsomely typeset announcement proposal left the dates blank and asked the *Aurora* of Philadelphia, "as the most complete channel of Republican communication in the United States," to reprint the proposal. In a few weeks the same striking columns had ap-

---

claims and the United States out of millions of acres." *Mississippi Herald* (Natchez), Mar. 15, 1805.

68. *Kentucky Gazette* (Lexington), Aug. 16, 1803.

peared in the most important Republican papers, with the date set for May 12, the anniversary festival of the decidedly Republican Tammany Society. On January 18 *Kline's Carlisle Weekly Gazette* republished it with the date in May confirmed, and inserted, "as published in the *Aurora*." On February 6 it was read aloud at a meeting of the Tammanyites in New York.[69]

When the actual celebration took place, Federalists in New York and elsewhere denounced it as a paper affair, manufactured by printers and made to look national when it was really sectional and partisan. The celebration, like Louisiana itself, stood as testimony to the fanciful imaginations of the administration and its supporters. Whatever its limitations in New York and New England, however, the May 12 festival fulfilled its purpose by creating an occasion for certain easterners and westerners to toast each other and by providing enough material for them to read all about it for weeks afterward. Perusers of New York's *American Citizen,* for example, learned of reprise celebrations of the Purchase in Lexington itself and in Lancaster, Ohio. By reperforming their celebrations according to eastern-mediated national cues, these Kentuckians provided yet more printed proof of their westernness, their Jeffersonian loyalties, and their Americanness. Even as they underlined their special western interests, they brought themselves more securely into the realm of nationalist geopolitics.[70]

Increasingly after 1803, the more secure patriots of Ohio, Kentucky, and the Mississippi Valley boasted of both their American heritage and their western virtues. Columbus served as their great pilgrim father while Lewis and Clark did duty as their John Smith. At a Fourth of July celebration in North Bend, Ohio, presided over by future senator John Cleves Symmes, the "respectable" demeanor of the participants helped them to claim the rights of self-government held by their ancestors—

69. *Kline's Carlisle Weekly Gazette* (Pa.), Aug. 31, Dec. 14, 1803, Jan. 18, 1804; *National Intelligencer* (Washington), Sept. 5, Dec. 18, 1803; *American Citizen* (New York), Jan. 8, 1804; Society of Tammany or Columbian Order, Minutebook, Feb. 6, 1804, New York Public Library. For Carlisle's place in the communication system, see the map in Meinig, *Atlantic America,* 402.

70. "Editor's Closet," *Balance, and Columbian Repository* (Hudson, N.Y.), III, no. 2 (1804), 62–63; *American Citizen* (New York), June 4, 1804; "Festival," *Kentucky Gazette* (Lexington), May 15, 1804; *Scioto Gazette* (Chillicothe, Ohio), Mar. 12, May 14, 21, 1804. By 1804 Ohio had its own branches of the Tammany Society to lead the celebration, against which Federalists founded local Washington Benevolent Societies and a short-lived Anti-Tammany Society.

and to link them to their campaign for statehood. At the same time, they insisted that they already contributed to union: "The Five Territories of the United States—which, more impregnable than the Chinese wall, oppose to the foe the western rampart of the American empire." The *"warriors of the back-woods"* would be first to defend "the Union" from domestic and foreign foes. At an Independence Day fete in 1810, inhabitants of Cincinnati portrayed the western states as an "asylum" for the coastal "sons of Liberty" overrun by "foreign influence." In Lexington, Kentucky, the previous year, "the Yankees and other Tories in America" were wished "passage over the river Styx."[71]

Those westerners who did not spend the War of 1812 on the march devoted at least a portion of it to toasting each other. Finally, westerners had a chance to show off their patriotism, to reenact the American Revolution by cursing the British and the Indians. In Kentucky, after the declaration of war, houses were lit up in Lexington, Winchester, Richmond, and Nicholasville; a militia company toasted: "The Twelfth Congress.—In declaring War against G[reat] Britain, they have only reechoed the sentiments of the people of Kentucky." Here the patriotism of the center is defined by that of the margins: for westerners, the cycle had been completed. They were the West; they were America. At the beginning of the war especially, Kentucky served the West as Massachusetts served New England: "the bulwark of the western country," the epitome of the regional ethos that was simultaneously national. By the end of the war the "Hunters of Kentucky" had been celebrated in a Boston-printed broadside for being "Half Horse and half Alligator" (see Figure 14). The "western states and territories" would be remembered by "a patriotic and enlightened posterity," proclaimed the citizens of New Albany, Indiana.[72]

Thanks to the War of 1812, westerners were once again able to claim Indian fighting—for a time a major source of frontier disorder and disloyalty—as an act of patriotic virtue. A Charleston victory festival

71. *Liberty Hall* (Cincinnati), July 7, 1807; "Tammany Society," *Scioto Gazette* (Chillicothe, Ohio), July 11, 1810, May 15, 1811; "The 4th of July," *Reporter* (Lexington, Ky.), July 4, 1809.

72. "Fourth of July," *Missouri Gazette* (Saint Louis), July 31, 1813; *Reporter* (Lexington, Ky.), July 1, 1812; *Hunter's of Kentucky; or, Half Horse and Half Alligator* (Boston, 1815); *Louisville Correspondent,* July 10, 1815. On the importance of the "Hunters of Kentucky" image in the 1820s, for background on the song, and for the text of a later edition, see John William Ward, *Andrew Jackson: Symbol for an Age* (New York, 1955), 13–29, 216–218 n. 1.

Half Horse, and Half Allegator.

Hunters of Kentucky.

Ye gentlemen and ladies fair
　Who grace this famous city
Just listen if ye've time to spare,
　While I rehearse a ditty ;
And for the ouportunity,
　Conceive yourselves quite lucky,
For 'tis not often that you see
　A hunter from Kentucky.
　　Oh, Kentucky ; the hunters of Kentucky,
　The hunters of Kentucky.

We are a hardy, free born race,
　Each man to fear a stranger;
Whate'er the game we join in chase,
　Despising toil and danger;
And if a daring foe annoys,
　Whate'er his strength and forces,
We'll shew him that Kentucky boys
　Are Alligator Horses.
　　　　Oh, Kentucky,

I 'spose you've read it in the prints,
　How Packenham attempted
To make old Hickory Jackson wince,
　But soon his scheme repented
For we, with rifles ready cock'd,
　Thought such occasion lucky,
And soon around the general flock'd
　The hunters of Kentucky.
　　　　Oh ! Kentucky.

You've heard I 'spose how New-Orleans
　Is fam'd for wealth and beauty—
There's girls of every hue it seems
　From snowy white to sooty,
So Packenham he made his brags,
　If he in fight was lucky,
He'd have their girls and cotton bags,
　In spite of old Kentucky.
　　　　Oh ! Kentucky.

But Jackson, he was wide awake,
　And was'nt scar'd at trifles ;
For well he knew what aim we take,
　With our Kentucky rifles.
So he led us down to Cypress swamp,
　The ground was low and mucky ;
There stood John Bull in martial pomp,
　And here was old Kentucky,
　　　　Oh ! Kentucky.

A bank was rais'd to hide our breast,
　Not that we thought of dying,
But that we always like to rest,
　Unless the game is flying ;
Behind it stood our little force,
　None wish'd it to be greater,
For every man was half a Horse,
　And half an Allegator.
　　　　Oh ! Kentucky.

They did not let our patience tire
　Before they shew'd their faces ;
He did not choose to waste our fire,
　So snugly kept our places ;
But when so near we saw them wink,
　We thought it time to stop 'em.
And 'twold have done you good, I think,
　To see Kentucky drop 'em.
　　　　Oh ! Kentucky.

They found, at last 'twas vain to fight
　Where lead was all their booty ;
And so they wisely took to flight,
　And left us all the beauty !
And now if danger e'er annoys,
　Remember what our trade is ;
Just send for us Kentucky boys,
　And we'll protect ye, ladies.
　　　　Oh ! Kentucky.

Printed and Sold at NO. 25, High Street, Providence, by the Hundred, Dozen or Single.

FIGURE 14. *Hunters of Kentucky.* Providence, 1815.
Courtesy Filson Club Historical Society Library

featured a transparency of an Indian about to be scalped. Southern Republicans were only too happy to toast the volunteers of Kentucky, Ohio, and Tennessee: "They have taught their elders practical patriotism." The Battle of New Orleans only completed this logic, providing another anniversary for many westerners to call their own, and another hero—Andrew Jackson—to play George Washington.[73]

By 1815 westerners were not only celebrating themselves as true sons of the Revolution; they were reading in their newspapers that some easterners, like the army officers at Burlington, Vermont, feted them in the same way:

14th. *The Western States*—Yesterday a wilderness . . . today cultured and blooming with industry, the *envied home of heroes* and patriots. . . .

15th. *The Eastern States*—Alas! how politically desolate. The minions of a crazy monarch look out from their windows, and revel undisturbed, in their habitations. Their warriors and sages, the pride of other times have ascended to heaven; forget what is—remember what was.

With the help of Republicans east and south, westerners had shifted the national center of gravity. In this last toast, the speakers acknowledge the patrimony of the eastern states only to place them in the past. Their insistence upon clinging to the past, and to England, only removes them from significance in the present. Once again, the real nation lay in the future, but now the future was the West. In this instance, expansion over space compensated for the passage of revolutionary time.[74]

73. "Grand Festival," *City Gazette and Commercial Advertiser* (Charleston, S.C.), Mar. 10, July 7, 1813; *Augusta Chronicle* (Ga.), July 9, 1813; *Southern Patriot, and Commercial Advertiser* (Charleston, S.C.), July 5, 1815; "National Character" (from *Baltimore Patriot*), *Muskingum Messenger* (Zanesville, Ohio), Mar. 22, 1815; "The Western Country" (from *National Intelligencer*), *Eagle* (Maysville, Ky.), July 4, 1817; "Toasts Given July 4th 1815 [Mantua, Ohio]," John Harmer Family Papers, box 1, folder 8, Western Reserve Historical Society; Anita Shafer Goodstein, *Nashville, 1780–1860: From Frontier to City* (Gainesville, Fla., 1989), 51; Ward, *Andrew Jackson*, 15.

On the larger cultural significance of Indian fighting in early America, see Slotkin, *Regeneration through Violence*. For the War of 1812 as crucial in the rise of nationalism in the West, see Reginald Horsman, *The Frontier in the Formative Years, 1783–1815* (New York, 1970), 166–186.

74. "The Nation of New England" (from *Green-Mountain Farmer* [Bennington, Vt.]), *Western American* (Williamsburg, Ohio), June 24, 1815; "New-Orleans; or, The Sons of the West," *The American Star: Being a Choice Collection of the Most Approved*

The increasing power of western regionalism and its successful conflation with American nationalism are apparent in the most popular new development in celebrations after 1815. These were the spectacles of progress, in which internal improvement projects were commenced and completed (often on the Fourth of July) with special parades, oratory, huge outdoor banquets, and toasts. The benefits of these canals and road-building ventures, insisted their proponents, would accrue not merely to locales they primarily served, nor even mainly to those whose resources would build them, but rather to "the union at large." Certainly the promoters of public works were right to celebrate the budding transportation revolution as a phenomenon that would materially bind the nation together. At the same time, in their linkage of "the true interest of the Western Country" with "this great national work," those who attended the groundbreaking of the Jeffersonville Ohio Canal had taken something of both strategy and substance from the New England forebears that many of them aggressively claimed. In ever-expanding America there was no necessary contradiction between an assertive regionalism and a commitment to the national future.[75]

Patriotic and Other Songs, 2d ed. (Richmond, Va., 1817), 51–53; Samuel Burnham, "An Oration, Delivered in Zanesville," *Zanesville Express, and Republican Standard* (Ohio), July 14, 1819. On expansion as the touchstone of the national Republican coalition emerging at this time, see Alexander Saxton, *The Rise and Fall of the White Republic: Class Politics and Mass Culture in Nineteenth-Century America* (London, 1990), 33–48. On time and space in post-Revolutionary politics and culture, see David Brion Davis, *The Problem of Slavery in the Age of Revolution, 1770–1823* (Ithaca, N.Y., 1975), 342.

75. "A Grand Project," *Western American* (Williamsburg, Ohio), Mar. 23, 1816; "Internal Improvement," *Muskingum Messenger* (Zanesville, Ohio), June 2, 1819; "Oration Delivered by Mr. Stephen F. Austin at Potosi, on the 4th of July, 1818," *Missouri Gazette* (Saint Louis), July 24, 1818; "From the Cincinnati Gazette; *The New England Thanksgiving,*" *Western Reserve Chronicle* (Warren, Ohio), Jan. 22, 1818; *American Mercury* (Hartford), July 19, 1825. On these spectacles and their meaning, see the insightful essays by John Seelye: " 'Rational Exultation': The Erie Canal Celebration," American Antiquarian Society, *Proceedings,* XCIV (1984), 261–287; and in *Beautiful Machine: Rivers and the Republican Plan, 1755–1825* (New York, 1991), 293–302, 319–353; and see also Carol Sheriff, *The Artificial River: The Erie Canal and the Paradox of Progress, 1817–1862* (New York, 1996), 27–29, 45–51. Seelye notes that, in the long run, the canals linked New England to the Midwest, isolating the South and the Southwest (*Beautiful Machine,* 338).

☆   ☆   ☆

Unfortunately for many self-identified New Englanders, southern and western improvements upon nationalist ideology and practice made it difficult for their own, classic version of regional nationalism to work effectively for them in the period between the adoption of the Constitution and the War of 1812. But this too would change. The shifting geopolitics of the antebellum era lie beyond the scope of this study. However, the striking use of the same tradition and strategies (or we might say, a tradition *of* strategies) by different regions over time suggests a different way of looking at the rescrambled regional conflicts of the era after the Missouri Crisis. It would be very difficult, if not impossible, for regionalists of the antebellum period to find a mode of dissent that did not partake of the nationalist logic and practices they had learned on the parade grounds and in the newspapers of the early Republic.

The very flexibility of the system of celebration and publicity made it possible to read the same national and regional attachments different ways, in acts of alliance and opposition; patriotism and sectionalism were in the eye of the beholder. But flexibility too has its costs. Earlier I suggested that celebrations, oratory, and the printed discourse that surrounded them constituted the true political public sphere of the early Republic. I also contended that this public sphere arose in order to mediate between local and national politics and that its limitations could be seen in the telling ways it pushed women and blacks to the margins of a political culture committed in theory to equality and popular participation. The geopolitics of national celebration had limits as well. Within this system of rhetorical alliances and oppositions, sections could resolve the seeming contradictions of regional and national attachments, both for themselves and to achieve interregional partisan alliances within the two-party system. In doing so, however, geopolitical celebration actually exacerbated regional enmities. It became all too easy to fight the Revolution all over again at home: for the evanescence of Revolutionary virtue in time to be relocated in, and blamed on, the inhabitants of un-American spaces. For the strength nationalism gained from the battles of regions, the nation itself would pay a heavy price.[76]

76. For the Civil War as a bloody battle among seekers of national identity, see Charles Royster, *The Destructive War: William Tecumseh Sherman, Stonewall Jackson, and the Americans* (New York, 1991).

6

MIXED FEELINGS:
RACE AND NATION

"Good feelings" animated the American nation in the victorious after-glow of the Battle of New Orleans, or so the textbooks tell us. A second contest with England had finally secured the national character against foreign disrespect and domestic discontent. Many had insisted that the War of 1812 would end in tragedy. Others, in the two centuries since, have dismissed the whole affair as a farce. But few failed to recognize the cultural and political power of being counted among history's winners.

If this was the dawn of a new era characterized by "the awakening of American nationalism," it was a most peculiar awakening, justified as it had been as a reenactment of the American Revolution. A younger generation of men had proven itself on the battleships and on the podiums of "Mr. Madison's War." As the Revolution became the stuff of legend, the new war, in its inflated military dimension, provided a link to the passing Revolutionary generation. The symbolic pull of the surviving revolutionaries grew continually stronger and yet, at the same time, became increasingly amorphous and abstract. In 1819, about two-thirds of the American population had been born after 1776. In 1820, a scandal over the nonpayment of Revolutionary war pensions spurred veterans to organize, parade, and present their claim forms on the Fourth of July. The collective guilt they inspired affected even the still-regnant rhetoric of sentimental display: "The grotesque appearance of these veterans and heroes of the Revolution, awakened the sensibility of all who beheld them . . . their claims to national gratitude seemed stamped on their visage." Spectacles such as these might have inspired Washington Irving's "Rip Van Winkle" (1819), in which the title charac-ter, who has slept through the Revolution, arrives at his favorite tavern only to interrupt the to-him-unfathomable rites of electioneering. The juxtaposition of past and present at these events could shock even those who, unlike Irving, intended to celebrate both. The sublime scenes of patriotism, still simultaneously imagined and embodied, could seem less beautiful than terrifying.[1]

Rather than being merely good, then, political feelings in America were truly mixed, and not the least because of the remarkable effort to promote and publicize "good feelings," an effort that denied the continuing conflicts Americans faced. The mixed feelings discernible in even the most patriotic celebrations should remind us that "good feelings" was as much an old ideological construct as it was a new political development. Partisan and related sectional differences continued to be the most obvious obstacle to joyous unity; at the same time, the dominant modes of nationalist thought and practice still encouraged attempts to celebrate America into a consensual, nonpartisan future.

Another dimension of difference haunted postwar American nationalism. This was the mixture of races that had characterized America since long before Independence—a mixture unacknowledged in the dominant rhetoric of Revolutionary and post-Revolutionary politics. This chapter views contemporary efforts to render America racially (as well as regionally and politically) homogeneous through the prism of the long-standing battle over the meaning of slavery and the place of free African Americans in the new nation. The formative rite of politi-

---

1. On the awakening: George Dangerfield, *The Awakening of American Nationalism, 1815–1828* (New York, 1965). Dangerfield could not resist titling his earlier, Pulitzer-prize winning book *The Era of Good Feelings* (New York, 1952), even though by his own estimate the good feelings lasted only about two years, from 1817 to 1819. For a treatment of the war's cultural politics, see Steven Watts, *The Republic Reborn: War and the Making of Liberal America, 1790–1820* (Baltimore, 1987).

On youth and the legacy of the Revolution, see David Brion Davis, "1819: Signs of a New Era," lecture, Yale University, February 1992. On the pensioners, see John P. Resch, "Politics and Public Culture: The Revolutionary War Pensions Act of 1818," *Journal of the Early Republic,* VIII (1988), 139–158.

For the spectacle of the veterans: "From the New York American: 'The Heroes of the Revolution,'" *Independent Chronicle and Boston Patriot,* July 22, 1820; *New-England Palladium and Commercial Advertiser* (Boston), July 14, 1820; Benjamin Gleason, *Anniversary Oration . . . Pronounced before the Republican Citizens of Charleston, July 5, 1819 . . .* (Charleston, S.C., 1819), 9–12; Washington Irving, "Rip Van Winkle," in Irving, *The Sketch Book of Geoffrey Crayon, Gent.* (New York, 1961), 37–55; Bryan Jay Wolf, *Romantic Re-Vision: Culture and Consciousness in Nineteenth-Century Painting and Literature* (Chicago, 1982), 153–167.

cal and regional "good feelings"—James Monroe's presidential tour—gained institutional expression in a patriotic organization dedicated to racial homogeneity: the American Colonization Society (ACS). The ACS's neocolonial white nationalism is best understood as a response to the black and white antislavery activists who used the forms of national celebration to challenge slavery after the Revolution. Meanwhile, northern urban free blacks appropriated nationalist celebration to their own ends. Their declarations of African identity, amid hostile white reactions, reveal the remarkable openness as well as the tragic limitations of American political culture.

NOTHING BUT UNION

After the War of 1812 as before, if there was one thing that white Americans could agree upon, it was their national greatness. As Fourth of July orators insisted at length, the United States was the "only Republic on earth." Europe remained "a degrading scene of regal turpitude and unmanly subjection." The Old World, like Asia and Africa, was probably not even "yet ripe for the establishment of a free government." Hence the self-evident virtues of America's national birthday: where foreigners were "compelled to pay homage at the shrines of titled nobility or kingly majesty," citizens of the United States joined "to render the free will offering of our own hearts to God and our common country."[2]

More important to the immediate consolidation of "good feeling"

2. John Mason, Jr., "Oration Delivered the 4th of July 1818 at Williamsburg Virginia," John Mason Commonplace Book, 1815–1818, Virginia Historical Society, Richmond; C[harles] A. Clinton, *Oration, Delivered on the 43d Anniversary of American Independence* . . . (Albany, N.Y., 1819), 6–9; Samuel Berrian, *An Oration, Delivered at Tammany Hall, on the 31st Day of March, 1817, in Commemoration of the Eighth Anniversary of the Columbian Society* (New York, [1817]), 12; Peter I. Clark, *An Address, Delivered at Flemington, on the Anniversary of American Independence* . . . (New Brunswick, N.J., 1817), quoted at 9. For similar remarks, see Selah North, *An Oration, Delivered at Goshen, July 4th, 1817* . . . (Hartford, Conn., 1817); J. P. C. Sampson, *An Oration, Delivered before the Members of the Law Institution, at Litchfield, on the Fourth of July, 1818* (New York, 1818), 5–7, 10–12; Dr. Samuel Jackson, *An Oration, Delivered at the County Court-House, Philadelphia, on the Forty-Second Anniversary of American Independence* (Philadelphia, 1818), 2–10; Henry Laurens Pinckney, *An Oration, Delivered in . . . Charleston, South-Carolina; on the Fourth of July, 1818* . . . (Charleston, S.C., 1818), 19–27. The only exception to the worldwide decline of liberty was seen in South America; see Pinckney, *Oration,* 28–29.

was the public renunciation of partisanship. The Fourth of July in 1817 marked a watershed as Federalists and Democrats in many locales came together for huge "mutual" celebrations. In Troy, New York, a correspondent noted how, before that day, the different parties had not celebrated together for seventeen years; he applauded the apparently "universal burst of American feeling." Orators made special efforts, often under instruction by committees, to avoid offending anyone. Austin Denny, the orator at Worcester in 1818, even forswore the generic recounting of American history in his oration—"The *past* might be the occasion of discord among those whose feelings are in unison when contemplating the *present,* and whose hearts beat with the same joyful anticipations of the *future.*"[3]

But bipartisan celebrations could not long hide the continuing conflict over the meaning of the Revolution. Many, especially those affiliated with the increasingly amorphous Democratic-Republicans, persisted in calling the birth of America "a new era in the history of man," in which the whole world would be inspired by America's example to break the chains of, at least, political slavery. "It is a lesson to the oppressed and an example to the oppressor," insisted Charles Ferris before New York's Tammanyites and tradesmen. Meanwhile, conservatives, especially in New England, still maintained that the American Revolution had merely conserved existing British liberties. Franklin Dexter, the Boston town orator for 1819, announced that true Americans should "find more appropriate modes of celebrating [the Fourth] than merely triumphing in our Independence, or anticipating our future grandeur." After all, the American Revolution had been mild, and its revolutionaries retained their gentility: "We are not emancipated slaves, but the sons of freemen. . . . Intemperate joy would seem

3. Edward D. Bangs to Nathaniel Howe, Aug. 1, 1817, Bangs Family Papers, American Antiquarian Society, Worcester, Mass.; Committee of Arrangements [Springfield, Mass.] to Herman Stebbins, July 2, 1818, Herman Stebbins Papers, Perkins Library, Duke University, Durham, N.C.; *Troy Post* (N.Y.), July 8, 1817; Henry A. DeSaussure, Fourth of July Oration, July 4th, 1817, DeSaussure Papers, South Carolina Historical Society, Charleston; Pliny Merrick, *An Oration, Delivered at Worcester, July 4, 1817* . . . (Worcester, Mass., 1817), 2; Clark, *An Address,* 3; Rollin C. Mallary, *An Oration, Addressed to an Assembly of United Citizens at Whitehall, New York, July 4, 1817* (Rutland, Vt., [1817]); Samuel Barlow Mead, *An Oration, Delivered at Amesbury, July 4, 1817* . . . (Newburyport, Mass., 1817), 11; Austin Denny, *An Oration Delivered at Worcester, (Mass.) July 4th 1818* (Worcester, Mass., 1818), 4.

like a reproach on our fathers."[4] One critic responded that, had the Revolution not occurred, Americans would indeed have been enslaved. Dexter lacked "that full glow of sentiments that ought to invigorate a nation of freemen, when celebrating this mighty achievement":

> Our rejoicings are not only for retaining our liberties, but for acquiring our national independence; and as this was done by the heroism and bravery of the WHOLE PEOPLE, under the direction of patriotic leaders, it is an incumbent duty on them, to appropriate this day to mirth, jollity, and public rejoicing.[5]

The display and witnessing of nationalist sentiment remained the most compelling link to the Revolution that most white Americans could possess, the most available method of claiming full citizenship and identifying with a "whole people."

The eastern tour of President James Monroe during the warm months of 1817 gave skeptics and enthusiasts alike the chance to cultivate "good feelings." Monroe's highly self-conscious and successful journey was the culmination of four decades of politically inspired sentimental spectacles—once again mobilized, as in 1789 and 1798, by a president when sectional and partisan developments led some to question whether the American union would endure. Newspapers followed the president's tour from Washington through Baltimore, New York, Philadelphia, and New England, invariably stressing the decline of par-

4. Andrew Dunlap, *An Oration, Delivered at Salem, on Monday, July 5, 1819* . . . (Salem, Mass., 1819); "For the Fourth of July," *The Columbian Songster: A Collection of the Most Approved Patriotic and Other Songs* (Pittsburgh, 1818), 21–22; Charles G. Ferris, *An Oration, Delivered before the Tammany Society, or Columbian Order, Hibernian Provident, and Columbian Societies, the Union of Shipwright's and Caulker's, Tailor's, Journeymen House Carpenter's, and Mason's Societies, in the City of New-York, on the Fourth Day of July, 1816* (New York, 1816), 3; Franklin Dexter, *An Oration, Delivered July 4, 1819* . . . (Boston, 1819), 8–10. For New Englanders like Dexter and their continuing efforts to promote a conservative public culture, see Harlow Elizabeth Walker Sheidley, "Sectional Nationalism: The Politics and Culture of the Massachusetts Conservative Elite, 1815–1836" (Ph.D. diss., University of Connecticut, 1990). As Sheidley notes, this elite saw public festivals and oratory as key modes of persuasion. Only on rare occasions, however, did they succeed in reconciling "their impulse to remove themselves from the masses they so deeply distrusted and their need to appeal to them directly and dramatically without sacrificing their self-proclaimed superior status as arbiters of the past" (324–325, 353–354).

5. "Communication: A Candid and Cautionary Criticism of Mr. Dexter's Oration," *Boston Patriot and Daily Mercantile Advertiser,* July 15, 1819.

tisanship that Monroe both inspired and brought to light. The president's patriotic progress provided answers to crucial public questions of 1817, such as military and technological improvements. A final western swing brought the politics of party, section, and empire together, allying Monroe and his national Republican consensus with material advancement and territorial expansion.[6]

Leaving Washington clad in breeches and homespun, topped off by his increasingly anachronistic wig, Monroe presented himself as a veteran of the Revolution and a man of the people. He affected surprise when surrounded by festive crowds. This last of the presidents in the Virginia dynasty disavowed all agency in the making of his triumphal progress: he had "chose[n] *rather to see* than *to be seen.*" This wish to avoid public show, according to one report, "could not be gratified," because the people themselves had to be gratified. By all accounts, Monroe kept a schedule of parades, dinners, addresses, and responses even more exhausting than did Washington himself, whom he imitated so conspicuously by mounting a white or gray horse.[7]

Like Washington (and Edmond-Charles Genêt) a quarter-century before, Monroe pronounced his intent to be the *reception* of impressions of the country, opening the door to all kinds of performances intended to impress him and everyone else. Already in New York and Phila-

6. *Genius of Liberty* (Leesburg, Va.), June 17, 1817; "President's Tour," *Georgia Journal* (Milledgeville), July 1, 1817; *Connecticut Courant* (Hartford), July 6, 13, 20, 27, 1817; John Seelye, *Beautiful Machine: Rivers and the Republican Plan, 1755–1825* (New York, 1991), 296–301. Other analyses of Monroe's tour include Dangerfield, *Era of Good Feelings,* 95–96; W. P. Cresson, *James Monroe* (1946; rpt. Hamden, Conn., 1971), 285–290; Harry Ammon, *James Monroe: The Quest for National Identity* (New York, 1971), 372–379; Herbert Adams, "Three Cheers for James Monroe," *Down East,* XXXIII (June 1987), 68–69, 83, 86–88.

7. S[amuel] Putnam Waldo, *The Tour of James Monroe, President of the United States, in the Year 1818* (Hartford, Conn., 1818), 44, 47; *A Narrative of a Tour of Observation, Made during the Summer of 1817, by James Monroe, President of the United States, through the North-Eastern and North-Western Departments of the Union: With a View to the Examination of Their Several Military Defenses* (Philadelphia, 1818), 14; "The President," *Genius of Liberty* (Leesburg, Va.), June 10, 1817; Edward D. Bangs to Nathaniel Howe, Aug. 1, 1817, Bangs Family Papers, AAS; James McCoy to R. W. McCoy, Aug. 28, 1817, Robert W. McCoy Papers, Ohio Historical Society, Columbus; Jeremiah Mason to Jesse Appleton, July 3, 1817, in G. S. Hillard, ed., *Memoir and Correspondence of Jeremiah Mason* (Cambridge, Mass., 1873), 163; *Diary of Sarah Connell Ayer* (Portland, Maine, 1910), 224; Blaine A. Guthrie, Jr., ed., "A Visit by That Confidential Character—President Monroe," *Filson Club Historical Quarterly,* LI (1977), 46.

delphia new voluntary associations like the Literary and Philosophical Society and the Society for the Encouragement of American Manufactures hastily organized special meetings to coincide with Monroe's visit —and to culminate in the election of the affable President as a member.[8] Monroe could then be invited to attend a meeting and promote these groups' ends. It would be hard to exaggerate the lure of these early-nineteenth-century media events. If the causes endorsed—expansion, self-improvement, capitalist development—were helping to create a "liberal America," the form itself espoused republican ideals that retained their resonance. Certainly, as another, more obsessively described, sentimental presidential journey, the tour revealed the power of patriotic spectacle in the continual remaking of America.

Monroe's enterprising reception in the middle states was only prelude to the orgy of nationalist expression that met his arrival in New England. With stops in many of the sizable coastal towns and a well-timed venture into Boston for Independence Day, the president gave Federalists every opportunity to atone for their well-known and effective opposition to the War of 1812. The Federalist *Columbian Centinel* in Boston coined the very term "era of good feelings" in describing the meeting of political enemies at the same table in honor of Monroe. In Salem, the preparations began almost three weeks in advance. The Reverend William Bentley noted a characteristically partisan contest over who should represent the town as its welcoming committee. When Monroe finally arrived, a local paper asserted, "The entire face of society changed." Where the locale lost its craggy features, the nation smoothed over its mountains of resentment. Salemites chose to deck their halls with scenes of naval battles rather than with portraits of Massachusetts's founders; there was no need to toast the Pilgrims when Monroe himself had raised his glass in honor of Massachusetts and its contributions to the Revolution. Along similar lines, when the Pittsburgh committee praised Monroe's former achievement in helping to secure navigation of the Mississippi, the president cautiously proclaimed himself "incapable of discriminating between the rights and interests of the eastern and western sections of the union." Concluding his semiofficial account of the tour, Samuel Putnam Waldo noted that, whatever the effects of the war, "its termination did much to eradicate sectional prejudices." Parties were inevitable outgrowths of the spread

8. *Narrative of a Tour of Observation,* 43–59.

of political knowledge—unhealthy in excess, but unavoidable. "Geographical distinctions," on the other hand, were the true disease for which events like Monroe's tour were an antidote.[9]

This much can be seen in Monroe's response to the town address of Kennebunk, Maine. The Kennebunk committee had prepared one of the more skeptical of the welcoming messages Monroe received. Alluding to the president's "paternal solicitude to make yourself acquainted with the various sections of the country," these New Englanders had pointed out the Virginian's, not their own, provinciality. They addressed the postwar political situation more directly by expressing a hope that Monroe, unlike his predecessor, would earn his plaudits for "an administration marked for its *wisdom,* its *mildness,* and *spirit of conciliation.*"[10] Faint praise indeed for the leader of the country and the Virginia Republican dynasty he inherited!

In response, Monroe reached deep into his store of sentimental performing arts. Speaking in general of his tour, he proclaimed himself "unable to express my emotions." "I have never before been so affected. Such distinguished attentions, such unexpected effusions of regard, as I experience from my fellow citizens, do indeed sink deep into my heart." Although he had not wanted such festivity to attend his tour, the arrangements had made possible the "personal interview" of the citizens with the one citizen they had chosen as chief magistrate.

> Nor can I ever regret that I have thus afforded myself so many opportunities of seeing and feeling how much we are one people; how strongly the ties by which we are united, do in fact bind us together; how much we possess in reality, a country not only of interest, but of sympathy and affection.

9. Jeremiah Mason to Rufus King, June 26, 1817, in Hillard, ed., *Memoir and Correspondence,* 160; *Columbian Centinel; Massachusetts Federalist* (Boston), July 12, 1817; *Connecticut Courant* (Hartford), July 6, 13, 20, 27, Aug. 3, 1817; William Bentley, *The Diary of William Bentley, D.D. . . .* (Salem, Mass., 1905–1914), IV, 459, 463; *Boston Patriot and Daily Chronicle* (paraphrasing the *Salem Register*), July 16, 1817; *Narrative of a Tour of Observation,* 213–215; Waldo, *Tour of James Monroe,* 270–272. One Virginian, a Federalist, wrote to a political ally: "Monroe will have been so feasted upon his northern tour that I think it highly probable that he will have the gout. He is a pretty statesman to call upon the widow Robert Morris." J. Marshall, Jr., to Charles Prentiss, July 10, 1817, Charles Prentiss Papers, AAS.

10. *Narrative of a Tour of Observation,* 146–147.

Reminding himself that his hearers might well doubt the harmony of the present, Monroe then appealed not only to what was but to what would be:

> The United States are certainly the most enlightened people on earth. We are certainly rapidly advancing on the road of national pre-eminence. Nothing but Union is wanting to make us a great people. The present time affords the happiest presages that this union is fast consummating. It cannot be otherwise. I daily see greater proofs of it: the further I advance in my progress, the more I perceive that we are all Americans. . . . Nothing could give me greater satisfaction than to behold a perfect union among ourselves . . . an union too, which is necessary to restore to social intercourse its former charms, and to render our happiness, as a nation, unmixed and complete.[11]

Union already existed but was always in a state of becoming; visible expressions of patriotic sympathies created the very thing they were supposed to reveal. This reprise of Washington's tour by itself sent America down "the road of national pre-eminence," toward that happy place where union would be "unmixed and complete."

The beginning of Monroe's administration coincided with another important and influential attempt to render America "unmixed": the American Colonization Society. Conspicuous among the important new progressive associations in Waldo's *Tour of James Monroe,* the Colonization Society's express purpose was the voluntary removal of free blacks —not slaves—beyond the geographic bounds of the United States. No voluntary association, even in that great age of voluntary associations, ever had a more auspicious, or a more national, beginning. At a first meeting in the chamber of the House of Representatives on December 28, 1816, a group of prominent citizens approved the society's constitution and elected a slate of officers that reads like an honor roll of early-nineteenth-century politics: Henry Clay, William H. Crawford, John Taylor of Caroline, Richard Rush, and even the western war hero, Andrew Jackson. Bushrod Washington, stepson of the father of his country, signed on to serve as president.[12]

11. Ibid., 149–150; see also Monroe's comments on returning to Washington, 228.

12. Waldo, *Tour of James Monroe,* 116–117; [American Colonization Society], *A View of Exertions Lately Made for the Purpose of Colonizing the Free People of Color, in the*

From its very first meetings the ACS made two facts about itself clear. First, the society presented itself as a patriotic, benevolent institution that deserved *national* support. Its secretary, Elias Caldwell, even suggested that the colonization of Africa should be funded by the federal government. Second, the colonizationists disclaimed any intention to meddle with slavery. Although some abolitionists (especially in New England) interpreted colonization as a way to ameliorate and ultimately eliminate slavery, the founders of the ACS explicitly denied that their scheme was a prelude to emancipation. Year after year the annual report insisted that the elimination of the free black population would actually reverse disturbing trends by making black bondpersons more obedient and reducing the likelihood of slave revolts. Colonization would ultimately secure present and future property in land and slaves.[13]

Having once again defeated British schemes to keep them in colonial dependence, the leaders of expanding America—especially those who hailed from the South and the West—sought a colonial answer to their own postcolonial problems. In one version that became increasingly popular, Africans would colonize Africa much as they had helped colonize America, reaping benefits for both whites and (supposedly) themselves. This scheme proved more satisfying than the idea of sending free blacks west, where they might interfere with the further colonization of native lands after the Indians' defeat in 1815. Although figures like Clay, Jackson, Crawford, Taylor, and Rush would later disagree about the ways and means of economic development, about the purview of the federal government, and about the role of ordinary white men in public life,

---

United States, in Africa, or Elsewhere (Washington, D.C., 1817); "Colonization of Free Blacks," *Union* (Washington, Ky.), Jan. 24, 1817. The standard accounts of the ACS's origins, those of Early Lee Fox and Philip Staudenraus, have been challenged by Douglas R. Egerton, " 'Its Origin Is Not a Little Curious': A New Look at the American Colonization Society," *Journal of the Early Republic*, V (1985), 463–480, which stresses that the ACS, whatever the motives of some of its later participants, was not in origin "a religiously inspired, benevolent, mildly emancipationist reform movement." For similar interpretations, see Winthrop D. Jordan, *White over Black: American Attitudes toward the Negro, 1550–1812* (Chapel Hill, N.C., 1968), 546–577; Lawrence J. Friedman, *Inventors of the Promised Land* (New York, 1975), 185–219.

13. [ACS], *View of Exertions*, 7, 10; *The First Annual Report of the American Society for Colonizing the Free People of Color, of the United States* (Washington, D.C., 1818), 15; *The Second Annual Report of the American Society for Colonizing the Free People of Colour in the United States*, 2d ed. (Washington, D.C., 1819), 9.

they shared a desire to replicate the British colonial system internally, in the expanding American empire, at the expense of free blacks and unassimilable natives, who were both to be removed and recolonized.[14]

Throughout the upper southern, western, and middle states, the ACS received very favorable initial press reports. For many whites, the national problem was not slavery. It was the problem of freedom vested in a population whose equality they denied. In their earliest published statements colonizationists expressed great discomfort with free blacks' "anomalous and indefinite relations to the political and social ties of the community." Unbound Africans, explained Henry Clay, were really neither slave nor free. White America's "unconquerable prejudices" made it necessary to "drive them off" to some other realm. Early members of the ACS displayed considerable ideological flexibility in blaming the condition of this "intermediate class" simultaneously on white racism and on that class's own tendency to "pervert the shadow of liberty which they enjoy, into purposes of crime, and self-debasement." All this could change, however—with their removal from America. Once in Africa, now the bearers of American civilization, these Africans would become "changed and respectable," even to the point of Christianizing Africa and providing an outlet for American manufactures. It is little wonder that during the 1820s the ACS would take to the streets every Fourth of July.[15]

14. Gary B. Nash, *Race and Revolution* (Madison, Wis., 1990), 42–50; John Ashworth, *Slavery, Capitalism, and Politics in the Antebellum Republic,* I, *Commerce and Compromise, 1820–1850* (New York, 1995), 44–45; Robert E. Berkhofer, Jr., *The White Man's Indian: Images of the American Indian from Columbus to the Present* (New York, 1978), 134–166; Brian W. Dippie, *The Vanishing American: White Attitudes and U.S. Indian Policy* (Middletown, Conn., 1982), 51, 56–78.

15. "Colonization of Africa," *Poulson's American Daily Advertiser* (Philadelphia), Jan. 2, 1817; "Colonization of the Blacks" (from New York), *Eagle* (Maysville, Ky.), Nov. 6, 1817; "American Colonization Society: Memorial," *Weekly Messenger* (Russellville, Ky.), Mar. 21, 1820; [ACS], *View of Exertions,* 5, 14; George Washington Edwards Philips Journal, 1817, typescript, 110–111, Special Collections Library, Duke University; Minutes of the Virginia Branch of the American Colonization Society, Jan. 16, 1826, MS Minutebook, Virginia Historical Society; Friedman, *Inventors of the Promised Land,* 188; Leonard I. Sweet, "The Fourth of July and Black Americans in the Nineteenth Century: Northern Leadership Opinion within the Context of the Black Experience," *Journal of Negro History,* LXI (1976), 260–261; *Connecticut Mirror* (Hartford), June 20, July 4, 11, 1829, July 9, 1831.

Interestingly, the Manumission and Colonization Society of North Carolina, founded literally the same week as the ACS, invoked the older rationale that slavery

The nationalist and neocolonial dimensions of the early colonization movement may be seen most vividly through the writings of one of its first publicists, the Reverend Robert Finley. Finley had corresponded with and met free blacks who had themselves proposed emigration, and he impressed some of them as genuinely interested in the welfare of African Americans.[16] His publications, however, epitomize a nationalist ideology that could comprehend nothing but a wholly white America.

Finley began his *Thoughts on the Colonization of Free Blacks* (1816) by asking, "What shall we do with the free people of color?" His answer—that they should be completely separated from whites in a colony placed far enough away to be unreachable by runaway slaves—could not but concede that the American dream of a virtuous, independent, nation had fallen upon hard times. "Most nations have had their colonies," insisted this citizen of the first postcolonial nation. After only forty years the rebels had to turn colonizers if they would solve their great national dilemma. The previously enslaved Africans would happily do the actual work of colonization: "Many have both the means and the disposition to go . . . where they could assume the rank of men, and act their part upon the great theatre of life." Nonetheless, Finley put little stock in black initiative. His plea for colonization addressed a white audience: "Remove them. Place them in some climate congenial with their color and constitution." As easily as they had been taken, they could be re-

---

was inconsistent with Revolutionary ideals. It did, however, forbid its members from speaking of manumission or colonization "in the presence of any person of colour . . . in such a manner as to hold out to him the idea of the liberation of the slaves." Constitution of the Manumission and Colonization Society of North Carolina, [Dec. 20, 1816], photocopy, Ohio Historical Society.

16. Floyd J. Miller, *The Search for a Black Nationality: Black Emigration and Colonization, 1787–1863* (Urbana, Ill., 1975), 45; Julie Winch, *Philadelphia's Black Elite: Activism, Accommodation, and the Struggle for Autonomy, 1787–1848* (Philadelphia, 1988), 36. Benjamin Quarles notes that Finley failed to persuade Philadelphia's free blacks to favor colonization *(Black Abolitionists* [New York, 1969], 4–5). Egerton, "'Its Origin Is Not a Little Curious,'" *Journal of the Early Republic,* V (1985), 463–480, downplays the importance of Finley in founding the ACS in favor of the Virginian, Charles Fenton Mercer. Yet Finley played a key role in garnering northern support for the organization—support that would crucially fashion a movement that was divided in its early years between slaveholders and nonslaveholders. Finley can be seen as a middle-state maverick who played both sides of the slavery-reform fence: a predecessor of those compromising characters who served such crucial functions in the compromises of 1820, 1850, and so many of the years in between.

moved. Whites would govern the colony until blacks had been raised high enough for self-government.[17]

After the ACS earned the vociferous objections of many free blacks, Finley had to resort to a more complex literary form in order to resolve the new obstacles to colonization. In his "Dialogues on the African Colony" (1818) Finley elevated the debate over America's racial future to heaven, where no personal interests or prejudices prevented an open discussion (and where he could put the right words into the mouths of dead men, black and white). Within the pearly gates, the father of American ethnic and religious tolerance, William Penn, asks two recently deceased black men their opinion on colonization: Paul Cuffe, the most active black proponent of emigration to Africa, and the Reverend Absalom Jones, whose Philadelphia black community had just condemned the ACS. Penn has heard of the colonization scheme and is concerned. Is it a violent attempt to rid America of its black population? Cuffe responds that it is quite the opposite: a benevolent plan to save Americans from "their deepest national sin, that of slavery." Jones, however, protests that free blacks rightly see colonization as merely the latest of the racist insults and material injuries they face in the United States every day. At the end of the first dialogue, Penn promises to consult with his good friend George Washington about the matter.[18]

In the second dialogue Penn returns from his conference with the founding father (who, it seems, even in heaven cannot be portrayed in conversation with black leaders). Not surprisingly, Washington and all his fellow champions of the rights of man stand resolutely in favor of colonization. When Jones expresses surprise, Penn explains the gentleness of the ACS plan: no one would be compelled to go to Africa, and only ten thousand settlers would be needed to initiate a viable colony. Why won't the government set aside western lands for free blacks? Penn replies that the white population is fast moving there; the "same scenes"

17. [Robert Finley], *Thoughts on the Colonization of Free Blacks* ([Washington, D.C.], 1816).

18. Robert Finley, "Dialogues on the African Colony," in Isaac V. Brown, ed., *Memoirs of the Rev. Robert Finley, D.D.* . . . (New Brunswick, N.J., 1819), 313–345, quoted at 317. This piece first appeared in the *Union* in June 1818. On Cuffe and colonization, see Miller, *Search for a Black Nationality*, 21–48; Lamont D. Thomas, *Rise to Be a People: A Biography of Paul Cuffe* (Urbana, Ill., 1986). On Jones, see Gary B. Nash, *Forging Freedom: The Making of Philadelphia's Black Community, 1720–1840* (Cambridge, Mass., 1988), 111–130, 237–240.

of racial conflict would inevitably occur. Equality and emancipation are "visionary expectations"; colonization, on the other hand, will even encourage manumissions. And when Jones insists that things are improving for blacks in the United States, Cuffe responds that white prejudice is inexorable: "If the Africans wish to elevate themselves to the rank and respectability of Americans and Europeans, let them establish a colony upon the coast of Africa."[19] Africans of any "rank" or "respectability" belong in Africa. They cannot be American.

Where Finley considers white racism, its sources, and its effects upon blacks, he ventriloquizes dead blacks to perform the task of exculpation for him. In this particular whitewashing of history, Jones and Cuffe speak wholly of the present and the future, saving Penn (not to mention Washington) from any inquiry into their own historical complicity in slavery or racial prejudice. The sins of the past and the present have no particular perpetrators. Because prejudice is long-standing, it is permanent; everyone theoretically (and thus no one practically) can be blamed. When Jones asks why slaveholding "southern nabobs" seem to love colonization, the politically neutral middle-state founder, Penn, steps in to blame northerners who promote sectionalism by speaking bitterly of southerners. In the end it is the original white founder who, backed by the invisible, higher word of Washington, insists that emancipation must be gradual and that colonization will allow America to repay Africa by giving her, over time, "an industrious and humanized people." Cuffe can only add that these industrious and humanized blacks will be effective Christian missionaries as well. "The day that beholds such an expedition embark from the shores of America," Penn concludes, "should be celebrated as a jubilee, throughout the civilized world."[20]

Finley's willingness to manipulate black voices reveals the consistency of his efforts. Although he found it necessary to work with African Americans to ensure their voluntary cooperation, for him the question remained, "What shall we do with the free people of color?" Yet even Finley's fantasy can be read for what it unintentionally reveals about African Americans' actions and desires. The last word is that of Absalom Jones, who accedes to colonization for the good of "the African

19. Finley, "Dialogues," in Brown, ed., *Memoirs of Finley*, 326, 330. Here, as elsewhere, Finley paraphrases Cuffe's actual words (from published letters) while wrenching them out of their context.

20. Ibid., 332–345.

nation." Here, Africans in America *are* a nation, whether they return to Africa or not: Jones asserts the black respectability that colonization ideology would defer to another time and place.

Ultimately, the reality of the growing free black community and the insistence of its leaders that their community was a nation within a nation made Finley's truly colonizing act of ventriloquism possible in the first place. Abolitionism and black nationalism fed the imagination of the American Colonization Society; the colonizationists' white nationalism sought to deflate the criticisms, aspirations, and appropriations of black abolitionists and their white allies. Even the rhetorical flourish by which Finley made the whitening of America a cause for jubilation was probably responding to more radical uses of the Fourth of July than those that Finley and his heaven-bound founders had ever imagined.

"DECLARATION OF INDEPENDENCE! WHERE ART THOU NOW?"

The Revolution brought great changes to the lives of blacks in America. In the South, tens of thousands of slaves left their masters when the opportunity arose, especially after the British forces under Lord Dunmore offered freedom to runaways. Slave revolts increased during the era, as they always had during periods of social and political disorder. The Revolution itself can be viewed as a "triangularity of events" in which the efforts of slaves to secure their freedom decisively shaped white military strategies and encouraged tories and whigs alike to make promises of liberty to blacks. That both sides often failed to keep these promises did not prevent tens of thousands of slaves from gaining their freedom. Migration and an increase in manumissions also led to the growth of the free population in the North, where African Americans began to establish the religious and secular institutions that would shape black communal life in the coming century.[21]

21. Ira Berlin, "The Revolution in Black Life," in Alfred F. Young, ed., *The American Revolution: Explorations in the History of American Radicalism* (DeKalb, Ill., 1976), 349–382; Benjamin Quarles, "The Revolutionary War as a Black Declaration of Independence," in Ira Berlin and Ronald Hoffman, eds., *Slavery and Freedom in the Age of the American Revolution* (Urbana, Ill., 1983), 283–301; Peter H. Wood, "'Liberty Is Sweet': African-American Freedom Struggles in the Years before White Independence," in Alfred F. Young, ed., *Beyond the American Revolution: Explorations in the History of American Radicalism* (DeKalb, Ill., 1993), 149–184; Sylvia R. Frey, *Water from the Rock: Black Resistance in a Revolutionary Age* (Princeton, N.J., 1991), 55; Gary B.

No one was quicker to perceive the tensions between the Revolution's rhetoric of freedom and the reality of slavery than the slaves, ex-slaves, and kin of slaves themselves. Petitions sent to the Massachusetts and Connecticut legislatures by slaves in the early and middle 1770s are quite explicit about blacks' "natur[a]l right to our freedom" and in linking the patriots' "present glorious struggle for liberty" to liberation for the patriots' slaves. "We expect great things from men who have made such a noble stand against the designs of their *fellow-men* to enslave them," wrote four Boston bondmen in a follow-up missive to their 1773 petition. Even before Independence, literate and nonliterate blacks managed to turn around the central metaphor of "slavery" to highlight the injustices they had long suffered and continued to suffer from the partisans of "liberty." The sharp irony of these petitions undercuts the hubris of Anglo-American claims to virtue.[22]

Despite the considerable material and political interests that made even discussion seem dangerous, during the next several decades a near cultural consensus emerged that American slavery was an anomaly, inconsistent with progressive ideals.[23] In his initial draft of the Declaration of Independence, Jefferson blamed this anomaly, as he blamed everything else, on the king of England. But after the success of the Revolution and the post-Revolutionary identification of all progress in liberty with America and its future, the contradiction of slavery in a free land could not be so easily foisted upon past generations. Whatever the Constitution permitted or forbade in national legislation regarding slavery, the existence of the nation made it possible to define slavery as a *national* sin. If America was a genuine republic and "genuine republicanism" dictated that "all men are equal," American slavery

---

Nash, "Forging Freedom: The Emancipation Experience in the Northern Seaport Cities, 1775–1820," in Berlin and Hoffman, eds., *Slavery and Freedom*, 3–48.

22. Petitions in Herbert Aptheker, ed., *A Documentary History of the Negro People in the United States* (New York, 1951), I, 7, 8, 10; Sidney Kaplan and Emma Nogrady Kaplan, *The Black Presence in the Era of the American Revolution*, rev. ed. (Amherst, Mass., 1987), 26–31; Thomas J. Davis, "Emancipation Rhetoric, Natural Rights, and Revolutionary New England: A Note on Four Black Petitions in Massachusetts, 1773–1777," *New England Quarterly*, LXII (1989), 248–263; Dickson D. Bruce, Jr., "National Identity and Early African-American Colonization, 1773–1817," *Historian*, LVIII (1995), 15–28.

23. Why this consensus emerged and what difference it made are the subject of David Brion Davis, *The Problem of Slavery in the Age of Revolution, 1770–1823* (Ithaca, N.Y., 1975).

could be only "an inconsistency with their national character," "inconsistent with the declared principles of the American Revolution." Even as the northern states passed gradual-emancipation laws and Federalists began to fear the South as a menacing slave power, antislavery writers, orators, and Fourth of July celebrants continued to call slavery a "national calamity," "the disgrace of our country," and a "Spot on our National Character."[24]

Although antislavery made its first gains in state-by-state campaigns, antislavery activists spoke in a nationalist idiom. Scholars have begun to analyze the ways in which nationalism provides a context and a justification for racism. The two -isms have often reinforced each other, in ways that differ according to specific historical contexts. In the case of post-Revolutionary America, it was *antiracism* (as antislavery) that first achieved historical articulation within nationalism. Racism preceded nationalism just as slavery long preceded the Revolution. Later, the American Colonization Society would set a pattern for the "white nationalism" of the nineteenth century.[25] That racist nationalism, how-

24. Othello, "Negro Slavery" (1788), in Carter G. Woodson, ed., *Negro Orators and Their Orations* (New York, 1969), 19; "To Marcus," *Freeman's Journal* (Cincinnati), Mar. 5, 1799; *American Citizen and General Advertiser* (New York), July 12, 1802; "Slavery Authorized by Law in the Indiana Territory," *National Intelligencer and Washington Advertiser*, Mar. 7, 1806; "A Spot on Our National Character," *Columbian Centinel; Massachusetts Federalist*, July 17, 1816; Joseph Pope, *An Oration, Pronounced July 4th, 1804* . . . (Portland, Maine, [1804]), 20–21; "The Sons of Columbia, O Hail the Great Day," *Odes for the 4th of July—1807* (n.d., n.p.), Broadsides Collection, AAS; Nathan Perkins, *The National Sins, and National Punishment in the Recently Declared War; Considered in a Sermon Delivered, July 23, 1812* . . . (Hartford, Conn., 1812), 16–18. The nationalization of slavery by the Constitution was one of the Antifederalist Luther Martin's main objections to the document (Davis, *Problem of Slavery in the Age of Revolution*, 323; Nash, *Race and Revolution*, 26, 142–143).

25. Etienne Balibar and Immanuel Wallerstein, *Race, Nation, Class: Ambiguous Identities* (London, 1991), 9, 50, 52; George M. Fredrickson, *The Black Image in the White Mind: The Debate on Afro-American Character and Destiny, 1817–1914* (1971; rpt. Middletown, Conn., 1987), 1–42, 97–164. Considering both native Americans and African Americans in white discourse, Carroll Smith-Rosenberg argues for the constitutive role of racism in the construction of the national subject at the time of the debate over the Constitution. See Smith-Rosenberg, "Dis-Covering the Subject of the 'Great Constitutional Discussion,' 1786–1789," *Journal of American History*, LXXIX (1992–1993), 841–873; "Subject Female: Authorizing American Identity," *American Literary History*, V (1993), 481–511; "Captured Subjects / Savage Others: Violently Engendering the New American," *Gender and History*, V (1993), 177–195.

ever, was in part a reaction to the nationalist abolitionism of the post-Revolutionary era.

From the very moment of national Independence, black and white abolitionists seized upon the Declaration of Independence to show that the American Revolution meant equality for all people, at least as much as it meant American national autonomy. Indeed, they insisted that the one was meaningless without the other. The most striking example of this is the black preacher Lemuel Haynes's long buried manuscript, "Liberty Further Extended" (1776), which quotes the Declaration's injunction, "All men are created equal," on its very first page. Likewise, Abraham Bishop pointed to the Declaration in praising the Saint Domingue slave revolts: "We did not say, all *white* men are *free*, but *all men* are free." If the Declaration was the prooftext of freedom, July Fourth, its anniversary, could only be the date when all unrequited claims to liberty and the pursuit of happiness should be most publicly presented. "And why should not Afric's sons be happy too?" asked William Rogers in his 1789 Independence Day oration.[26]

During the early 1790s the abolition societies of Maryland and Pennsylvania began to hold their annual meetings on Independence Day. Their orators challenged the complacent assumption that the new nation was the seat of perfect enlightenment. "While the Americans celebrate the anniversary of Freedom and Independence," noted George Buchanan before a Baltimore audience, "abject slavery exists in all her states but one."

Deceitful men! Who could have suggested that American patriotism would at this day countenance a conduct so inconsistent; that while

26. Ruth Bogin, "'Liberty Further Extended': A 1776 Antislavery Manuscript by Lemuel Haynes," *William and Mary Quarterly*, 3d Ser., XL (1983), 85–105; Abraham Bishop, "Rights of Black Men" (1791), in Tim Mathewson, "Abraham Bishop, 'The Rights of Black Men,' and the American Reaction to the Haitian Revolution," *Journal of Negro History*, LXVII (1982), 153; letter of "Humanitas" (from *Baltimore Evening Post*), *Dunlap's American Daily Advertiser* (Philadelphia), July 5, 1793; "Constitution of the Chester-town Society for Promoting the Abolition of Slavery, and the Relief of Free Negroes, and Others, Unlawfully Held in Bondage," *Delaware Gazette* (Wilmington), June 14, 1792; William Rogers, *An Oration, Delivered July 4, 1789 . . .* (Philadelphia, 1789), 15; see also Robert Porter, *An Oration, to Commemorate the Independence of the United States of North-America . . .* (Philadelphia, 1791), 23; Samuel Miller, *A Sermon, Preached in New-York, July 4th, 1793 . . .* (New York, [1793]), 27; Samuel Worcester, *An Oration, Delivered at the College Chapel, Hanover, on the Anniversary of American Independence, July Fourth, 1795* (Hanover, N.H., 1795), 7–9, 11.

America boasts of being a land of freedom, and an asylum for the oppressed of Europe, she should at the same time foster an abominable nursery for slaves to check the shoots of her glorious liberty?

The connection between the acts of national celebration and the solution to the problem of slavery was soon written into law by New York and New Jersey. The New York Gradual Emancipation Act provided eventual freedom for all slaves born after July 4, 1799 (men upon their twenty-eighth birthday, women upon their twenty-fifth). Similarly, in 1804 New Jersey freed all the blacks born in the state after the following Fourth of July.[27]

Throughout the 1790s and early 1800s, some revelers used Independence Day and other national celebrations to damn slavery or to toast its end. Although Federalists claimed the most prominent abolitionists in the northern states, some Republicans still threw caution (and the national Jeffersonian alliance) to the winds, as Cincinnati Republicans did in 1802 when they raised their glasses to "The Enslaved Sons of Africa." After all, even if Jefferson was a slaveholder, he was also the author of the Declaration of Independence. Surveying the world battle of liberty against slavery, Boston's Jeffersonian orator of 1805 noted the sad fate of the kidnapped Americans in Tripoli—and "the Africans in our own country."[28]

On July 10, 1800, a remarkable antislavery oration appeared in Con-

27. *Independent Gazetteer, and Agricultural Repository* (Philadelphia), July 9, 1791; *Maryland Journal* (Baltimore), July 5, 1793, July 7, 1794; George Buchanan, *An Oration upon the Moral and Political Evil of Slavery* . . . (Baltimore, 1793), 13; Arthur Zilversmit, *The First Emancipations: The Abolition of Slavery in the North* (Chicago, 1967), 181–182, 193; Shane White, *Somewhat More Independent: The End of Slavery in New York City, 1770–1810* (Athens, Ga., 1991), 38, 53–54.

28. New York City Society of Tammany or Columbian Order, Committee of Amusements, Minutebook, 1791–1795, 17, New York Public Library; *General Advertiser and Political, Commercial, and Literary Journal* (Philadelphia), Oct. 20, 1792 (New York), Feb. 12, 1793 (Brookline); *Dunlap's American Daily Advertiser* (Philadelphia), Aug. 2, 1794 (Deerfield); *New York Commercial Advertiser*, July 9, 1798; Joseph Locke, *An Oration, Pronounced at Billerica, July 5, 1802* . . . (Boston, 1802), 20; "Pickaway Plains, July 5, 1802," *Scioto Gazette* (Chillicothe, Ohio), July 10, 1802; *Aurora; General Advertiser* (Philadelphia), July 10, 1804, July 15, 1806; Hosea Ballou, *An Oration, Pronounced in the Meeting-House in Hartland, on the Fourth of July, 1807* (Randolph, Vt., 1807), 14; *Western Spy, and Hamilton Gazette* (Cincinnati), July 10, 1802; Ebenezer French, *An Oration, Pronounced July 4th, 1805, before the Young Democratic Republicans, of the Town of Boston* . . . (Boston, 1805), 6–7.

necticut's decidedly Jeffersonian *American Mercury.* It maintained that, if the Fourth had any meaning at all, it lay, not in "mere national independence," but rather in "the genuine, universal principles of the declaration of independence," which established that "all men are created EQUAL." The Declaration had inspired revolutions all over the world, including the revenge of the black race upon their enslavers in Saint Domingue. The author hoped that the Fourth would inspire "Ethiop," asking of blacks: "Curse us not—some of us have principles of justice and bowels of compassion—we will raise thee to freedom, if we do not restore thee to long lost Africa!" Meanwhile, for anyone who held to the true principles of the Declaration, slavery could be only a source of shame. "Citizens, my soul shrinks from herself, and startles at the name of Africa! . . . Declaration of Independence! Where art thou now?"[29]

National celebrations were not merely a convenient venue for critiques of slavery. Rather, they were integral to making the case that slavery was a national problem that contradicted the nation's founding ideals. A number of the first published attacks on slavery in the new nation took the form of (probably undelivered) festival orations. President Washington's February 19, 1795, national Thanksgiving provided the occasion for *Tyrannical Libertymen: A Discourse upon Negro-Slavery in the United States* to appear. Taking issue with the argument that the affairs of the separate states, including slave laws, were no business of the inhabitants of other states, the anonymous author retorted that, if this were so, "Our joining together in the celebration of this national thanksgiving is altogether a farce." The nation's churches were "probably ringing with *rights and privileges*" on such a day:

> But shame to the whole union, that more than a seventh part of the human beings in these states can, with no manner of propriety, join in any of these topics. They are not of the nation; and therefore, have no national blessings to acknowledge. They have no share in the commonwealth. They are politically nothing. And by celebrating this day, we subscribe to their nonexistence.[30]

29. See "An Oration Delivered by a Citizen of the United States, on the 4th of July," *American Mercury* (Hartford), July 10, 1800, also reprinted in *An Oration Delivered on the Fourth Day of July 1800, by a Citizen of the United States, to Which Is Added the Female Advocate, Written by a Lady* . . . (Springfield, Mass., 1808).

30. *Tyrannical Libertymen: A Discourse upon Negro-Slavery in the United States: Composed at* ———, *in New Hampshire; on the Late Federal Thanksgiving-Day* (Hanover, N.H., 1795), 10–11. The only scholar who seems to have noticed this remarkable

In well-publicized acts of celebration Americans "subscribe" to nationality and become, politically, something. In doing so they also subscribe to the continual exclusion of slaves and free blacks from American nationality.

Although the eloquence of these anonymous writers may shock us into a realization of what was at stake on the Fourth of July, they were hardly the only contemporaries to notice the whiteness of the rites, as well as of the rights, of American liberty. As I have noted earlier, free blacks made the point themselves through their persistent presence at the margins of festivity. If they could truly have been made invisible, there would have been no need for Charleston's Vauxhall Gardens to advertise for the Fourth in 1799, "No admittance for people of Color." What is admitted aloud must be resolved somehow, and the distinctions made on every holiday came to seem especially telling in the South. Thomas Holland, the 1807 Independence Day orator in Rutherford, North Carolina, though he would have "like[d] to say that Liberty and Equality reign here triumphant," concluded: "There remains still an objection: my countrymen, look at our own slaves." Edward Hooker, a Yale graduate who taught school in South Carolina, experienced culture shock when he attended his first southern Independence Day in 1805:

> The tables were served by negro slaves under the superintendence of the managers. What an incongruity! An independence dinner for freemen and slaves to wait upon them. I couldn't keep the thought out of my mind the whole time I was feasting.

Two years later, in Columbia, Hooker served on a committee to draw up a list of July Fourth toasts. When he proposed a fairly innocuous rights of man toast ("The principles of rational liberty—May the blessed period ere long arrive when they shall prevail through the globe"), his hosts suddenly grew silent. Though Hooker explained that he referred to the liberty of nations, not slaves, the native South Carolinians prevailed: the toast was not accepted. In an age of slave revolts, the

---

piece is Winthrop Jordan in his magisterial *White over Black,* 547–548. Jordan mainly notes that the author's "fervent equalitarianism led directly to Negro removal." The text, however, plainly suggests that blacks should be encouraged to settle a western American territory that eventually should receive representation in Congress—a mark of equality that few, if any, later colonizationists would propose (*Tyrannical Libertymen,* 10).

celebration of liberty and its extension to all nations remained a risky business.[31]

As Eugene D. Genovese has observed, it is striking how often black revolutionaries planned slave revolts for the days of jubilee. A failed plot in Camden, South Carolina, had been set for July 4, 1816; Denmark Vesey planned his rebellion for July 14, Bastille Day; and Nat Turner himself scheduled the "work of death" to begin on Independence Day. Holidays, of course, provided opportunities to catch whites off guard. Yet when we begin to see African Americans, slave and free, as partaking of a cultural and political milieu that reached beyond the slave quarters and black neighborhoods, it becomes easier to understand why one of the defendants in the trial of Gabriel's conspiracy of 1800 compared his actions to George Washington's. Gabriel and many of his followers, after all, were members of a multiracial "Atlantic working class" that, clustered in or near seaport towns, had ample exposure to the ideals of the democratic revolutions in both hemispheres.[32]

31. "Vauxhall Garden," *South-Carolina State Gazette, and Timothy's Daily Advertiser* (Charleston), July 4, 1799; "Oration Delivered by Thomas Holland," *Miller's Weekly Messenger* (Pendleton, S.C.), July 30, Aug. 5, 1807; "The Fourth of July," *Raleigh Register, and North-Carolina State Gazette,* Aug. 6, 1807; J. Franklin Jameson, ed., "The Diary of Edward Hooker, 1805–1808," American Historical Association, *Annual Report,* 1896 (Washington, D.C., 1897), I, 900, 904–905.

32. Eugene D. Genovese, *From Rebellion to Revolution: Afro-American Slave Revolts in the Making of the Modern World* (New York, 1981), 129–130; Aptheker, ed., *Documentary History,* I, 50–51; "Insurrection of the Negroes," *Yankee* (Boston), July 26, 1816; *Camden Gazette* (S.C.), July 11, 1816; Henry W. DeSaussure to Timothy Ford, July 8, 1816, Ford-Ravenel Papers, South Carolina Historical Society; Herbert Aptheker, *American Negro Slave Revolts,* rev. ed. (New York, 1974), 257; *The Confessions of Nat Turner* (1831), excerpted in David Brion Davis, ed., *Antebellum American Culture* (Lexington, Mass., 1979), 317; Douglas R. Egerton, *Gabriel's Rebellion: The Virginia Slave Conspiracies of 1800 and 1802* (Chapel Hill, N.C., 1993), 34–68, 102; John Lofton, *Denmark Vesey's Revolt: The Slave Plot That Lit a Fuse to Fort Sumter,* rev. ed. (Kent, Ohio, 1983), 54–74. Peter Linebaugh and Marcus Rediker's forthcoming work will trace the lineaments of the "Atlantic working class"; see Linebaugh, "Jubilating; or, How the Atlantic Working Class Used the Biblical Jubilee against Capitalism, with Some Success," *Radical History Review,* L (1991), 143–180; Linebaugh and Rediker, "The International Working Class in the Age of Revolution," paper presented at meeting of the Organization of American Historians, Atlanta, April 1994; Rediker, "A Motley Class of Rebels: Sailors, Slaves, and the Coming of the Revolution," in Ronald Hoffman and Peter J. Albert, eds., *The Transforming Hand of Revo-*

According to a letter between two abolitionists in 1862, blacks who plotted an insurrection near Charleston in 1813 sang a "Hymn of Freedom" to open and close their meetings. Sterling Stuckey and other scholars have rightly cited this hymn as evidence of a "nationalist or separatist thrust" in early-nineteenth-century black thought. Yet this "Hymn" can hardly be said to be a product of African culture. It was actually a riff on one of the most popular American nationalist songs of the era: "Hail, Columbia" (1798) (reprinted overleaf).[33]

African culture did have its influence on free blacks as well as slaves.[34] There can be no doubt that shared cultural traditions, of whatever ori-

lution: Reconsidering the American Revolution as a Social Movement (Charlottesville, Va., 1995), 155–198. Paul Gilroy writes of a black Atlantic diaspora formed by the population shifts, voluntary and involuntary, that characterize the last several centuries: *The Black Atlantic: Modernity and Double Consciousness* (Cambridge, Mass., 1993).

33. Sterling Stuckey, "Classical Black Nationalist Thought" (1972), in his *Going through the Storm: The Influence of African American Art in History* (New York, 1994), 85; Stuckey, *Slave Culture: Nationalist Theory and the Foundations of Black America* (New York, 1987), 49; John Hammond Moore, "A Hymn of Freedom—South Carolina, 1813," *Journal of Negro History,* L (1965), 50–53. According to Archie Epps (who offers no source), this song was also sung at Denmark Vesey's meetings ("A Negro Separatist Movement," *Harvard Review,* IV [1966], 75); this was picked up and amplified by Sterling Stuckey in "Through the Prism of Folklore: The Black Ethos in Slavery" (1968), in Stuckey, *Going through the Storm,* 10. In the introduction to his pathbreaking anthology *The Ideological Origins of Black Nationalism* (Boston, 1972), Stuckey made the song a sign of the singers' Africanness; later, in *Slave Culture,* he modified this claim: "The principles of the Age of Reason and those of African nationalism were joined, illustrating their compatibility for the blacks who sang. . . . African and European political as well as religious ideals at times mingled and united, the one preparing the ground for the other" (49). Vincent Harding also speculated on a connection between these singers and Vesey's conspiracy, and placed the song in the Atlantic context of black rebellions, in *The Other American Revolution* (Los Angeles, 1980), 24–25; and in *There is a River: The Black Struggle for Freedom in America* (New York, 1981), 62–63.

For the text, see Joseph Hopkinson, *The Favorite Song Adapted to the Federal Song President's March* (Philadelphia, 1798), reproduced in Vera Brodsky Lawrence, *Music for Patriots, Politicians, and Presidents: Harmonies and Discords of the First Hundred Years* (New York, 1975), 144–145. For the writing of the song, see Burton Alva Konkle, *Joseph Hopkinson, 1770–1842: Jurist: Scholar: Inspirer of the Arts* (Philadelphia, 1931), 69–84.

34. Stuckey, *Slave Culture;* Stuckey, *Going through the Storm;* William D. Piersen, *Black Yankees: The Development of an Afro-American Subculture in Eighteenth-Century New England* (Amherst, Mass., 1988).

gin, contributed to African-American solidarity in the eighteenth and nineteenth centuries. But the outspoken nationalism of these Northern and Southern blacks drew less on recognized and preserved Africanisms than on the nationalist popular political culture that pervaded American public life at this time. These Africans invented Africa in the New World, in response to revolutionary conditions and out of Revolutionary rhetoric. By the time Nat Turner set his sights on the Fourth of July, African Americans had been appropriating the practices of American nationalism for more than half a century.

Much of Phillis Wheatley's poetry, for example, participated directly in the Revolutionary politics of celebration. For Wheatley to publish at all made her an effective agent for antislavery: for decades her achievement was cited as evidence of black capabilities. And a few of the poems do even more. Though less well known today, her occasional verses celebrating figures and events of the Revolution aroused particular interest in her day. "On the Death of General Wooster" (1777) is an elegy for a hero who "nobly perished in his country's cause." That cause—national independence—is also the cause of freedom, and Wheatley paints Wooster, in his last breath, praying for freedom's extension to slaves:

> But how, presumptuous shall we hope to find
> Divine acceptance with th'almighty mind—
> While yet (O deed ungenerous!) they disgrace
> And hold in bondage Afric's blameless race?
> Let virtue reign—And thou accord our prayers
> Be victory our's, and generous freedom theirs.

Wheatley's act of ventriloquism, the device whites so often used to ridicule blacks, enables her to redefine victory and virtue, the causes for celebration and mourning. "Liberty," in the poem "America," by "wond'rous instinct" lets "Ethiopians speak." What they speak indicates the possibilities of appropriation: "Sometimes by Simile a victory's won." [35]

35. Julian D. Mason, Jr., ed., *The Poems of Phillis Wheatley*, rev. ed. (Chapel Hill, N.C., 1989), 170–172; David Grimsted, "Anglo-American Racism and Phillis Wheatley's 'Sable Veil,' 'Length'ned Chain,' and 'Knitted Heart,'" in Ronald Hoffman and Peter J. Albert, eds., *Women in the Age of the American Revolution* (Charlottesville, Va., 1989), 425–435; Phillip M. Richards, "Phillis Wheatley and Literary Americanization," *American Quarterly*, XLIV (1992), 163–191; Betsy Erkkila, "Phillis Wheatley and the Black American Revolution," in Frank Shuffleton, ed., *A Mixed Race: Ethnicity in Early America* (New York, 1993), 225–240.

1. *Hail! all hail ye Afric clan*
    Hail! ye oppressed, ye Afric band
    Who toil and sweat in Slavery bound;
        (Repeated)
    And when your health & strength are gone
    Are left to hunger & to mourn
    Let *Independence* be your aim,
    Ever mindful what 'tis worth.
    Pledge your bodies for the prize
    Pile them even to the skies!

Chorus. Firm, united let us be,
    Resolved on death or liberty
    As a band of Patriots joined
    Peace & Plenty we shall find.

2. *Look to Heaven with manly trust*
    And swear by Him that's always just
    That no white foe with imipous hand
        (Repeated)
    Shall slave your wives & daughters more
    Or rob them of their virtue dear.
    Be armed with valor firm & true,
    Their hopes are fixed on Heaven & you
    That truth & justice will prevail
    And every scheme of bondage fail.

                [*Chorus*]

3. *Arise! Arise! shake off your chains*
    Your cause is just, so Heaven ordains
    To you shall Freedom be proclaimed.
        (Repeated)
    Raise your arms & bare your breasts,
    Almighty God will do the rest.
    Blow the clarion! A warlike blast!
    Call every Negro from his task!
    Wrest the scourge from Buckra's hand,
    And drive each tyrant from the land.

                [*Chorus*]

Hail! Columbia happy land
Hail ye Heroes, heav'n born band!
Who fought and bled in freedom's cause
Who fought and bled in freedom's cause
and when the storm of war was gone
enjoy'd the peace your valor won
let Independence be our boast
ever mindful what it cost
ever grateful for the prize
let its Altar reach the Skies

Chorus. Firm united let us be
rallying round our Liberty
as a band of Brothers join'd
peace and safety we shall find.

Immortal Patriots rise once more
Defend your rights—defend your shore
Let no rude foe with impious hand
Let no rude foe with imipous hand
Invade the shrine where sacred lies
Of toil and blood the well-earnd prize
While offering peace sincere and just,
In heav'n we place a manly trust
That truth and justice will prevail
And every scheme of bondage fail

Firm—united &c

Sound sound the trump of fame
Let Washingtons great name
Ring thro the world with loud applause
Ring thro the world with loud applause
Let every clime to Freedom dear
Listen with a joyful ear—
With equal skill with god-like powr,
He governs in the fearful hour
Of horrid war or guides with ease
The happier times of honest peace—

Firm—united &c

The late-eighteenth-century cult of sensibility also deeply informed abolitionism and became a useful tool for early black nationalists. As we have seen, the evocation and display of true feeling was central to the nationalist cultural politics of the whig rebels and, later, to supporters of the Constitution, Federalists of the 1790s, and their Jeffersonian opponents. At the same time, the slaves' ability to feel made them truly human and even (to some whites) the possessors of the most natural virtues. Scenes of broken black families, whose devastated members then often committed suicide, pervaded abolitionist poetry, fiction, and essays, appearing in the most mainstream and popular publications, such as almanacs and newspapers. American as well as English readers followed the adventurer Mungo Park into the wilds of Africa, where he "discovered" the natives to be kind, generous, sentimental, and humane. In ascribing true sentiment to blacks, many abolitionist writers "unwittingly enhanced historically negative attitudes toward Africans" and even "silenced the objects of their benevolence."[36] At the same time, it was in this literature that "Africans" were first widely defined as a nation by whites—and blacks. The national sin found a national martyr in wronged Africans. For whites, the nationalization of the black martyr opened up the possibility of American national reform and national benevolence. For blacks, nationhood could prove

36. "The Slave," *The Pennsylvania, Delaware, Maryland, and Virginia Almanack and Ephemeris, for . . . 1790* (Baltimore, 1789); *Tyrannical Libertymen*, 13–15; "Quashy; or, The Coal-Black Maid," *Time-Piece* (New York), Jan. 24, 1798; "The Negro Boy," *The Columbian Harmonist; or, Songster's Repository* (New York, 1814), 15–16; "The Slave Ship," *New-England Palladium* (Boston), Mar. 11, 1815; David Brion Davis, *The Problem of Slavery in Western Culture* (Ithaca, N.Y., 1966), 356–357; Mary Louise Pratt, *Imperial Eyes: Travel Writing and Transculturation* (New York, 1992), 69–85, on Mungo Park; Mukhtar Ali Isani, "'Far from Gambia's Golden Shore': The Black in Late Eighteenth-Century American Imaginative Literature," *WMQ*, 3d Ser., XXXVI (1979), 353–372; Keith A. Sandiford, *Measuring the Moment: Strategies of Protest in Eighteenth-Century Afro-English Writing* (Selinsgrove, Pa., 1988), esp. 64–71; Moira Ferguson, *Subject to Others: British Women Writers and Colonial Slavery, 1670–1834* (New York, 1992), quoted at 91, 108. The importance of these themes in the cultural politics of the late eighteenth century has been stressed by Julie Ellison, "Race and Sensibility in the Early Republic: Anna Eliza Bleecker and Sarah Wentworth Morton," *American Literature*, LXV (1993), 445–474, and in "Cato Discourse, the Carthage Syndrome, and the Shores of Tripoli," paper presented at the First Annual Conference of the Institute of Early American History and Culture, Ann Arbor, Mich., June 1995. See also John Saillant, "The Black Body Erotic and the Republican Body Politic," *Journal of the History of Sexuality*, V (1995), 403–428.

their peoplehood and thus a certain kind of equality that, they argued, was utterly inconsistent with the institution of slavery.

In *The Interesting Narrative of the Life of Olaudah Equiano; or, Gustavus Vassa, the African* (1789, first American edition 1791), Equiano is more than willing to set himself up as "the African" for a white audience, and in doing so he constructs a decidedly national, even more than racial, concept of Africanness. The "chief design" of *The Narrative*, writes the man whose life epitomized the geographical wanderings and cultural commerce of the black diaspora, "is to excite . . . a sense of compassion for the miseries which the Slave-Trade has entailed on my unfortunate countrymen." The first two chapters are just like a travel narrative, introducing Europeans to the habits and situation of Equiano's native country. The description proves the humanity and virtue of his nation, even presenting whiteness as a relative "deformity" in the eyes of Africans, and white slave traders as "savage" from the perspective of the enslaved.[37]

With race foregrounded, nationhood appears to have a more specific meaning, especially when Equiano is initially kidnapped by slavetraders from another African nation. Yet even the "sable destroyers of human rights" retain true feelings: they treat him well and are "affected" when the kidnapped Equiano is briefly reunited with his sister. Only when he is taken out of Africa by whites do all Africans, even those on the slave ship, become his "countrymen."[38] A similar redefinition of Africa as one nation can be seen in virtually all contemporary black writing. Zaama, the author of "The Appeal of an Hapless African, to the Rising Generation of America" (1802), also describes his capture as a tragedy in which his former homeland becomes the true land of the free: "Could I but return to that country where every man is free and slavery is unknown . . . then I shall be happy!" Casting Americans and

37. Olaudah Equiano, *The Interesting Narrative of the Life of Olaudah Equiano; or, Gustavus Vassa, the African* (1814 ed.), in Henry Louis Gates, Jr., ed., *The Classic Slave Narratives* (New York, 1987), 3, 11–24, 34. Equiano was first taken to Virginia and, later, as a mariner, actually witnessed the celebrations for the repeal of the Stamp Act in Charleston and also spent time in Savannah and Philadelphia (39, 94, 102, 116–118, 170). For more biographical information, see Sandiford, *Measuring the Moment*, 118–148.

38. Equiano, *Interesting Narrative*, in Gates, ed., *Classic Slave Narratives*, 25–26, 29, 36, 39, 53. On the rise of pan-Africanism in this period, see, especially, Miller, *Search for a Black Nationality;* and Bruce, "National Identity and Early African-American Colonization," *Historian*, LVIII (1995), 15–28.

Africans as national types, he can assert national equality in sentimental terms: "The sun shines—the rain descends, upon the African as well as the American." Zaama grants the Americans their great national act, the Declaration of Independence, but insists that it has been perverted by politicians' loose rhetorical usage of "liberty" versus "slavery":

> If "Republicanism means any thing or nothing," away with your political professions.—Let me return to Africa, and live under a despotism, without tyranny—a royal government, without slavery![39]

Insistently, explicitly, African Americans turned the discourse of race to one of nation. The new benevolent societies they formed in northern cities took names like that of Newport's African Benevolent Society; these organizations associated with the African Methodist Episcopal Church and other African churches to found African schools. They also began to regularly sponsor addresses like *The Sons of Africans: An Essay on Freedom* (1808). In this piece, spoken by a member of the Boston African Society and printed for its members, the antislavery uses of black nationalism reached their logical culmination. During the Revolution, noted the orator, America had faced the end of its national freedom and had felt justified in asking other nations for aid. If national freedom was "so desirable to America as that they exerted all their powers to obtain it, why then are they not willing to have it universal?"

> America hath an equal right to their privileges with any nation of the earth. Well, if so, what must be said of America, or especially that part which treats the African in ways similar to those which we have mentioned? This we leave for their own consciences to answer.[40]

39. Zaama, "The Appeal of an Hapless African, to the *Rising Generation of America*," in *The African Miscellanist; or, A Collection of Original Essays, on the Subject of Negro Slavery* (Trenton, N.J., 1802), 27–38, quoted at 30, 33, 37.

40. "Constitution of the African Benevolent Society," in William Patten, *A Sermon, Delivered at the Request of the African Benevolent Society, in the Second Congregational Church, . . . Newport, 12th April, 1808* (Newport, R.I., [1808]); *Constitution of the African Improvement Society of New Haven* (n.d., n.p.), broadside, Beinecke Library, Yale University, New Haven, Conn.; Nash, "Forging Freedom," in Berlin and Hoffman, eds., *Slavery and Freedom*, 45–46; Ira Berlin, *Slaves without Masters: The Free Negro in the Antebellum South* (New York, 1974), 78; Jacob Oson, *A Search for Truth; or, An Inquiry for the Origin of the African Nation: An Address, Delivered at New-Haven in March, and at New-York in April, 1817* (New York, 1817); *The Sons of Africans: An Essay on Freedom, with Observations on the Origin of Slavery, by a Member of the African Society in*

The Declaration of Independence, and white nationhood generally, served less as the inspiration than as the rhetorical and political fulcrum upon which blacks pressed their own continuing American Revolution.

"THE AFRICANS AND THEIR DESCENDANTS, WILL CELEBRATE . . ."

Students of black nationalism and African American identity have been most concerned with whether free blacks endorsed "separatism" or endorsed "assimilationism." To some extent, these very categories reflect a later period's somewhat different political and cultural alternatives.[41] Yet scholars of the antebellum period have found ample evidence among African Americans both of a separatist impulse and of an assimilationist desire to be incorporated into American institutions on an equal basis. These paths, it is acknowledged, need not have been mutually exclusive. Free black communities were increasingly diverse, and the very conditions of African Americans' lives early fostered a Du Boisian double consciousness.[42]

Those who have explicitly addressed early African American celebra-

Boston (Boston, 1808), 10. The last oration is also available in Dorothy Porter, ed., *Early Negro Writing, 1760–1837* (Boston, 1971), 13–27.

41. George A. Levesque, "Interpreting Early Black Ideology: A Reappraisal of Historical Consensus," *Journal of the Early Republic,* I (1981), 269–287. In this, of course, histories of black nationalism and black identities differ little from scholarly debates over "American identity," with the possible caveat that the latter tradition, no less polemical or political, has more often succeeded in hiding its political valences in the penumbra of scholarly objectivity. For separation and assimilation as a "false dichotomy," see James Oliver Horton and Lois E. Horton, *In Hope of Liberty: Culture, Community, and Protest among Northern Free Blacks, 1700–1860* (New York, 1997), xii.

42. Miller, *Search for a Black Nationality;* Stuckey, *Slave Culture;* Robert L. Harris, Jr., "The Free Black Response to American Racism, 1790–1863" (Ph.D. diss., Northwestern University, 1974); V. P. Franklin, *Black Self-Determination: A Cultural History of African American Resistance,* 2d ed. (New York, 1993), esp. 83–102; Sweet, "The Fourth of July and Black Americans in the Nineteenth Century," *Journal of Negro History,* LXI (1976), 256–275; William B. Gravely, "The Dialectic of Double Consciousness in Black American Freedom Celebrations, 1808–1863," *Journal of Negro History,* LXIX (1982), 302–317; Ernest Allen, Jr., "Afro-American Identity: Reflections on the Pre–Civil War Era," *Contributions in Black Studies,* VII (1985–1986), 55–56.

tions and blacks' uses of the Fourth of July have tried to resolve this interpretive problem by employing a variant of the double-consciousness
theme, but with a decidedly assimilationist emphasis. "Black nationalism provided the creative thrust for black demands of American nationality," writes Leonard I. Sweet. "Their nationalism did not preempt
their demands for inclusion as Americans." African American critiques
of patriotism's verities, after all, were a kind of engagement with them,
revealed in a "hate-love attitude" toward the Fourth of July. Free blacks'
public rejections of the Fourth and their inventiveness regarding their
own celebrations "carried them into the era of Reconstruction with the
conviction that being black was a distinctive way of being American."[43]

This argument for separatist means to assimilationist ends may capture the dominant black political strategy of the nineteenth century.
But it underestimates the integrity of black nationalism itself as a product of blacks' political needs in the late eighteenth and early nineteenth
centuries. During the period 1790–1820, as during the Revolutionary
era, free black communities grew rapidly, in part because of manumissions and gradual-emancipation laws. Not coincidentally, many states
began to fashion laws and ordinances that policed the black community and denied free black men the right to vote.[44] African Americans
were more concerned with communal survival and growth and the fate
of slavery than with the possibilities for true integration. The struggles
of the post-Revolutionary generation might not have led them to articulate or stress their Americanness, for doing so might not have been
the most effective way of forging community or fighting slavery.

Moreover, the argument of separatist means to assimilationist ends
tends also to underestimate blacks' engagement with the dominant
nationalist political culture, which they had effectively combated on its
own terms since the 1770s. Closer attention to their celebrations from
1808 to 1820 of the end of the slave trade alters somewhat the emphasis that historians have placed on the separatist or nationalist means

43. Leonard I. Sweet, *Black Images of America, 1784–1870* (New York, 1976), 5–6;
Benjamin Quarles, "Antebellum Free Blacks and the 'Spirit of '76,'" in Quarles, *Black
Mosaic: Essays in Afro-American History and Historiography* (Amherst, Mass., 1988), 92–
108; Gravely, "Dialectic of Double Consciousness," *Journal of Negro History*, LXIX
(1982), 312. See also Genevieve Fabre, "African American Commemorative Celebrations in the Nineteenth Century," in Fabre and Robert O'Meally, eds., *History
and Memory in African American Culture* (New York, 1994), 72–91.

44. Leon F. Litwack, *North of Slavery: The Negro in the Free States, 1790–1860* (Chicago, 1961).

that free blacks later used to achieve assimilationist, or Americanizing, ends. Rather, free blacks appropriated white political culture for the purposes of antislavery activity and cultural autonomy. They used the tools of American nationalism to create black nationalism.[45]

In order to recognize the nature of this appropriation, it is necessary to break down the notion of *wholly* autonomous black and white cultures while still recognizing the crucial importance of race—of perceptions of whiteness and blackness—in the shared culture. Historians of slave culture have made us aware of the critical edge in slave songs and other forms of black expression that derive from plantation life.[46] Too great an emphasis on the autonomy of the slave community, though, has at times drawn our attention away from the importance of white-black interactions in the making of this slave culture—and of the dominant white culture. Even on the plantation, everyday life acquired a theatricality born of the necessary performances of whiteness (by masters) and blackness (by slaves). Moreover, from the late eighteenth century onward, it is clear that blacks and whites imitated each other in culturally charged enactments of their deeply felt feelings of desire and disgust. Early black festivals and parades like Negro Election Day "were tinged with burlesque, as blacks lampooned whites." Here and in the interracial public spaces of northern cities lie the complex origins of blackface minstrelsy. Although we rightly think of such cultural interchanges, where whites imitated blacks imitating whites, as the epitome of white racism, the number of turns in even this equation should hint that there was more going on on both sides of the culturally porous racial divide.[47]

45. I have been influenced here by the formulation in Priscilla Wald's essay, "Terms of Assimilation: Legislating Subjectivity in the Emerging Nation," in Amy Kaplan and Donald E. Pease, eds., *Cultures of United States Imperialism* (Durham, N.C., 1993), 59–84, esp. 67–68, where Wald argues that the nationalist Cherokees who formed their own constitution imitated rather than assimilated to United States nationalism. Doing so made them an even greater threat to the American nation than the Cherokees who stressed the need to remain culturally Cherokee. See also William G. McLoughlin, *Cherokee Renascence in the New Republic* (Princeton, N.J., 1986).

46. See especially Lawrence W. Levine, *Black Culture and Black Consciousness: Afro-American Folk Thought from Slavery to Freedom* (New York, 1977); Eugene D. Genovese, *Roll, Jordan, Roll: The World the Slaves Made* (New York, 1974); Stuckey, *Slave Culture*, chap. 1.

47. Roger D. Abrahams, *Singing the Master: The Emergence of African-American Culture in the Plantation South* (New York, 1993), xxii–xxiii, 33, 46–47, 126–127, 137;

THE BATTLE OF PLATTSBURG—Tune,...Banks of the DEE.
Together with the Siege of Plattsburg, sung in the
Character of a Black Sailor.—Tune.—"Boyn-Water."

TWAS autumn, around me the leaves were descending,
  And lonely the wood-pecker peck'd on the tree :
Whilst thousands their freedom & rights were defending,
The dim of their arms sounded dismal to me,
For Sandy, my love, was engag'd in the action,
His death would have ended my life in distraction ;
Without him I valued this world not a fraction,
As lonely I stray'd on the Banks of Champlain.

  Then turning to list to the cannons' loud thunder,
My elbow I lean'd on a rock near the shore :
The sound nearly parted my heart strings asunder,
I thought I should see my dear shepherd no more,
But soon an express all my sorrows suspended,
My thanks, to the Father of Mercies, ascended ;
My shepherd was safe and my country defended,
By freedom's brave sons, on the banks of Champlain.
Wip'd from my eyes the big tear that had started,
And hastened to parents the news for to bear ;
Who sad for the loss of relations departed,
And wept at the tidings that bani hed all care,
The cannon ceas'd roaring, the drums still were beating,
The foes of our country for the North were retreating.
The neighboring damsels each other were greeting,
With songs of delight, on the Banks of Champlain.
  They sung of the heroes whose valor had made us,
Sole nation on earth, independent and free ;
And so we'll remain with kind Heaven to aid us,
In spite of invaders, by land or by sea.
New York, the Green Mountain, M'Comb, & M'Donnough
The Farmer, the soldier, the sailor, and Gunner ;
All parties united had plighted their honor,
To conquer or die, on the Banks of Champlain.
  Our squadron triumphant, our army victorious,
With laurels unfaded, our spartans' return'd ;
My eyes never dwelt on a scene half so glorious,
My heart with such raptures, before never burn'd,
For Sandy my darling, that moment appearing,
His presence to ev'ry countenance cheering,
Was render'd to me more than doubly endearing,
By the feats he'd perform'd, on the Banks of Champlain.
  But should smiling peace, with her blessings & treasures,
Soon visit the plains of Columbia again,
What pen can describe the enrapturing pleasures,
Which I shall experience, through life, with my swain,
For now no wild savage will come to alarm us,
No worse British foe, send their millions to harm us ;
But nature and art will continue to charm us,
While so happy we'll live, on the Banks of Champlain.

BACK side Albany stan' Lake Champlain,
  One little pond, half full a' water,
Plat-te-bug dare too, close pon de main,
Town small he grow bigger do hereafter.
    On Lake Champlain
    Uncle Sam set he boat,
And Massa M'Donough he sail 'em,
    While Gen'ral M'Comb
    Make Plat-te-bug he home,
  Wid de army, who courage nebber fail 'em.

On 'lebenth day of Sep tem ber,
In eighteen hund'red an fourteen,
Gubbener Probose, an he British roger,
Come to Plat-te-bug a-tea party courtin ;
    An he boat come too
    Arter uncle Sam boat ;
Massa Donough do look sharp out de winder,
  D n Gen'ral Mc Comb.
  (Ah ! he always at home.)
Catch fire too, jis like a tinder.

Bang ! bang ! bang !' den de cannons gin
    t'roar
In Plat-te-bug an all 'bout dat quarter ;
Gubbener Probose try he hand 'pon de shore,
While he boat take he luck 'pon de water,
    But Massa M'Donough
    Knock he boat in he head,
Break he heart broke he shin, 'tove he caf-
    fin in,
    An General Mc Comb,
    Start ole Probose home,
Tot me soul den, I mus die a lassa.

Probose scare so, he lef all behine,
Powder, ball, cannon, tea-pot an kittle,
Some say he catch a cole, trouble in he mine,
Cause he eat so much raw an cole vittle.
    Uncle Sam berry sorry,
    To be sure, for he pain ;
Wish he nuss heself up well an hearty,
For Gen'ral Mc'Comb, an Massa 'Donough
    home,
When he notion for a nudder tea party.

———

☞ Printed by Nathaniel Coverly, Jun.

FIGURE 15. *The Battle of Plattsburg.* Boston, 1815.
The first minstrel song. Courtesy Boston Public Library

Perhaps it is no accident, then, that the first minstrel song, later known as "Backside Albany," first appeared side by side with a song celebrating the American victory at Lake Champlain in the War of 1812. "Backside Albany" presents a black dialect version of the victory song, "The Siege of Plattsburg, Sung in the Character of a Black Sailor": while it certainly participates in what was becoming a tradition of racist parody, it also acknowledges the real contribution of African American seamen in the American war effort (see Figure 15).[48] An important part of black or African American culture, then, consisted of the imitation and criticism of white culture; and an important part of white-dominated American culture consisted of playing black. At certain crucial moments, as we have seen, the imitation both of black culture and of blacks imitating whites, in acts of literary blackface, helped white partisans police the racial boundaries of their political culture. Given this context, blacks marching through the streets of an American city had meanings far more complex and dangerous than when any other groups, even other ethnic groups, went on parade.

The meanings of parades changed for blacks because of the importance parades had acquired for whites. National celebrations became principal venues for political participation and for debates concerning what American identity was and what it meant. A stress on the need for respectability, expressed by the upper class in tasteful displays of patriotic sentiments, meshed uneasily with the unceasing pressure from

---

Shane White, "'It Was a Proud Day': African Americans, Festivals, and Parades in the North, 1741–1834," *JAH*, LXXXI (1994–1995), 13–50, quoted at 27; Eric Lott, *Love and Theft: Blackface Minstrelsy and the American Working Class* (New York, 1993). White finds that African American parades were a "significant departure" from the more African-influenced festivals of the earlier period. He rightly concludes that they evinced a new kind of political engagement on the part of the free black community—though the beauty of White's approach is that he also brings out the subversive aspects of the earlier festivals, which have too often been seen as imitative, if black-oriented. That the parades were recognized as a political challenge accounts for the increasing hostility they faced in the 1810s.

48. *The Battle of Plattsburg—Tune, . . . Banks of the Dee* (Boston, n.d.). On "Backside Albany" as the first blackface song, see Lott, *Love and Theft*, 41, 46; and William J. Mahar, "'Backside Albany' and Early Blackface Minstrelsy: A Contextual Study of America's First Blackface Song," *American Music*, VI (1988), 1–27. Later minstrel songs, such as T. D. Rice's "Jim Crow" and G. W. Dixon's "Zip Coon," also commemorated the Battle of New Orleans; see Jon W. Finson, *The Voices That Are Gone: Themes in Nineteenth-Century American Popular Song* (New York, 1993), 164–165, 170.

below for the democratization of public life. Around the turn of the century, blacks' efforts to be part of this democratization spurred whites of both political parties to erect them as symbols of inappropriate participation. Black resentment of this treatment can be seen in the group of young black Philadelphians who, on July 4, 1804, formed an ad hoc military group and took over the city streets, knocking down the whites who stood in their way. They repeated their actions the next night, "damning the whites and saying that they would shew them *St. Domingo*." Whites retaliated the next year on the Fourth by driving all the blacks off the park in front of Independence Hall. In the coming years, African Americans would often be hustled out of urban public space by the working-class whites who increasingly claimed the Fourth as their own.[49]

Important as this racial battle over the streets was, it is nonetheless important not to reduce black celebrations (as historians have too often done to white celebrations) to the parades alone. To do so would remove these celebrations from the context of the full-fledged nationalist political culture that they appropriated and contested. Black American nationalists formed committees, took out advertisements in newspapers, held religious services, gave and listened to orations, and, in a surprising number of cases, had these orations printed and distributed—all in honor of their *national* holiday. The very complexity of these new black nationalist celebrations reveals how determined and successful African Americans were in adapting white American nationalism for their own purposes. These purposes, like those of white festivals, included community-based organizing, public political protest, and the promotion of a national identity.

The first recorded black nationalist celebration took place in New York City on July 5, 1800. In honor of the state's Gradual Emancipation Act (which would eventually free slaves born after July 4, 1799), New York's African Americans held a parade on the day after Independence Day—reportedly because the Tammany Society, merchants, and me-

49. White, "'It was a Proud Day,'" *JAH*, LXXXI (1994–1995), 34; Nash, *Forging Freedom*, 176–177; *Freeman's Journal, and Philadelphia Daily Advertiser*, July 7, 9, 1804; Paul A. Gilje, *The Road to Mobocracy: Popular Disorder in New York City, 1763–1834* (Chapel Hill, N.C., 1987), 159; Susan G. Davis, *Parades and Power: Street Theatre in Nineteenth-Century Philadelphia* (Berkeley, Calif., 1986). On the white working class and racism in this era, see, especially, David R. Roediger, *The Wages of Whiteness: Race and the Making of the American Working Class* (New York, 1991).

chanics objected to a black parade on the Fourth. In 1807, some blacks from Boston joined those in Salem for a "public parade of the African Society" on July 16.[50] Although no earlier Boston July 14 festivities have been uncovered, the next year Boston blacks established an annual tradition by celebrating on that day the end of the slave trade in Great Britain, Denmark, and the United States.

The abolition of the United States slave trade had taken effect on January 1, 1808, and African Americans in New York and Philadelphia made this their annual holiday. (After 1804, January 1 had also marked the anniversary of Haitian independence.) The idea that the celebration ought to be annual and national originated with the festivals' first organizers. The Reverend Absalom Jones, who chaired a May 10, 1807, planning meeting, asked in his sermon that "the first of January, the day of the abolition of the slave trade in our country, be set apart in every year, as a day of public thanksgiving for that mercy." The Philadelphians who belonged to another black church likewise proclaimed January 1 "THE DAY OF OUR POLITICAL JUBILEE." Black New Yorkers the next year advertised "the National Jubilee." Early on there were suggestions that white abolitionists too might join in rejoicing, especially at the church services, where donations were often collected for the Manumission Society and the African School. Yet the advertisements taken out by the all-black committees of arrangements were explicitly placed for "the Africans and People of Colour."[51]

50. Robert J. Swan, "John Teasman: African-American Educator and the Emergence of Community in Early Black New York City, 1787–1815," *Journal of the Early Republic*, XII (1992), 343–344; Bentley, *Diary*, III, 309; *The Sons of Africans*.

51. Absalom Jones, *A Thanksgiving Sermon, Preached January 1, 1808, in St. Thomas's, or the African Episcopal Church, Philadelphia: on Account of the Abolition of the African Slave Trade, on That Day, by the Congress of the United States* (Philadelphia, 1808), 19; "An Address to the Africans and People of Colour . . . ," *Poulson's American Daily Advertiser* (Philadelphia), Jan. 1, 1808; "National Jubilee of the Abolition of the Slave Trade," *Mercantile Advertiser* (New York), Jan. 2, 1809; "Meeting of Africans," *New-York Evening Post*, Dec. 16, 1807, reprinted in Paul A. Gilje and Howard B. Rock, eds., *Keepers of the Revolution: New Yorkers at Work in the Early Republic* (Ithaca, N.Y., 1992), 238–239; "Abolition of Slavery," *Boston Gazette*, July 13, 1809, "African Celebration," July 8, 1811, July 15, 1813; "African Celebration," *Columbian Centinel* (Boston), July 8, 1811; *Independent Chronicle* (Boston), July 13, 1812.

The Brooklyn African Woolman Benevolent Society, founded in 1810, along with the New York African Wilberforce Society, paraded down Fulton Street on Jan. 1, 1819. Daniel Perlman, "Organizations of the Free Negro in New York City,

In all three cities, free blacks marched through the central streets to their place of meeting, and sometimes back, "with their badges and banners, accompanied with a band of music." The procession routes were carefully delineated in advance and often published in the papers. In New York and possibly elsewhere, the services included a reading of Congress's act abolishing the slave trade, much as white celebrants read the Declaration of Independence, Jefferson's inaugural address, or other texts. Songs and prayers were interspersed with the rest of the exercises. In Boston, white ministers generally gave sermons, though they were sometimes assisted in leading the congregation by Thomas Paul, a black Baptist minister. But in New York and Philadelphia, African Americans gave orations, often introduced by another black speaker. These orations (discussed below) took the form—but altered the content—of Fourth of July orations. And in Boston, some African Americans dined together after the service and gave patriotic toasts.[52]

On one all too rare occasion, in 1810, the *Columbian Centinel* included in its brief account a list of toasts given by the African Americans at their dinner:

1800–1860," *Journal of Negro History,* LVI (1971), 185; Sandra Shoiock Raff, "The Brooklyn African Woolman Benevolent Society Reconsidered," *Afro-Americans in New York Life and History,* X (1996), 56–57.

52. "Notice," *Poulson's American Daily Advertiser* (Philadelphia), Jan. 1, 1813, "African Procession," Dec. 29, 1815, "African Meeting," Jan. 1, 1819; "National Jubilee," *Mercantile Advertiser* (New York), Jan. 2, 1809; "Order of the Celebration of the Day," in Peter Williams, *An Oration on the Abolition of the Slave Trade; Delivered in the African Church, in the City of New-York, January 1, 1808* (New York, 1808), 8; "Order of the Day," in Henry Sipkins, *An Oration on the Abolition of the Slave Trade: Delivered in the African Church in the City of New-York, January 2, 1809* (New York, 1809), 3; *American Citizen* (New York), Dec. 30, 1809; "Fourth Anniversary of the Abolition of the Slave Trade," in Adam Carman, *An Oration Delivered at the Fourth Anniversary of the Abolition of the Slave Trade, in the Methodist Episcopal Church . . . January 1, 1811* (New York, 1811); "Celebration of the Abolition of the Slave Trade," *Columbian* (New York), Dec. 31, 1810; "Sons of Africa," *Independent Chronicle* (Boston), July 18, 1814, July 18, 1816; "African Society," *New-England Palladium* (Boston), July 14, 1818; "Abolition of the Slave Trade," *Independent Chronicle* (Boston), July 15, 1820; John S[ylvester] J[ohn] Gardiner, *A Sermon, Preached before the African Society, on the 14th of July, 1810, the Anniversary of the Abolition of the Slave Trade* (Boston, 1810); Paul Dean, *A Discourse Delivered before the African Society, at Their Meeting-House, in Boston, Mass. on the Abolition of the Slave Trade . . .* (Boston, 1819); *Boston Gazette,* July 18, 1808.

1. —The Day; and the memory of the land of our Forefathers.
2. *Mr. Wilberforce,* and other members who advocated the abolition of the slave trade in the British Parliament.
3. The Governor of this State, and the Government of the U. States.
4. The Trustees of the African School in *Boston*.
5. The memory of *Hancock, Franklin,* and *Sullivan;* and all who have advocated the cause of the Africans.
6. The Chaplain of the Day.
7. *Great Britain,* the U. States and *Denmark.*—May all nations imitate their exertions in favor of the race of *Africa*.
8. Liberty to our African brethren in *St. Domingo,* and elsewhere.
9. The present *Engines* of Peace and Liberty—May their copious streams extinguish the fire of party spirit.[53]

At the service earlier that day, the African Americans who gave these toasts had been told by their invited white speaker, "You cannot be too thankful for the blessings you enjoy in this happy country, though your situation in civil society will probably always remain subordinate."[54] The toasts, however, do not particularly thank America for the blessings of freedom. Only the particular friends of abolition earn plaudits. Nor do these celebrants assume or accept any subordination in the public sphere. To toast their African nation and to comment on the actions of other nations toward Africa and Africans are to participate equally among fellow nationals in a multinational "civil society." Yet neither do they accept émigré status. They toast not just the federal government but the governor—in Boston, always a potentially controversial, even partisan act. They even presume to comment upon "party spirit."

Although primarily celebrations of African American autonomy, the observances of January 1 and July 14 regularly commented on the partisan political practices that preceded and followed them on the cal-

53. "Abolition of the Slave Trade," *Columbian Centinel* (Boston), July 18, 1810; toasts also appear in "Celebration of Freedom," July 18, 1821. It is reasonable to assume that the celebrants dined and toasted annually, especially since satires of the celebration—the Bobalition broadsides—feature fake black toasts in dialect. See also *Boston Daily Advertiser,* July 17, 1817; "African Celebration," *Columbian Centinel,* July 13, 1822.

54. Gardiner, *A Sermon,* 17–18. Gardiner added that African Americans were far more blessed than other Africans: "In their native country they are mere savages, continually making war on each other, and selling their prisoners to white men."

endar. On more than one occasion, free blacks used their national holiday to display partisan affiliations. They were tempted to do so because abolition, the central focus of the occasion, remained politically charged. In its second year, New York's celebration of January 1 split along party lines. The years 1808 and 1809 were marked by intense courtship of black voters by the Federalists, which Republicans ridiculed by labeling the Federalist slate "The African Ticket." When black Jeffersonians and neutrals discovered that the originally planned festival would have a distinctly Federalist cast, they arranged their own procession and two additional orations. While speakers Henry Sipkins and William Hamilton avoided partisan endorsements, the Federalist Joseph Sidney, appearing before the Wilberforce Philanthropic Association and the New York Manumission Society, jumped squarely into the sectionalized partisan fray. Noting that suffrage was a right and a duty, Sidney maintained that most southerners were democrats, and most democrats southerners—"the very people who hold our African brethren in bondage." "These people, therefore, are the *deniers* of our *rights*." For Sidney, opposing the Jeffersonians made it possible to be simultaneously an African and an American patriot: "Will you flock to the *slavery-pole* of democracy?—Or will you patriotically rally round the *standard of liberty?*" By voting Federalist, at least some free blacks, like white party members, could hope that "every return of this anniversary may be accompanied with additional cause for JOY AND REJOICING."[55]

As their toasts indicate, Boston free blacks also made partisan political statements as part of their appearance in public. They also found other ways to display their Federalism. In the course of observing Afri-

---

55. *American Citizen* (New York), Apr. 30, 1808; *A Black Joke* (New York, 1808), Broadsides Collection, New York State Library; Dixon Ryan Fox, "The Negro Vote in Old New York," *Political Science Quarterly*, XXXII (1917), 252–275; Litwack, *North of Slavery*, 80–81; Sipkins, *An Oration;* William Hamilton, *An Address to the New York African Society for Mutual Relief, Delivered in the Universalist Church, January 2, 1809*, in Porter, ed., *Early Negro Writing*, 33–41; Joseph Sidney, *An Oration, Commemorative of the Abolition of the Slave Trade in the United States; Delivered before the Wilberforce Philanthropic Association, in the City of New-York, on the Second of January, 1809* (New York, 1809), 7–15. It is interesting to note that 1809 was the same year that the white, mostly Federalist New York Manumission Society tried to dissuade free African Americans from parading. See John L. Rury, "Philanthropy, Self-Help, and Social Control: The New York Manumission Society and Free Blacks, 1785–1810," *Phylon*, XLVI (1985), 240; Swan, "John Teasman," *Journal of the Early Republic*, XII (1992), 349.

can American Federalism in 1813, a writer in a Republican paper seemed at first to pay them a rare compliment:

> The *African Society,* which paraded on Thursday, was composed of an assemblage of very good looking *coloured people,* and made upon the whole, almost as respectable an appearance as any procession we have seen in *Boston* the present year. Some of their marshals were mistaken, by many, for officers of the *Washington Benevolents;* and this small mistake was occasioned by their wearing the WHITE ROSE, and carrying pillar-standards, and wearing *tearing* high *chapeau-de-bras.*

As the writer surely knew, however, his subjects knew exactly what they were doing; there had been no mistake. As in New York and elsewhere, free blacks had formed chapters of the Federalist political club, the Washington Benevolent Society. The unmistakable Federalism of the Washington Society inspired the inversion of this compliment into a racial joke suggesting that, even if blacks knew how to parade, they were not in control of the language of politics:

> From this respectable body of *negro-citizens* were selected a corps of guards, with golden epaulets, espontoon, and swords, some metallic, and some made of wood; the latter to denote that they belonged to "*the Peace Party.*" We understand that this select corps is to continue embodied; and to be trained like the other independent companies; and that they mean to apply for a Charter, under the name and title of "*The Washington Benevolent Federal Black-Guards*"! *Vive la Republique!*

Once again, when blacks enter public space with their own versions of politicized speech and ritual, they must be ridiculed to justify their continued marginalization by whites. That same year, Boston Jeffersonians included a dialect satire and a visual caricature of the black Washingtonians in their anti-Federalist publications.[56]

But silence was just as effective in reinforcing the dialect jokes: both silence and satire maintained the illusion that blacks were not really acting and speaking politically. The most detailed accounts we have of black festivals are the paid ads placed in newspapers (usually Federalist) by the participants themselves. Not coincidentally, virtually the only

56. "Communication: Black and White Roses," *Boston Patriot,* July 17, 21, 1813; *The First Book of the "Washington Benevolents"; Otherwise Called, The Book of Knaves* (Boston, 1813), 12. For blacks in the Washington Benevolent Society, see Fox, "Negro Vote in Old New York," *Political Science Quarterly,* XXXII (1917), 252–275.

sympathetic accounts of black celebrations that appeared at all (and even these are generally cursory) are to be found in diehard Federalist publications, such as the following, published in a short-lived Boston magazine, the *Idiot; or, Invisible Rambler,* in 1818:

> The Anniversary of the *Abolition of the Slave Trade,* was on Wednesday last celebrated in this town, by a number of respectable people of colour. Their proceedings on the joyful occasion, were not only decent, but such as would have done honor to any assemblage, whatever. If it becomes *us* to celebrate the natal day of our country's Independence, how much more does it become the descendants of the sorely oppressed Africans to celebrate the day when the laws of the land forbid that we should longer separate husband and wife, parents and children—force them from their native land, and doom them to perpetual bondage! [57]

Republican and Federalist papers found plenty of column space for Independence Day toasts for weeks into the month of July. Nonetheless, they found little or no room for what was probably the most striking and innovative civic spectacle of the year.

Poor and nonexistent press coverage is of course the main reason why even specialists remain unaware that hundreds of free blacks annually marched through the streets of early-nineteenth-century Boston, Philadelphia, and New York City, protesting slavery and proclaiming

57. *Idiot; or, Invisible Rambler* (Boston), July 18, 1818; see also "On Seeing the African Procession on Wednesday Last," *Boston Kaleidoscope and Literary Rambler,* July 17, 1819. Blacks were able to gain some notice through their purchasing power and partisanship. The greatest number of notices appeared in the *Columbian Centinel* and the *Boston Gazette,* the two papers most identified with the Federalists. After the blacks took out an ad in 1812, the fiercely Republican *Independent Chronicle* included brief notices of their celebrations in 1814, 1816, and 1820 (July 13, 1812, July 18, 1814, July 18, 1816, July 15, 1820). Black New Yorkers took out ads in the *American Citizen,* a daily paper of similar Republican politics, but no accounts appeared (Dec. 31, 1808, Dec. 30, 1809). In Philadelphia, announcements appeared in the moderately Federalist *Poulson's American Daily Advertiser* and once in the *Political and Commercial Register,* also a Federalist paper. No notices appeared in the *Aurora,* or in the *Democratic Press,* in *Relf's Philadephia Gazette; and Daily Advertiser,* or in the *True American and Commercial Advertiser* after the initial resolution and celebration in 1807. *Poulson's American Daily Advertiser,* Jan. 1, 1808, Jan. 1, 1813, Jan. 1, 1814, Dec. 29, 1815, Dec. 31, 1817, Dec. 31, 1818; *Political and Commercial Register,* Dec. 26, 1807, Dec. 30, 1811; *Relf's Philadelphia Gazette,* Dec. 30, 1807; *Democratic Press,* Dec. 31, 1807.

their African identity. Apparently, the one aspect of American nationalism that African Americans could not easily appropriate was newspaper reportage—precisely what, as I maintain throughout this study, allowed celebrations to serve as the centerpieces of every nationalist political subculture. The quasi-official silence regarding blacks' nationalistic practices signified white America's unwillingness, even inability, to recognize its own mirror image.

This is not to say that black celebrations were ignored. One Bostonian, Elijah Clark, recorded purposefully "walking into State Street" to see "the African procession, it being the anniversary of their emancipation." One way or another, Clark had learned that this parade carried an emancipatory political message, even if it did not explicitly commemorate the end of slavery in Massachusetts. Black parades drew large crowds—a decidedly mixed blessing, because paraders faced increasing intimidation as the novelty wore off and the processions got bigger. In 1813, black Philadelphians made a point of obtaining and publishing the mayor's "cordial approbation" of their parade. In 1819 the Bostonians thanked the town selectmen for their "protection and countenance." Nevertheless, the next year they faced dirt-throwing boys. By 1821, Boston whites had broken out of their silence in the newspapers to disagree publicly about the propriety of the black festival, which by that time brought out hundreds of paraders and many more spectators. One editor launched a lengthy critique, and an approving reader echoed his complaints: The celebration "has a tendency to make the soot-headed race more impudent, and of course more lazy. They should be made to correctly understand their station in society. . . . My bootblack had the hardihood to refuse to clean my boots last Monday morning." These racist attacks prompted responses from two sympathetic editors, one of whom fingered the stakes quite explicitly: "We are glad that there is one day in the year, in which the sons of Africa may know that they are men, and exercise something like national feeling."[58]

58. Elijah Clark Diary, July 14, 1814, Massachusetts Historical Society, Boston (thanks to Mitchell Snay for pointing me to this source); "Notice," *Poulson's American Daily Advertiser* (Philadelphia), Jan. 1, 1813; *New-England Palladium* (Boston), July 16, 1819; "African Independence," *New England Galaxy and Masonic Magazine* (Boston), July 14, 1820, July 21, 1821; "Celebration of Freedom," *Columbian Centinel* (Boston), July 18, 1821; "African Celebration," *Boston Recorder,* July 28, 1821. In 1826, some Boston whites rioted against blacks on July 14, an event that itself provoked a new variety of Bobalition broadside. See *Dreadful Riot on Negro Hill!,* Broadsides Collection, Beinecke Library, Yale University; Peter P. Hinks, *To Awaken*

FIGURE 16. *Invitation . . . the Commemoration of the "Abolition of the Slave Trade."* Salem, Mass., 1816. The first surviving Bobalition broadside. Courtesy Boston Public Library

For the most part, when Boston Republicans did deign to notice the slave trade celebrations in print, they did so satirically, in a way designed to challenge not just the parades but the very idea of blacks' presenting their nationalist performances in print. By 1816 printed broadsides ridiculing the "GRAND AND SPLENDID BOBALITION OF SLAVERY" began to appear all over Boston in advance of July 14 (see Figure 16). Going behind the scenes of the political other's celebration and exposing it as artifice, the "Bobalition" broadsides took on the properties of anticelebratory discourse that partisans had been practicing since the Revolution. In doing so they also drew upon the particular tradition that I have called literary blackface—in which whites, employing exaggerated dialect and malapropisms, imitated black speech in order to ridicule black pretensions to speak (and write) as whites did. By 1821 these broadsides had begun to take a standard form. They begin with a fake letter from a black procession organizer to one of his marshals, giving the "Order of de Day." A "Bosecrip" lists the toasts supposedly given and a sentimental song sung by a participant: both are burlesqued into nonsense, as in the 1816 toast to: "De Orator of de day. His eloquence demonish de Afrikin, and almost make my sould die a laffin."[59] Or *almost* nonsense: they make enough sense to reveal blacks' nationalist and antislavery political discourse, but make that discourse an example of African Americans' *lack* of cultural independence and real equality. In the inverted world of Bobalition, blacks reveal their inability to be respectable or politically effective in their very act of imitating whites. Black leaders keep "de most perfect disorder."

There can be no doubt that the Bobalition broadsides were part and parcel of whites' purposeful, if at times subtle, marginalization of blacks in public life during the early nineteenth century. They spoke for blacks so that blacks would not be heard. Reacting to the appropria-

---

My Afflicted Brethren: David Walker and the Problem of Antebellum Slave Resistance (University Park, Pa., 1997), 83–84.

59. Boston *Daily Advertiser,* July 15, 1817, July 15, 20, 1820; White, "It Was a Proud Day," *JAH,* LXXXI (1994–1995), 35–38; *Invitation, Addressed to the Marshals of the "Africum Shocietee," at the Commemoration of the "Abolition of the Slave Trade," July 14th, 1816* (Boston, 1816), Broadsides Collection, Boston Public Library; *Grand Celebration! Of the Abolition of the Slave Trade* (Boston, [1817?]), photocopy courtesy of Philip Lapsansky, Library Company of Philadelphia; *Grand Bobalition: or, "Great Annibersary Fussible"* (Boston, 1821), Broadsides Collection, AAS; *Grand and Splendid Bobalition of Slavery* (Boston, 1822), Broadsides Collection, AAS; *Grand Bobalition of Slavery! By De Africum Shocietee* (Boston, [1820?]), Library Company of Philadelphia.

tion of white nationalist rituals by African Americans, blackface satire exaggerated the cultural, intellectual, and physical differences between blacks and whites, suggesting differences so absolute as to be innate. The true meaning of Africanness, here, is racial inferiority. In this respect the Bobalition broadsides are important artifacts in the history of American racism. They probably also contributed to the physical and verbal abuse that African Americans received on the streets of Boston. Yet these broadsides also have their uses in the quest to understand the politics and practices of black nationalism, which must be understood from both the free black perspective and in the context of the larger public culture of Boston and the urban North.

Boston in the 1810s, like the other northern seaboard cities, relied upon an international commerce linking the Atlantic world. For this reason, in part, Boston was the site of fierce political partisanship and opposition to the War of 1812. At the same time, African Americans working in the seaborne trade moved between Boston and other cities just as other blacks, including the recently freed, flocked there from the countryside in search of livelihoods. The city would soon become the hub of the antislavery movement, black and white. If whites were looking for principles of agreement, they certainly could have found them in responses to the increasingly public activities of Boston's black population, much as they sought them in President Monroe's ritual of "good feelings." All such public events and issues—the president, the army, bank legislation, the Hartford Convention, the Fourth of July, colonization—are alluded to in the broadsides, especially in the toasts, where blacks explicitly comment on these variously divisive and unifying matters, but in a way that discredits the blacks themselves, rather than any other class or partisan group. Northern cities had also begun to exhibit a newly racialized (as well as class) pattern of residential segregation that by the 1820s had clearly contributed to the emergence of the antebellum race riot. Blacks were becoming both more urban and more cosmopolitan, more politically active and more separate in their daily lives from the whites they often worked for and with. The Bobalition broadsides reveal these facets of black life, despite their racist intent, by portraying blacks as remarkably aware of contemporary news and passionately committed to the particular meanings that public culture might have for them (including, as we shall see, the broadsides themselves).[60]

60. On Boston and abolition, see James Brewer Stewart, "Boston, Abolition, and the Atlantic World, 1820–1861," in Donald M. Jacobs, ed., *Courage and Conscience:*

Most of all, the broadsides tell us that whites were quite aware of the importance of these annual celebrations to African Americans and that these events were irreducibly nationalist. In the 1821 broadside, for example, blacks toast "De fourt of Uly"—but only to say that it is "no better day dan dis." Another toast refers to Monroe's tour: "De President of de Nited Tate—Spose he com dis way agin, we make Bobalition No. 2." The next year, the letter of "Cudjoe Crappo," president of the day, to his chief marshal portrays the African American committee's desire to make the July Fourteenth even "more splendum" than the Republican and Federalist July Fourth fetes, but for specifically black nationalist reasons: "De day is one of dose great nashumnal hepox wich call fort de sensumbility and de heraw of good feelum of ebery son and daughter of Africa in dis world, and good many udder place beside, which you no find tell of in de jography." In every instance, such revelations of black aspiration must be stretched to dimensions beyond this world, to make it seem absurd. This genre, after all, ridicules black mimicry of whites: a mimicry that itself was often part ridicule. The Bobalition broadsides are unthinkable without *both* the real black appropriations of white American national culture *and* white denial of the very possibility of those appropriations. Thus at every turn they reveal their dual origins in white racism and in African American resistance.

Not surprisingly, given their multiple meanings, the Bobalition broadsides spurred their own rebuttals following the constraints of the genre. This *Reply to Bobalition* series portrays dialogues among African Americans *after* the celebration has occurred and the Bobalition broadsides have appeared (see Figure 18).[61] Also in dialect (but with far fewer

---

Black and White Abolitionists in Boston (Bloomington, Ind., 1993), 101–125; Hinks, *To Awaken My Afflicted Brethren*, chap. 3. On residential segregation and riots in urban spaces, see Nash, *Forging Freedom*, 164–171; Horton and Horton, *In Hope of Liberty*, 90–91; Gilje, *Road to Mobocracy*, chap. 6. For black seafaring men and their importance in the emergence of an African American identity, see W. Jeffrey Bolster, "An Inner Diaspora: Black Sailors Making Selves," in Ronald Hoffman, Mechal Sobel, and Fredrika J. Teute, eds., *Through a Glass Darkly: Reflections on Personal Identity in Early America* (Chapel Hill, N.C., 1997), 419–448.

61. White discusses and reprints *Reply to Bobalition* (Boston, 1821), Broadsides Collection, AAS, in " 'It Was a Proud Day,' " *JAH*, LXXXI (1994–1995), 35, 37. See also *Reply to Bobalition of Slavery!* (1819), Broadsides Collection, Beinecke Library, Yale University; *Reply to the Grand and Splendid Bobalition of Slavery* (Boston, 1822), Broadsides Collection, Historical Society of Pennsylvania; *Bosson Artillerum Election; or, The African's Reply to the Burlesque on Their Late Celebration of the Abolition of the*

Grand & Splendid
BOBALITION
OF SLAVERY,

And "Great Annibersary Fussible," by de *Africum Shocielee* of Bosson.

BOSSON, ULY 15, 1822 1-2.

Order of de Day.

DE sheef Marshal send he most dispectful ompliment to he Debiltry,

Gritting:

SIR—I want you now to take tickelar tention to what I say.—As it happen one two tree time afore, since de Africum Shocietee become independent, and set he whole race at liberty, sept dem who still be kept slave at de sout and good many place more beside, de glorious * ambersary fussible" come dis year one day later, cause he no come soon nuff to bide folks catch um Saturday. Derefore, he go out town Sunday, and stay till dis morning, and bring de fifteent of Uly to make up for he absence in keeping de fourteent out of de Almanack.

Now, Sir, de destruction I gib to you is sactly de same as I gib to your brudder debiltry marshal; and if you no mind um, you cubber yourself wid such disgrece, dat soap-sud and salt-water hab no power to wash um out. You will recollect den, dat your character for good conduck be most greatly concern in de manner in which your good haviour show on dis blessed and superdanglous occashun.

De day is one of dose great nashumnal hepox wich call fort de sensitability and de heraw of good feelum of ebery son and daughter of Africa in dis world, and good many udder place beside, which you no find tell of in de jography, cause I spose Massa Morse what make um, dont know wedder deir any such place or not.

De committee of derangement hab gib me full power to make de debiltry marshal mind what I say—else dey stand chance to get shin kick cause he no take de hint and act just like raw soger, who know nothing bout militntary disumpleen.

You know, sir, dat de white folk, on de fourt of Uly, when deir company turn out, some of um take de lock and key step, same what de Cadet do, when dey come here and build tent on de commos, and lib dere a week, and pay no rent for um. Some udder of um, cause he no got men nuff to make much show when he march close together, tring out he section two rod apart, to make folks tink dere be a debil of a lot of um. But de fack is, in our selebrashum, we got member and skollar nuff to make all do folks stare, and darken de face of heaven and earth, as Massa Shakespole say.

But to de point of de subject matter of dis destruction. You no doubt see de publicum and de feddless, and de midillum interest folks sellybrate de fourt of Uly—bery well—de committee of derangement hab determine to make sellybrashum more splendum as dat, just same as de Sun more bigger as two cent candle.— Derefore, you muss pay de gratest tention to your duty, and mind all de order of de sheef marshal, whedder lie hab any reason in um or not.

For de order of de proceshum, you muss call at "*my office,*" No. 164, Lampblack-street, round de corner, up Shoeblack-ally, down two pair stairs, sign of de mink and musquash. I shall dere gib you such furder information na' what you want to know; and you must be sure to be dere in good season, so dat de company no hab to wait same as Gubberner Brook and udder grate folk do, while de marshal quarrel bout what he do fusser.

Nudder ting, I wish you take notice, dat arter de exumcise at de meetum-house be ober, and de company eat he dinner, dat you see de little boys and gals no make sturbance outside de hall, cause he bery sirable dat good fellowship be no broke up by de little debils, when dey get too much ginger-pop on de head. I telk you dis now, cause you needent forget um, when I no time to tink bout um myself.

I remain, sir,

Wid de gratest speck,

Your berry good friend,

CUDJOE CRAPPO,

Sheef Marshal.

Bosecrip.

For de better guberment of your conduck, and dat you may know when to grin, when to gib 40 cheer and tree quarter, I send you copy of de regular tose, and such number of Boluntear, as my friends intend shall get drunk.

TOASTS.

De day we sellumbrate—

De Jubilee hab come once more,

Why he no sooner come before?

70 cheer—Moosic—Hail Liberty.

De tate of Masser ———'— He no more like Africa, dan brickbat like ——ius Watch Seal.

40 cheer—Song—Our natib home.

De Fourt of Uly—Guess he no better dan de fifteent, sept he make more broken head.

40 cheer—4 grin all round de mout.

De Presidumpt of de Nited Tate—Guess he glad when he serve he tune out, and set up for heself, and let tudder prentice try he hand at it.

3 gree—5 sober look.

De City of Bosson—Now he got a mare, he turn de old horse out to pasture. Wonder if he get so much good feed he use to?

2 wink—7 sly look—Song " Poor old horse, let him die !"

De Hartford Convention—Chah ! let de dead rest, and no sturb um till he wake up heself.

Tin Pot—Wonder if de mail go regular now to Wess-Bosson—Guess de House of Industry start an opposition line of hand-cart.

9 cheer—Moosic, Hark away.

Broad-treet—Dont know what to make of um, dat is one end ont, mose in de middle— hope he no go to be de Hill No. 2.

' Song—Cesar, what you tink.

De new Banks—what de debil dey want more shaving-mill for—tough' dey scrape de beard off pretty well afore.

15 guess—Song, When I're money I am merry.

De City Mills—What de debil dey call um so for when dey way out of town ? Guess dey want to get too much perk for a shilling.

6 laff—Song, great way off at sea.

De Police Court—Guess some of de old Just tice of Peace look radder sour at um, cause " Othello's occupation's gone," as Massa Shakespole say good while ago.

300 cheer, grin all de time.

Missy Squantum—No hear about um lately —Guess she dug up de hatchet what she bury two tree year ago, and clear out for de woods.

Moosic—I love de rural shade.

De Firework on de Common fourt of Uly— How lucky he no set de pond afire. Guess salt pêtre not so plenty now as when Massa Schaffer make um.

Song—He rise like de rocket, and fall like de stick.

De Africum Fair Sex—May ebery true son of Africa crasp to he trobbing bosom de brushing virgin he adore : for as Massa Walter Scott, de poet say,

O, woman in de hour of ease,

How deblish hard you be to please,

But when we sick and ake de head,

You fetch de priest before we dead.

[When dis tose be gib out, de company will all rise, and listen bery tentively to de following song which will be sung by one of de debiltry marshal.]

SONG.

Tune—*"Soldier's Gratitude.*

O love is like de pepper-corn,

It make one act so cute,

It make de bosom feel so warm,

And eye shine like new boot.

I meet Miss Phillis tudder day,

In berry pensive mood ;

She almost cry her eye away,

For Pomp's ingratitude.

O lubly brushing-maid, say I,

What make look so sad ?

Ah ! Scip, de booteous virgin cry,

I feel mose deblish bad.

For Pomp he stole my heart away,

Me tought him bery good,

But he no lub me now he pay,

Chah ! what ingratitude.

I mope about de whole day long,

And when de night do come,

I sing de lonesome lub-lorn song,

And sit and bite my thumb.

And when de bell ring nine I go

To find my pillow good,

But ah ! I sleep none for de wo

Cause by ingratitude.

O, lubly Phillis, I reply,

Den tink no more more ;

Here on dis faitful bosom lie,

Dy charms I long adore)

And now de booteous maid again,

In chirk and chipper mood,

Wid me do laugh in hearty strain,

Bout Pomp's ingratitude.

Arter dis song be encore two tree time, de company will den sit down, and charge he half mug for de following

BOLUNTEARS.

De tate of New-England—De son of Africa here set under de vine-tree and fig leaf, widout nobody to molest or make him scare. Song—When me leetle boy.

De Banger Bank bill—Hope dey no pay de boot-black with um fore next December. 20 sober look.

De new invented ink—No such ting ; he made long ago as when Adam little boy.

De nordern division of de Army—Some trouble in de camp lately—but de commander begin to "look gay" agin. —Song—Who come dere.

De suddern division of de Army—When he disband, wonder what come of de old General—guess he go into "dignified retirement." Song—Rural Felicity.

De gremmen of de Navy—Cause he good fellow once he no business to act like de debil arterward, and take away he young brudder jack-knife and coat-button, and keep um two year. Song—De topsails shiver in de wind.

De man who dare be honest masc any time—and not build sixteen house, and meetum-house beside, and make Uncle Sam pay um.

De memory of Peter Guss—De recollecahum of he virtue lib in de heart of ebery true son of Africa.

De Africum School—Bime bye guess de little debils know nuff to tell de white folks dey no fool.

Moosic—De sun of science.

De Artful knave, who take de clothes off de line, and den set de brewer to watch and see if de owner come for um—Guess dere aint many Merchants make such good Haul.

Sold by the Flying Booksellers.

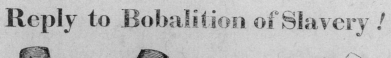

FIGURE 18. *Reply to Bobalition of Slavery!* Boston, 1819.
One of the earliest extant Bobalition replies. Courtesy Beinecke Rare Book
and Manuscript Library, Yale University

malapropisms), the Bobalition replies criticize the whites who physically and verbally abuse black celebrants. They also draw attention to the politics of a print culture that guaranteed that whites would always have the last word:

> We no sturb dem on the fourt of July, lection day nor no oder time. But no sooner dey get well sober arter deir Independence, den dey begin to brackguard our Independent day fore we sellybrate him.— Spose now we write Bobalition bout dem on the fourt of July, and scatter him bout town all day, why dey would take us up for salt and baterum direckly.

Slave Trade (Boston, n.d.), photocopy in the possession of Philip Lapsansky, Library Company of Philadelphia. The Boston Public Library possesses a copy of the 1821 *Reply to Bobalition* printed on the same sheet as the *Grand Bobalition; or, Great Annibersary Fussible.*

Where the Bobalition broadsides expose the production of black nationalist celebration, the reply to Bobalition exposes its satirical white
reproduction in print or lack thereof. The two black protagonists in the
1821 version go on to ask why the newspapers fail to publish accounts of
black celebrations. They conclude that the printers, in printing Bobalition, filling the papers with Fourth of July celebrations, and ignoring
July Fourteenth, are probably influenced by money. Even in the materi-
alist analysis, however, the whiteness of the Fourth and the blackness of
the Fourteenth are clear: "Jus go wid a five dollar bill in your hand, and
he print bout our sellybrashun juss as quick as he would bout he own."

It is hard to know whether this reflexive moment is itself an appeal on behalf of the printer, who obviously has been paid to produce
this broadside and who claims that the "Dialogue" had been "handed"
to him. As if by apology (or self-advertisement), the reply ends with
a positive, three-sentence, newspaper-style account of the black celebration, of the kind that so often followed white commemorations but
rarely appeared in print after black festivals. ("The celebration yesterday was more splendid than any recollected, since the formation of the
Society. . . . No disturbance took place, and every thing was conducted
with the utmost harmony.") Perhaps it is more revealing that both Bobalition replies contain a gesture to an African American community that
goes beyond West Boston and whose knowledge of itself is mediated by
print. In the 1819 broadside, both of the included dialogues are "occasioned by reading the account of Bobalition proceedings." The 1821
reply includes a letter from "Marco Mushee," a friend from Northampton, who turns out to have more than a little interest in Boston's celebration—and who asks his friend to "sens me latest news in depapers next
time you write me better." Both white racist satire and its preemptive
self-criticism were predicated upon blacks' reading as well as parading.

The Boston Bobalition replies were at best one, inherently limited,
way of contesting the racist cultural politics of nationalist celebration.
But they were hardly the only one. In New York and Philadelphia, where
there were no Bobalition broadsides, blacks produced printed versions
of the orations given at their national jubilee. They did so as part of
a larger effort to promote abolition and to prove their own abilities—
their national virtues—to black and white audiences. African American
leaders placed great emphasis on these performances and their reproduction in print. At the end of an 1810 pamphlet attacking slavery, the
Reverend Daniel Coker, the African Methodist minister in Baltimore,

gave a list of eight "descendants of the African race, who have given proofs of talents" in orations. Of the eight orators Coker cited, six had published their speeches. Russell Parrott of Philadelphia sent one of his published January First orations to Roberts Vaux, a wealthy white abolitionist and, later, colonizationist. (In 1817, Parrott and James Forten would cowrite and publish the Philadelphia black community's reply to the American Colonization Society.) And during his 1809 January First address, William Hamilton actually held up in his hand "a specimen of African genius": a copy of the last year's printed oration. "If we continue to produce specimens like these, we shall soon put our enemies to the blush; abashed and confounded they shall quit the field, and no longer urge their superiority of souls."[62]

Hamilton did not engage in mere flattery. Observing an American popular political culture that had national significance precisely because of its ability to produce printed descriptions of itself, he was suggesting that black nationalists could achieve their ends through the same system of performance and publicity. Knowing that accounts of their exploits would not appear magically in the newspaper, the African American oration pamphlets often included accounts of the day's proceedings. With the advertisements that black organizers placed in the newspapers, the orations are the only accounts that we have in African Americans' own words. For this reason alone the surviving slave trade orations deserve the close attention this study gives to the rhetoric of reportage and to white nationalist oratory. By combining parades with the printing and reprinting of what has too often been dismissed as mere rhetoric, white Americans created a nationalist political culture that had lasting historical consequences. Not the least of these consequences was the inspiration of an African American nationalist cultural politics decades before David Walker or Martin Delany. Blacks performed their nationalism and their abolitionism for white as well as black audiences. As centerpieces of the celebrations, these speeches

---

62. Daniel Coker, *A Dialogue between a Virginian and an African Minister* (Baltimore, 1810), 42–43; Russell Parrott to Roberts Vaux, n.d., Historical Society of Pennsylvania; Nash, *Forging Freedom*, 236–240, 341 n. 30; Porter, ed., *Early Negro Writing*, 265–268; Hamilton, *An Address*, in Porter, ed., *Early Negro Writing*, 37. Coker mentioned Absalom Jones, Peter Williams, Jr., James Varrick, Henry Sipkins, William Hamilton, William Miller, Henry Johnson, and James Forten. The pamphlet Hamilton held up contained the attestation of four white men (including two ministers) that Peter Williams, a black man, had actually written the oration (Williams, *An Oration*, 27–28).

and pamphlets fought American racial injustice while inventing and establishing black nationality.

☆   ☆   ☆

The slave trade orations place Africa on the world stage as resolutely as Independence Day rhetoric placed America at the center of world history. They construct a diasporic African nation—the "Africans and descendants of Africans"—who are invited to listen to their own history and prospects recounted in sympathetic detail. Where American July Fourth orators dated national history from emigration through Revolution to recent politics, diasporist African history commenced with the arrival in Africa of white slave traders. Absalom Jones defined the slave trade as "wars fomented among the different tribes of Africans in order to procure captives"; later orators left no more doubt who was at fault in the downfall of "our mother country." White men had found Africans "a peaceable, simple, unsuspicious people." Bent on gain, "the white man's God," they had brought Africans "to do the drudgery of the New World." The histories of the African diaspora and the making of America are joined here, at the rape of Africa.[63]

Just as slavery had led to the downfall of Africa, it more than accounts for the lowly status of dispossessed, despised Africans in America. When educated, the orators insist, Africans are as capable as any humans. Having portrayed the first, flagrantly evil actions of Europeans in Africa, Adam Carman wondered aloud how "those infernal miscreants that ravaged the wide fields of our country . . . these very savage man-stealers" could possibly "brand us with inferiority of sensibility." Rhetorically, the slave trade orations prove the equality, even superiority of African sensibilities by describing the scenes of enslavement and its subsequent effects. Russell Parrott asked his hearers to imagine an African man, with his beloved wife, "when, in the midst of his domestic enjoyment, a fiend steals in and mars all his happiness." "No tears, no entreaties, will avail; in vain he tells him that numer-

63. Jones, *A Thanksgiving Sermon*, 11; Williams, *An Oration*, 14–18; Russell Parrott, *An Oration on the Abolition of the Slave Trade . . . Delivered the First of January, 1812 at the African Church of St. Thomas* (Philadelphia, 1812), 4–5; Sipkins, *An Oration*, 8–11; "Introductory Address by Mr. Adam Carman," in Henry Johnson, *An Oration on the Abolition of the Slave Trade . . . Delivered in the African Church in New-York, January 1, 1810* (New York, 1810), 5–8; William Hamilton, *An Oration, on the Abolition of the Slave Trade . . . January 2, 1815* (New York, 1815), in Porter, ed., *Early Negro Writing*, 391–399, quoted at 395–397.

ous offspring depend on him for sustenance; that an affectionate wife, looks on with an anxious solicitude for his return; he shrieks with all the violence of desperate anguish—all, all is lost!" Afterward, the enslaved suffer a loss of faculties: ". . . insulated and alone, debarred from the benefits which a refined state of society affords. . . . Even those benevolent feelings, that glow with such vehemance at the ideal distreses of others, lose their ardour" in the African heart "when the sufferer's 'skin is not coloured like their own.'" An unsentimental education in slavery makes blacks—like, not coincidentally, their white masters—unfeeling and inhumane.[64]

As in most abolitionist literature, these sentimental scenes evoke compassion for blacks and a hatred of slavery, but they also prove the true sensibility of the African, the orator who describes them, and the audience, if they too are touched. If racism, slavery, and the lack of sensibility are linked, so are freedom, true feeling, and nationality. The anniversary occasion itself, "a day which in some degree renovates the primeval tranquility of our forefathers," should awaken good feelings that should be displayed proudly and conspicuously:

> He that has the last drop of African blood in his veins, and does not witness the warm emotion of gratitude on this auspicious and exalted occasion, he is degenerated from his country, and the sable race disowns him.

Displaying and thus creating national joy on national holidays, African Americans also paid tribute to their national heroes: the virtuous whites who had fought long and hard for an end to the slave trade and slavery (even though God got most of the credit). They congratulated the African American community on its achievements. And black leaders, like white ones on such occasions, urged their constituents to be, at all costs, respectable, for the sake of the nation. The orator, in particular, models and evokes sentimental nationality, proving, in the

---

64. Carman, *An Oration*, 19–20; Carman, "Introductory Address," in Johnson, *An Oration*, 6; [Russell Parrott], *An Oration on the Abolition of the Slave Trade* (Philadelphia, 1814), 7; Parrott, *An Address, on the Abolition of the Slave-Trade, Delivered before the Different African Benevolent Societies, on the 1st of January, 1816* (Philadelphia, 1816), 5. See also Parrott, *An Oration* (1812), 3–6; George Lawrence, *An Oration on the Abolition of the Slave Trade, Delivered on the First Day of January, 1813, in the African Methodist Episcopal Church* (New York, 1813), in Porter, ed., *Early Negro Writing*, 377–379; Johnson, *An Oration*, 10–11.

meetinghouse and again in print, that blacks are capable of citizenship in their own or any nation.[65]

Yet black nationalists also echoed Fourth of July forms in order to point out that holiday's failings. Parrott decried "the fatal influence of slavery . . . in this land of liberty and equal rights." With ample tongue in cheek William Hamilton convened the African American community "to celebrate an act of congress of the United States of America, which for its justice and humanity outstrips any that have ever passed that honorable body." Later, he praised the white, mainly Federalist founders of the New York Manumission Society, the group whose present-day members had tried to dissuade the blacks from celebrating that very day:

> a number of gentlemen of the first respectability, who were strongly attached to the principles of liberty and the rights of man; they, possessing the true spirit of patriotism, felt for the honor of their country; they saw that while the siren song of Liberty and equality was sung throughout the land, that the groans of the oppressed made the music very discordant, and that America's fame was very much tarnished thereby.

During the War of 1812, George Lawrence reminded his January First audience that they celebrated "the birthday of justice," a day that marked "the epoch that has restored to us our long-lost rights." Expertly contrasting the available styles of celebration like any good July Fourth orator, Lawrence allied the black festivity with God's rule and

65. Carman, *An Oration*, 9, 11, 15–16; Williams, *An Oration*, 20–24; Parrott, *An Oration* (1812), 8–11; Hamilton, *An Oration*, in Porter, ed., *Early Negro Writing*, 398; Sipkins, *An Oration*, 15–19; Hamilton, *An Address*, in Porter, ed., *Early Negro Writing*, 35–36; "Anthems, Composed by R. Y. Sidney," in Joseph Sidney, *An Oration*, 19–20; [Parrott], *An Oration* (1814), 10–12; Johnson, *An Oration*, 13–14; Parrott, *An Address*, 7–8. During the ensuing years, the modes of rejoicing—particularly the choice of whether or not to parade—would be the site of a class-based conflict within black communities over cultural and political styles, similar to that which would change the character and meaning of parades for whites in the 1830s and after. For discussions of the split celebrations of New York African Americans on July 4 and 5, 1827, in this context, see Alessandra Lorini, "Public Rituals, Race Ideology, and the Transformation of Urban Culture: The Making of the New York African-American Community, 1825–1918" (Ph.D. diss., Columbia University, 1991), chaps. 1–2; and White, " 'It Was a Proud Day,' " *JAH*, LXXXI (1995–1996), 37–48. On the meanings of parades in the 1820s and beyond, see Davis, *Parades and Power;* Mary P. Ryan, *Women in Public: Between Banners and Ballots, 1825–1880* (Baltimore, 1990), 19–57.

universal liberties, against the anxious festivals of the local Republicans: "It's not to celebrate a political festivity, or the achievement of arms by which the blood of thousands were spilt, contaminating [God's] pure fields with human gore!" [66]

It is little wonder that even the satirical Bobalition broadsides have African Americans describing the Fourth as "no better day dan dis," "no better dan de fifteent, sept he make more broken head." [67] For more than a generation, patriotic Americans had been telling themselves that their celebrations, like their nation, were politically and morally superior to the complacent, forced festivals of monarchy still held in the Old World, and to the tainted toasts and parades of their particular partisan opponents. When we learn that African Americans had truly done them one better—that, in celebrating their own African nation, they bid for a glory that put the salvos of electoral politics and the armed victories of New World republicanism to shame—it is less surprising that white Americans responded to these jubilees of justice with incredulous ridicule, occasional violence, and cold silence.

That silence as well as that satire revealed white Americans' bad faith and the cultural feat they were performing in turning from a postcolonial into a colonizing nation. Both silence and satire were necessary because, while white Americans furiously reenacted the Revolution in a costly war and in increasingly uncanny rites of reunion, African Americans invented the African nation out of the borrowed tools of nationalist political culture. Their appropriation, in fact, mimicked that of the Americans vis-à-vis the British four decades before: they claimed what had been denied them and made something both old and new in the process. Free blacks, the greatest critics of American political culture, paid that culture its greatest compliment: they used it to forge their own structures of celebration and mourning.

The language of slavery and the practices of nationality, in all their sentimental excess, had come back to haunt white Americans, like an awakened Rip Van Winkle or the legend of a headless Hessian horseman. As whites struggled again for economic self-determination and sovereignty over the seas and the frontier and fought among themselves

66. Parrot, *An Address*, 4; Hamilton, *An Address*, in Porter, ed., *Early Negro Writing*, 35, 39; Lawrence, *An Oration*, 376, 382.

67. *Grand and Splendid Bobalition* (1822); *Grand Bobalition* (1821).

in partisan warfare that had increasingly sectional overtones, blacks asserted their ability to become national subjects as well as the subjects of a national debate. Meanwhile, native Americans too, within and between their tribes, began to act according to their own understandings of the logic of nationality.[68] The mainstream white response to both—removal and colonization—reveals that, however successful the making of American nationalism had been by the second decade of the nineteenth century, it would have to be remade as well.

68. McLaughlin, *Cherokee Renascence;* Gregory Evans Dowd, *A Spirited Resistance: The North American Indian Struggle for Unity, 1745–1815* (Baltimore, 1992). For white cultural responses to Indian presences that were also characterized by forms of ventriloquism, see Philip J. Deloria, "Playing Indian: Otherness and Authenticity in the Assumption of American Indian Identity" (Ph.D. diss., Yale University, 1994).

☆ ☆ ☆

EPILOGUE

"YOU MAY REJOICE, I MUST MOURN"

On January 8, 1836, a mixed-blood Pequot Indian named William Apess took the stage at the Odeon Theater in Boston to give an anniversary oration. The subject of his speech was not Andrew Jackson, though it might have been, given that other Americans spent part of that day celebrating the president and the anniversary of his victory 21 years earlier at the Battle of New Orleans. Instead, Apess called attention to the death of King Philip, the Pequot sachem and warrior, 160 years before: "a martyr to [a] cause, though unsuccessful, yet as glorious as the *American* Revolution."

The italics that Apess gave to the word *"American"* in print spoke volumes. Apess, a veteran of the War of 1812 (on the American side) and a leader of the Mashpee Indian revolt of 1833, had already helped fashion an Indian Declaration of Independence in defense of Mashpee sovereignty over Indian lands and an *Indian Nullification of the Unconstitutional Laws of Massachusetts,* another ironic appropriation of current political rhetoric. But he knew that in order to contest the present he also had to challenge reigning conceptions of the past. At the theater on Federal Street he retold New England and American history from a native American point of view that questioned the usual celebrations of the Pilgrim Forefathers' Day and of American national independence. "Let every man of color wrap himself in mourning," he implored, "for the 22nd of December and the 4th of July are days of mourning and not of joy."[1]

1. Barry O'Connell, ed., *On Our Own Ground: The Complete Writings of William Apess, a Pequot* (Amherst, Mass., 1992), xxxvi, xx–xxi, lxix, lxxiii–lxxv, 164, 277, 286; Kim McQuaid, "William Apes, Pequot: An Indian Reformer in the Jackson Era," *New England Quarterly,* L (1977), 605–625; Donald M. Nielsen, "The Mashpee Indian Revolt of 1833," *New England Quarterly,* LVIII (1985), 400–420; Karim M. Tiro, "Denominated 'Savage': Methodism, Writing, and Identity in the Works of William Apess, a Pequot," *American Quarterly,* XLVIII (1996), 653–679. Apess and the Mashpees were not the only native Americans to seize Fourth of July forms for their own purposes. See William G. McLoughlin, *Cherokee Renascence in the New*

The history of dissent in America is filled with countercelebrations: protests against the celebratory mode that themselves employ celebratory forms. "What to the American slave is your Fourth of July? . . . To him, your celebration is a sham; your boasted liberty, an unholy license," said Frederick Douglass from a platform on the day after the Fourth, in 1852. "The Fourth of July is *yours,* not *mine. You* may rejoice, *I* must mourn." A contemporary of Douglass, Henry David Thoreau made sure to tell readers of *Walden* that he began his experiment in living "deliberately" on the Fourth of July 1846. Nine years later he gave an antislavery address on Independence Day. In 1901, the Socialist leader Eugene V. Debs annexed the national birthday to a new generation's radicalism: "I like the Fourth of July. It breathes the spirit of Revolution." Most recently, on the twenty-fifth anniversary of the Stonewall riot, in 1994, Tony Kushner observed: "Stonewall, the festival day of lesbian and gay liberation, is followed closely by the Fourth of July; they are exactly one summer week apart. The contiguity of these two festivals of freedom is important. . . . Lesbian and gay freedom is the same freedom celebrated annually on the Fourth of July."[2]

One way of thinking about these critics of American nationalism and the social movements that have produced them is to celebrate their commitment to American ideals of freedom, ideals that these dissenters cherished even as they rejected the prevailing wisdom of their day. This interpretation ratifies, posthumously, the true Americanism of these figures, awarding them a place in our celebrated past. A related though less common mode of interpretation mourns the ways in which American dissenters who joined "celebration and lament" participated in a "ritual of consensus." This ritual ultimately works as a peculiarly Ameri-

---

Republic (Princeton, N.J., 1986), 388; George Copway, *The Life, Letters, and Speeches of Kah-Ge-Ba-Gah-Bowh; or, G. Copway, Chief, Ojibway Nation* (New York, 1850), 189–190; Wolfgang Hochbruck, " 'I Ask for Justice': Native American Fourth of July Orations," in Paul Goetsch and Gerd Hurm, eds., *The Fourth of July: Political Oratory and Literary Relations, 1776–1876* (Tübingen, 1992), 155–166.

2. Paul Goetsch, "Thoreau and the Fourth of July," in Goetsch and Hurm, eds., *The Fourth of July,* 185–203; Frederick Douglass, "What to the Slave Is the Fourth of July? Extract from an Oration at Rochester, July 5, 1852," in Douglass, *My Bondage and My Freedom* (New York, 1855), 441; Nick Salvatore, *Eugene V. Debs: Citizen and Socialist* (Urbana, Ill., 1982), 192; Tony Kushner, "Fireworks and Freedom," *Newsweek,* June 27, 1994, 46.

can strategy of containment by ultimately reducing every struggle to another ratification of the American dream.[3]

Both interpretations are true enough. Figures like Thoreau and Eugene Debs certainly claimed the true heritage of the Revolution for themselves and, in doing so, put forth the Revolution as the model for political action. Douglass, as a Fourth of July mourner, expertly appropriated the dialectic of celebration and anticelebration that had already characterized political practice in America for more than a century. Yet he continued to do so for half a century, eventually championing Emancipation Day and Memorial Day as ways to remember abolition as the great victory of the Civil War. Douglass did not find the possibilities of "celebration and lament" impoverishing, though he had ample cause to feel disappointed. Instead, he continued to combine celebration and criticism, fighting the Gilded Age's "racialization of patriotism" in ways that still inspire.[4] Likewise, William Apess insisted on having something to say about the Fourth of July and the Pilgrims and thus called attention to his own Americanness. But he also insisted on creating his own, differently native holiday. Apess's critique of the Pequots' oppression in America contained within it the affirmation of a part of that past— an affirmation more damning than even his rhetorical mourning of the Fourth of July. His affirmation of King Philip questioned the politics of celebrating a certain version of the American past, a version that

3. For the former interpretation, compare the use of Frederick Douglass and Martin Luther King, Jr., in Arthur M. Schlesinger, Jr., *The Disuniting of America* (New York, 1992); and in Michael Lind, *The Next American Nation: The New Nationalism and the Fourth American Revolution* (New York, 1995). For the latter thesis, see Sacvan Bercovitch, *The Rites of Assent: Transformations in the Symbolic Construction of America* (New York, 1993), chap. 2; for an equally challenging perspective on "outsider" strategies, see R. Laurence Moore, *Religious Outsiders and the Making of Americans* (New York, 1986).

4. Although he spoke of "this glorious anniversary," Douglass delivered his protest oration on July 5. Douglass actively participated in African American celebrations and on at least one occasion explicitly characterized January 1 as greater than July 4. Peter Linebaugh, "Jubilating; or, How the Atlantic Working Class Used the Biblical Jubilee against Capitalism, with Some Success," *Radical History Review*, no. 50 (1991), 177; David W. Blight, "'For Something beyond the Battlefield': Frederick Douglass and the Struggle for the Memory of the Civil War," *Journal of American History*, LXXV (1998–1989), 1156–1178; Cynthia O'Leary, "'Blood Brotherhood': The Racialization of Patriotism, 1865–1918," in John Bodnar, ed., *Bonds of Affection: Americans Define Their Patriotism* (Princeton, N.J., 1996), 53–81.

erased certain actors completely. For Apess, King Philip could be considered "the greatest man that ever lived upon the American shores." In saying so he reminded his audience that it was only the success of earlier celebrations that made them seem to be more than partial. Consensus, in effect, erased all traces of the political, and thus of history.[5]

Some contemporary proponents of a national culture decry a divisive "identity politics" and hold up an inclusive civic culture as a true source for national identity. The task of American history, maintains Arthur M. Schlesinger, Jr., is to celebrate and inculcate that national culture. The history of national celebration, however, shows us that America's common political culture consists of a series of contests for power and domination, contests over the meaning of the Revolution, the development of the United States, and who counted as truly "American." Insofar as the making of American nationalism included broadening the promise of the American Revolution, American nationality may indeed be cause for celebration. But insofar as it encouraged practicing American nationalists to live in what Alexis de Tocqueville called "the perpetual utterance of self-applause," to participate all too joyfully in a political system that did not easily address the exclusion of many Americans from citizenship (much less the distribution of power and wealth in the United States), nationalist festivity may not provide the usable past we need.[6] Perhaps what is most usable in our nationalist past is less the unity Americans invoked on the Fourth of July than the ways in which some of them challenged those affirmations: their willingness not just to observe holidays but to invent them.

5. Apess, *On Our Own Ground*, 290; Laura J. Murray, "The Aesthetic of Dispossession: Washington Irving and Ideologies of (De)Colonization in the Early Republic," *American Literary History*, VIII (1996), 223–224. Apess drew on a heated and long-standing struggle over the memory of King Philip's War. See Jill Lepore, *The Name of War: King Philip's War and the Origins of American Identity* (New York, 1998).

6. Alexis de Tocqueville, *Democracy in America* (New York, 1945), I, 275. For a useful corrective to Schlesinger, see Nathan Irvin Huggins, "American History and the Idea of a Common Culture," in his *Revelations: American History, American Myths*, ed. Brenda Smith Huggins (New York, 1995), 166–173.

☆ ☆ ☆

INDEX